Community Emergency Management, Disaster Recovery and Resilience

Richard Skiba

Skiba, Richard (author)

Community Emergency Management, Disaster Recovery and Resilience

ISBN 978-978-1-7635743-3-5 (paperback) 978-1-7635743-4-2 (eBook) 978-1-7635743-5-9 (Hardcover)

Non-fiction

Contents

Contents

Preface

Natural disasters have become a significant global concern due to their increasing frequency and impact on populations worldwide. According to the Centre for Research on the Epidemiology of Disasters (CRED), the global community experiences an average of 384 natural disasters per year, affecting close to 200 million people and causing annual average damages of around $162 billion [1]. These disasters have led to over 1.6 million fatalities worldwide since 1990 and resulted in an annual economic loss of about $260-310 billion [2]. The World Health Organization reports an average of 11,000 deaths from natural disasters annually [3].

The frequency of natural disasters has been on the rise over the past decades, with an average of more than 500 natural disasters worldwide per year affecting a significant number of people or requiring international assistance [4]. The number of natural disasters has been growing globally, with roughly 6,800 natural disasters occurring annually [5]. This increase is attributed to factors such as climate change, which is expected to further escalate the frequency and severity of natural disasters in the future [6].

The impact of natural disasters extends beyond immediate casualties and damages, affecting various sectors such as healthcare, economics, and infrastructure. With the growing number of disasters, there is a greater focus on disaster management, rehabilitation services, and understanding the implications of these events on mental health [7-9]. Additionally, the fragility of cultural heritage sites has not received adequate protection despite the escalating frequency of natural disasters due to climate change [10].

The global occurrence of natural disasters is a pressing issue that demands attention and proactive measures to mitigate their impact on human lives, economies, and the environment. The increasing frequency of these events underscores the importance of disaster preparedness, resilience building, and international cooperation to address the challenges posed by natural disasters.

The disaster management cycle provides a structured framework that outlines the various stages of managing a disaster [11]. This cycle is crucial for organizations and individuals alike, enabling them to prepare for and respond effectively to all types of disasters, whether natural, technological, or human-made. It guides professionals in identifying potential hazards, assessing associated risks, and devising strategies to prevent, mitigate, and respond effectively to these threats.

Disasters can occur unexpectedly, but with a well-prepared disaster management plan derived from this cycle, it is possible to minimize the worst impacts and establish a foundation for a more efficient recovery process. The stakes are high, often involving significant property loss, environmental damage, or even fatalities. Thus, the capacity to respond swiftly and efficiently is essential. For example, in the event of a flooding, a comprehensive disaster plan might include activating communication systems, blocking roads, coordinating evacuations, or assisting victims in retrieving valuable possessions.

A key goal of disaster management is to provide timely assistance to those affected. When disaster strikes, individuals may suffer injuries, require evacuation, or need immediate medical care. Disaster management teams are prepared to offer crucial support, such as mobilizing medical personnel, securing evacuation sites, and supplying essentials like water, food, and shelter.

Recovery is an integral component of the disaster management cycle, focusing on both individuals and their properties. This phase may encompass rebuilding efforts, providing medical care, ensuring safety, and may extend to restoring an area's infrastructure, economy, ecological balance, and community life.

Different types of disasters necessitate distinct response strategies to maximize prevention efforts and facilitate a quick return to normalcy when prevention is not possible. The expertise of trained professionals is vital, as they are equipped to assess the situation and determine the necessary level and type of response. For instance, while the response to a wildfire might centre on extinguishing the fire, the approach to a hurricane might focus more on survivor search and rescue operations.

1

Disasters Exemplified

A disaster is commonly defined as a serious disruption that results in widespread human, material, economic, or environmental losses, surpassing the affected community's or society's ability to manage using its own resources [12]. This definition underscores the overwhelming impact disasters have on communities, highlighting the need for external assistance for recovery. Disasters are characterized by their severity, which can vary across different types of disasters but always lead to significant disruptions [13]. The concept of disaster resilience is closely linked to disasters, with resilience representing the ability of communities to recover and bounce back following a disaster, often with minimal external aid [14].

Further, the Australian 2011 National Strategy for Disaster Resilience defines a disaster as a significant interruption to community life that poses a threat or actual harm to people or damages property [15]. This disruption surpasses the routine capabilities of local statutory authorities, necessitating the special coordination and deployment of resources not typically at their disposal. According to the Strategy, disasters and emergencies stem from the interaction between a hazard and a vulnerable population, disrupting lives and communities [15]. For those in recovery roles, understanding the origins of an emergency is helpful for context, but the focus often shifts more towards managing the aftermath and addressing the community's immediate needs.

Moreover, disasters are events that severely disrupt the structural, organizational, and functional capacities of communities, families, and individuals, resulting in acute social crises [16]. According to the World Health Organization and the United Nations, a disaster is defined as a breakdown in the ecological relationships between humans and their environment, necessitating extraordinary efforts to cope, often with external assistance [17]. This definition emphasizes the need for exceptional measures to address the scale of the disruption caused by disasters.

In essence, disasters overwhelm the capacity of a community or society to cope using its own resources, leading to significant losses and disruptions that require external assistance for recovery and rebuilding. While the severity and impact of disasters may vary, they always entail a level of destruction that exceeds the affected entity's ability to manage independently. Resilience plays a critical role in mitigating the effects of disasters and facilitating the recovery process, underscoring the importance of preparedness and response strategies in disaster management.

Despite advances in predictive technologies and warning systems, emergencies remain predominantly unpredictable and chaotic in nature and impact. Compounding this issue is a common human tendency to underestimate personal risk, leading many to avoid preparing for such events. Thus, emergencies, whether minor or major, share two characteristics: they are unforeseen and they disrupt individuals, households, livelihoods, and communities [15].

The following are examples of disasters that fit within the various definitions of disaster outlined above:

Hurricane Katrina (2005): This hurricane is a textbook example of a disaster causing widespread human, material, economic, and environmental losses that overwhelmed the local and federal government's ability to manage with existing resources. The severity of the hurricane led to significant disruptions in New Orleans and other affected areas, necessitating massive external assistance for recovery and reconstruction.

Figure 1: West End Marina, New Orleans, after Hurricane Katrina. Jeff Albert, CC BY-SA 2.0, via Wikimedia Commons.

Hurricane Katrina is one of the most notorious and devastating natural disasters in the history of the United States. It formed over the Bahamas on August 23, 2005, and crossed southern Florida as a moderate Category 1 hurricane, causing some deaths and flooding there before growing to catastrophic proportions in the Gulf of Mexico. By August 28, it had intensified into a Category 5 hurricane with winds of up to 175 mph (280 km/h). The loss of life, particularly in New Orleans, was significant due to the storm surge and subsequent flooding caused by the failure of levees [18].

Landfall and Impact: Katrina made its second and more devastating landfall on August 29, 2005, as a Category 3 hurricane near Buras-Triumph, Louisiana, with sustained winds of 125 mph (205 km/h). The storm surge caused severe flooding in many parts of the Gulf Coast, but it was particularly catastrophic in New Orleans, Louisiana. Although the city was known to be vulnerable to flooding because it is located below sea level and protected by levees, the levees failed during Katrina, leading to widespread flooding.

Consequences:

- **Human Toll:** Over 1,800 people lost their lives due to the hurricane and subsequent floods, making it one of the deadliest hurricanes in U.S. history.

- **Displacement:** More than a million people in the Gulf region were displaced, with hundreds of thousands needing temporary housing.
- **Economic Damage:** Katrina caused an estimated $125 billion in damage, making it one of the costliest natural disasters in U.S. history [19].
- **Infrastructure:** The infrastructure damage was extensive, including destroyed homes, businesses, and critical infrastructure like bridges and roads.

Response and Criticism: The response to Hurricane Katrina involved local, state, and federal agencies, including the Federal Emergency Management Agency (FEMA). However, the response was widely criticized for being slow and inadequate. Delays in rescue and relief operations exposed significant gaps in disaster preparedness and response capabilities at all levels of government.

Long-term Effects: Katrina had a lasting impact on the demographics and economy of New Orleans and the broader Gulf region. Many residents who evacuated were unable to return, leading to significant demographic shifts. The disaster also spurred reforms in emergency management and disaster preparedness, emphasizing the need for better planning, communication, and coordination.

The event highlighted the manufactured flood risk in New Orleans, exacerbated by engineering and construction defects that led to severe flooding and loss of life [20]. Additionally, the environmental impact of Katrina, such as high levels of mold and allergens post-disaster, had implications for public health, particularly for children with asthma [21].

Cultural Impact: The hurricane also had a profound impact on the culture and community spirit of New Orleans. It influenced music, literature, and film and brought national and international attention to issues of socio-economic disparity and government accountability.

Figure 2: FEMA special debris Contractors work on removing this boat from Highway 23. National Archives at College Park - Still Pictures, Public domain, via Wikimedia Commons.

The legacy of Hurricane Katrina remains a reminder of the vulnerability of coastal regions to natural disasters and the importance of effective disaster preparedness and response strategies.

2011 Tōhoku Earthquake and Tsunami, Japan: This disaster highlights the interaction between a natural hazard (earthquake and subsequent tsunami) and a vulnerable population. The magnitude of the event surpassed the capacity of local and national authorities to respond effectively without significant international aid. The disaster disrupted lives, destroyed communities, and caused a severe nuclear incident.

The 2011 Tōhoku earthquake and tsunami was a devastating natural disaster that struck Japan on March 11, 2011. It is also commonly referred to as the Great East Japan Earthquake.

Figure 3: An aerial view of Ishinomaki, Japan, a week after a 9.0 magnitude earthquake and subsequent tsunami devastated the area. U.S. Marine Corps photo by Lance Cpl. Ethan Johnson, Public domain, via Wikimedia Commons.

The 2011 Tōhoku Earthquake and Tsunami in Japan exemplified the devastating impact of a natural disaster on a vulnerable population. The disaster resulted in over 15,000 deaths, thousands of injuries, and many missing individuals, underscoring the human toll of the event [22]. Additionally, hundreds of thousands of people were displaced from their homes due to the combined effects of the tsunami and the subsequent nuclear disaster, highlighting the widespread displacement caused by the catastrophe [23].

Earthquake Details:

- **Magnitude and Epicentre:** The earthquake had a magnitude of 9.0-9.1, making it the most powerful earthquake ever recorded in Japan and one of the five most powerful earthquakes in the world since modern record-keeping began. The epicentre was located approximately 70 kilometres east of the Oshika Peninsula of Tōhoku and the hypocentre at an underwater depth of around 29 kilometres.

- **Seismic Activity:** The earthquake caused significant seismic activity, including numerous aftershocks, many of which were over magnitude 6.0.

Tsunami:

- **Wave Heights:** The earthquake triggered a massive tsunami with waves reaching heights of up to 40.5 meters (133 feet) in Miyako in Tōhoku's Iwate Prefecture [24]. These waves travelled up to 10 kilometres (6 miles) inland in the Sendai area.
- **Destruction:** The tsunami devastated coastal areas, sweeping away cars, homes, buildings, and other structures. It also caused numerous fires, including a major one in Kesennuma [25].

Figure 4: Kesennuma earthquake damage. Caleb Eames, U.S. Marine Corps, Public domain, via Wikimedia Commons.

Nuclear Crisis:

- **Fukushima Daiichi Nuclear Power Plant:** The tsunami caused a series of equipment failures, nuclear meltdowns, and releases of radioactive materials at the Fukushima Daiichi Nuclear Power Plant. This was the most severe nuclear accident since the Chernobyl disaster in 1986 and was rated a Level 7 on the International Nuclear Event Scale.

Casualties and Damage:

- **Loss of Life:** The disaster resulted in over 15,000 deaths, thousands of injuries, and many people missing [22].
- **Displacement:** Hundreds of thousands of people were displaced from their homes due to the tsunami and nuclear disaster.
- **Economic Impact:** The total economic cost was estimated at approximately $235 billion, making it the costliest natural disaster in world history [26].

Figure 5: 2011 Japan earthquake - House turned upside-down by the force of tsunami. DFID - UK Department for International Development, CC BY 2.0, via Wikimedia Commons.

Response and Recovery:

- **Immediate Response:** Japan's response included a massive mobilization of rescue workers, including the Japanese Self-Defense Forces, alongside countless international aid agencies and foreign governments.
- **Rebuilding Efforts:** Rebuilding efforts were extensive and ongoing, with significant focus on enhancing coastal defenses and rebuilding infrastructure.
- **Safety Regulations:** The disaster prompted a re-evaluation of earthquake and tsunami safety and nuclear power policies in Japan and internationally.

Global Impact and Lessons Learned:

- **Global Awareness:** The disaster raised global awareness about the risks of nuclear power in earthquake-prone regions, leading to changes in nuclear safety standards worldwide.
- **Scientific Research:** It also contributed to significant advancements in earthquake and tsunami research and monitoring technology.

The 2011 Tōhoku earthquake and tsunami remains a stark reminder of the potential power of natural disasters and the need for preparedness, resilient infrastructure, and effective crisis management.

COVID-19 Pandemic (2019-Present): Although not a traditional natural disaster, the pandemic fits the definitions as it disrupted the structural, organizational, and functional capacities of communities worldwide. It created acute social crises and required extraordinary efforts to cope, with extensive reliance on external assistance in terms of healthcare, economic aid, and social support systems.

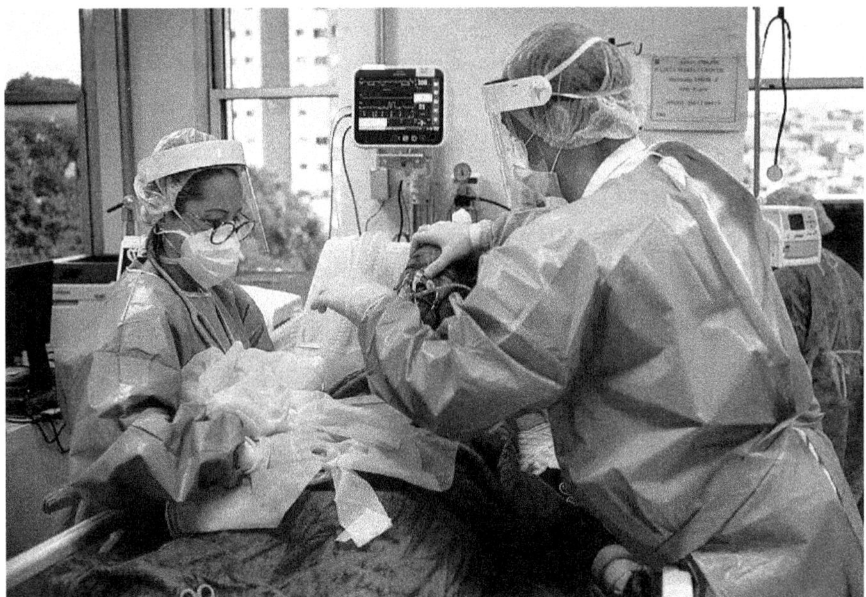

Figure 6: A team of doctors, nurses and physiotherapists take care of critical patients with COVID-19 in the ICU of the Vila Nova Cachoeirinha hospital, north of São Paulo. Gustavo Basso, CC BY-SA 4.0, via Wikimedia Commons.

The COVID-19 pandemic is a global health crisis caused by the novel coronavirus SARS-CoV-2, which emerged in late 2019. It has led to widespread and profound impacts on health systems, economies, and daily life around the world. Here are key details about the pandemic:

Origin and Spread:

- **Initial Outbreak:** The virus was first identified in December 2019 in Wuhan, a city in the Hubei province of China. It is believed to have originated in a seafood market where live wild animals were also sold, suggesting a zoonotic origin [27].

- **Global Spread:** COVID-19 quickly spread globally, leading the World Health Organization (WHO) to declare it a pandemic on March 11, 2020 [28]. The virus spread to almost every country, with the United States, India, Brazil, and many European countries being heavily affected [29].

The origins of COVID-19 have been a subject of intense research and speculation. Two major hypotheses have been proposed to explain the emergence of the virus. One hypothesis suggests that COVID-19 originated from a seafood market in Wuhan, China [27]. Another hypothesis posits that the virus may have been developed in a laboratory in Wuhan [30]. Genomic analysis has revealed that SARS-CoV-2, the virus responsible for COVID-19, is phylogenetically related to bat viruses, indicating that bats could be the possible primary reservoir [31].

Research has also explored the possibility of intermediate hosts in the transmission of the virus. Pangolins have been suggested as potential hosts, with comparisons of viral genomes indicating that 2019-nCoV might have originated from a recombination of a Pangolin-CoV-like virus with a Bat-CoV-RaTG13-like virus [32]. However, there is no conclusive evidence to definitively identify the exact origin of the virus [33].

The COVID-19 outbreak, which began in Wuhan, China, has led to various conspiracy theories and beliefs about its origins. These theories range from natural origins to lab-based origins, influencing public perceptions and attitudes towards the virus and vaccination efforts [34]. Understanding the origins of SARS-CoV-2 is crucial not only for determining its zoonotic source but also for developing effective prevention and control strategies for future zoonotic events [35].

The origins of COVID-19 remain a complex and evolving area of study. While research has provided insights into potential reservoirs and transmission pathways, ongoing investigations are necessary to fully elucidate the origins of the virus and its implications for public health and disease prevention.

Impact on Health:

- **Symptoms:** COVID-19 presents a range of symptoms, from none at all (asymptomatic) to severe pneumonia and death. Common symptoms include fever, cough, and difficulty breathing [36].

- **Fatalities and Infections:** As of now, millions of people have been infected worldwide, and several million have died from the disease, making it one of the deadliest pandemics in history [37].

- **Healthcare Systems:** The pandemic has placed enormous strain on healthcare systems worldwide, leading to shortages of hospital beds, critical care facilities, and medical supplies [38].

Economic and Social Effects:

- **Lockdowns and Quarantines:** In an effort to control the spread of the virus, many countries implemented strict lockdowns, curfews, and quarantine measures, disrupting normal life, causing widespread economic disruption, and exacerbating mental health problems [39].

- **Economic Downturn:** The global economy suffered a significant downturn, with millions losing their jobs, businesses closing, and significant contractions in GDP across the world [40].

- **Social and Cultural Impact:** The pandemic has had profound social and cultural impacts, including changes in how people work, learn, and interact, with a significant shift towards remote and digital platforms [41].

Response and Management:

- **Public Health Measures:** Countries implemented various measures to manage the outbreak, including social distancing, mask mandates, travel restrictions, and contact tracing.

- **Vaccine Development:** An unprecedented global effort led to the development, testing, and deployment of several effective COVID-19 vaccines within a year of the virus's emergence. Mass vaccination campaigns have been critical in controlling the spread of the virus.

- **Ongoing Challenges:** Variants of the virus, such as Delta and Omicron, have posed ongoing challenges by increasing transmissibility and impacting the effectiveness of vaccines.

Figure 7: COVID-19 Vaccine at the Orange County Convention Center. Whoisjohngalt, CC BY-SA 4.0, via Wikimedia Commons.

Scientific and Technological Advances:

- **Rapid Research:** The pandemic accelerated research in virology, epidemiology, vaccine technology, and public health response, leading to significant scientific advancements.

- **Technology and Innovation:** The crisis spurred innovation in technology, including the use of artificial intelligence in diagnostics, the expansion of telemedicine, and the development of new platforms for digital collaboration and communication.

The COVID-19 pandemic continues to affect global society, with ongoing efforts to manage new cases and outbreaks, vaccinate populations, and address the socio-economic impacts. The lessons learned from this pandemic are expected to shape health policies and emergency preparedness for future global health crises.

Research has shown that lockdowns and quarantines have not only affected the economy but have also had adverse psychological effects on individuals, including stress, anxiety, and mental disorders [42]. The economic downturn from these measures has caused financial stress and mental health concerns among populations [43]. Additionally, the pandemic has highlighted the role of social media in disseminating information and influencing behaviours during crises [44].

Studies have examined the impact of lockdown strategies on the basic reproductive number of COVID-19 cases, emphasizing the need for ongoing assessment of the effectiveness of such strategies to justify their economic impact [45]. The strict enforcement of lockdowns and quarantines is predicted to have long-lasting social, economic, and psychological effects [46]. Moreover, the pandemic has underscored the importance of social capital, cultural values, and local wisdom in responding to its impact [47].

The COVID-19 pandemic has not only presented significant economic challenges but has also profoundly affected the social and cultural dynamics of societies worldwide. The interaction between lockdowns, economic downturns, and social transformations highlights the necessity for comprehensive strategies to address the multifaceted impacts of global crises.

2004 Indian Ocean Earthquake and Tsunami: This disaster caused tremendous loss of life and widespread destruction across several countries bordering the Indian Ocean. The scale of the disaster overwhelmed the affected countries' abilities to respond, leading to an extensive international humanitarian effort. This event also highlights the importance of disaster resilience and preparedness, as many regions were caught unprepared for such a large-scale disaster.

Figure 8: A village near the coast of Sumatra lays in ruin after the Tsunami that struck South East Asia. U.S. Navy photo by Photographer's Mate 2nd Class Philip A. McDaniel, Public domain, via Wikimedia Commons.

The 2004 Indian Ocean earthquake and tsunami, also known as the Sumatra-Andaman earthquake, was one of the deadliest natural disasters in recorded history, affecting multiple countries around the Indian Ocean. Here are the key details:

Date and Origin:

- **Date:** The disaster occurred on December 26, 2004.
- **Epicentre:** The earthquake's epicentre was off the west coast of northern Sumatra, Indonesia.
- **Magnitude:** It was an undersea megathrust earthquake with a magnitude of 9.1–9.3, making it one of the most powerful earthquakes ever recorded globally. The earthquake was 2.5 times larger than initially reported, making it the second-largest recorded earthquake in history, following the 1960 Chilean earthquake [48].

Tsunami:

- **Trigger:** The earthquake caused the sea floor to uplift, displacing a massive amount of water and triggering a series of devastating tsunamis.

- **Impact Areas:** The tsunamis affected coastal and island communities across the Indian Ocean, from Indonesia, Thailand, and the northern coast of Malaysia to distant shores in Sri Lanka, India, the Maldives, and as far away as the east coast of Africa.

- **Wave Heights:** In some places, the waves reached heights of up to 30 meters (100 feet).

Casualties and Damage:

- **Fatalities:** The disaster resulted in an estimated 230,000 to 280,000 deaths across 14 countries, with Indonesia, Sri Lanka, India, and Thailand experiencing the highest number of casualties [49].

- **Displacement:** Millions of people were displaced by the destruction, with many communities losing homes, livelihoods, and infrastructure.

- **Economic Impact:** The economic damage was immense, with billions of dollars needed for reconstruction and recovery.

Response and Recovery:

- **International Aid:** The magnitude of the disaster prompted an unprecedented international humanitarian response, with billions of dollars in aid contributed by governments, international organizations, and private donors.

- **Reconstruction:** The recovery and reconstruction process varied by country and region but involved rebuilding homes, restoring livelihoods, and improving infrastructure to better withstand future disasters.

- **Improvements in Tsunami Warning Systems:** One of the critical outcomes was the establishment of improved tsunami warning systems in the Indian Ocean to provide early alerts for similar events in the future.

Scientific and Societal Impacts:

- **Scientific Research:** The event significantly advanced scientific understanding of plate tectonics and tsunami science, leading to improved risk assessment models.

- **Awareness and Preparedness:** It also increased global awareness about the risks of tsunamis, leading to better preparedness measures in tsunami-prone regions worldwide.

The 2004 Indian Ocean earthquake and tsunami marked a pivotal moment for disaster management and humanitarian response, emphasizing the need for better preparedness and cooperation at international levels to handle such large-scale natural disasters.

Figure 9: Street in downtown Banda Aceh after 2004 tsunami. Michael L. Bak, Public domain, via Wikimedia Commons.

2010 Haiti Earthquake: This devastating earthquake severely disrupted the Haitian society's structural, organizational, and functional capacities. The disaster resulted in significant human casualties and material destruction, overwhelming the local government's ability to manage the crisis without substantial external aid. The recovery and rebuilding efforts have been prolonged and complex, further underscoring the critical role of resilience and external support in disaster management.

Figure 10: Haiti Post Earthquake January 2010. Colin Crowley, CC BY 2.0, via Wikimedia Commons.

The 2010 Haiti earthquake was a catastrophic natural disaster that struck Haiti on January 12, 2010. Here are the key details about the earthquake [50-53]:

Magnitude and Epicentre:

- **Magnitude:** The earthquake had a magnitude of 7.0 Mw.
- **Epicentre:** It was centred approximately 25 kilometres (16 miles) west-southwest of Port-au-Prince, the capital of Haiti.
- **Depth:** The earthquake occurred at a shallow depth of about 13 kilometres (8.1 miles), which contributed to its destructive power.

Impact and Damage:

- **Casualties:** The earthquake caused extensive loss of life, with estimates of the death toll ranging from 100,000 to over 300,000 people. It was one of the deadliest earthquakes in recent history.
- **Injuries:** More than 300,000 people were injured.
- **Displacement:** Approximately 1.5 million people were displaced, leading to a

major humanitarian crisis with many Haitians living in makeshift camps.

- **Infrastructure:** The earthquake caused massive damage to infrastructure, including homes, schools, and hospitals, as well as historic buildings. The Presidential Palace and the Port-au-Prince Cathedral were among the structures that sustained severe damage.

Humanitarian Response:

- **International Aid:** The international response was substantial, with countries and organizations around the world sending aid, rescue teams, and medical assistance. However, the response was also criticized for coordination problems and for not effectively addressing the long-term needs and development goals of Haiti.

- **Relief Efforts:** Relief efforts included providing emergency medical care, food, water, and temporary shelter to the survivors. Non-governmental organizations played a significant role in these efforts.

Recovery and Reconstruction:

- **Challenges:** The reconstruction process has been slow, hampered by political instability, economic problems, and logistical challenges. Ten years after the earthquake, many Haitians were still in need of adequate housing and basic services.

- **Development Issues:** The earthquake exacerbated pre-existing development challenges in Haiti, which is one of the poorest countries in the Western Hemisphere.

Lessons Learned:

- **Preparedness and Building Codes:** The disaster highlighted the critical need for improved building codes and construction practices in earthquake-prone regions. Haiti's vulnerability to earthquakes was increased by weak building standards.

- **Disaster Management:** It also underscored the importance of local capacity building in disaster response and recovery to ensure more effective management of aid and reconstruction efforts.

Figure 11: Haiti Earthquake building damage. Photo Marco Dormino/ The United Nations United Nations Development Programme, CC BY 2.0, via Wikimedia Commons.

The 2010 Haiti earthquake remains a poignant reminder of the devastating impact of natural disasters, particularly in regions with limited economic resources and insufficient infrastructure to withstand such events. The ongoing struggles of the Haitian people emphasize the need for sustained international support and effective disaster preparedness and management strategies.

A further notable example of an Australian bushfire disaster that fits within these definitions is the **2019-2020 Black Summer bushfires**. This event dramatically underscores the challenges described in disaster management definitions and highlights the need for resilience and external assistance. Here are the details [54-57]:

Scope and Impact:

- **Duration and Extent:** The bushfires began in late 2019 and continued into early 2020, affecting large swathes of Australia, particularly New South Wales, Victoria, and South Australia.

- **Severity:** The fires were extraordinarily severe, with flames reaching unprecedented heights and temperatures, resulting in widespread destruction of forests, wildlife, and communities.

- **Environmental Impact:** An estimated 18.6 million hectares were burned, and the fires led to significant ecological and environmental damage, including the loss of nearly three billion animals (killed or displaced).

Human and Material Losses:

- **Casualties:** At least 33 people lost their lives directly due to the fires. Many more suffered from respiratory issues and other health complications related to air quality and stress.

- **Property Damage:** Thousands of homes and buildings were destroyed, leading to massive economic and personal losses for the affected communities.

Response and Recovery:

- **External Assistance:** The scale of the fires surpassed the coping capacities of local fire services and communities, necessitating significant national and international aid. This included firefighting support from countries like the United States, Canada, and New Zealand.

- **Community and Government Response:** There was a substantial mobilization of resources, including military assistance and community fundraising efforts. The Australian government announced billions of dollars in recovery funds.

Resilience and Recovery:

- **Community Resilience:** The event highlighted the resilience of affected communities, with many stories of individuals and groups organizing relief efforts and supporting rebuilding initiatives.

- **Policy and Preparedness:** Post-disaster, there was a strong focus on reevaluating and enhancing bushfire management and preparedness strategies, including better resource allocation, building codes, and land management practices to reduce future bushfire risks.

Lessons and Legacy:

- **Scientific Research and Awareness:** The disaster prompted significant research into climate change impacts, fire management strategies, and community resilience models.

- **Awareness and Preparedness:** It raised global awareness about the risks of bushfires in the era of climate change, emphasizing the need for improved preparedness and adaptive strategies at community, national, and global levels.

The 2019-2020 Black Summer bushfires illustrate how severe disasters challenge existing capacities and necessitate extraordinary recovery efforts, underscoring the critical role of resilience in disaster management and the importance of global cooperation in times of crisis.

The Black Summer bushfires underscored the urgent need for disaster resilience and external assistance in managing such crises. The event highlighted the challenges faced in disaster management and emphasized the importance of preparedness, response, and recovery efforts in the face of such extreme events. The impact of the bushfires on health, biodiversity, community well-being, and emergency response systems necessitated a comprehensive and coordinated approach to address the aftermath of the disaster [54-57].

These examples encompass a range of disaster types, from natural disasters like hurricanes and tsunamis to pandemics, illustrating the various ways in which disasters can severely impact and overwhelm communities, necessitating external aid and significant recovery efforts.

Causes of Disaster

Disasters can arise from a myriad of natural, technological, and human-induced factors. These primary causes can be broadly categorized as follows:

Natural Causes include several types of disasters:

- **Geological Disasters** such as earthquakes, which involve sudden movements of the Earth's tectonic plates, can cause ground shaking, surface rupture, and tsunamis. Volcanic eruptions can result in lava flows, ash clouds, pyroclastic flows, and lahars. Landslides and avalanches are typically triggered by factors like rainfall, earthquakes, volcanic activity, and human activities.

- **Meteorological Disasters** include hurricanes, typhoons, and cyclones, which are large storm systems characterized by strong winds, heavy rainfall, and storm surges. Tornadoes are violently rotating columns of air connected to both the Earth's surface and a cumulonimbus cloud, or occasionally a cumulus cloud.

Extreme temperatures, such as heatwaves and cold spells, can cause health emergencies and affect agriculture.

- **Hydrological Disasters** such as floods can be caused by heavy rainfall, dam breaks, or snowmelt exceeding the carrying capacity of river systems and coastal defences. Tsunamis are typically triggered by underwater earthquakes or volcanic eruptions.

- **Climatological Disasters** involve droughts, extended periods of deficient rainfall leading to water shortages, and wildfires, which may be triggered by human activity or natural factors like lightning.

Technological and Man-Made Causes include:

- **Industrial Accidents** such as chemical spills, where hazardous chemicals are released from industrial plants or storage facilities, and nuclear accidents, which involve radiation leaks from nuclear power plants or improper disposal of nuclear waste.

- **Structural Failures** like building collapses that occur due to poor construction, earthquakes, or explosions, and bridge failures, often due to structural deficiencies, poor maintenance, or natural disasters.

- **Transportation Accidents** such as airplane crashes can lead to significant loss of life and environmental damage, while train derailments and maritime disasters often involve hazardous materials and can lead to widespread environmental damage.

Human-Induced Causes include:

- **Terrorism and Conflict** such as bombings and armed attacks are deliberate actions intended to cause widespread fear, injury, and damage. Biological and chemical warfare involves the use of hazardous agents to cause illness, death, and panic.

- **Cyberattacks** target critical infrastructure such as power grids, water systems, and healthcare systems or involve data breaches that compromise personal data and can disrupt financial and personal security.

Environmental Degradation such as deforestation, land degradation, and urban sprawl can increase the vulnerability of regions to natural disasters such as floods and landslides.

Disasters often result from a combination of these factors, where natural hazards meet vulnerable and unprepared societies. Effective disaster management involves understanding these causes and implementing strategies to mitigate their impacts.

Disasters and Climate Change: Globally, changing climate conditions and demographic shifts are expected to pose new challenges for disaster recovery. Communities worldwide may find themselves increasingly vulnerable, which could impact health and well-being as well as the stability of local infrastructure and economies. Projected impacts of climate change include:

- An increase in the frequency and intensity of extreme weather events, such as hurricanes, droughts, and heatwaves.
- Greater potential for property damage and disruptions to critical infrastructure.
- Changes in wind patterns could affect sectors like agriculture and energy, necessitating adjustments in building codes and farming practices. These shifts may challenge existing disaster management theories and necessitate new approaches to recovery.

The impact of climate change on extreme weather events such as droughts, heatwaves, and wind pattern changes has significant implications for disaster management, property damage, and critical infrastructure. The Commonwealth Scientific and Industrial Research Organisation (CSIRO) highlighted the potential consequences of these shifts, necessitating adjustments to building codes and new recovery approaches [58-61].

The increase in extreme weather events, including droughts and heatwaves, poses challenges to the agricultural sector, leading to changes in rainfall patterns and more frequent extreme climate events. These changes have implications for adaptation strategies in agriculture. Additionally, the durability of building materials under changing climate conditions is a critical consideration, as weathering can accelerate the degradation of building structures, emphasizing the need for resilience in construction practices.

The impact of climate change on wind patterns can affect sectors such as agriculture and energy, requiring adjustments to building codes to enhance structural resilience. The need for paradigm shifts in building construction practices to address climate change challenges is evident, with strategies like raising floors, using local materials, and orienting buildings based on sun and wind directions being crucial for adaptation [61, 62].

Terrorism: Terrorism, defined as acts or threats intended to advance political, ideological, or religious causes by coercing governments or the public, includes:

- Causing serious harm to people or property.
- Creating significant public health and safety risks.
- Seriously disrupting trade, infrastructure, or electronic systems. Global events such as the September 11 attacks in the United States and the 2002 Bali bombings have heightened perceptions of vulnerability and led to significant investments in national security, the development of anti-terrorism laws, and increased security awareness in both public and private sectors. These incidents have challenged notions of multiculturalism and tolerance, potentially reducing social cohesion and complicating recovery processes.

Figure 12: Explosion following the plane impact into the South Tower (September 11 attacks). rds323, Public domain, via Wikimedia Commons.

Crimes of Extreme Violence: Internationally, events like the 2011 Norway attacks and the 2016 Nice truck attack illustrate the complexities of recovering from acts of extreme violence, which result in numerous casualties and widespread psychosocial impacts. The unpredictable and heinous nature of such crimes poses significant challenges for emergency response and long-term recovery.

Figure 13: Government building in Oslo after the bombing on 22 July 2011. Johannesen, Nærings- og handelsdepartementet, CC BY 2.0, via Wikimedia Commons.

Biosecurity: Biosecurity emergencies, such as outbreaks of pest insects, animal, or plant diseases, can devastate economies, environments, and communities across the globe. Historical examples include the 2000 foot and mouth disease outbreak in the United Kingdom and the spread of avian influenza in various countries, which had significant economic and psychological impacts. The emergence of zoonotic diseases also poses risks, potentially leading to disproportionate fear and undermining business confidence.

Human Pandemics: Historical pandemics like the 1918 Spanish Flu and more recent ones like H1N1 in 2009 have demonstrated the potential for significant societal disruption. The unpredictable nature of pandemics underscores the importance of global readiness and the need for robust pandemic preparedness plans.

Figure 14: 2,500 people line up in a mall in Texas City, Texas to receive a dose of the H1N1/Swine Flu vaccine from the Galveston County Health Department. Nsaum75, CC BY-SA 3.0, via Wikimedia Commons.

Infrastructure Failures: Our globalized world heavily depends on essential services such as electricity, water, fuel, gas, and telecommunications. Disruptions to these services, whether from natural disasters, extreme weather, or human actions like cyberattacks, can have extensive consequences. Examples include the 2003 Northeast blackout in the United States and Canada, and more recent cyberattacks on critical infrastructure, which have highlighted the profound impacts on business operations and public safety.

These examples underscore the interconnected nature of modern challenges in disaster management and the importance of international cooperation and preparedness to mitigate their effects.

2

Phases of Disaster, Emergency Management, Recovery and Resilience

Disaster management is structured around several critical phases that guide communities on how to effectively prepare for, respond to, recover from, and mitigate disasters. These stages are collectively known as the "Emergency Management Cycle", which consists of four main phases: mitigation, preparedness, response, and recovery.

Mitigation, or prevention, focuses on preventing future emergencies or minimizing their effects before they occur. This phase includes actions such as enforcing building codes and zoning laws, conducting vulnerability analyses, educating the public, and reinforcing infrastructure to withstand natural and human-made hazards like hurricanes, earthquakes, and floods.

Preparedness is aimed at getting ready to handle an emergency effectively. This involves preparing people to respond appropriately when a disaster is imminent. Key activities during this phase include developing emergency response plans, conducting disaster drills and training, establishing emergency communications and warning systems, and stocking essential food and emergency supplies.

The Response phase kicks in once an emergency occurs, focusing on ensuring a safe and effective reaction to the disaster. This phase typically involves the mobilization of necessary emergency services and first responders such as firefighters, police, and ambulance crews. Activities include evacuation, search and rescue operations, providing immediate assistance, assessing damage, and continuing to deliver emergency relief to affected individuals.

Recovery seeks to restore the affected area to its previous state, or even improve it, after the immediate response has concluded. This involves rebuilding homes and infrastructure, restoring essential services, processing claims for disaster assistance, and implementing disaster mitigation programs to prevent future disasters. Recovery efforts also address the health and mental well-being of the survivors, aiming to return life to normal as efficiently as possible.

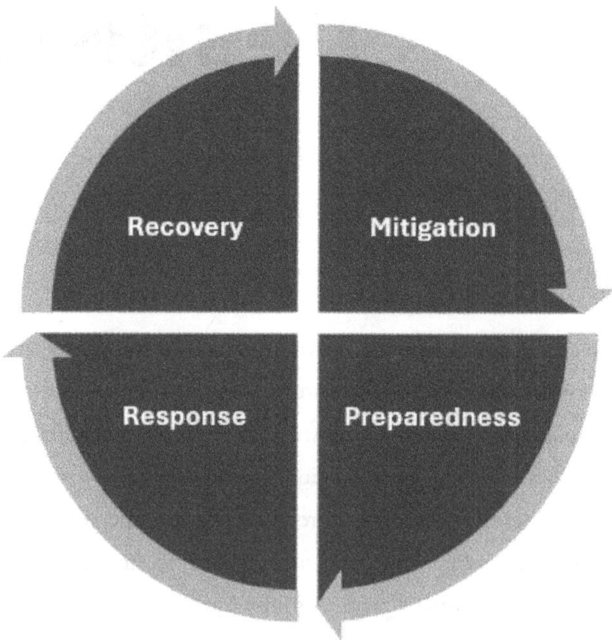

Figure 15: Emergency Management Cycle.

Incorporated within these phases is the broader concept of Resilience in disaster management, which underscores the ability of individuals, communities, organizations, and states to adapt to and recover from disasters or threats with minimal long-term disruption. Resilient systems utilize strategies across all phases of the disaster management cycle to ensure that communities can bounce back quickly and effectively, thereby minimizing social, economic, and environmental impacts.

Understanding and effectively managing these phases of disaster management not only reduces the impact of disasters but also enhances a community's ability to cope with and recover from unforeseen incidents, reinforcing the overall resilience of the society.

Mitigation

Mitigation strategies are essential in disaster management, focusing on preventing future emergencies or minimizing their effects before they occur. This proactive phase involves various actions such as enforcing building codes and zoning laws, conducting vulnerability analyses, educating the public, and reinforcing infrastructure to withstand natural and human-made hazards like hurricanes, earthquakes, and floods [63-66].

Research emphasizes the significant benefits of investing in natural hazard mitigation programs, where each dollar spent in such initiatives saves society an average of $4 in future avoided losses [63]. Similarly, research highlights the importance of cost-benefit analyses for risk mitigation actions, providing insights into the effectiveness of mitigation strategies for earthquakes and floods [64].

Studies focusing on specific disasters, such as Hurricane Harvey in Houston, Texas, underscore the importance of disaster preparedness, home structure flood hazard mitigation, and the relationship between preparedness, mitigation, health effects, and recovery [65]. Additionally, research demonstrates the risk-reduction capacity of various mitigation strategies, such as dry-proofing and wet-proofing, in residential areas prone to flooding [66].

Mitigation efforts are crucial for reducing the impact of disasters on communities and infrastructure. Researchers have highlighted the complementary roles of mitigation and insurance in managing catastrophic risks, emphasizing the importance of specific risk mitigation measures in reducing losses and improving resilience [67, 68]. Furthermore, initiatives like disaster mitigation education in schools and community-based disaster risk reduction programs are essential for enhancing preparedness and resilience at the grassroots level [67, 69].

Effective mitigation strategies are vital for reducing the vulnerability of communities to disasters and enhancing their capacity to withstand and recover from adverse events. By integrating mitigation measures into planning, policy development, and public awareness campaigns, societies can build resilience and mitigate the impacts of future emergencies.

Preparedness

Preparedness in emergency management is a crucial phase aimed at effectively handling emergencies by preparing individuals to respond appropriately when a disaster is imminent. This phase involves key activities such as developing emergency response plans, conducting disaster drills and training, establishing emergency communications and warning systems, and stocking essential food and emergency supplies [70, 71].

Research emphasizes that emergency preparedness is the initial phase of emergency management, followed by response, recovery, and mitigation [72]. It mainly focuses on emergency planning, training, and exercising aspects. Similarly, research highlights the importance of education in disaster management and emergencies, defining a new European course to enhance preparedness and response to disasters [73].

Studies focusing on the effectiveness of disaster drills and simulations in improving knowledge, attitude, and self-efficacy for disaster management among healthcare professionals underscore the significance of continuous training and preparedness exercises [74, 75]. Furthermore, highlights the value of earthquake drills and simulations in community-based training and preparedness programs, emphasizing the role of short simulation exercises in enhancing emergency department nurses' self-efficacy for initial disaster management [74, 75].

The integration of tabletop exercises, continuous training, and disaster drills is essential for enhancing knowledge, attitude, and self-efficacy in disaster preparedness among healthcare professionals and emergency responders [74]. Additionally, discuss the challenges of policy implementation and the ritualization of public health emergency plans in urban communities, further emphasizing the importance of effective emergency preparedness strategies in responding to public health emergencies like the COVID-19 pandemic.

The preparedness phase in emergency management plays a crucial role in ensuring effective response and mitigation of disasters. By focusing on planning, training, and exercising, individuals and organizations can enhance their readiness to handle emergencies and protect the well-being of communities.

As a specific example preparedness strategy, the Tokyo Rinkai Disaster Prevention Park, also known as Tokyo Rinkai Koiki Bosai Koen, is strategically located in the waterfront area of Tokyo. It is specifically designed to enhance public knowledge about disaster preparedness and doubles as a critical emergency evacuation site during major disasters, such as earthquakes or tsunamis. This park is a vital component of Tokyo's comprehensive disaster management strategy.

Figure 16: The Tokyo Rinkai Disaster Prevention Park. □□, CC BY-SA 3.0, via Wikimedia Commons.

Key Features and Functions of the Park:

Education and Training: The park features a comprehensive disaster preparedness learning centre, where visitors can participate in realistic simulations and interact with exhibits that teach them how to react in various disaster scenarios. The centre educates on the science behind disasters, emergency response strategies, and essential life-saving techniques, aiming to equip citizens with the knowledge and skills needed to handle emergencies effectively.

Evacuation Facility: Designed to serve as a primary evacuation zone in the event of a significant disaster, the park is equipped with facilities to support the needs of displaced individuals. These facilities include temporary shelters, medical stations, and centres for the distribution of essential supplies, all of which are essential for immediate disaster response and recovery.

Advanced Infrastructure: The infrastructure of the park is engineered to withstand severe natural disasters, including earthquakes and tsunamis. It includes expansive open spaces that are crucial for accommodating large numbers of evacuees safely and efficiently.

Community Engagement: To foster a culture of preparedness, the park regularly conducts drills and training sessions for local residents and organizations. These activities not only enhance community readiness and resilience but also promote active participation, ensuring that the local population is well-prepared and aware of necessary actions during disasters.

Overall, the Tokyo Rinkai Disaster Prevention Park exemplifies how urban areas, particularly those vulnerable to natural disasters, can integrate safety, education, and community involvement into public spaces. This integration significantly enhances the area's overall resilience and preparedness, serving as a model for disaster readiness worldwide.

Response

The Response phase of emergency management is a critical period that activates once an emergency or disaster strikes. This phase is dedicated to ensuring a safe and effective reaction to the immediate impacts of the disaster. Its primary goal is to address the urgent needs of those affected and to stabilize the situation as quickly as possible.

During this phase, a coordinated effort is made to mobilize all necessary emergency services and first responders. This includes firefighters, police officers, and ambulance crews who are often the first on the scene. Their actions are crucial in managing the immediate dangers and providing essential aid to victims.

Figure 17: Firefighters break through concrete during the search for survivors in the remains of the Plaza Towers Elementary School after a tornado struck Moore, Okla., May 20, 2013. MAJ Geoff Legler, Public domain, via Wikimedia Commons.

The Response phase in emergency management is a critical stage that comes into play once an emergency occurs, focusing on ensuring a safe and effective reaction to the disaster. This phase typically involves the mobilization of essential emergency services and first responders, such as firefighters, police, and ambulance crews, to address the immediate needs of the affected population. Activities during the Response phase include evacuation procedures to move individuals out of harm's way, conducting search and rescue operations to locate and assist those in distress, providing immediate medical assistance to the injured, assessing the extent of damage caused by the disaster, and continuing to deliver emergency relief to support affected individuals [76-78].

Key activities in the Response phase encompass a wide range of urgent actions. Evacuation procedures may be implemented to move people away from imminent threats to safer locations. Search and rescue operations are conducted to locate and save victims trapped or injured by the disaster. Providing immediate assistance is also a priority, which includes medical care, distributing emergency supplies like food and water, and offering temporary shelter to those displaced.

Figure 18: Members of Fairfax County Urban Search and Rescue conduct a rescue operation in a collapsed section of the Hotel Montana in Port-au-Prince, Haiti during a search for survivors. U.S. Navy photo by Mass Communication Specialist 1st Class Joshua Lee Kelsey, Public domain, via Wikimedia Commons.

Emergency response efforts are essential for mitigating the impact of disasters and saving lives during crisis situations. The coordination and collaboration among various response agencies and organizations play a vital role in ensuring a swift and effective response to emergencies. Timely actions, such as setting up emergency shelters, establishing communication channels, and deploying resources to the most affected areas, are crucial components of the Response phase. Additionally, the provision of medical care, food, water, and other essential supplies to those impacted by the disaster is vital in addressing immediate needs and ensuring the well-being of individuals in distress [79-81].

Additionally, the Response phase involves assessing the extent of the damage caused by the disaster. This assessment is vital for understanding the scope of the impact and for planning subsequent recovery efforts. Throughout this phase, efforts continue to deliver emergency relief and support to affected individuals, ensuring that the most critical needs are met and that the groundwork is set for the recovery process that follows.

The Response phase is characterized by rapid decision-making, resource allocation, and the implementation of emergency protocols to address the evolving situation. Effective communication and information dissemination to the public regarding safety measures, evacuation procedures, and available support services are key aspects of the Response phase. Furthermore, the deployment of specialized response teams, such as urban search and rescue teams and medical response units, enhances the capacity to provide timely assistance and support to individuals affected by the disaster. Overall, the Response phase plays a critical role in managing the immediate aftermath of emergencies and laying the foundation for subsequent recovery and rebuilding efforts [82, 83].

Figure 19: Volunteers with the Missouri Lutheran Church Disaster Response team are helping survivors clean up after the deadly May 20 tornado. Volunteers provide much needed personal services and are important FEMA partners in disaster recovery. National Archives at College Park - Still Pictures, Public domain, via Wikimedia Commons.

Recovery

The recovery phase in disaster management begins once the immediate emergency response has ended. It is a crucial stage that focuses on both restoring and enhancing the affected area. The overarching aim of recovery is comprehensive, addressing not only the repair of physical damages but also strengthening the community's resilience against future disasters.

The recovery phase involves various critical activities, including rebuilding homes and infrastructure, restoring essential services, processing claims for disaster assistance, implementing disaster mitigation programs, and addressing health and mental well-being [84-86].

The recovery phase encompasses a variety of critical activities:

- Rebuilding Homes and Infrastructure: The construction and repair of residential buildings, roads, bridges, and public facilities form a major part of recovery efforts. These structures, damaged or destroyed by the disaster, are rebuilt to quickly provide safe and functional living and working conditions. This helps support the return to daily life and restore normalcy [87-89].

- Restoring Essential Services: Recovery efforts also prioritize the restoration of vital services such as water, electricity, healthcare, and sanitation. These services are crucial for meeting basic needs and play a significant role in preventing secondary health crises among the affected populations.

- Processing Claims for Disaster Assistance: Recovery includes the administrative processes necessary to help disaster victims receive financial aid. This assistance is vital for helping individuals and businesses cope with financial losses and is integral to the economic recovery of the community.

- Implementing Disaster Mitigation Programs: Learning from the disaster is a key component of recovery. Steps are taken to mitigate the effects of similar future disasters. This might involve updating building codes, improving flood defences, and refining evacuation plans to enhance community safety and resilience.

- Addressing Health and Mental Well-being: The psychological impact of the disaster on survivors is also a critical focus of the recovery phase. Mental health support, counselling, and community support programs are implemented to help individuals deal with trauma and loss, fostering a resilient and supportive community environment.

The recovery phase is not merely about physical reconstruction but is geared towards building back better. It aims for a swift and sustainable return to normalcy while enhancing the community's preparedness and resilience to future disasters.

Leadership and Management

For disaster management leaders to effectively oversee the management cycle, they must cultivate a range of essential skills tailored to each stage:

Prevention: At the prevention stage, leaders require strong analytical skills to identify potential threats, hazards, and high-risk areas. Equally important are problem-solving skills, which are crucial for determining the most effective ways to prevent or reduce the chances of catastrophic events [90-92].

The prevention stage in disaster management is a critical phase aimed at reducing the potential impacts of disasters before they occur. Leaders play a pivotal role during this stage by utilizing their analytical and problem-solving skills to proactively safeguard communities against potential emergencies. Analytical skills are essential for leaders to identify and assess potential threats, hazards, and high-risk areas by analysing environmental data, historical disaster records, and current trends [93]. This analysis helps in pinpointing where and how disasters might occur, enabling leaders to predict outcomes and implement pre-emptive measures [94].

In addition to analytical skills, problem-solving abilities are indispensable at the prevention stage. Leaders must devise strategic solutions such as developing policies to protect vulnerable areas, enhancing public infrastructure, and initiating educational programs to inform the public about risk reduction practices [95]. This combination of insightful analysis and creative problem-solving is crucial for preventing or mitigating the adverse effects of disasters, ultimately protecting lives and reducing economic losses [96].

Leadership in disaster prevention involves strategic planning, risk assessment, and the development of preventive measures to safeguard communities and infrastructure. By analysing vulnerabilities, assessing potential hazards, and implementing mitigation strategies, leaders can enhance the resilience of communities and reduce the likelihood of disasters. Effective prevention strategies may include developing regulations, conducting risk analyses, providing training on mitigation strategies, and promoting community awareness of disaster risks.

Mitigation: Planning skills are vital during the mitigation stage, as leaders must devise strategies and implement structural changes that mitigate potential threats. Raising awareness is also key; it is essential that community members understand the proactive steps they can take to mitigate risks. Examples of effective mitigation include updates to building codes post-Hurricane Andrew in 1992 and the strengthening of infrastructure in coastal areas responding to sea-level rise and climate change. Similarly, coastal regions threatened by sea-level rise have strengthened their infrastructure by constructing sea walls and improving water management systems [97].

The mitigation stage in disaster management is a crucial phase that focuses on reducing the impact of potential disasters by implementing strategic and structural changes to lessen both the probability and consequences of adverse events. Effective mitigation heavily relies on strong planning skills, where leaders in disaster management must develop comprehensive strategies to address identified risks [98]. This involves organizing resources, coordinating with stakeholders, and creating actionable plans to ensure community preparedness and resilience [99].

Structural changes play a key role in mitigation efforts, aiming to reduce risks to life and property. Examples include reinforcing buildings against earthquakes, elevating homes in flood-prone areas, and improving drainage systems to manage heavy rainfall effectively [100]. These changes require careful planning and investment but are essential for reducing vulnerability and enhancing safety within communities.

Raising awareness through education and community engagement is another vital component of mitigation. It is crucial for community members to be aware of the risks they face and the steps they can take to mitigate these risks. Effective communication strategies can inform the public about disaster risk reduction practices, such as adhering to building codes and participating in preparedness programs [101].

Preparedness: In the preparedness phase, the ability to train people effectively for disaster response is crucial. Organizational skills ensure that preparations are comprehensive and systematic, while strong oral and written communication abilities are necessary to effectively prepare both laypeople and emergency responders for potential worst-case scenarios.

The preparedness phase in disaster management is a critical component that focuses on ensuring communities and emergency responders are well-equipped and ready to efficiently handle potential disasters. This phase relies on thorough training, organizational skills, and effective communication to build resilience and enhance disaster response capabilities.

raining programs play a crucial role in the preparedness phase, equipping both emergency responders and the general public with the necessary skills and knowledge to respond effectively during disasters [102]. These programs often include drills, simulation exercises, and educational workshops covering various topics such as first aid, survival techniques, evacuation procedures, and emergency communication.

Strong organizational skills are essential for leaders in disaster management during the preparedness phase to ensure comprehensive planning and execution of disaster preparedness activities [103]. This includes organizing drills, managing resources, coordinating with multiple agencies, and ensuring all aspects of disaster preparedness are covered systematically.

Effective communication is another critical element in the preparedness phase, enabling leaders to convey information clearly to a wide audience, including laypeople and professional emergency responders [104]. Clear communication through verbal and written materials such as manuals and emergency plans ensures that everyone understands their roles and responsibilities during a disaster.

Historical examples and research studies demonstrate the importance of disaster preparedness in mitigating the impact of disasters. By setting up structures, conducting rigorous training, and fostering effective communication, disaster management professionals can prepare individuals and communities to respond swiftly and effectively to emergencies, ultimately reducing risks and enhancing safety when disasters occur.

Response: This stage requires the ability to make swift decisions, as responding to disasters is highly time-sensitive. Another critical skill is the capacity to delegate essential tasks efficiently to volunteers or emergency responders, ensuring that response efforts are effective and timely.

Figure 20: EU Emergency Response Coordination Centre in Brussels. Gillmti, CC BY-SA 4.0, via Wikimedia Commons.

The Response stage in disaster management is a critical phase that necessitates immediate and effective action to address the immediate impacts of a disaster. This stage is characterized by its urgency, demanding quick and decisive actions to mitigate the effects of the disaster and provide relief to affected individuals. Swift decision-making is crucial during this stage as disaster scenarios evolve rapidly, requiring leaders and responders to assess situations quickly and make informed choices to save lives and minimize damage [105]. Effective delegation of tasks is equally vital in the Response stage to ensure optimal utilization of resources and personnel, leading to a coordinated and successful response. Leaders must assign responsibilities based on skills, expertise, and proximity to the needs, emphasizing the importance of understanding team capabilities and situational demands [106].

Furthermore, effective delegation involves providing team members with necessary information and resources to perform tasks efficiently, avoiding duplication of efforts and ensuring comprehensive coverage of critical aspects of the disaster response without delay [106]. The Response stage of disaster management demands decisive and precise actions. Swift decision-making and efficient task delegation are essential for managing emergencies effectively, ensuring timely and effective response efforts. These skills are instrumental in navigating the chaos typical of disaster situations and achieving the best possible outcomes for those affected.

Recovery: During recovery, the key skills include empathy, understanding, and relationship-building. Trust is fundamental; without it, recovery efforts may not be fully successful. Leaders must work closely with their communities, understanding their needs and challenges to facilitate a successful recovery.

The recovery phase in disaster management is a critical period that goes beyond physical reconstruction to encompass healing and strengthening the social fabric of affected communities. Effective leadership during this phase is paramount, relying heavily on interpersonal skills to foster a supportive and collaborative environment. Empathy plays a crucial role as it allows leaders to genuinely understand the needs and concerns of affected individuals, enabling tailored recovery efforts [107]. Building trust-based relationships within the community is vital, facilitating open communication and ensuring well-supported recovery plans [108]. Trust not only aids in communication but also mobilizes community members to actively participate in the recovery process, contributing positively to rebuilding efforts [109].

Successful recovery hinges on leaders' abilities to employ empathy, understanding, and relationship-building skills effectively. These interpersonal skills are instrumental in gaining the trust and cooperation of the community, ultimately determining the success of recovery endeavours. By closely engaging with communities, understanding their specific needs, and challenges, leaders can facilitate a recovery process that not only reconstructs physical structures but also restores lives and enhances community resilience [110].

Disaster management demands a comprehensive skill set that varies across different phases of the disaster management cycle. Each stage requires specific competencies that contribute to the overall effectiveness of disaster preparedness, mitigation, response, and recovery efforts.

3

Emergency Management

Emergency management is a multidisciplinary field that involves preparing for, responding to, recovering from, and mitigating the impacts of disasters and emergencies. It encompasses various aspects such as resource allocation, social equity, and effective response strategies. Emergency management involves the coordination of resources and personnel to address crises promptly and efficiently [111]. It aims to reduce vulnerability to hazards and cope with disasters effectively [112]. Social equity is a crucial aspect of emergency management, requiring continuous efforts to reduce social vulnerability and equalize the impacts of hazards on all groups [113].

Furthermore, emergency management involves not only immediate response but also long-term care to ensure the well-being of individuals affected by emergencies [114]. Stakeholders involved in emergency management view resilience as an essential ability that encompasses both emergency management activities and personal responsibility, emphasizing the need for a comprehensive approach to building resilience [115]. Overall, emergency management is a dynamic field that requires continuous adaptation, collaboration, and preparedness to effectively address a wide range of emergencies and disasters.

As such, emergency management encompasses far more than just the immediate response to incidents; it is a dynamic and ongoing process that involves meticulous planning, organizing, coordinating, and executing strategies through all phases of the emergency management cycle. This extensive process ensures comprehensive readiness and effective response to any crisis situation.

Key Components of Emergency Management:

- Public Education and Awareness: One fundamental aspect is educating the community about potential risks and the proper preparations for emergencies. This involves disseminating information and educating people on how to respond in various emergency situations, which is vital for ensuring community safety.

- Training and Exercises: Regular training and exercises are crucial for emergency responders and officials. Through simulations and drills, these professionals hone their skills, ensuring they are prepared to act swiftly and efficiently during real-life emergencies.

- Community Engagement: Involving the community in the planning and decision-making process is essential. This engagement ensures that emergency management strategies are well-rounded and reflect the actual needs and capabilities of the population, leading to more effective and inclusive approaches.

- Technology Integration: The use of advanced technology plays a significant role in improving prediction, communication, resource management, and coordination during emergencies. Technology enhances the capabilities of emergency management by providing accurate data and facilitating better decision-making.

- Interagency Collaboration: Effective emergency management requires the collaboration of various entities, including governmental and non-governmental organizations, businesses, and the public. This collaboration leverages diverse resources and capabilities, enhancing the efficiency and comprehensiveness of the response.

Emergency management is not the sole responsibility of any single entity or sector; rather, it involves a collective approach that includes local, state, and federal governments, the private sector, non-profits, and the general public. Each stakeholder plays a critical role in mitigating risks and managing the effects of disasters. By working together, these diverse groups not only improve the immediate response to emergencies but also bolster the community's overall resilience against future disasters.

Emergency management is a comprehensive system aimed at reducing vulnerability to hazards and managing disasters effectively. While emergency management encompasses various phases such as mitigation, preparedness, response, and recovery, it primarily focuses on handling disasters that exceed a community's capacity to manage independently [116]. The activities within emergency management involve a combination of efforts from individuals, households, organizations, and different levels of government [117]. The ultimate goal of emergency management is to prevent disasters and minimize their adverse impacts on communities [118].

Effective crisis and disaster management typically involve planning and preparedness activities, immediate response during a crisis, and efforts to restore or improve the situation post-crisis [119]. Furthermore, the evaluation of emergency response capabilities is crucial and can be assessed based on aspects like prevention, monitoring, response, and recovery [120]. The evolution of emergency management has led to a holistic approach that spans the entire disaster life cycle, including mitigation, preparedness, response, and recovery phases [121].

Disaster management information systems play a vital role in assisting managers in analysing situations, making informed decisions, and recommending actions based on existing emergency plans [122]. Additionally, the use of technology, such as Digital Twin applications, has been explored to enhance civil and infrastructure emergency management [123]. Moreover, the roles of local emergency managers have evolved to encompass coordination across mitigation, preparedness, response, and recovery activities [124].

Emergency management is a comprehensive and systematic process aimed at efficiently coordinating and utilizing resources across all phases of emergencies and disasters. This process encompasses planning, organizing, coordinating, and implementing strategies that mitigate risks, prepare for potential emergencies, respond effectively during crises, and facilitate recovery afterward. Below is a detailed step-by-step guide on how to effectively implement emergency management.

Risk Assessment:

- **Identify Hazards**: It's crucial to recognize all potential natural, technological, and human-made hazards that could impact the area.

- **Assess Vulnerabilities**: Evaluate how susceptible the community, infrastructure, and environment are to these identified hazards.

- **Analyse Potential Impacts**: Understand the likely consequences if these hazards were to materialize, which helps in prioritizing planning efforts.

Mitigation:

- **Implement Mitigation Strategies**: Develop and put in place measures to reduce the identified risks, such as updating building codes, improving infrastructure, or erecting barriers against natural disasters.

- **Public Education**: Engage the public by informing them about the risks and promoting practices that reduce vulnerability.

Preparedness:

- **Emergency Plans**: Craft detailed emergency response plans that are tailored to various disaster scenarios, clearly outlining roles, responsibilities, and procedures.

- **Training and Drills**: Conduct regular training sessions and simulation drills for both emergency responders and community members to ensure readiness.

- **Resource Allocation**: Ensure that necessary resources are secured and logistics are in place for efficient distribution during a disaster.

Response:

- **Activate Emergency Plans**: Quickly implement the emergency response plan once a disaster strikes.

- **Emergency Operations Center (EOC)**: Set up an EOC to act as the hub for directing operations and managing communications.

- **Rescue and Relief Operations**: Perform search and rescue efforts, provide medical aid, and distribute emergency supplies.

Recovery:

- **Short-term Recovery**: Address immediate needs by providing temporary housing, restoring services, and supporting affected individuals and businesses.

- **Long-term Recovery**: Focus on rebuilding infrastructure, revitalizing the economy, and restoring community life, incorporating lessons learned into future plans.

- **Community Involvement**: Actively involve the community in the recovery process to ensure that their needs and preferences are met.

Evaluation and Improvement:

- **After-Action Reviews**: Post-disaster, conduct thorough debriefings and evaluations to assess the effectiveness of the emergency response.
- **Update Plans and Training**: Continuously revise emergency plans and training programs based on new insights and information.

Continuous Improvement:

- **Stay Informed**: Keep abreast of new technologies and methods in emergency management.
- **Community Engagement**: Maintain an ongoing dialogue with the community to ensure they remain informed and involved.

Technologies and Tools:

- **Utilize Technology**: Leverage tools such as emergency notification systems, GIS for mapping and tracking hazards, and online resource management systems to enhance the efficiency and effectiveness of emergency management processes.

Implementing a robust emergency management system requires a coordinated effort from multiple stakeholders, including government agencies, private sector partners, non-profit organizations, and the community. A successful approach to emergency management involves thorough preparation, efficient execution, and ongoing improvement, ensuring that communities are resilient and can recover swiftly from disasters.

Risk Assessment in Emergency Management

Risk assessment is a foundational element in emergency management, serving as the first step in a proactive approach to preventing and mitigating disasters. This process involves several critical activities aimed at understanding and preparing for potential risks.

Identifying Hazards: The initial stage in risk assessment involves identifying all possible hazards that could affect an area. This includes natural disasters like earthquakes, hurricanes, and floods; technological hazards such as chemical spills or nuclear accidents; and human-made hazards, including terrorism or civil unrest. The goal is to compile a comprehensive list of threats by gathering data from historical records, scientific research, and other relevant sources. This comprehensive identification helps ensure that all potential risks are considered in the planning process.

Assessing Vulnerabilities: Once hazards are identified, the next step is to evaluate the vulnerability of the community, infrastructure, and environment to these threats. This involves analysing how susceptible the identified entities are to damage or disruption caused by each hazard. Factors such as the condition and age of buildings, the robustness of local infrastructure, the preparedness level of the community, and the resilience of the local environment are all considered. Vulnerability assessment helps to pinpoint where weaknesses exist and which areas or aspects are most at risk.

Analysing Potential Impacts: Understanding the potential impacts of each hazard is crucial for prioritizing emergency management efforts. This analysis involves estimating the likely consequences should the identified hazards materialize. Impact analysis looks at both the direct and indirect effects of disasters, including loss of life, economic losses, environmental damage, and societal disruption. This step helps emergency managers understand the scale and scope of potential disasters and is essential for developing effective mitigation strategies, emergency response plans, and recovery processes.

Scenario Example: Risk Assessment in a Coastal City

Context: A coastal city located near a major fault line is also vulnerable to hurricanes and flooding due to its geographical location. The city's economy thrives on its port activities and tourism, which makes it densely populated and bustling with infrastructure that is critical to both local and regional economies.

Identifying Hazards:

- **Natural Disasters**: The city faces multiple natural threats. Its proximity to a fault line increases the risk of earthquakes. The coastal location subjects it to hurricanes during the storm season and associated flooding risks both from storm surges and heavy rainfall.

- **Technological Hazards**: The port facilities handle various hazardous materials; thus, chemical spills are a significant risk. Additionally, the city's reliance on an aged power grid poses a risk of significant power outages and related accidents.

- **Human-made Hazards**: Given its economic importance and high population density, the city could be a target for terrorist activities. Civil unrest could also erupt as a result of economic disparities in densely populated areas.

Assessing Vulnerabilities:

- The building infrastructure in older parts of the city is not up to current earthquake standards, posing a high risk in the event of a seismic event.

- Many residential areas below sea level with inadequate drainage systems are particularly vulnerable to flooding.
- The port's security measures and hazardous material handling protocols need updating to mitigate risks of terrorism or accidental spills.
- Emergency services are well-trained but underfunded and lack sufficient equipment to handle large-scale disasters effectively.

Analysing Potential Impacts:

- **Earthquake**: Potential destruction of non-retrofitted buildings, disruption of transportation networks, damage to the power grid, and secondary impacts like fires or gas leaks.
- **Hurricanes and Floods**: Extensive property damage, especially in low-lying areas, loss of life, disruption of commerce and daily life, and potential environmental contamination from flooded industrial areas.
- **Chemical Spills**: Potential for significant health hazards, long-term environmental damage, and disruption of port activities.
- **Terrorism**: Risk of mass casualties, severe damage to critical infrastructure, and long-term economic and psychological impacts on the community.

Based on this risk assessment, the city's emergency management team can prioritize upgrading building codes, enhancing flood defences, improving port security and hazardous materials handling, and boosting the capacity and capabilities of emergency response services. Additionally, public education programs on earthquake preparedness and evacuation routes in case of hurricanes or chemical spills can be implemented to enhance community resilience. This comprehensive approach ensures that the city is not only prepared to respond effectively to emergencies but also equipped to recover swiftly from their impacts.

Mitigation in Emergency Management

Mitigation is a proactive approach in emergency management that focuses on reducing or eliminating risks before a disaster strikes. This phase is crucial because effective mitigation can significantly lessen the impact of disasters, saving both lives and resources. Mitigation involves a variety of strategies and actions aimed at addressing both the causes of disasters and their potential impacts.

Implementing Mitigation Strategies:

The first step in mitigation is to develop and implement strategies that reduce the identified risks. This could involve several practical measures:

- Updating Building Codes: One common mitigation strategy is to update local building codes to ensure that structures are able to withstand potential disasters such as earthquakes, floods, or hurricanes. This might mean mandating stronger materials, better construction practices, or retrofitting older buildings to meet new standards.

- Improving Infrastructure: Strengthening infrastructure is another key area of focus. This could include upgrading water management systems to prevent flooding, reinforcing bridges and roads to withstand earthquakes, or improving electrical grids to reduce the likelihood of outages during natural disasters.

- Erecting Barriers: In some cases, physical barriers can be effective in mitigating certain types of natural disasters. For instance, levees or sea walls can be constructed to protect coastal communities from storm surges and tsunamis.

Public Education:

Educating the public about risks and how to effectively reduce vulnerabilities is another critical component of mitigation. Public education can empower individuals and communities, making them more resilient to disasters:

- Informing About Risks: Clear communication about the types of disasters that could occur, their potential impacts, and the measures being taken to mitigate these is essential. This can be achieved through public campaigns, workshops, school programs, and the use of mass media.

- Promoting Vulnerability-Reducing Practices: Public education efforts should also focus on promoting behaviours and practices that reduce vulnerability. This could include teaching people how to prepare emergency kits, secure furniture and heavy objects in earthquake-prone areas, or create defensible space around properties in wildfire-prone regions.

- Engagement and Training: Encouraging public participation in community-based disaster preparedness programs can further enhance mitigation efforts. This can involve training sessions for emergency preparedness, community drills, and encouraging volunteerism in local disaster response and recovery efforts.

By integrating these mitigation strategies and public education efforts, communities can significantly reduce the risk of disaster-related damage and ensure a quicker, more efficient recovery process. This dual approach of structural changes combined with informed and prepared community members creates a robust defence against the inevitable challenges posed by natural and man-made disasters.

Scenario Example: Mitigation in Emergency Management in a Coastal City

Context: A coastal city prone to hurricanes and seasonal flooding has implemented a comprehensive mitigation strategy to minimize potential disaster impacts. This city, located near a large delta, has historically faced severe storm surges and water management issues, exacerbated by the effects of climate change and sea-level rise.

Mitigation Strategies Implemented:

1. **Updating Building Codes:**

    - The city council updated local building codes to require that all new constructions in flood-prone areas be elevated above the base flood elevation level. Additionally, all critical infrastructure and commercial buildings are mandated to use hurricane-resistant materials and designs. Existing structures in high-risk zones are also subject to mandatory retrofitting to enhance their resilience against hurricanes and floods.

2. **Improving Infrastructure:**

    - The city has invested significantly in upgrading its water management systems, including the construction of new stormwater retention basins and the expansion of existing drainage systems to effectively manage heavy rainfall events.

    - Key bridges and roads have been reinforced to withstand higher loads and more intense seismic activity, anticipating potential earthquakes from nearby fault lines.

- The electrical grid has been modernized with the addition of underground cables in critical areas and the installation of smart grid technologies to enhance grid resilience and reduce the likelihood of extended power outages.

3. **Erecting Barriers:**
    - In response to the increasing threats of storm surges, the city built a series of levees and sea walls designed to protect the most vulnerable coastal communities. These barriers are engineered to defend against projected sea levels and storm surge heights for the next fifty years.

Public Education Efforts:

1. **Informing About Risks:**
    - The city has launched an extensive public education campaign utilizing various media platforms to inform residents about the risks of hurricanes, floods, and earthquakes. This campaign includes detailed information on the city's mitigation strategies and what those mean for individual preparedness.
2. **Promoting Vulnerability-Reducing Practices:**
    - Workshops and school programs are regularly held to teach community members how to prepare emergency kits, secure furniture and valuables, and understand evacuation routes and procedures. Special emphasis is placed on securing heavy objects and vital documents, especially in areas most susceptible to quick flooding and high winds.
3. **Engagement and Training:**
    - The city encourages active community participation in disaster preparedness through neighbourhood drills and volunteer programs that support local emergency services. These initiatives aim to build a network of trained volunteers who can assist in times of disaster, particularly in conducting initial damage assessments and basic rescue operations.

Outcome: By integrating robust physical mitigation measures with an aggressive public education strategy, the city has significantly enhanced its resilience against natural disasters. The updated infrastructure and community preparedness efforts have not only reduced the potential for severe damage and loss of life but have also ensured that the city can recover more quickly and effectively when disasters do occur. This dual approach demonstrates a comprehensive defence strategy against the challenges posed by both natural and potential human-made disasters.

Preparedness in Emergency Management

Preparedness is a crucial phase in emergency management, focusing on establishing plans and procedures that ensure effective and coordinated response to disasters. This phase is about setting the groundwork to minimize the impacts of potential disasters by ensuring that all necessary systems, resources, and personnel are ready to act when needed.

Emergency Plans: Creating comprehensive emergency response plans is the cornerstone of preparedness. These plans are developed to address various disaster scenarios, such as natural disasters, technological incidents, or human-caused events. The plans should detail the specific roles and responsibilities of all involved parties, including emergency services, government agencies, and community organizations. They must outline clear procedures for communication, evacuation, resource deployment, and other critical operations. Each plan should be tailored to the unique characteristics of the community and the specific types of hazards it faces, ensuring that responses are effective and pertinent to the actual risks.

Training and Drills: Regular training sessions and simulation drills are essential to test and reinforce these emergency plans. Training helps to ensure that all emergency responders and relevant personnel are familiar with their roles and responsibilities and can perform them effectively under pressure. Drills, on the other hand, simulate disaster scenarios to practice coordination and response procedures. This not only helps to identify any gaps or weaknesses in the emergency plans but also improves the readiness and confidence of both responders and the community. Drills should involve realistic scenarios and include as many participants as possible to ensure a thorough and practical test of the emergency systems.

Resource Allocation: Ensuring that resources are properly allocated and logistics systems are in place is another critical aspect of preparedness. This involves stockpiling necessary supplies, such as food, water, medical kits, and emergency equipment. It also includes planning for the efficient distribution of these resources during a disaster. Logistics plans should account for potential disruptions and include alternative strategies for transporting and distributing supplies in case standard routes or methods are compromised. This level of planning ensures that resources are available where and when they are needed most, thereby significantly improving the effectiveness of the disaster response.

By focusing on these key aspects of preparedness—meticulous planning, regular training and drills, and strategic resource allocation—communities can enhance their ability to manage and mitigate the impacts of disasters effectively. This not only saves lives and reduces damage but also speeds up the recovery process, helping communities to bounce back more quickly from emergencies.

Scenario Example: Preparedness in Emergency Management in a Midwestern City

Context: A mid-sized city in the Midwest, known for experiencing a range of natural disasters including tornadoes, severe winter storms, and occasional flooding, has developed a comprehensive emergency management preparedness program. This program is designed to protect its residents and infrastructure by ensuring all necessary measures, resources, and personnel are effectively coordinated and ready to respond to emergencies.

Emergency Plans: The city's emergency management team has crafted detailed response plans tailored to each type of natural disaster the city might face. For tornadoes, the plan includes specific protocols for early warning systems, community shelters, and post-event search and rescue operations. For winter storms, the plan details procedures for road treatment and clearing, as well as guidelines for maintaining essential city services. For floods, there are strategies focusing on sandbag distribution, evacuation routes, and water rescue. Each plan delineates clear roles and responsibilities for local government agencies, emergency services, and community organizations, and outlines communication procedures to keep the public informed and safe.

Training and Drills: The city conducts regular training sessions for all emergency personnel, including firefighters, police, medical staff, and utility workers, ensuring they are familiar with their specific roles under different disaster scenarios. Community-wide drills are held bi-annually, simulating each type of disaster to practice evacuation procedures, the opening and operating of shelters, and the coordination among different emergency response teams. These drills are critical for identifying any gaps in the plans and for building confidence and readiness among both emergency responders and residents.

Resource Allocation: The city has established a robust system for resource management, which includes stockpiling necessary supplies like non-perishable food, water, medical kits, and emergency equipment in accessible locations throughout the city. Detailed logistics plans have been developed to ensure the quick distribution of these resources to impacted areas, with alternative strategies in place should standard routes be disrupted by the disaster. This system ensures that resources are available quickly and efficiently when and where they are needed, which is crucial for effective disaster response.

Outcome: By prioritizing these aspects of preparedness—meticulously developing emergency response plans, conducting regular training and realistic drills, and ensuring efficient resource allocation—the city has significantly enhanced its ability to manage and mitigate the impacts of natural disasters. This comprehensive approach not only helps to save lives and reduce damage during disasters but also accelerates the recovery process, allowing the community to recover more swiftly and effectively from emergencies.

Response Phase in Emergency Management

The response phase is a critical component of emergency management, activated immediately after a disaster occurs. This phase focuses on addressing the immediate needs to ensure safety, reduce casualties, and manage chaos efficiently. Effective execution of this phase relies heavily on well-coordinated actions, quick decision-making, and pre-established emergency plans.

Activating Emergency Plans: Once a disaster strikes, the immediate step is to activate the relevant emergency response plan. These plans should have been meticulously developed during the preparedness phase and tailored to specific types of disasters, whether they are natural, technological, or human-induced. Activation includes mobilizing all designated emergency personnel and resources according to predefined roles and responsibilities. Quick implementation is crucial and relies on clear communication channels established beforehand to alert all stakeholders and responders without delay.

Setting Up an Emergency Operations Center (EOC): An essential structure in the response phase is the Emergency Operations Center (EOC). The EOC serves as the central command and control facility responsible for carrying out the principles of emergency preparedness and emergency management, or disaster management functions at a strategic level in an emergency situation, and ensuring the continuity of operation of a company, political subdivision, or other organization. An effective EOC is equipped with the necessary technology and communications infrastructure to coordinate efforts, make strategic decisions, and manage resources effectively. It acts as the nerve centre for operations, gathering real-time information, assessing rapidly changing scenarios, and deploying resources where they are needed most.

Conducting Rescue and Relief Operations: Rescue and relief operations are the most visible aspects of the disaster response phase. These operations include deploying search and rescue teams to locate and save victims trapped by the disaster, providing immediate medical aid to the injured, and distributing essential supplies such as food, water, and medical kits to survivors. For these operations to be effective, they must be well-coordinated and quick. This requires that all responding teams know their roles and have the necessary equipment and training to carry out their tasks under pressure. Moreover, logistical support must ensure that supplies reach those in urgent need without significant delays.

Scenario Example: Response Phase in Emergency Management During a Major Earthquake

Context: A major earthquake has struck a large metropolitan area, causing significant structural damage to buildings, rupturing gas lines, and disrupting power and communication lines. The local emergency management team, having anticipated such an event, has a well-organized response plan ready for activation.

Activating Emergency Plans: Immediately following the earthquake, the local government activates its earthquake response plan. Emergency alerts are sent out via various channels, including radio, television, and emergency notification apps, informing residents of the quake and providing initial safety instructions. Emergency response teams, including firefighters, medical personnel, and search and rescue units, are mobilized according to their predefined roles. Each team has specific assignments, ensuring a swift and organized response to various aspects of the disaster.

Setting Up an Emergency Operations Centre (EOC): An Emergency Operations Centre (EOC) is quickly established at a pre-designated location known to all major stakeholders. This location is equipped with backup power generators and emergency communication systems to ensure operational effectiveness despite the power outage. The EOC serves as the command hub where leaders gather real-time data from various sources, including field teams and satellite imagery. They assess the extent of the damage, prioritize response actions, and deploy resources to critical areas, such as collapsed buildings or neighbourhoods reporting the highest casualties.

Conducting Rescue and Relief Operations: Search and rescue teams are immediately dispatched to areas with the most severe damage. These teams include specially trained dogs and personnel equipped with life-detection equipment to locate survivors trapped under debris. Concurrently, medical teams set up triage centres near the impacted zones to provide immediate medical care to the injured. Mobile units distribute emergency supplies, including water, food, and blankets, to displaced residents.

Volunteers and community organizations play a crucial role, assisting with minor injuries and helping to comfort those affected. Coordination with nearby cities and states is initiated to request additional resources like medical supplies and additional rescue teams if the local capacity is overwhelmed.

Outcome: Thanks to the rapid activation of the emergency response plan and the efficient functioning of the EOC, the initial response is effective in managing the chaos caused by the earthquake. The quick deployment of rescue and relief operations helps minimize further casualties and provides immediate aid to those in need. The response phase's success sets a solid foundation for the forthcoming recovery efforts, focusing on rebuilding and restoring normalcy in the affected areas.

This scenario illustrates the importance of preparedness and the need for a well-coordinated response strategy during disasters. By having a clear plan, trained personnel, and a functional EOC, communities can significantly improve their resilience and capacity to handle major disasters.

Recovery Phase in Emergency Management

The recovery phase is a critical component of emergency management, following the immediate response to a disaster. It is divided into two main stages: short-term and long-term recovery, each with distinct objectives and actions necessary for a community to heal and rebuild.

Short-term Recovery: Short-term recovery focuses on addressing the immediate needs that arise in the aftermath of a disaster. The primary goal during this stage is to ensure that affected individuals and businesses receive the support they need to begin the normalization process. This includes providing temporary housing for those whose homes have been damaged or destroyed. Temporary housing solutions might range from setting up shelters in schools and community centres to providing trailers or other forms of temporary accommodation.

Restoring essential services is another critical aspect of short-term recovery. This involves re-establishing electricity, water, sewage, and other utilities that are often disrupted by disasters. It's essential for public health and safety that these services be returned to operational status as quickly as possible. Additionally, support for affected individuals and businesses includes distributing emergency aid, such as food and water, medical care, and financial assistance to help them cope with immediate post-disaster challenges.

Long-term Recovery: Long-term recovery begins once the immediate crisis has passed and focuses on rebuilding and revitalizing the community's infrastructure and economy. This stage involves more substantial reconstruction efforts, which may include repairing roads, bridges, and public buildings or completely rebuilding areas that were extensively damaged. Economic revitalization is also a crucial focus, which may involve support for reopening businesses, attracting new investments, and assisting unemployed individuals back into work.

Long-term recovery also includes efforts to restore community life. This can involve rebuilding schools, parks, and community centres, and resuming regular community events and activities, which help restore a sense of normalcy and community cohesion. Importantly, this phase should incorporate lessons learned from the disaster to improve the community's resilience and preparedness for future incidents. This could mean updating building codes, enhancing flood defences, or revising emergency management plans.

Community Involvement: Active community involvement is essential throughout the recovery process to ensure that the recovery activities align with the specific needs and preferences of the community members. Engaging local residents, business owners, and community groups in the planning and implementation of recovery initiatives ensures transparency and that the recovery efforts are relevant and effective. This involvement can take the form of public meetings, surveys, and inclusion of community representatives in recovery planning committees.

Communities that actively involve their residents in recovery efforts tend to experience more successful and swifter recoveries, as these efforts are rooted in a deep understanding of local needs and priorities. Additionally, involving the community helps to strengthen social ties and mutual support, which are vital for overcoming the psychological impacts of disasters.

Overall, the recovery phase is about rebuilding not just the physical infrastructure but also the social fabric of the community, making it better prepared and more resilient against future disasters.

Scenario Example: Recovery Phase Following a Major Hurricane in a Coastal Town

Context: A large hurricane has just swept through a small coastal town, resulting in significant property damage, loss of utilities, and disruptions to everyday life. The town has now entered the recovery phase of emergency management, tackling the challenges of both short-term and long-term recovery to rebuild and strengthen the community.

Short-term Recovery: Immediately after the hurricane, the town's priority is addressing the immediate needs of its residents. Emergency management teams set up temporary housing using local schools and community centres to shelter those whose homes are either destroyed or severely damaged. Additionally, mobile home units are brought in to accommodate displaced families during the rebuilding process.

Simultaneously, utility companies, supported by regional aid, work around the clock to restore essential services. Crews are quickly deployed to repair downed power lines and restore electricity, while water service teams address breaks in the water mains to ensure residents have access to clean water. Emergency aid stations are set up to distribute food, water, and basic medical care to those affected. Financial assistance offices are established to help residents and business owners apply for emergency funds to cover critical expenses.

Long-term Recovery: As the initial chaos stabilizes, the focus shifts to long-term recovery efforts. The town begins extensive projects to repair roads, bridges, and public buildings damaged by the hurricane. An economic recovery plan is implemented, offering loans and grants to help local businesses reopen and recover from financial losses. Efforts are made to attract new investments to diversify and strengthen the town's economic base.

Efforts to restore community life are also a major focus. Schools are repaired and reopened to provide children with stability and routine. Parks and community centres are restored to help rekindle community spirit and provide safe spaces for residents to gather. Plans drawn from lessons learned during the disaster lead to the updating of local building codes to improve storm resilience, and enhancements to the town's flood defences are made to mitigate the impact of future hurricanes.

Community Involvement: Throughout the recovery process, the town actively involves its residents. Community feedback forums and surveys are conducted to identify the most pressing needs and preferences of the community members. Recovery planning committees include representatives from various community groups to ensure that all voices are heard and considered. This inclusive approach not only ensures that the recovery efforts are closely aligned with the community's needs but also strengthens the social fabric and resilience of the town.

Outcome: The proactive and inclusive approach to recovery helps the coastal town not only to rebuild but also to improve its preparedness for future disasters. By addressing immediate needs swiftly and focusing on sustainable rebuilding and economic revitalization, the town emerges from the recovery phase more resilient and unified, ready to face future challenges.

Evaluation and Improvement in Emergency Management

Evaluation and improvement are critical components of the emergency management cycle, aimed at enhancing the effectiveness and efficiency of responses to future emergencies. This phase involves systematic review of the actions taken before, during, and after an emergency to identify both strengths and areas for improvement. The process is iterative, ensuring that emergency management practices evolve based on lessons learned and new developments in the field.

After-Action Reviews: After-action reviews (AARs) are essential for a comprehensive evaluation of the emergency response. These reviews are typically conducted after the response phase of an emergency has concluded. The goal is to gather all key stakeholders involved in the emergency response—including first responders, government officials, community leaders, and other relevant parties—to discuss what happened, what was done well, and what could have been done better.

During these debriefings, participants examine the sequence of events, the effectiveness of the emergency response, and the outcomes. They assess the functionality of the implemented emergency plans, the adequacy of resource allocation, the effectiveness of communication systems, and the coordination among different teams and organizations. Feedback from these sessions is critical as it provides first hand insights into the practical aspects of the response efforts and highlights unexpected challenges that were encountered.

Update Plans and Training: Based on the insights gained from after-action reviews, emergency management plans and training programs should be continuously updated. This includes making necessary adjustments to strategies that may have shown weaknesses during the last deployment or incorporating new techniques and technologies that can improve future responses. For example, if an AAR identifies that communication between different emergency services was problematic, improvements might include upgrading communication equipment or revising protocols to ensure clearer and more reliable lines of communication.

Training programs should also be revised to address any shortcomings identified during the emergency. New scenarios that reflect recent experiences should be included in training exercises to prepare responders for similar or worse situations in the future. This ongoing revision and improvement of training and planning ensure that emergency response teams are not only well-prepared but also adaptive to changing circumstances and emerging threats.

In addition to internal reviews, seeking external feedback through community engagement sessions can also provide valuable perspectives on the public's view of the response effectiveness. This helps ensure that the community's needs and concerns are considered in the planning process.

The evaluation and improvement phase is integral to developing a robust emergency management system. By systematically reviewing actions and outcomes through after-action reviews and continuously updating plans and training programs, emergency management can become more effective and responsive. This not only enhances the capability to deal with future emergencies but also builds public trust in the preparedness and response mechanisms of local and regional authorities.

Scenario Example: Evaluation and Improvement Following a Major Flood Event

Context: A medium-sized river town experienced severe flooding after days of torrential rainfall, leading to the activation of the town's flood response plan. The flood affected numerous residential areas, disrupted local businesses, and resulted in significant infrastructural damage. After the floodwaters receded and the initial response phase was concluded, the local emergency management team initiated a comprehensive evaluation and improvement process.

After-Action Reviews (AARs): The town's emergency management director convened an after-action review meeting involving first responders, local government officials, representatives from affected communities, and volunteers who participated in the response efforts. This review aimed to critically analyse every aspect of the flood response.

During the AAR, stakeholders discussed the effectiveness of the evacuation orders, the adequacy of the shelters provided, the speed and efficiency of the rescue operations, and the distribution of emergency supplies. It was noted that while the evacuation was timely, communication between different emergency services was sometimes delayed, causing some confusion at evacuation points. The feedback collected was detailed and constructive, highlighting strengths such as strong community volunteer turnout and areas for improvement, notably in communication and logistics.

Update Plans and Training: Based on the insights from the AAR, the emergency management team decided to revise their flood response plan. Key updates included enhancing the communication protocols to incorporate more reliable technology and establishing clearer lines of authority and processes for rapid information sharing. The plan's revisions also involved a new partnership with local technology companies to develop an improved emergency notification system.

Furthermore, the training programs for first responders and volunteers were updated to include more realistic drill scenarios that mimic the challenges encountered during the recent flood. New training sessions were scheduled to focus specifically on inter-agency coordination and logistics management, ensuring that all teams could work more seamlessly in future emergencies.

Community Involvement: Recognizing the importance of community feedback, the emergency management team also organized community engagement sessions. These forums allowed residents to share their experiences and offer suggestions directly to planners and responders. This direct feedback was invaluable and was used to further refine emergency plans, particularly concerning community needs and expectations.

Conclusion: The systematic approach to evaluating and improving the flood response strategies helped the town enhance its preparedness and response capabilities significantly. The iterative process of revising emergency plans and training programs, informed by both structured after-action reviews and community input, ensured that the emergency management practices were not only up-to-date but also responsive to the specific needs and conditions of the community. This ongoing commitment to evaluation and improvement solidified the community's trust in local emergency management and increased its resilience against future disasters.

Continuous Improvement in Emergency Management

Continuous improvement is a crucial strategy in emergency management, ensuring that the practices and procedures employed are always evolving to better meet the needs of the community and to utilize the latest advancements in technology and methodology. This process is essential not only for enhancing the effectiveness of emergency responses but also for fostering a resilient community that can adapt to new challenges.

Staying Informed: To ensure continuous improvement, it is vital for emergency management professionals to stay informed about the latest developments in the field. This includes keeping up-to-date with new technologies that can improve disaster response and recovery efforts, such as drones for damage assessment, advanced communication tools for better coordination, or more sophisticated data management systems that can provide real-time analysis during emergencies. Additionally, understanding new methods and best practices from around the world is crucial. This could involve participating in professional development opportunities, attending conferences, workshops, and seminars, and subscribing to relevant publications and journals. By staying informed, emergency managers can integrate innovative solutions and cutting-edge strategies into their existing protocols, thereby enhancing their overall effectiveness and efficiency.

Community Engagement: Another key aspect of continuous improvement is maintaining an active and ongoing dialogue with the community. This engagement is vital because it helps ensure that the needs and preferences of the community are continuously being addressed in emergency planning and response efforts. Community engagement can take many forms, including regular public meetings, surveys, and interactive workshops that invite community input on emergency management strategies. These interactions not only allow for the collection of valuable feedback from community members but also serve to educate the public about disaster preparedness and response procedures, which is essential for ensuring effective community action during disasters.

Moreover, community engagement helps to build and strengthen relationships between emergency management professionals and community members, fostering a sense of trust and cooperation that is critical in times of crisis. It also empowers residents, giving them a voice in how their community prepares for and responds to emergencies, which can lead to more effective and culturally appropriate strategies.

Continuous improvement in emergency management is about constantly seeking ways to do better through innovation, learning, and community interaction. By staying informed about new technologies and methods and engaging regularly with the community, emergency management organizations can ensure that their strategies remain relevant, effective, and responsive to the needs of those they serve. This ongoing process not only improves the capacity to handle emergencies but also builds a stronger, more resilient community.

Scenario Example: Continuous Improvement in Emergency Management in a Coastal City

Context: A coastal city prone to hurricanes has implemented a robust emergency management system, which has been developed through a culture of continuous improvement. Following significant impacts from previous hurricanes, the city's emergency management team identified key areas where ongoing updates and community involvement could enhance their response efforts and overall resilience.

Staying Informed: The city's emergency management team regularly updates their knowledge and skills by integrating new technological advancements and methodologies. For instance, after learning about the efficacy of drones in damage assessment from international conferences and workshops, the city invested in drone technology. These drones are now used to quickly assess affected areas post-disaster, which significantly speeds up the decision-making process regarding where to send first responders and aid. The team also implemented an advanced data management system that gathers real-time data during emergencies, allowing for a more dynamic response.

Additionally, the emergency management team participates in yearly professional development sessions that focus on the latest trends in disaster response and recovery. This includes training in new software for crisis management and simulations that use virtual reality to mimic emergency scenarios, providing practical experience in a controlled environment.

Community Engagement: The city has established a regular schedule of community engagement events that include town hall meetings, surveys, and interactive workshops. These forums are designed to gather input from residents on the effectiveness of current emergency plans and to discuss potential improvements. For example, after feedback from the community indicated that many people were unclear on the evacuation routes during a hurricane, the city launched a campaign to educate residents about these routes through interactive apps and community drills.

These engagement strategies not only ensure that the community's needs and preferences are continuously addressed but also help to educate the public on emergency preparedness. Moreover, by involving community members in the planning process, the city fosters a sense of ownership and cooperation, which is crucial during actual disaster responses.

This approach to continuous improvement in emergency management has enabled the coastal city to enhance its preparedness and response capabilities effectively. By staying informed of new developments and maintaining an active dialogue with the community, the city's emergency management team ensures that their strategies are not only current but also deeply integrated with the needs and capabilities of the residents. As a result, the city has seen improved outcomes in disaster response and a stronger, more resilient community capable of facing future challenges.

Utilizing Technologies and Tools in Emergency Management

In the complex and dynamic field of emergency management, the use of advanced technologies and tools is crucial for enhancing the effectiveness and efficiency of responses to disasters. By leveraging these modern solutions, emergency managers can improve data accuracy, speed up response times, and increase the overall resilience of communities. Here's how to effectively integrate and utilize these technologies:

Emergency Notification Systems: Emergency notification systems are vital for disseminating information quickly and efficiently to the public during emergencies. These systems can send alerts via text messages, emails, social media, and other digital platforms to ensure that critical information reaches a wide audience promptly. For implementation, emergency managers need to choose platforms that can handle the scale of messages required for their specific region and ensure that the system is capable of segmenting messages geographically. This enables targeted alerts that are relevant to specific areas within a community, enhancing the relevance and urgency of the messages.

GIS for Mapping and Tracking Hazards: Geographic Information Systems (GIS) are powerful tools that allow emergency managers to visualize, analyse, and interpret data to understand relationships, patterns, and trends regarding hazards. GIS can be used to map hazard-prone areas, track the progression of ongoing disasters (like wildfires or hurricanes), and plan evacuation routes and strategies. To effectively use GIS, emergency managers should work with skilled GIS professionals to develop maps and models that are tailored to the specific hazards their community faces. These tools should be regularly updated with the latest data and integrated into training exercises to ensure familiarity and ease of use during actual disasters.

Online Resource Management Systems: Online resource management systems are crucial for the efficient allocation and deployment of resources during emergencies. These systems help manage inventories of supplies like food, water, medical kits, and other essential emergency resources. They also track resource needs and logistics, ensuring that supplies are replenished and delivered to where they are needed most. To implement these systems, it's essential for emergency managers to choose software that is robust, secure, and capable of integrating with other emergency management tools. Training for personnel on how to use these systems effectively should be conducted regularly, and systems should be tested during drills to ensure they function as expected under the stress of an actual emergency.

Integration for Maximized Effectiveness: The most effective approach to utilizing these technologies is to integrate them into a cohesive system where data and resources can be shared quickly and seamlessly. Integration ensures that information from GIS can inform decisions in the emergency notification system and resource management tools, creating a dynamic, real-time workflow that adapts to the evolving nature of the disaster. Collaboration with technology experts and regular updates based on the latest technological advances can further enhance these systems.

By embracing these technologies and tools, emergency management professionals can transform the speed and accuracy of their response efforts, ultimately saving lives and reducing the impact of disasters on their communities. Regular training, updates, and strategic integration of these technologies into the emergency management process ensure that teams are ready and equipped to handle any emergency situation.

Scenario Example: Utilizing Technologies and Tools in Emergency Management During a Wildfire

Context: A large-scale wildfire breaks out in a rural county with diverse terrain, threatening residential areas, wildlife, and extensive forest land. The local emergency management team, equipped with advanced technological tools, mobilizes to combat the wildfire effectively and minimize damage.

Emergency Notification Systems: As soon as the wildfire is detected, the emergency management team activates the emergency notification system. This system sends out immediate alerts via SMS, emails, and push notifications through a mobile app specifically designed for emergency communications. The alerts inform residents about the wildfire's proximity, provide instructions for immediate evacuation, and direct them to the nearest safe zones. The system is configured to segment messages geographically, ensuring that residents who are in the most imminent danger receive the most urgent and relevant instructions.

GIS for Mapping and Tracking Hazards: The team utilizes Geographic Information Systems (GIS) to track the spread of the wildfire in real-time. GIS data, including satellite imagery and aerial reconnaissance, helps create dynamic maps that show the fire's current location, the rate of spread, and the topography of the surrounding areas. These maps are crucial for planning evacuation routes and strategizing firefighting efforts. They are also shared with local news outlets and public platforms to keep the community informed. Additionally, GIS helps in identifying critical infrastructure at risk, such as power plants and water supply networks, guiding efforts to protect these assets.

Online Resource Management Systems: An online resource management system is used to coordinate the logistics of firefighting resources, such as water bombers, ground crews, and medical units. The system tracks resource availability, deployment status, and resupply needs, ensuring that all teams have the necessary equipment, such as fire retardants, medical kits, and food supplies. This system is particularly useful in managing the allocation of resources in remote areas, optimizing response times and ensuring that efforts are not duplicated.

Integration for Maximized Effectiveness: The integration of these technologies proves essential for a coordinated response. Information from the GIS is used to update emergency notification messages and to redirect resources managed through the online system as the fire spreads to new areas. This cohesive technology framework allows for a flexible, adaptive response strategy that evolves with the situation on the ground, significantly enhancing the effectiveness of the emergency management operations.

Outcome: By leveraging these advanced technologies and tools, the emergency management team is able to conduct a highly efficient and effective response to the wildfire. The prompt and precise emergency notifications help ensure resident safety, while the GIS and resource management systems enable a well-orchestrated firefighting effort that minimizes damage to property and the environment. Post-incident analysis shows that the integrated use of technology not only saved lives but also preserved significant areas of forest and wildlife, underscoring the importance of continuous technological integration in emergency management practices.

Responsibility for Emergency Management

Emergency management involves a complex network of responsibilities distributed among various entities. The National Preparedness System outlines key roles in emergency management, highlighting the significance of an incident command manager and an emergency management office in task assignment, resource management, and decision-making [125]. These roles are crucial for ensuring effective coordination and response during crises.

Responsibility for emergency management is typically shared across various levels of government, private entities, non-profit organizations, and the community itself. The collaborative effort is essential because it allows for comprehensive planning, response, recovery, and mitigation activities to be effectively coordinated. Here's a breakdown of the roles at different levels:

Federal Government: The federal government plays a crucial role in setting standards, providing guidance, and offering resources to support state and local emergency management efforts. In the United States, for example, the Federal Emergency Management Agency (FEMA) is the primary federal agency responsible for coordinating the federal government's response to natural and man-made disasters. FEMA supports state and local governments in their response efforts with financial, technical, and logistical aid and leads the integration of federal disaster response activities.

State Government: State governments are responsible for managing public health and safety within their jurisdictions, including emergency management. Each state has its own emergency management agency that coordinates disaster response and recovery efforts, liaises with federal and local agencies, and develops state-wide disaster management policies and plans. These agencies also often provide training and resources to local emergency management teams.

Local Government: Local governments, including cities, towns, and counties, are typically the first responders to emergencies and are directly responsible for protecting public health and safety in their areas. They develop emergency plans tailored to their specific regional risks, conduct training and public education campaigns, and manage local resources and personnel during emergencies. Local emergency management efforts are crucial because they involve direct interaction with the affected populations and on-the-ground management of disaster response and recovery.

Tribal Government: In regions with significant indigenous populations, such as in the United States, tribal governments also play a critical role in emergency management within their territories. Tribal governments work to prepare for and respond to emergencies affecting their communities, often coordinating with federal, state, and local agencies.

Private Sector: Businesses and corporations are responsible for managing risks and planning for emergencies that could impact their operations, employees, and customers. This includes implementing business continuity plans that enable them to maintain essential functions during and after a disaster. The private sector can also play a significant role in community response efforts by providing resources, expertise, and other forms of support.

Non-Profit Organizations and NGOs: Non-profit organizations, including humanitarian and disaster relief organizations, often assist in emergency management by providing critical services such as emergency food, water, shelter, and medical care. These organizations work in coordination with government agencies and are essential in addressing the needs of vulnerable populations both during and after disasters.

Individuals and Communities: Finally, individuals and communities play a key role in emergency management. Individuals are responsible for understanding the risks they face, preparing emergency kits and plans for their families, and adhering to safety instructions during emergencies. Community involvement is crucial for enhancing local resilience, with community-based organizations often participating in planning processes and helping to disseminate information during emergencies.

Effective emergency management requires coordination across all these levels and sectors, ensuring a cohesive and united response to disasters.

Emergency management also heavily relies on cognition, particularly in recognizing emerging risks and taking appropriate actions based on available information [126]. This cognitive aspect is essential for understanding the level of risk a community faces and responding proactively to mitigate potential impacts.

Communication emerges as a fundamental tool in emergency management, facilitating coordination among different stakeholders and ensuring information dissemination

[127]. Effective communication is vital for seamless collaboration and response efforts during emergencies.

At a strategic level, emergency managers play a pivotal role in managing operational needs and addressing the requirements of political leaders involved in crisis management [128]. Their responsibilities extend to coordinating emergency operations, maintaining communication channels, and linking with policymakers to ensure a comprehensive response.

Moreover, emergency management involves a mix of public and private sector responsibilities, with some activities falling under government jurisdiction, others under private sector entities, and some requiring shared responsibility [129]. This shared responsibility underscores the need for collaboration and cooperation across different sectors to enhance overall emergency management effectiveness.

In emergency management, various national organizations across different countries have developed structured frameworks and dedicated agencies to handle disasters effectively.

Australia: In Australia, Emergency Management Australia (EMA) is the primary government agency responsible for emergency management. The country, known for its susceptibility to natural disasters like heatwaves, bushfires, and floods, emphasizes the importance of a prepared community. EMA works to strengthen community resilience and preparedness through comprehensive emergency management strategies and public education initiatives.

Canada: In Canada, Public Safety Canada (PSC) serves as the national emergency management agency, coordinating and supporting the efforts of federal organizations while overseeing emergency management in federal jurisdictions. Most emergency management activities, however, are administered at the local, provincial, and territorial levels, in alignment with Canada's constitutional setup which places municipalities under provincial jurisdiction. PSC steps in to assist under specific circumstances at the request of provincial or territorial governments.

China: China's emergency management is stratified across various government levels. The State Council oversees major public emergency incidents, delegating natural disaster management to the Ministry of Emergency Management depending on the severity of the event. This system allows for a scalable response where provincial and prefectural governments manage lesser emergencies.

Germany: Germany's emergency management is coordinated by the Federal Office of Civil Protection and Disaster Assistance. It oversees several programs including the Technisches Hilfswerk (Technical Relief) and the Zivilschutz (Civil Protection). Alongside governmental efforts, private organizations such as the German Red Cross and the Johanniter-Unfall-Hilfe play significant roles in emergency relief.

India: The National Disaster Management Authority leads India's efforts in disaster management, focusing on strategic risk management, mitigation, and building response capacity. The National Disaster Response Force specializes in rapid response to natural and man-made disasters, providing critical search, rescue, and rehabilitation services.

Japan: Japan's Central Disaster Prevention Council leads a highly centralized emergency management system, coordinating with lower levels of government to manage disasters in a country prone to earthquakes, tsunamis, and other natural events.

Malaysia: The National Disaster Management Agency (NADMA) is the focal point for managing disasters in Malaysia, established under the Prime Minister's Department, particularly after the 2014 floods. It coordinates with various ministries and agencies to handle emergency management effectively.

Nepal: Nepal's approach to disaster risk management is guided by the National Strategy for Disaster Risk Management and the Nepal Risk Reduction Consortium, which aligns with global frameworks like Hyogo's to promote sustainable disaster risk management strategies.

The Netherlands: The Ministry of Justice and Security in the Netherlands handles emergency management at a national level, operating through regional safety regions that integrate emergency services like fire, medical care, and crisis management for coordinated responses to incidents.

New Zealand: In New Zealand, the Ministry of Civil Defence & Emergency Management oversees national emergency management efforts, activating mutual-support arrangements and coordinating responses through the National Crisis Management Centre when local capabilities are overwhelmed.

Philippines: The National Disaster Risk Reduction and Management Council in the Philippines coordinates national efforts to prepare for and respond to emergencies, ensuring the protection and welfare of people during disasters.

Russia: In Russia, the Ministry of Emergency Situations (EMERCOM) handles tasks related to firefighting, civil defence, and search and rescue operations following both natural and human-made disasters.

Somalia: In Somalia, the Federal Government endorsed a proposal for establishing the Somali Disaster Management Agency (SDMA) in May 2013, introduced by the Ministry of Interior. The SDMA aims to coordinate responses to natural disasters as part of a broader initiative to rebuild national institutions. The Federal Parliament is set to review and potentially endorse this legislation after necessary amendments.

Turkey: Turkey's Disaster and Emergency Management Presidency, established in 2009 and headquartered in Ankara, is responsible for managing all forms of disasters and emergencies across the nation. This agency coordinates comprehensive emergency management efforts, including preparedness, mitigation, response, and recovery operations, and reports directly to the Turkish Ministry of Interior.

United Kingdom: Following significant events like the 2000 fuel protests and the foot-and-mouth disease crisis in 2001, the UK enacted the Civil Contingencies Act 2004 to define and enhance emergency preparedness and response strategies. Managed by the Civil Contingencies Secretariat and implemented through Regional Resilience Forums and local authorities, the act categorizes organizations as either Category 1 or 2 responders, each with specific responsibilities. Training for disaster management is widely available through professional courses, and qualifications can be earned at various academic levels from institutions across the country, including a specialized program at the University of Bonn.

United States: In the United States, the Federal Emergency Management Agency (FEMA), a component of the Department of Homeland Security (DHS), is the primary federal agency overseeing emergency management. While local authorities initially manage disasters, FEMA steps in to coordinate at the national level if the situation escalates beyond local control. FEMA organizes the country into ten regions for structured management and supports state authorities without overriding them. The agency works closely with other organizations, such as the Citizen Corps and the Red Cross, to prepare for and respond to emergencies. Volunteer efforts are significant to U.S. disaster response, with many religious and non-profit organizations playing key roles in providing immediate aid and ongoing support.

These diverse structures reflect each nation's unique geographical, political, and social landscapes, showcasing tailored approaches to managing emergencies effectively.

Emergency Management Teams

Forming an effective emergency management team involves incorporating a variety of roles that contribute essential skills and expertise for managing disasters efficiently. Here's who should be included and why:

1. Emergency Management Director: This leader coordinates all emergency response activities and decisions, ensuring cohesive and effective management across various agencies. The director is crucial for overseeing the development and implementation of emergency plans.

2. Public Safety Officials (Police, Fire, EMS): These first responders are critical for immediate rescue operations, maintaining public order, and providing medical assistance. Their early actions can save lives, prevent chaos, and stabilize the affected areas.

3. Public Health Officials: Vital for addressing potential public health crises resulting from emergencies, such as disease outbreaks or environmental health hazards. They ensure that health services continue to operate and public health is protected throughout the emergency.

4. Local Government Representatives: These officials provide insight into the community's needs and priorities and can mobilize local resources and facilitate legal and logistical support necessary for effective emergency response and recovery.

5. Communications and Information Technology Specialists: These team members manage the communications infrastructure, ensuring that critical information is reliably disseminated to all stakeholders and the public quickly and efficiently.

6. Logistics and Supply Chain Managers: Responsible for the procurement, allocation, and transportation of essential resources and supplies during emergencies, these managers ensure that all operational teams have what they need to perform their tasks effectively.

7. Infrastructure Experts (e.g., Engineers): They assess and report on the integrity of critical infrastructure, advise on necessary repairs or constructions, and help prioritize infrastructure recovery efforts.

8. Community and Volunteer Coordinators: These coordinators engage with the community and manage volunteers and NGO contributions, which are often substantial. They help harness local efforts and ensure that volunteer resources are used effectively.

9. Legal Advisors: Essential for ensuring that all emergency management activities comply with local, state, and federal laws, and for advising on issues related to liability and regulatory compliance.

10. Meteorologists or Environmental Scientists: When dealing with natural disasters, these experts provide forecasts and analyses of environmental conditions that can greatly influence emergency operations and planning.

11. Mental Health Professionals: They offer necessary psychological support to survivors and responders, helping manage the mental and emotional impacts of disasters, which are crucial for long-term recovery.

12. Financial Analysts or Grant Managers: These professionals manage the financial aspects of emergency operations, including the sourcing and allocation of funds, which are critical for sustained response and recovery efforts.

Each of these roles brings a unique and necessary skill set to the emergency management team, ensuring a comprehensive approach to disaster preparedness, response, recovery, and mitigation. Their combined expertise enables the community to not only respond more effectively to emergencies but also recover and rebuild stronger than before.

Capacity for Emergency Management

Capacity for Emergency Management refers to the resources, systems, and capabilities that a community, organization, or government has to effectively prepare for, respond to, and recover from emergencies and disasters. This capacity encompasses a broad range of elements, from personnel and training to infrastructure and technology, each playing a crucial role in enhancing the overall resilience and readiness of the community. The following provides a deeper look into what constitutes capacity in emergency management:

1. Human Resources and Training

The foundation of emergency management capacity is skilled and trained personnel. This includes not only emergency responders such as firefighters, police, and medical professionals but also those involved in planning, logistics, communication, and recovery operations. Comprehensive training programs, regular drills, and simulations ensure that these personnel remain prepared to handle various emergency scenarios effectively.

The ability to respond efficiently to disasters relies heavily on the skills and readiness of the personnel involved in all facets of emergency management.

Skilled and Trained Personnel

The backbone of emergency management consists of the personnel who are directly involved in the response and recovery phases of emergencies. This group includes frontline responders like firefighters, police officers, and emergency medical technicians (EMTs), who are often the first to arrive at a disaster site and take immediate action to save lives and property. However, the scope of emergency management extends beyond these first responders to include professionals engaged in critical behind-the-scenes roles such as:

- **Emergency Planners**: These individuals design comprehensive emergency response plans tailored to specific types of disasters and community needs.
- **Logistics Coordinators**: They manage the supply chain of emergency resources, ensuring that necessary supplies like food, water, and medical equipment are procured and distributed efficiently.
- **Communications Specialists**: These experts handle internal and external communications, crucial for coordinating response efforts and disseminating information to the public and media.
- **Recovery Specialists**: They plan and manage the recovery phase, focusing on restoring services and infrastructure and helping communities return to normalcy.

Comprehensive Training Programs

To ensure these personnel are effective during emergencies, comprehensive training programs are essential. These training initiatives equip them with the necessary skills and knowledge to perform their duties under the high-pressure conditions of disaster response. Training programs often include:

- **Technical Skills Training**: This involves specific instructions on handling equipment, performing rescue operations, administering first aid, and other critical tasks.

- **Scenario-Based Drills**: These drills simulate real-life emergency situations, providing personnel with practical experience in responding to various scenarios. These exercises help teams refine their strategies and improve coordination.

- **Regular Simulations**: Simulations test the readiness of emergency teams and the effectiveness of communication and operational plans. They help identify gaps in response plans and provide a controlled environment to practice complex procedures.

Importance of Regular Drills

Regular drills and simulations play a pivotal role in maintaining the preparedness of emergency teams. They help ensure that all team members are familiar with their roles and can execute emergency plans swiftly and efficiently. Drills also help reinforce the importance of teamwork and communication, which are essential during actual disaster situations.

Human resources and training are fundamental to building robust emergency management capacity. By investing in the ongoing training and development of emergency management personnel, communities can enhance their ability to manage disasters effectively, minimizing damage and speeding up recovery times. This comprehensive approach to preparedness is crucial for safeguarding lives and maintaining public safety during emergencies.

2. Planning and Preparedness

Effective emergency management requires detailed planning and preparedness strategies. This involves creating and regularly updating emergency plans that address potential risks specific to the area or organization. Plans typically include evacuation routes, resource allocation, communication strategies, and recovery processes. Preparedness also involves public education initiatives that inform community members about how to prepare for and respond to emergencies.

Effective planning and preparedness form a critical foundation for emergency management, significantly enhancing the capability to manage and mitigate the impacts of disasters. These efforts are vital in ensuring that communities and organizations are ready to respond swiftly and effectively when emergencies arise.

Emergency Planning

Emergency planning is the process of developing procedures and protocols to manage and respond to potential emergencies. This comprehensive planning involves:

- **Risk Assessment**: Identifying and analysing the specific risks that a community or organization may face. This could include natural disasters like earthquakes and floods, technological incidents like chemical spills, or human-caused events such as terrorism.

- **Development of Emergency Plans**: Creating detailed action plans that outline the steps to be taken before, during, and after an emergency. These plans include:

  - **Evacuation Routes**: Clearly marked and accessible paths for safely evacuating people from danger zones.

  - **Resource Allocation**: Strategies for the distribution and use of resources such as personnel, equipment, and supplies during an emergency.

  - **Communication Strategies**: Plans for how information will be communicated to stakeholders, responders, and the public, including the use of emergency notification systems.

  - **Recovery Processes**: Guidelines for how to quickly and effectively begin recovery efforts post-emergency.

Preparedness Activities

Preparedness extends beyond the mere existence of plans to how these plans are implemented and practiced. Key preparedness activities include:

- **Training and Exercises**: Regular training sessions for emergency response teams and support staff to ensure they understand their roles and can perform them effectively under pressure. Exercises might include drills, simulations, and tabletop exercises that practice the execution of emergency plans.

- **Public Education Initiatives**: Programs designed to inform the public about the risks they face and how to prepare for emergencies. These might include:

  - **Educational Campaigns**: Distributing brochures, holding workshops, and using media to educate the public on how to prepare emergency kits, develop family emergency plans, and recognize and respond to different types of emergencies.

- **Community Engagement**: Encouraging active participation from community members in preparedness activities such as community response team trainings or public planning sessions.

- **Alert Systems**: Ensuring the public is signed up for and familiar with local alert systems that notify them of imminent threats through various communication channels.

Regular Updating of Plans

A crucial aspect of planning and preparedness is the regular review and updating of emergency plans and protocols. This ensures that plans remain relevant and effective, incorporating new insights from recent emergencies, changes in the physical and demographic landscape, and advancements in technology and best practices. Regular updates also involve revisiting risk assessments to account for new threats or vulnerabilities.

Planning and preparedness are dynamic components of emergency management that require continual attention and improvement. By meticulously planning and preparing, communities and organizations can enhance their resilience against emergencies, minimize the impact of disasters, and ensure a quicker, more structured response. This ultimately saves lives, reduces economic losses, and helps communities recover more swiftly from emergencies.

3. Technology and Information Systems

Technological capacity in emergency management includes the use of advanced software and hardware that aid in risk assessment, communication, resource management, and response coordination. For example, Geographic Information Systems (GIS) are used to map hazard zones and critical infrastructure, while emergency notification systems can alert citizens about imminent threats. The integration of these technologies enables more precise and timely decision-making.

In the modern landscape of emergency management, technology and information systems play a pivotal role in enhancing the efficiency and effectiveness of operations before, during, and after emergencies. These tools are essential for risk assessment, communication, resource management, and coordination, facilitating more informed and timely decision-making across all phases of emergency management.

Figure 21: MERS Mobile Emergency Operations Vehicle at Disaster Site. George Armstrong, Public domain, via Wikimedia Commons.

Advanced Software and Hardware

The technological capacity in emergency management encompasses a broad range of advanced software and hardware, including:

- **Geographic Information Systems (GIS)**: GIS technology is crucial for mapping and analysing geographic data related to hazards. It allows emergency managers to visualize hazard zones, vulnerable populations, and critical infrastructure in real-time. By overlaying various data sets, GIS can provide a comprehensive view of the risks specific to different areas, helping planners to anticipate problems and prioritize response efforts effectively.

- **Emergency Notification Systems**: These systems are designed to disseminate information rapidly to the public during emergencies. Using a variety of channels such as SMS, email, social media, and dedicated mobile apps, these systems ensure that critical alerts and updates reach a broad audience efficiently. This is vital for instructing residents on evacuation procedures, providing updates on emergency conditions, and guiding the public on how to respond during different types of emergencies.

- **Resource Management Software**: In emergency management, having the right resources at the right time can save lives. Resource management software helps in tracking and allocating supplies, personnel, and equipment during disasters. This technology ensures that logistical operations are streamlined and that resources are distributed effectively, avoiding shortages and redundancies.

- **Decision Support Systems (DSS)**: These systems integrate and analyse data from various sources to aid in decision-making. For example, a DSS can analyse weather data, population density, and current resource allocation to provide recommendations on where to focus response efforts or how to best evacuate an area.

Integration for Enhanced Coordination

The integration of these technologies into a cohesive system is what truly amplifies their effectiveness. By ensuring that different technologies communicate and work together seamlessly, emergency managers can:

- **Enhance Situational Awareness**: Integrated systems allow for a real-time view of the evolving situation, providing emergency managers with up-to-date information that is crucial for making informed decisions.

- **Improve Response Coordination**: When information flows smoothly between different systems and teams, coordination is enhanced. For example, GIS mapping can be directly linked to resource management software to quickly redirect supplies and personnel as the situation on the ground changes.

- **Streamline Communication**: Integrated communication systems ensure that all stakeholders—from emergency responders to the public—are kept informed and can communicate effectively amongst themselves. This reduces confusion and ensures that everyone has the information they need to act swiftly and appropriately.

The strategic application of technology and information systems in emergency management not only enhances the capability to manage disasters more effectively but also contributes to building resilience within communities. As technology evolves, so too does the potential for its application in emergency preparedness, response, and recovery, making continuous evaluation and adaptation of these technologies essential for staying ahead of future challenges.

4. Logistical Capability

Logistics play a critical role in emergency management, involving the procurement, management, and deployment of resources such as food, water, medical supplies, and shelters before and after disasters. Effective logistical systems ensure that these resources are available where and when they are needed most, without significant delays.

Logistical capability is a fundamental aspect of emergency management that ensures the right resources are available at the right time and place to effectively respond to and recover from disasters. This capability encompasses several critical functions, from procurement and storage to distribution and management of essential supplies and equipment. Understanding and enhancing logistical capability can significantly impact the success of emergency operations.

Key Components of Logistical Capability:

- **Procurement**: This involves the acquisition of necessary supplies and equipment required during emergencies. Efficient procurement systems are crucial for ensuring that a sufficient stockpile of resources such as food, water, medical supplies, and other essentials is maintained. Procurement also needs to be flexible and fast-responding to adapt to the changing needs during a disaster.

- **Storage and Inventory Management**: Once resources are procured, proper storage and inventory management ensure they remain in good condition and are readily accessible when needed. This includes maintaining secure and strategically located warehouses that can quickly dispatch supplies to affected areas. Inventory systems should be robust, with real-time tracking capabilities to monitor supply levels and expiration dates, preventing shortages and wastage.

- **Distribution**: The ability to distribute supplies efficiently to impacted areas is a critical function of logistics. This involves not only the physical transportation of goods but also the planning of delivery routes, especially in scenarios where infrastructure may be damaged. Utilizing GIS technology can aid in identifying accessible routes and prioritizing distribution based on urgency and need.

- **Resource Allocation**: During a disaster, resources must be allocated in a manner that maximizes their impact. This requires an understanding of the needs of the affected population and the ability to adjust distribution plans as the situation evolves. Effective resource allocation ensures that supplies reach the most vulnerable populations and critical services, such as hospitals and shelters, without unnecessary delays.

Challenges in Emergency Logistics

Logistical operations during emergencies face several challenges:

- **Rapidly Changing Conditions**: Disasters can evolve quickly, and logistical plans must be equally adaptable to respond to new information and changing circumstances.
- **Damaged Infrastructure**: Roads, bridges, and communications systems may be damaged during disasters, complicating delivery routes and coordination efforts.
- **Resource Shortages**: High demand and disrupted supply chains can lead to shortages of critical supplies. Planning for these contingencies is essential for maintaining supply stability.

Enhancing Logistical Capability

Improving logistical capability involves several strategic initiatives:

- **Advanced Planning**: Developing comprehensive logistics plans that include scenarios for different types of emergencies and potential complications.
- **Technology Integration**: Utilizing technology such as supply chain management software, drones for delivery in inaccessible areas, and real-time tracking systems to enhance visibility and control over logistics operations.
- **Partnerships**: Establishing partnerships with local businesses, NGOs, and government agencies can expand resource networks and facilitate quicker responses. International cooperation may also be necessary for large-scale disasters.
- **Training and Simulations**: Regular training and simulation exercises for logistics personnel help prepare them for the pressures and challenges of managing supplies during emergencies.

Effective logistical systems are crucial for the success of emergency management. By ensuring that essential resources are procured, managed, and deployed efficiently, emergency management professionals can significantly enhance their response and recovery efforts, ultimately saving lives and reducing the impact of disasters on affected communities. Continuous improvement and adaptation of logistical strategies to new technologies and methodologies are key to maintaining robust emergency response capabilities.

5. Infrastructure

Robust infrastructure is crucial for effective emergency response and recovery. This includes not only physical structures like roads, bridges, and public buildings that must be designed to withstand disasters but also the infrastructure for utilities such as power, water, and communication systems. Strengthening infrastructure resilience through retrofitting and improved design standards is a key part of building emergency management capacity.

Infrastructure plays a vital role in emergency management, forming the backbone of a community's ability to respond to and recover from disasters efficiently. The resilience and robustness of infrastructure determine not only the immediate ability to perform emergency responses but also the long-term recovery and stability of the affected area.

Types of Critical Infrastructure:

- **Transport Infrastructure**: Roads, bridges, and transportation networks are essential for facilitating the swift movement of emergency services, resources, and evacuees. When disasters strike, the accessibility and integrity of these networks can significantly impact response times and the overall effectiveness of the emergency operations.

- **Utility Infrastructure**: Utilities such as power, water, and sewage systems are crucial for sustaining life and maintaining sanitation in disaster-stricken areas. Power outages and water supply disruptions can severely hinder emergency response efforts and prolong recovery times. Reliable communication systems are also critical for effective coordination among emergency responders and for disseminating information to the public.

- **Public Buildings**: Hospitals, schools, emergency operation centres, and other public buildings serve as key hubs for emergency operations, shelters for evacuees, and centres for medical care. Ensuring these buildings are resilient and functional during disasters is essential for effective community support and recovery.

Enhancing Infrastructure Resilience

The resilience of infrastructure is enhanced through several strategies:

- **Retrofitting**: Existing infrastructure often needs upgrades to meet modern standards of disaster resilience. Retrofitting involves modifying structures to make them more resistant to disasters, such as reinforcing buildings to withstand earthquakes or elevating roads in flood-prone areas.

- **Improved Design Standards**: New infrastructure projects should incorporate advanced design standards that consider a range of potential disaster scenarios. This includes using materials and construction techniques that can endure extreme weather conditions and incorporating redundancy in critical systems like communications and power supplies.

- **Regular Maintenance**: Continual maintenance is key to ensuring infrastructure remains in good condition and can perform as expected during emergencies. This includes routine inspections and repairs of roads, bridges, and utility systems to prevent failures when they are most needed.

Challenges in Infrastructure Management

Managing infrastructure for emergency preparedness involves addressing several challenges:

- **Funding Constraints**: Infrastructure projects, especially retrofitting and upgrading, require substantial investment. Securing adequate funding is a constant challenge for many communities, particularly in economically constrained environments.

- **Technological Changes**: Keeping up with rapid technological advancements can be difficult. Integrating new technologies into existing infrastructure systems often requires significant redesign and investment.

- **Environmental and Geographical Factors**: Different regions face unique risks based on their environmental conditions and geographical settings, necessitating customized infrastructure solutions to address specific vulnerabilities.

Strategic Importance

Robust infrastructure not only supports the immediate response to emergencies but also underpins the long-term recovery and resilience of communities. Investment in infrastructure is an investment in a community's safety and stability, reducing the overall risk and impact of disasters. Effective management, regular maintenance, and strategic upgrading of infrastructure are therefore essential components of comprehensive emergency management planning.

6. Legal and Institutional Frameworks

A strong legal and institutional framework supports effective emergency management. This includes laws and regulations that govern emergency procedures, funding allocations, and the roles and responsibilities of various agencies involved in disaster management. Institutions need to be empowered with the authority to act swiftly in emergencies and have clear, pre-established coordination mechanisms.

Legal and institutional frameworks form the backbone of effective emergency management by establishing the authority, responsibilities, and procedures necessary for coordinated disaster response and recovery efforts. These frameworks are crucial for ensuring that all actions taken during an emergency are well-regulated, transparent, and effective.

Role of Legal Frameworks

- **Governance of Emergency Procedures**: Legal frameworks provide the foundation for all emergency management activities by defining how emergencies are declared, the steps to be followed during different phases of emergency management (preparedness, response, recovery, mitigation), and the criteria for ending a state of emergency. These laws ensure that there is a structured approach to handling disasters, which helps in minimizing chaos and ensuring that responses are timely and effective.

- **Funding Allocations**: Laws and regulations also govern how funds are allocated for emergency management. This includes funding for emergency response activities, as well as for rebuilding and recovery efforts post-disaster. Legal provisions ensure that funds are allocated swiftly and are used appropriately, according to the needs that arise during and after emergencies.

- **Defining Roles and Responsibilities**: A clear definition of the roles and responsibilities of various stakeholders involved in disaster management is another critical aspect covered by legal frameworks. This includes delineating the responsibilities of federal, state, and local governments, as well as those of private sector entities and non-governmental organizations. Clear roles help in avoiding overlap and confusion during the actual execution of emergency plans.

Importance of Institutional Frameworks

- **Authority to Act**: Institutions involved in emergency management must be empowered with the authority to act decisively and swiftly in the face of disasters. This authority is often derived from legal frameworks that empower agencies such as FEMA in the U.S. or similar organizations worldwide to take necessary actions during emergencies without undue delay.

- **Coordination Mechanisms**: Effective emergency management requires excellent coordination among various agencies and organizations. Institutional frameworks establish coordination mechanisms such as emergency operations centres (EOCs) and integrated command systems to facilitate this. These mechanisms are crucial for ensuring that resources are used efficiently and that efforts are not duplicated.

- **Compliance and Enforcement**: Institutions not only implement emergency management policies but also ensure compliance with laws and regulations. They have the responsibility to enforce building codes, zoning laws, and other regulations that reduce risk and enhance safety, thereby mitigating the impact of potential disasters.

- **Continuous Improvement**: Institutions are also involved in evaluating and improving emergency management strategies. After-action reviews, updating of emergency plans, and revising legal frameworks based on recent experiences are all institutional responsibilities that play a significant role in enhancing the overall effectiveness of emergency management.

Challenges and Considerations

- **Up-to-Date Legislation**: One of the significant challenges in maintaining effective legal and institutional frameworks is ensuring that laws and regulations keep pace with the changing nature of risks, technological advancements, and lessons learned from past incidents.

- **Interagency Collaboration**: Effective collaboration among various agencies and organizations, each with different mandates and priorities, can be challenging but is essential for integrated emergency management.

Robust legal and institutional frameworks are critical to ensuring that emergency management is conducted effectively and efficiently. They provide the necessary authority, define responsibilities, ensure accountability, and facilitate coordinated actions among various stakeholders. By strengthening these frameworks, communities enhance their ability to manage disasters more effectively, minimizing damage and accelerating recovery.

7. Financial Resources

Financial capacity is critical to support all stages of emergency management. This includes funds set aside for emergency response and recovery, as well as financial mechanisms like insurance and aid programs that can help mitigate the economic impact of disasters. Efficient financial management ensures that funds are used effectively and are available immediately when needed.

Financial resources play a pivotal role in the entire spectrum of emergency management, from preparedness and response to recovery and mitigation. The availability and efficient management of financial resources determine not only the immediacy and quality of the emergency response but also the speed and extent of recovery and rebuilding efforts after a disaster.

Funding for Emergency Response and Recovery

- **Emergency Response Funds**: Having readily available funds specifically designated for emergency response is crucial. These funds are used to cover the immediate costs of disaster response activities, including but not limited to, deploying emergency services, setting up shelters, providing medical care, and ensuring the availability of essential supplies like food and water. Quick access to these funds is vital to ensure that response efforts are not delayed.

- **Recovery Funds**: Post-disaster recovery can be lengthy and expensive, involving rebuilding infrastructure, restoring services, and helping communities return to normal life. Recovery funds are therefore essential to support these activities over the months or even years it can take to fully recover from major disasters. This funding can come from national budgets, international aid, or recovery-specific fundraising efforts.

Financial Mechanisms for Mitigation

- **Insurance**: Insurance plays a critical role in mitigating the financial impact of disasters on individuals, businesses, and governments. Property and casualty insurance, business interruption insurance, and special disaster policies can provide the necessary funds to repair and rebuild without the undue financial burden falling entirely on the disaster victims or government entities.

- **Aid Programs**: Various aid programs, both governmental and non-governmental, provide financial assistance to those affected by disasters. These programs can help cover costs that are not insured and provide a safety net for the most vulnerable populations.

Efficient Financial Management

- **Budget Allocation and Oversight**: Effective emergency management requires not only having sufficient funds but also managing these funds efficiently. This involves careful budgeting, forecasting potential costs, and setting aside reserves specifically for emergency use. Financial oversight is also crucial to ensure that funds are spent appropriately, avoiding mismanagement and corruption.

- **Rapid Disbursement**: In the aftermath of a disaster, the ability to quickly disburse funds can significantly impact the effectiveness of the response and the speed of recovery. Systems must be in place to ensure that financial resources can be mobilized and accessed without bureaucratic delays.

- **Long-term Financial Planning**: Besides immediate disaster response and recovery, long-term financial strategies are essential for reducing future risks and enhancing community resilience. This includes investing in infrastructure improvements, funding public education programs about disaster preparedness, and supporting research and development in technologies that can mitigate disaster impacts.

Challenges in Managing Financial Resources

- **Sustainability**: Ensuring that there are always sufficient funds available for emergency management while balancing other fiscal priorities can be challenging.

- **Equity**: Distributing financial resources in a manner that equitably addresses the needs of all affected populations, including marginalized and vulnerable groups, is another significant challenge.

Financial resources are a critical component of effective emergency management. Ensuring their availability, effective management, and equitable distribution supports not only immediate disaster response efforts but also broader objectives of reducing disaster risk, enhancing community resilience, and supporting comprehensive recovery and mitigation strategies. As such, continuous evaluation and adaptation of financial strategies are essential to meet the evolving nature of risks and community needs.

8. Community Involvement and Collaboration

Finally, the capacity for emergency management is strengthened by active community involvement and collaboration among various stakeholders. Engaging community members in planning and response efforts not only improves the relevance and effectiveness of strategies but also builds local resilience. Collaboration between governments, businesses, non-profits, and the public enhances resource sharing and innovation.

Community involvement and collaboration are foundational elements that enhance the effectiveness and sustainability of emergency management efforts. By actively engaging various stakeholders within the community, emergency management becomes a more inclusive and comprehensive process. This approach leverages the unique strengths and resources of different groups, leading to improved strategies, enhanced resilience, and more robust recovery efforts. Here's a closer look at the importance of these elements:

Benefits of Community Involvement

- **Enhanced Relevance of Plans**: When community members are involved in the emergency planning process, the plans that emerge are more attuned to local needs, preferences, and risks. Residents can provide valuable insights into vulnerabilities and resources that external planners might overlook. This makes the strategies more relevant and practical.

- **Increased Public Awareness**: Engaging the community helps to raise awareness about the risks and the necessary preparations for potential emergencies. Through educational programs, workshops, and simulations, communities become better prepared to handle disasters, which can significantly reduce the impact when they do occur.

- **Empowerment and Capacity Building**: Active involvement empowers residents by giving them a role in their safety and preparedness. Training community members in basic first aid, emergency response, and disaster recovery can significantly enhance the overall community response capability during an emergency.

The Role of Collaboration

- **Pooling Resources**: Collaboration among various sectors — government agencies, businesses, non-profit organizations, and community groups — allows for pooling of resources, which can significantly enhance the response to and recovery from disasters. For example, local businesses might provide supplies, non-profits can offer volunteer labour, and government agencies can give technical support and funding.

- **Innovative Solutions**: Working together can foster innovative solutions to complex problems. Diverse groups bring different perspectives and expertise, which can lead to more creative and effective approaches to disaster management and resilience building.

- **Coordinated Response and Recovery Efforts**: Collaboration ensures that the actions of various groups are coordinated and not redundant. It helps in establishing a unified command or a coalition that can streamline decision-making and resource allocation during emergencies, making the response more efficient and effective.

Challenges in Implementing Community Involvement and Collaboration

- **Coordination Complexity**: Managing a collaborative approach can be complex, especially when it involves numerous stakeholders with varying objectives, capabilities, and levels of commitment.

- **Sustaining Engagement**: Keeping community members and organizations engaged over the long term, especially outside of immediate disaster periods, can be challenging.

- **Equitable Participation**: Ensuring that all parts of a community, especially marginalized and vulnerable groups, are represented and have a voice in the planning and response efforts.

Strategies for Effective Community Involvement and Collaboration

- **Establish Clear Communication Channels**: Regular and clear communication is essential for effective collaboration. This includes not only during emergencies but also in planning and preparation stages.

- **Create Formal Partnerships and Agreements**: Formalizing partnerships through memoranda of understanding (MOUs) or other agreements can clarify roles and expectations, making collaboration more structured and reliable.
- **Regular Training and Joint Exercises**: Conducting joint training sessions and simulations involving all stakeholders ensures everyone understands their roles and how to work together effectively.
- **Community Forums and Advisory Boards**: Establishing forums or advisory boards that include community representatives can ensure ongoing involvement and feedback, which is crucial for maintaining engagement and adapting strategies as community needs evolve.

Community involvement and collaboration are not just beneficial but essential for effective emergency management. They turn passive recipients of aid into active participants, enhance the relevance of emergency strategies, and build a more resilient community capable of facing disasters. As such, fostering these aspects should be a priority for all involved in emergency management.

Building capacity for emergency management is a continuous and dynamic process that requires ongoing evaluation and adaptation. Strengthening these capacities is essential for communities to effectively handle emergencies, mitigate the impact of disasters, and recover promptly and robustly. Community resilience is crucial for disaster readiness and includes adaptive capacities such as Economic Development, Social Capital, Information and Communication, and Community Competence [130]. Research highlights the importance of human initiative in enhancing community emergency management capacity resilience, emphasizing the significance of residents' reorganizational capacity and collective behaviour in bolstering post-disaster community resilience [131].

Furthermore, the availability of health services during emergencies is vital for effective disaster management and community health resilience. Research emphasizes the need to develop strategies to enhance organizations' emergency management systems, focusing on improving adaptability and response capabilities under new circumstances [132]. Other research underscores the global priority of strengthening community emergency management capacity building and cultivating resilience to disasters [133].

Effective community resilience interventions involve leadership, team building, communication, and risk management skills, which are essential for enhancing community resilience activities [134]. The Whole Community Approach to Emergency Management stresses the importance of individual preparedness and community engagement to enhance overall community resiliency and security [135]. Additionally, active community involvement in building their capacity to prepare for, respond to, and recover from natural hazards is crucial for effective emergency management planning [136].

4

Principles of Disaster Resilience

Disaster resilience is a fundamental goal in emergency management, focusing on the ability of individuals, communities, organizations, and systems to withstand, adapt to, and recover from disasters. Developing resilience involves a holistic approach that integrates various principles across planning, response, recovery, and mitigation efforts.

Understanding and Managing Risk

Resilience begins with a comprehensive understanding of the risks a community or organization faces. This involves identifying potential hazards, assessing vulnerabilities, and analysing the potential impacts of different types of disasters. Effective management of these risks through mitigation strategies, such as strengthening infrastructure or revising building codes, is essential to reducing the potential damage and disruption caused by disasters.

Resilience in the face of disasters relies on a comprehensive understanding of risks, which includes hazard identification, vulnerability assessment, and impact analysis [137]. Mitigation strategies are essential for effective risk management and involve actions such as strengthening infrastructure and updating building regulations to minimize the potential harm caused by disasters [137].

Disaster Risk Reduction (DRR) is a critical concept aimed at reducing disaster risks through systematic measures and addressing the adverse consequences of disasters [138]. Effective disaster risk communication is crucial, as emphasized in a systematic review highlighting the importance of communication strategies in reducing risks [139]. Mainstreaming risk reduction in urban planning and housing poses a challenge for international aid organizations, underscoring the necessity of integrating risk reduction practices into development initiatives [140].

Local wisdom-based disaster mitigation literacy is recognized as a valuable asset, emphasizing the significance of community knowledge and practices in reducing disaster risks [141]. Post-disaster assessments are vital for evaluating hazard mitigation efforts, as demonstrated by studies analysing mitigation actions following disasters in various regions [116]. Disaster risk reduction through education involves diverse strategies such as integrating disaster learning in schools and conducting disaster mitigation simulations [142].

Risk communication is a crucial component of disaster management, as shown in studies focusing on the preventive and mitigatory aspects of risk communication in various contexts, including the COVID-19 pandemic [143]. Policy implementation is key in disaster risk reduction, with a focus on empowering students and fostering a culture of safety and resilience [144]. Guiding documents outline priority actions for disaster risk reduction, emphasizing the importance of understanding risks, strengthening governance, investing in management, and enhancing preparedness [145].

Inclusive disaster mitigation education in schools encompasses various elements such as self-initiated education, infrastructure modifications, diverse learning methods, child empowerment, school management strategies, and stakeholder involvement [146]. The Sendai Framework for Disaster Risk Reduction acknowledges the role of persons with disabilities in disaster risk reduction policies, ensuring their inclusion in decision-making processes [147]. Stakeholders play a vital role in disaster risk reduction efforts, contributing to systematic analyses, vulnerability reduction, effective land management, and enhanced preparedness [148].

Integration

Disaster resilience requires the integration of emergency management activities across various sectors and levels of responsibility, from individual and local to national and international scales. This integration is crucial for ensuring that planning and response efforts are unified and comprehensive, considering the needs and capacities of all stakeholders. It also involves incorporating disaster risk considerations into all aspects of development planning, policies, and practices [149, 150].

To achieve effective disaster resilience, it is crucial to incorporate resilience principles into various domains. For example, in healthcare systems, establishing resilient health systems and hospital disaster planning is essential. This includes using incident and hospital incident command terminology and integrating disaster risk reduction strategies into planning and operations [151, 152]. Similarly, in facilities management, focusing on resilience from a facilities perspective and implementing mitigation interventions can significantly reduce an organization's vulnerability to disasters [153].

Furthermore, resilience extends beyond individual sectors. Public-private partnerships are essential in developing disaster-resilient communities by promoting critical infrastructure and social system development, crisis mitigation, emergency response, and facilitating post-disaster recovery [154]. Additionally, integrating disaster resilience into tourism management plans can enhance the resilience of tourist destinations to natural disasters, ensuring the sustainability of the tourism industry [155, 156].

Disaster resilience planning should adopt a multi-dimensional approach, considering factors such as community narratives, stakeholder engagement, and the effectiveness of flood resilience plans for urban sustainability [157, 158]. By integrating these diverse perspectives and strategies, disaster resilience can be enhanced at various levels, contributing to more effective disaster preparedness, response, and recovery efforts.

Collaboration and Partnership

Building resilience against disasters requires collaboration and partnerships among government agencies, private businesses, non-profit organizations, and the general public [159]. Research emphasizes the importance of collaboration in enhancing resilience, acting as the "glue" that binds organizations together during crises [160]. Partnerships play a crucial role in building urban community resilience and are essential for effective humanitarian supply chains [161].

Partnerships extend to school-family-community collaborations, fostering educational resilience and opportunities in urban schools [162]. Public-private partnerships are integral in enhancing urban community resilience, including critical infrastructure resilience [163]. Leveraging public-private partnerships is a strategy to improve community resilience during disasters [164].

Proactive Investment

Investing proactively in disaster resilience is a strategic approach that can yield significant benefits by reducing the costs and damages associated with emergency responses and recovery efforts. This proactive investment involves various key components such as research and innovation to develop new solutions and technologies, enhancing early warning systems, and building resilient infrastructure. Additionally, funding education and training programs to increase public awareness and preparedness plays a crucial role in disaster resilience [165, 166].

By focusing on assets that build resilience rather than deficits, proactive investment can lead to more effective disaster preparedness and response strategies. This approach emphasizes the importance of developing innovative solutions to address complex social issues that impact high-risk populations' resilience [167]. Furthermore, it involves incorporating social and technological aspects to enhance disaster resilience, highlighting the need for a comprehensive approach that considers various factors such as social relationships and community capacities [168, 169].

The concept of resilience, as defined by various researchers, encompasses the ability to survive, cope with, and recover from disasters with minimal impact and damage. It involves the capacity to reduce losses, contain disaster effects, and recover with minimal social disruption [169-171]. Moreover, resilience is not only about bouncing back from disasters but also about adapting, transforming, and building stronger systems to withstand future challenges [172, 173].

Community Empowerment

Empowering communities to participate actively in their own resilience-building processes is crucial. This involves engaging local leaders and community groups in disaster planning, decision-making, and implementation of resilience strategies. Community empowerment ensures that resilience-building efforts are culturally appropriate, widely supported, and sustainable [174].

Community involvement ranges from planning and decision-making to the implementation of disaster resilience strategies. When community members, especially local leaders and groups, are actively engaged, the outcomes of these strategies are not only more effective but also more sustainable.

Significance of Community Empowerment:

- **Local Knowledge and Expertise**: Communities possess deep knowledge of their local geography, climate patterns, vulnerabilities, and available resources. This local insight is invaluable in enhancing the precision and relevance of disaster resilience planning. Leveraging this expertise allows emergency management strategies to be specifically tailored to meet the unique needs and conditions of the area.

- **Increased Engagement and Ownership**: Active involvement in resilience-building initiatives fosters a greater sense of ownership and commitment among community members. This heightened engagement leads to more enthusiastic participation in preparedness activities, such as training and drills, thereby boosting the overall effectiveness of these efforts.

- **Cultural Appropriateness**: Given the diversity within communities, it is essential that resilience strategies are culturally sensitive. Community empowerment ensures that the plans and actions taken are culturally appropriate, promoting wider acceptance and long-term sustainability.

- **Enhanced Support and Sustainability**: Empowered communities are more likely to support and sustain resilience efforts over the long term. A strong sense of personal stake in their safety and recovery encourages community members to maintain and build upon resilience initiatives, even when immediate threats are not present.

Implementing community empowerment includes:

- **Inclusive Planning Processes**: Ensuring that community insights and needs are integrated from the onset of the planning process is crucial. This can be achieved through public meetings, focus groups, and advisory committees where community representatives work alongside emergency management professionals.

- **Building Local Capacities**: Educating and training community members not only prepares them to respond effectively during disasters but also helps in building local capacities. This includes training in basic first aid, disaster response techniques, and recovery processes.
- **Decentralized Decision-Making**: Allowing for decentralized decision-making empowers local leaders and groups to act based on their firsthand understanding of the situation, which can lead to quicker and more effective responses to dynamic disaster conditions.
- **Leveraging Local Resources**: Communities often have readily mobilizable resources that can be crucial in an emergency. Planning for the use of local shelters, equipment, and skilled volunteers can significantly enhance emergency response efforts.
- **Feedback and Continuous Improvement**: Continuous improvement is fostered by actively engaging the community in post-disaster reviews and ongoing resilience planning. This feedback is vital for refining strategies to better meet the community's needs.

Figure 22: In Midhega Tola Woreda, men and women community members are engaged in the participatory disaster risk assessment. USAID in Africa, Public domain, via Wikimedia Commons.

Community empowerment transcends being merely beneficial—it is essential for effective disaster resilience. By ensuring that community members are involved at every stage of disaster resilience planning, communities can significantly enhance their ability to withstand and recover from disasters more effectively. This approach guarantees that resilience strategies are well-informed, culturally relevant, enthusiastically supported, and sustainable.

Adaptability and Flexibility

Resilience requires the capacity to adapt and be flexible in response to changing circumstances during a disaster. Systems and plans should be designed to be adjustable in the face of unforeseen challenges. This adaptability extends to learning from past disasters and incorporating those lessons into future planning and preparedness efforts.

Resilience in the face of disasters necessitates adaptability and flexibility to effectively respond to changing circumstances. This adaptability involves the ability to adjust systems and plans to unforeseen challenges and incorporate lessons learned from past disasters into future preparedness efforts [175, 176]. The concept of adaptability extends to learning from previous disasters and integrating these insights into future planning and response strategies [177].

Studies emphasize the importance of adaptive governance in managing resilience to natural hazards. Adaptive governance involves flexible, collaborative, and learning-oriented approaches to enhance resilience at various scales [178-180]. Furthermore, the ability to adapt to environmental changes and manage responses efficiently is crucial for community resilience and disaster management [91, 181].

Resilient hospitals play a vital role in disaster reduction efforts, as recognized in global policies like the Sendai Framework for Action [182]. Hospital resilience involves the capacity to resist, absorb, respond to shocks, and recover or adapt to new conditions while maintaining essential services [182]. Additionally, the promotion of safe and resilient hospitals is highlighted as a key component in disaster reduction initiatives [183].

Incorporating flexibility, redundancy, diversity, efficiency, autonomy, strength, interdependence, adaptability, and collaboration into systems can enhance their resilience to disasters [184]. A change and adaptation-oriented organizational culture are fundamental for self-adapting disaster management systems [185]. Moreover, a focus on priority work and the flexibility required of community-based social workers are essential in post-disaster environments [186].

Redundancy

Redundant systems are those that have backup or alternative options in case the primary system fails during a disaster. This might include having multiple routes for evacuation, backup communication systems, or alternative water and power supplies. Redundancy enhances resilience by ensuring that the failure of one component does not lead to the collapse of the entire system.

Redundancy is a critical concept in emergency management, referring to the integration of backup systems or alternatives that can be utilized if primary systems fail during a disaster. This principle is essential for maintaining functionality and continuity in critical services, thereby enhancing the overall resilience of communities and organizations against emergencies.

The main goal of incorporating redundancy into emergency management is to ensure that the failure of one component does not compromise the ability to manage and respond to a disaster effectively. Redundancy operates within various emergency management contexts through:

- **Multiple Evacuation Routes**: Having several predefined evacuation routes is crucial, especially in areas prone to natural disasters like wildfires or floods. If one route is blocked or unsafe, alternative routes ensure that evacuation can proceed smoothly without significant delays, increasing the safety of residents.

- **Backup Communication Systems**: Communication is vital during an emergency for both coordination of response efforts and dissemination of information to the public. Redundant communication systems might include a mix of radio, satellite, and internet-based technologies. If one system fails, others can take over to maintain critical lines of communication between emergency services, government authorities, and the public.

- **Alternative Water and Power Supplies**: Essential utilities such as water and electricity are often disrupted during severe disasters. Having alternatives such as portable water tanks, generators, or solar power systems ensures that there is no complete outage, which can be critical for hospitals, shelters, and other key facilities during emergencies.

Redundancy in emergency management offers several crucial benefits that enhance the overall safety and efficiency of disaster response and recovery processes including:

- **Enhances Resilience**: By allowing systems and services to remain operational despite failures, redundancy enhances the resilience of a community or organization. This capacity to absorb and quickly recover from disruptions is vital for minimizing the impact of disasters.

- **Prevents Systemic Collapse**: Redundancy prevents the cascade of failures that can occur when interconnected systems depend solely on one another. By having alternatives, the failure of one component doesn't lead to the breakdown of the entire system.

- **Increases Flexibility and Adaptability**: Redundant systems provide the flexibility to adapt to unexpected situations. During a disaster, conditions can change rapidly, and having multiple options available allows responders to shift strategies quickly.

Implementing redundancy involves strategic planning and investment. Key considerations include:

- **Identifying Critical Systems and Functions**: Determine which systems and functions are most critical to operations and public safety. These are the areas where redundancy should be prioritized.

- **Cost-Benefit Analysis**: Implementing redundant systems involves additional costs. A thorough cost-benefit analysis can help in deciding how much redundancy is necessary and sustainable.

- **Regular Testing and Maintenance**: Redundant systems must be regularly tested and maintained to ensure they are operational when needed. This includes drills that involve switching to backup systems to simulate their use during actual emergencies.

Redundant systems are a fundamental aspect of robust emergency management practices. They provide a necessary buffer and flexibility during disasters, ensuring that essential services and functions continue uninterrupted. By planning for and investing in redundancy, communities and organizations can significantly enhance their preparedness and resilience against various emergencies.

Reflective Learning

After a disaster, resilient communities take the time to reflect on the response efforts and learn from them. This involves conducting thorough after-action reviews, identifying successes and failures, and modifying plans and protocols accordingly. Reflective learning helps to continuously improve disaster response strategies and resilience over time.

Reflective learning is an essential component of enhancing community resilience and improving disaster management strategies over time. After a disaster, it is crucial for communities and organizations to engage in a process of reflection to evaluate the effectiveness of their response efforts. This reflective process not only aids in understanding what occurred but also helps in identifying areas for improvement.

Conducting After-Action Reviews: The cornerstone of reflective learning is the after-action review (AAR), a structured debrief process that is conducted after each disaster event. This review involves all key stakeholders who were part of the emergency response, including emergency responders, local government officials, community leaders, and other relevant organizations. The AAR aims to assess the effectiveness of the disaster response by examining what actions were taken, the outcomes of these actions, and how well the emergency plans and protocols worked in practice.

Identifying Successes and Failures: During the after-action review, participants discuss both the successes and failures of the disaster response. Successes are celebrated and analysed to understand what factors contributed to effective outcomes, ensuring that these practices can be replicated in future. Conversely, failures are critically examined to determine their causes—whether they were due to inadequacies in planning, gaps in communication, resource limitations, or other factors. This honest appraisal is crucial for learning and growth, as it highlights the areas where improvements are needed.

Modifying Plans and Protocols: The insights gained from the after-action review are then used to modify existing disaster response plans and protocols. This might involve updating evacuation routes, refining communication strategies, reallocating resources, or implementing new training programs for responders. The goal is to address the shortcomings identified during the AAR and to strengthen the community's overall disaster response capabilities.

Continuous Improvement: Reflective learning is a continuous process that contributes to the iterative improvement of disaster management practices. By regularly engaging in this process after each disaster, communities can evolve their strategies to better meet their unique challenges and needs. This ongoing learning and adaptation process is vital for building long-term resilience, as it ensures that disaster management strategies remain effective and responsive to new information and changing conditions.

Inclusivity

Building disaster resilience requires the integration of inclusivity by considering the needs and perspectives of all segments of society, especially vulnerable and marginalized groups, in the planning and execution of resilience strategies. Inclusive approaches are essential to ensure that resilience measures protect all individuals, particularly those most at risk during disasters [187, 188].

In the context of hospital disaster resilience, inclusivity involves enhancing hospitals' capacity to withstand, absorb, and respond to disasters while maintaining essential functions and eventually recovering to their original or an adaptive state. This highlights the importance of addressing the diverse needs of all individuals, including vulnerable populations, to ensure hospitals can effectively endure and recover from disasters [189].

Resilient health facilities, particularly hospitals, play a crucial role in post-disaster settings by contributing to the responsiveness of local health systems. Their resilience is vital for ensuring the continuity of care and services during and after disasters, underscoring the significance of inclusive strategies in healthcare resilience [183].

In the broader scope of disaster resilience planning, inclusive practices are fundamental for addressing the diverse challenges faced by communities. Studies emphasize the importance of outreach programs to facilitate access to inclusive resilience-building strategies and resources, enabling communities, especially vulnerable groups, to better cope with disaster risks In the broader scope of disaster resilience planning, inclusive practices are fundamental for addressing the diverse challenges faced by communities. Studies emphasize the importance of outreach programs to facilitate access to inclusive resilience-building strategies and resources, enabling communities, especially vulnerable groups, to better cope with disaster risks [190].

The Role of Resilience in Disaster Management

Resilience in disaster management refers to the ability of individuals, communities, organizations, and systems to withstand, adapt to, and recover from the impacts of disasters. It encompasses a broad range of activities and capabilities that aim to minimize the physical, economic, and social disruptions caused by emergencies. Understanding and enhancing resilience is central to effective disaster management, as it not only involves immediate reactive measures but also proactive planning and continuous improvement. Here's a detailed exploration of the role of resilience in disaster management:

Absorbing Shock and Minimizing Impact

At its core, resilience enables a community or system to absorb the shock of a disaster with minimal disruption. This involves having robust infrastructures, such as flood defences and earthquake-resistant buildings, that can withstand the initial impacts of disasters. It also includes having effective emergency response systems that can quickly mobilize resources, such as medical aid, shelters, and emergency supplies, to meet immediate needs and stabilize the situation.

Resilience is a crucial concept that enables communities and systems to withstand and recover from disasters with minimal disruption. This involves the presence of robust infrastructures like flood defences and earthquake-resistant buildings that can endure the initial impacts of disasters [170]. Additionally, effective emergency response systems play a crucial role in quickly mobilizing resources such as medical aid, shelters, and emergency supplies to address immediate needs and stabilize the situation [191].

Community resilience, as highlighted in various studies, encompasses adaptive capacities that promote effective disaster readiness and response [192]. It involves building the capacity of communities to enhance their ability to withstand and recover from disasters, which is considered essential for post-disaster reconstruction and recovery [193]. Resilience is not merely about withstanding adversity but also about accessing resources necessary to sustain well-being and support communities in times of crisis [194].

Resilience is closely linked to sustainable development, particularly in lower-income and disaster-prone countries, as it enhances the agility and flexibility of infrastructure against future hazards while reducing disaster risks [191]. The concept of resilience has been integrated into disaster management policies, where it has been superimposed on existing frameworks to enhance disaster preparedness and response [195].

Adapting to Changing Conditions

Resilience in disaster management also involves the capacity to adapt to changing conditions during a disaster. This adaptability is crucial because disasters can evolve unpredictably, presenting new challenges that require flexible response strategies. For example, during a prolonged drought, a resilient community may shift its water usage policies to ensure sustainability [196, 197]. Similarly, during a pandemic, adaptability might involve modifying public health strategies in response to emerging scientific knowledge.

The notion of resilience in disaster management has gained prominence in disaster risk reduction programs, emphasizing the interconnectedness between disaster recovery and the resilience of affected communities [14]. Resilience, when integrated into operational disaster management, builds upon pre-existing concepts and frameworks, highlighting the need for adaptability and flexibility in responding to evolving disaster scenarios [195].

Community resilience plays a fundamental role in post-disaster reconstruction and recovery, with a focus on enhancing the capacity of communities to withstand and bounce back from disasters [193, 194]. This resilience is underpinned by adaptive capacities that enable effective disaster readiness and response, emphasizing the importance of promoting community resilience as a strategy for comprehensive disaster management [158, 192].

In the context of specific disasters like the COVID-19 pandemic, adaptability involves modifying public health strategies based on emerging scientific knowledge, showcasing the dynamic nature of resilience in disaster management. Furthermore, the ability to anticipate, absorb, accommodate, and recover from hazardous events efficiently is central to resilience in disaster management, emphasizing the preservation, restoration, or enhancement of essential structures and functions.

Rapid Recovery

A key component of resilience is the ability to recover quickly from disasters. Rapid recovery reduces the long-term social and economic impacts of disasters and helps restore normalcy. This requires not only physical rebuilding but also restoring economic activities and community services. Efficient recovery processes are supported by pre-disaster planning, such as recovery frameworks and financial mechanisms like insurance and reserve funds, which enable communities to initiate rebuilding efforts immediately after a disaster.

The relationship between disaster recovery and community resilience has been a central focus in disaster risk reduction programs since the adoption of The Hyogo Framework for Action 2005-2015 [14]. It is underscored that psychological resilience is a crucial component in long-term disaster recovery efforts, highlighting the necessity to address both psychological and community resilience factors to enhance mental health outcomes [198]. Moreover, the significance of place and social capital in community disaster resilience is emphasized, suggesting a re-evaluation of disaster recovery processes to consider the importance of place in the recovery journey [199].

Efforts to assess recovery and enhance flood resilience stress the importance of developing response capabilities to natural disasters and subsequent recovery to establish disaster-resilient communities [200]. Additionally, the evolution of the federal role in supporting community recovery after disasters underscores the importance of governmental intervention in facilitating and supporting the community recovery process [201]. The concept of resilience, encompassing resistance and recovery, is crucial in evaluating resilience under disastrous conditions, focusing on both the reduction of functional capacities and the restoration of these capacities to a normal state [202].

Learning and Improving

Resilience is not static; it involves continuous learning and improvement. After a disaster, resilient communities engage in reflective learning processes, such as after-action reviews, to analyse their response and identify lessons learned [203]. This information is then used to update plans, train personnel, and improve infrastructure, thus enhancing resilience for future events. This cycle of preparation, response, recovery, and improvement is fundamental to resilience in disaster management.

After a disaster strikes, resilient communities undertake a critical assessment of their response through reflective learning processes, such as after-action reviews. These reviews are comprehensive evaluations conducted by stakeholders involved in the disaster management efforts, including emergency responders, government agencies, community organizations, and sometimes the affected public. The goal is to dissect what happened, what was done, how effectively the actions were implemented, and what could be improved.

During the reflective learning process, communities analyse various aspects of their response to identify both strengths and weaknesses. They look at the adequacy of their preparedness measures, the effectiveness of their response strategies, and the efficiency of their recovery operations. Key questions might include: Did the emergency plans work as expected? Were communications effective? How well did the infrastructure withstand the disaster? Were resources adequate and appropriately allocated? This analysis helps to pinpoint successful tactics that should be continued or expanded, as well as failures or gaps that need to be addressed.

The lessons learned from these reviews are crucial for updating existing disaster management plans. This might involve revising evacuation procedures, improving data collection and sharing, updating training programs for responders, and reinforcing physical infrastructure. For instance, if an after-action review reveals that communication breakdowns were a major issue, future updates may focus on enhancing communication systems and backup methods.

Based on the identified lessons, training programs for personnel are updated to include new tactics, technologies, or procedures that could improve their effectiveness in future disasters. Similarly, infrastructure improvements are prioritized based on vulnerabilities that were exposed during the disaster. This might involve upgrading buildings to be more earthquake-resistant, enhancing flood defences, or expanding the capacity of emergency shelters.

This ongoing cycle of preparation, response, recovery, and improvement forms the cornerstone of resilience in disaster management. Each phase is interconnected, with the insights gained from one disaster informing the preparations for the next. This cyclical process ensures that disaster management strategies are continuously refined, thereby enhancing the community's resilience with each iteration.

Community Engagement and Empowerment

At the heart of resilience is the active involvement and empowerment of the community. Resilient communities are those where local stakeholders — from government and businesses to individual citizens — are engaged in resilience-building activities [204]. This includes participating in planning processes, undertaking preparedness activities, and contributing to recovery efforts. Community engagement ensures that disaster management strategies are relevant, culturally appropriate, and widely supported.

Research has highlighted the significance of community empowerment in disaster management. Studies emphasize that enhancing capacities, reducing vulnerability, and building resilience require increased participation of local communities, aligning with approaches long encouraged in development research and practice [204]. Community empowerment is essential for building the capacity of individuals in disaster-prone areas to enhance their resilience to disasters [205].

Furthermore, the concept of community-based disaster management (CBDM) has been recognized as a salient feature in building resilience to natural perturbations [206]. This approach emphasizes participatory action to empower individuals, enabling them to take proactive measures during crises based on their preparedness [207]. Additionally, the Community Management Disaster Risk Reduction (CMDRR) approach has been identified as a means to manage disasters effectively, reduce poverty, and address vulnerabilities collectively [208].

Collaboration Across Sectors

Resilience requires collaboration across various sectors and disciplines. This includes partnerships between government agencies, private businesses, non-profits, and the academic community [154, 209-211]. Such collaborations can bring in diverse resources and expertise, facilitating innovative solutions and comprehensive strategies that enhance resilience.

These partnerships are instrumental in promoting the development of resilient communities, critical systems, and facilitating post-disaster recovery and learning [154]. By bringing together different sectors, collaborative arrangements can enhance performance and promote greater public accountability [212]. Moreover, partnerships are vital for supporting sustainable business models that underpin socio-ecological resilience [211]. They also contribute to building community resilience through interdisciplinary research and cross-sector partnerships [213].

In disaster management, public-private partnerships have been shown to play a significant role in achieving resilience by increasing societal resilience through strategic, operational, and tactical effects [214]. Additionally, partnerships are crucial in community engagement and multi-sector collaborations, aligning with various models emphasizing the importance of partnerships for disaster resilience [215]. These collaborations are essential for integrating ethnically-diverse communities and organizations to enhance overall resilience [215].

5

Risk Assessment and Hazard Analysis

Risk assessment and hazard analysis play crucial roles in emergency management, disaster recovery, and resilience planning. Risk assessment involves the comprehensive identification, analysis, and evaluation of potential risks that could impact an organization, community, or system, aiming to comprehend the likelihood and impact of various hazards on people, property, the environment, and the economy. The process encompasses several key steps, including the identification of hazards [216] such as natural disasters (e.g., earthquakes, floods, hurricanes), technological hazards (like chemical spills, nuclear accidents), and human-made threats (such as terrorism). Following hazard identification, vulnerability assessment comes into play, evaluating the susceptibilities of systems or communities, considering factors like infrastructure, socio-economic elements, and environmental conditions. Subsequently, risk analysis is conducted, employing both quantitative and qualitative methods to assess the likelihood and consequences of each identified hazard. This analysis facilitates risk evaluation, determining the level of risk posed by each hazard and prioritizing them based on their significance.

On the other hand, hazard analysis focuses on pinpointing specific hazards and evaluating their characteristics, potential consequences, and likelihood of occurrence. It involves steps like hazard identification, where all possible hazards within a given area or system are identified, and hazard characterization, which delves into understanding the nature of each hazard, encompassing factors like source, magnitude, duration, and spatial extent. Consequence analysis follows, assessing potential impacts such as human casualties, property damage, economic losses, and environmental ramifications. Additionally, probability analysis estimates the likelihood of each hazard occurring, drawing from historical data, scientific models, and expert insights. The overarching purpose of hazard analysis is to furnish detailed insights into specific hazards, which inform the development of effective mitigation, preparedness, response, and recovery strategies. By grasping the characteristics and potential impacts of hazards, authorities can tailor planning efforts to address the unique challenges posed by each hazard.

In the realm of emergency management, disaster recovery, and resilience planning, risk assessment and hazard analysis serve as foundational pillars. These processes equip stakeholders with the understanding needed to comprehend the threats they face, enabling them to devise proactive strategies to mitigate risks and enhance preparedness. Through these measures, communities and organizations can fortify their resilience, adapt to evolving conditions, and mount effective responses to and recoveries from disasters.

Interdisciplinary research and collaboration are essential for developing hazard and disaster theories that encompass environmental, human, and infrastructure systems at various scales and units of analysis [217]. Additionally, hazard analysis of meteorological disasters is significant for disaster prevention, mitigation, risk management, and crisis response [218].

Identification of Hazards

In emergency management, the identification of hazards is a fundamental step in understanding the potential threats that could impact an organization, community, or system. These hazards encompass a broad spectrum, including natural disasters, technological hazards, and human-made threats. Natural disasters such as earthquakes, floods, hurricanes, and wildfires arise from environmental phenomena and can cause widespread devastation. Technological hazards involve incidents like chemical spills, industrial accidents, or nuclear incidents, often stemming from human activities or technological failures. Human-made threats, such as terrorism or cyberattacks, are deliberate acts intended to cause harm or disruption.

Once hazards are identified, the next crucial step is assessing vulnerabilities. This involves evaluating the susceptibility of the system or community to the identified hazards. Vulnerabilities can manifest in various forms, including weaknesses in infrastructure, socioeconomic disparities, environmental degradation, or inadequate emergency response capabilities. Understanding vulnerabilities provides insights into the potential areas of weakness that could exacerbate the impact of hazards, guiding efforts to strengthen resilience and preparedness.

Following vulnerability assessment, risk analysis is conducted both quantitatively and qualitatively. Quantitative risk analysis involves using mathematical models, data, and statistics to assess the likelihood and consequences of each identified hazard. This method quantifies risks in terms of probabilities and potential impacts, enabling stakeholders to make informed decisions based on empirical evidence. Qualitative risk analysis, on the other hand, relies on expert judgment, historical data, and scenario-based assessments to evaluate risks subjectively. It considers factors such as the severity of potential consequences, the likelihood of occurrence, and the effectiveness of existing mitigation measures.

After analysing risks, the next step is evaluating and prioritizing them based on their significance. Risk evaluation involves determining the level of risk posed by each hazard, considering factors such as its potential impact on human life, property, the environment, and the economy. Risks are then prioritized based on their severity, likelihood, and the resources available for mitigation and response efforts. This prioritization ensures that limited resources are allocated effectively, focusing on addressing the most critical risks first.

The process of identifying hazards, assessing vulnerabilities, analysing risks quantitatively and qualitatively, and evaluating and prioritizing risks based on their significance forms the cornerstone of effective emergency management, disaster recovery, and resilience planning. By systematically understanding and addressing these aspects, stakeholders can develop robust strategies to mitigate risks, enhance preparedness, and build resilience against a diverse range of threats.

As an example of the process, imagine a coastal city preparing for potential disasters as part of its emergency management plan. The city's authorities begin by identifying hazards that could threaten the community's safety and infrastructure. Among these hazards are natural disasters such as hurricanes, which are common in the region due to its proximity to the ocean. They also recognize the risk of flooding, particularly during heavy rainfall or storm surges, as well as the possibility of wildfires during dry seasons.

In addition to natural disasters, the authorities consider technological hazards that could occur within the city. They acknowledge the risk of chemical spills from nearby industrial facilities and the potential for accidents involving hazardous materials during transportation. Furthermore, the threat of a nuclear incident from a nearby power plant is included in their hazard identification process.

Moreover, the city's emergency management team assesses human-made threats that could disrupt the community. They recognize the potential for terrorism, given the city's population density and status as a hub for tourism and commerce. Additionally, the increasing reliance on digital infrastructure prompts concerns about cyberattacks targeting critical systems, such as power grids and communication networks.

Having identified these hazards, the authorities proceed to assess vulnerabilities within the city. They recognize weaknesses in infrastructure, such as aging flood defences and inadequate drainage systems, which increase the city's susceptibility to flooding. Socioeconomic disparities are also identified, with certain neighbourhoods lacking access to evacuation routes or emergency shelters. Environmental degradation, including coastal erosion and loss of wetlands, further exacerbates the city's vulnerability to natural disasters.

With a comprehensive understanding of hazards and vulnerabilities, the emergency management team conducts risk analysis to quantify and qualify the potential impacts of various scenarios. They use mathematical models, historical data, and expert judgment to assess the likelihood and consequences of each hazard. This analysis enables them to prioritize risks based on their severity and the resources available for mitigation and response efforts.

Following risk analysis, the authorities evaluate and prioritize risks based on their significance to the community. They consider factors such as the potential loss of human life, damage to property, environmental impacts, and economic consequences. Risks with the highest potential impact, such as hurricanes and terrorism, are given top priority in the city's emergency preparedness plans.

In summary, the city's emergency management process involves a systematic approach to identifying hazards, assessing vulnerabilities, analysing risks, and prioritizing mitigation efforts. By understanding and addressing these aspects, the city can develop robust strategies to enhance preparedness and resilience, ultimately reducing the impact of disasters on the community.

Hazard Analysis

Hazard analysis is a systematic process aimed at understanding and evaluating specific hazards, their characteristics, potential consequences, and likelihood of occurrence. This process involves several key steps that collectively provide insights crucial for effective emergency management and disaster preparedness.

Disaster hazard analysis involves a comprehensive process known as risk analysis, which aims to understand the nature of identified hazards, estimate the associated risks, and evaluate the potential consequences that could lead to a disaster [219]. This analysis considers the causes and sources of risks, their positive and negative outcomes, and the likelihood of these consequences occurring [219]. Understanding Earth processes and dynamics is fundamental to hazard analysis, as it provides insights into various disaster risk drivers, which are essential for managing and reducing disaster risk [220].

Moreover, risk analysis plays a crucial role in identifying different types of hazards, measuring their potential risk levels in terms of disaster impacts, and determining the actions needed to prevent, estimate, and address multi-hazard coupling disasters [221, 222]. It involves assessing the vulnerability of hazard-affected bodies, the fragility of disaster-prone environments, and the danger posed by hazard factors to establish a risk assessment system for specific disaster scenarios [223].

The first step in hazard analysis is hazard identification, where all possible hazards within a given area or system are systematically identified. This step involves comprehensive research, consultation with experts, and consideration of historical data to ensure that no potential threat is overlooked. By identifying hazards, emergency planners can establish a comprehensive understanding of the threats facing the community or organization.

Following hazard identification, the next step is hazard characterization. This step involves delving into the nature of each identified hazard, including its source, magnitude, duration, and spatial extent. Understanding these characteristics is essential for assessing the potential impacts of each hazard and determining appropriate mitigation and response measures. For example, in the case of a flood hazard, understanding factors such as the duration and spatial extent of potential flooding events can help authorities develop evacuation plans and flood control measures.

Consequence analysis is another critical component of hazard analysis. This step involves assessing the potential impacts of each hazard, including human casualties, property damage, economic losses, and environmental ramifications. By quantifying the potential consequences of different hazard scenarios, emergency planners can prioritize resources and develop targeted response strategies to minimize the impact on affected communities.

Additionally, probability analysis is conducted to estimate the likelihood of each hazard occurring. This analysis draws from historical data, scientific models, and expert insights to assess the probability of different hazard scenarios. By understanding the likelihood of various hazards, emergency planners can prioritize mitigation efforts and allocate resources effectively to address the most probable threats.

Overall, the overarching purpose of hazard analysis is to provide detailed insights into specific hazards, their characteristics, potential consequences, and likelihood of occurrence. These insights inform the development of effective mitigation, preparedness, response, and recovery strategies tailored to address the unique challenges posed by each hazard. By systematically analysing hazards, authorities can develop proactive measures to enhance community resilience and minimize the impact of disasters on lives, property, and the environment.

Conducting hazard analysis involves a systematic approach to identifying, evaluating, and understanding specific hazards and their potential impacts. Here's a detailed explanation of how to conduct hazard analysis:

- **Hazard Identification**:
  - Begin by compiling a comprehensive list of potential hazards that could affect the area or system under consideration. This involves gathering information from various sources such as historical data, scientific studies, government reports, and expert opinions.
  - Consider a wide range of hazards, including natural disasters (e.g., earthquakes, floods, hurricanes), technological hazards (such as chemical spills, industrial accidents), and human-made threats (like terrorism, cyberattacks).
  - Use tools such as hazard maps, historical records, and hazard inventories

to ensure that all possible threats are identified. Collaborate with subject matter experts in relevant fields to ensure thorough hazard identification.

- **Hazard Characterization**:
  - Once hazards are identified, delve into understanding the characteristics of each hazard. This includes examining factors such as the source, magnitude, frequency, duration, and spatial extent of potential hazard events.
  - Gather data and information on the physical processes driving each hazard, as well as any factors that could influence its severity or impact.
  - Consider the vulnerability of exposed elements (e.g., infrastructure, population, natural resources) to each hazard, taking into account local conditions and socio-economic factors.
- **Consequence Analysis**:
  - Assess the potential consequences of each identified hazard on human life, property, the environment, and the economy.
  - Quantify the potential impacts in terms of human casualties, injuries, property damage, economic losses, disruption of critical services, and environmental degradation.
  - Use available data, modelling tools, and scenario-based assessments to estimate the severity and extent of potential consequences under different hazard scenarios.
- **Probability Analysis**:
  - Estimate the likelihood or probability of each hazard occurring within a given timeframe. This involves analysing historical data, statistical trends, and scientific models to assess the probability of different hazard events.
  - Consider factors that could influence the probability of hazards, such as climate change, land-use changes, technological advancements, and human activities.

    - Use expert judgment and consultation with relevant stakeholders to validate probability estimates and account for uncertainties.

- **Integration and Interpretation**:

    - Integrate the findings from hazard identification, characterization, consequence analysis, and probability analysis to develop a comprehensive understanding of the overall risk landscape.

    - Interpret the results to identify priority hazards, areas of high risk, and potential gaps in existing mitigation and preparedness measures.

    - Use the insights gained from hazard analysis to inform decision-making, prioritize resource allocation, and develop targeted risk reduction strategies tailored to address the specific challenges posed by each hazard.

- **Documentation and Communication**:

    - Document the findings of hazard analysis in a clear and concise manner, including details on identified hazards, their characteristics, potential consequences, and probability estimates.

    - Communicate the results to relevant stakeholders, including policymakers, emergency managers, community members, and other decision-makers.

    - Ensure that hazard analysis results are accessible and understandable to all stakeholders, facilitating informed decision-making and fostering collaboration in risk reduction efforts.

By means of an example of this processes, let us consider:
Scenario: Hazard Analysis for a Coastal Community

- **Hazard Identification**:

    - The coastal community of Seaview Harbor identifies several potential hazards that could impact the area, including natural disasters, technological hazards, and human-made threats.

- **Hazard Characterization**:

  - Hurricanes: Considering the region's history and meteorological data, the likelihood of hurricanes making landfall is assessed as moderate to high, particularly during the hurricane season.
  - Oil spills: The likelihood of oil spills is evaluated based on the frequency of maintenance and safety protocols on offshore drilling platforms. While the probability is relatively low, the potential consequences are severe.
  - Terrorism: The likelihood of terrorist attacks is assessed based on intelligence reports and threat assessments. While the probability may be low, the potential impact is considered significant.
- **Consequence Analysis**:
  - Hurricanes: Potential consequences include damage to infrastructure, displacement of residents, loss of life, and environmental degradation due to flooding and erosion.
  - Oil spills: Consequences may include contamination of water bodies, harm to marine life, economic losses, and health risks for residents.
  - Terrorism: Potential impacts encompass loss of life and injuries, damage to infrastructure, economic disruption, and social unrest.
- **Probability Analysis**:
  - Hurricanes: Probability estimates are based on historical storm data, climate projections, and hurricane forecasting models.
  - Oil spills: Probability analysis considers factors such as the effectiveness of spill response measures and the frequency of incidents in similar regions.
  - Terrorism: Probability estimates are based on intelligence reports and historical data on terrorist activities.
- **Integration and Interpretation**:
  - The hazard analysis findings are integrated to develop a comprehensive understanding of the overall risk landscape facing Seaview Harbor. Priority

hazards and areas of high risk are identified.

- The community interprets the results to inform decision-making, prioritize resource allocation, and develop targeted risk reduction strategies.

- **Documentation and Communication**:
  - The results of the hazard analysis are documented in a hazard assessment report, detailing the identified hazards, their characteristics, potential consequences, and likelihood estimates.
  - The findings are communicated to relevant stakeholders through public awareness campaigns and engagement sessions.

The hazard assessment for Seaview Harbor provides valuable insights into the potential threats facing the coastal community, including natural disasters, technological hazards, and human-made threats. Here's what the hazard assessment tells us:

1. Identification of Hazards: The assessment identifies a range of hazards that could impact Seaview Harbor, including hurricanes, oil spills, and terrorism. This comprehensive identification ensures that all potential threats are considered in the community's risk management efforts.

2. Characterization of Hazards: By characterizing each hazard, the assessment provides detailed information about their characteristics, such as their sources, magnitude, and potential impacts. This understanding allows stakeholders to assess the severity of each hazard and prioritize their response efforts accordingly.

3. Assessment of Likelihood and Consequences: The hazard assessment evaluates both the likelihood of each hazard occurring and the potential consequences if they were to occur. This information helps stakeholders understand the probability of different hazard scenarios and the potential impacts on the community, including damage to infrastructure, loss of life, economic losses, and environmental damage.

4. Identification of High-Risk Areas: The assessment identifies areas within Seaview Harbor that are particularly vulnerable to certain hazards, allowing for targeted risk reduction strategies and investments in resilience measures.

5. Development of Risk Reduction Strategies: Based on the findings of the hazard assessment, stakeholders can develop tailored risk reduction strategies to enhance community resilience and minimize the impact of disasters. These strategies may include investments in infrastructure improvements, emergency preparedness and response plans, and measures to enhance cybersecurity and counter-terrorism efforts.

6. Communication and Awareness: The hazard assessment facilitates communication and awareness among stakeholders by providing clear and accessible information about the potential threats facing the community. This allows residents, businesses, and government agencies to make informed decisions and take proactive measures to mitigate risks and prepare for emergencies.

Overall, the hazard assessment serves as a valuable tool for Seaview Harbor in understanding and addressing the complex challenges posed by various hazards, ultimately contributing to the community's resilience and ability to adapt to changing conditions.

Hazard Mapping

Hazard mapping involves visually representing hazards and their spatial distribution within a specific area, offering valuable insights into the location, extent, and severity of various risks. This process enables stakeholders to pinpoint areas prone to specific hazards, aiding in the prioritization of mitigation and preparedness initiatives.

Process:

- Data Collection: Hazard mapping commences with gathering pertinent data, including historical records, scientific studies, satellite imagery, and topographic maps. These sources provide crucial information about the frequency, intensity, and spatial distribution of different hazards within the area of interest.

- Hazard Identification: Utilizing the collected data, hazards such as floods, earthquakes, landslides, wildfires, and industrial accidents are identified. Each hazard is assessed based on its likelihood of occurrence and potential impacts on the community.

- Spatial Analysis: Geographic Information Systems (GIS) technology is frequently employed to analyse and visually represent hazard data spatially. This facilitates the creation of maps illustrating hazard locations, extents, and factors that may exacerbate or alleviate their effects, such as terrain features, land use patterns, and existing infrastructure.

- Mapping Outputs: The culmination of hazard mapping efforts results in the production of hazard maps depicting the spatial distribution of hazards, vulnerability, and risk levels within the community. These maps often incorporate overlays of various hazard layers—such as flood zones, seismic zones, and areas of heightened wildfire risk—to offer a comprehensive understanding of the overall risk landscape.

Purpose:

- Risk Communication: Hazard maps serve as effective tools for communicating and raising awareness among stakeholders regarding potential threats confronting the community. By providing clear and accessible information, these maps empower residents, businesses, and government agencies to make informed decisions and take proactive measures to mitigate risks and prepare for emergencies.

- Planning and Decision-Making: Hazard maps inform crucial aspects of land-use planning, zoning regulations, infrastructure development, and emergency response planning. Decision-makers leverage these maps to identify high-risk areas and prioritize investments in risk reduction measures and resilience-building efforts.

- Emergency Preparedness and Response: Hazard maps play a pivotal role in enhancing emergency preparedness and response capabilities. By enabling emergency managers to anticipate potential hazards, develop evacuation plans, and allocate resources effectively during disasters, these maps contribute significantly to safeguarding lives and minimizing damage to property and infrastructure.

Types of Hazard Mapping

Flood Hazard Map: To minimize flood-related damage through efficient evacuation and flood prevention, flood hazard maps are produced. These maps illustrate the projected depth and duration of flooding in areas susceptible to inundation from river overflow during extreme rainfall events. They delineate the zones expected to be affected by river overflow and provide information on water depth in such scenarios, forming the basis for river flood prevention strategies.

Volcanic Hazard Map: Volcanic hazard maps delineate regions susceptible to various volcanic hazards such as pyroclastic flows, large cinder cones, and volcanic mudflows. These maps serve as foundational data for developing evacuation plans during normal conditions and devising disaster prevention measures like restricting mountain access, implementing evacuation protocols, and regulating land use during eruptions.

Seismic Hazard Map: Seismic hazard maps predict seismic activity levels, including the likelihood and intensity of earthquakes, and estimate potential damage. These maps may include probabilistic seismic motion prediction maps, specifying expected tremor levels, and earthquake motion prediction maps detailing potential shaking intensity based on source fault scenarios. Additionally, some maps forecast regional building damage and liquefaction risks.

Tsunami and Storm Surge Hazard Map: Tsunami and storm surge hazard maps delineate areas at risk of damage and predict the extent of potential damage from these disasters. They also provide crucial disaster management information such as evacuation sites and routes, aiding in resident evacuation and infrastructure planning.

Geo-Hazard Map: Geo-hazard maps categorize hazards triggered by heavy rainfall or seismic events, including collapses of mountains and cliffs, and flows of soil and rocks mixed with water. These maps offer residents information on disaster risks and evacuation procedures, aiding in disaster preparedness and response. Geo-hazards typically encompass rock falls, debris flows, and slides, each posing distinct risks and requiring specific mitigation strategies.

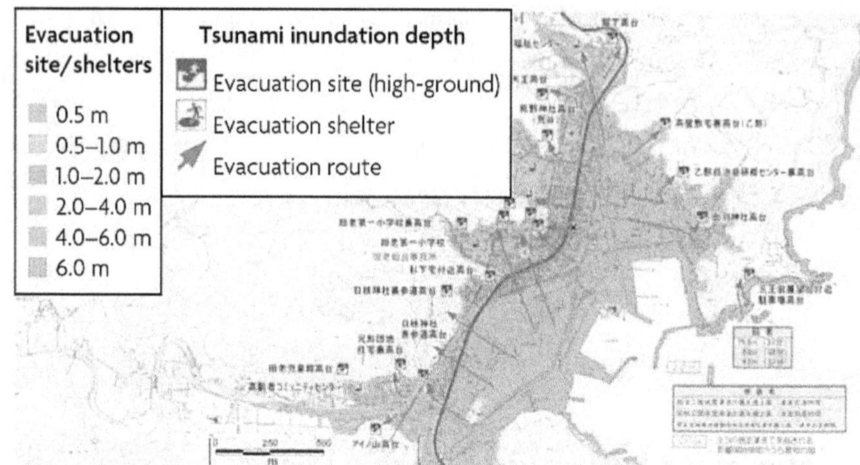

Figure 23: An example of a tsunami hazard map Miyako City Iwate Prefecture. Miyako City (Iwate Prefecture, Japan), CC BY 3.0 IGO, via Wikimedia Commons.

UNDRO (United Nations Disaster Relief Coordinator) defines hazard mapping as the process of determining where and to what extent specific phenomena are likely to pose a threat to people, property, infrastructure, and economic activities within a geographical area [224]. This entails identifying and visually representing the spatial distribution of hazard events or physical conditions, such as potential ground shaking, floodplains, hazardous material sites, and climate zones. The primary aim is to provide residents with information regarding the potential extent of damage and to facilitate disaster prevention activities. While hazard mapping cannot prevent disasters outright, its effective utilization can mitigate their magnitude.

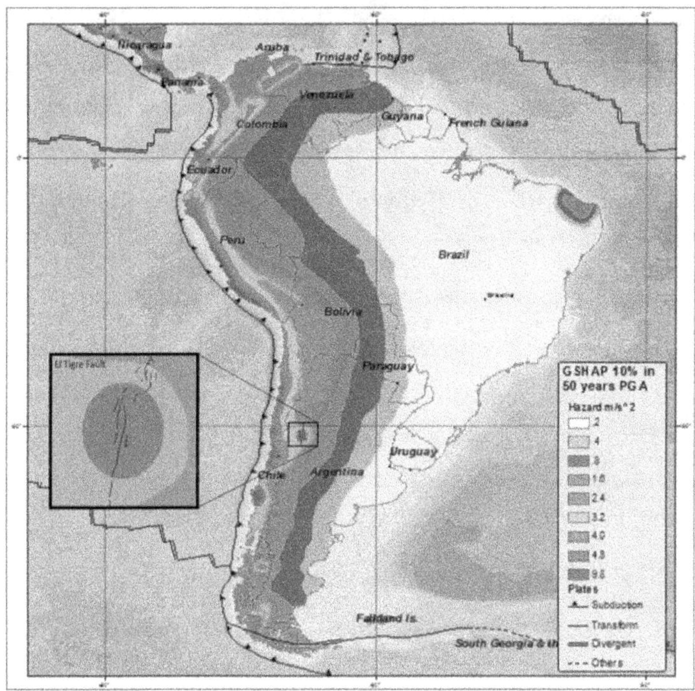

Figure 24: South America seismic hazard map with estimated El Tigre Fault location inset. Original map edited by user sara8s001, Public domain, via Wikimedia Commons.

Hazard maps, including flood maps, landslide maps, and shake maps, are specific types of hazard maps categorized into two main types [224]:

(a) Resident-Educating Type: These maps are designed to inform residents of a particular area about the risks they face.

(b) Administrative Information Type: These maps are intended to inform administrative bodies, aiding in the implementation of warning and evacuation systems.

The probability of hazard occurrence varies depending on the location.

Mapping techniques are essential for synthesizing data on natural hazards and integrating them with socioeconomic data, thereby enhancing analysis and communication among stakeholders involved in hazard management and decision-making processes. Two key techniques utilized in hazard mapping are [224]:

1. Multiple Hazard Mapping (MHM): This technique is typically employed in conjunction with new development projects. MHM combines information from various hazard maps of differing scales, coverage, and detail into a single

composite map, providing a comprehensive overview of the magnitude, frequency, and spatial extent of all natural hazards within a study area. Different scales of MHM are utilized depending on the planning stage and the specific requirements of the project, ranging from regional scale maps useful for regional development planning to large-scale maps necessary for infrastructure project site investigations.

2. Critical Facilities Mapping (CFM): CFM focuses on identifying and mapping man-made structures or improvements that possess characteristics making them capable of causing significant harm, property damage, or disruption to vital socioeconomic activities if damaged or destroyed. These critical facilities encompass structures with unique functions, sizes, service areas, or roles within a community. CFM is typically conducted with a focus on development within existing infrastructure.

MHM offers several benefits, including synthesizing information on natural phenomena and their impacts, identifying interconnected hazards, recommending mitigation techniques, and facilitating simultaneous consideration of all hazards in land-use decisions. Additionally, MHM has implications for emergency preparedness planning, such as equitable fund allocation, integrated response procedures, and cooperative agreements among relevant agencies and groups [224].

Selecting an appropriate base map is crucial for MHM, preferably utilizing existing maps or photographs to avoid the time and effort required to create a base map from scratch. The scale of an MHM depends on factors such as the number and severity of hazards, the area covered, and the intended use of the map.

While much hazard information may initially be in non-map formats, translating this data into maps is essential for effective communication with planners and decision-makers. Information on hazard location, likelihood of occurrence, and severity must be clearly conveyed on the maps. However, planners must acknowledge that the credibility and accuracy of an MHM are contingent upon the quality of the individual hazard information used to compile it. Despite its importance, an MHM is only as effective as the clarity and simplicity of its presentation.

The primary objective of CFM is to provide planners and decision-makers with clear and accurate information regarding the location, capacity, and service area of critical facilities. CFM allows for the simultaneous presentation of numerous critical facilities, aiding in decision-making processes. When combined with multiple hazard mapping (MHM), CFM can highlight areas requiring additional hazard information, different hazard reduction strategies, or immediate attention during hazardous events.

The benefits of CFM include:

- Clarifying the uniqueness of services provided by facilities in the area.
- Identifying facilities in need of upgrading or expansion.
- Assessing the impact of potential development on existing infrastructure.
- Highlighting the need for further hazard assessment.

Combining CFM with MHM offers several advantages in the development planning process. For instance, if a critical facility is located in a hazardous area, planners and decision-makers are alerted to potential future challenges. This allows for the analysis of the facility's equipment, use, and condition to evaluate its vulnerability.

Incorporating appropriate vulnerability reduction techniques into each stage of the planning process can help mitigate social and economic disasters. Strategies for reducing vulnerability may include avoiding hazardous areas, designing for resistance, or implementing minimal exposure practices. For existing critical facilities, mitigation measures may involve relocation, strengthening, retrofitting, redundancy enhancement, operational revisions, and the adoption of emergency preparedness, response, and recovery programs [224].

The benefits of combining CFM and MHM include:

- Providing awareness of hazards to existing and proposed critical facilities before project implementation.
- Determining the potential impact of existing critical facility failure or disruption on new development due to natural events.
- Facilitating the determination of realistic benefit-cost ratios for new development projects.
- Identifying sub-areas necessitating different assessments, emergency preparedness measures, immediate recovery actions, or specific vulnerability reduction techniques.

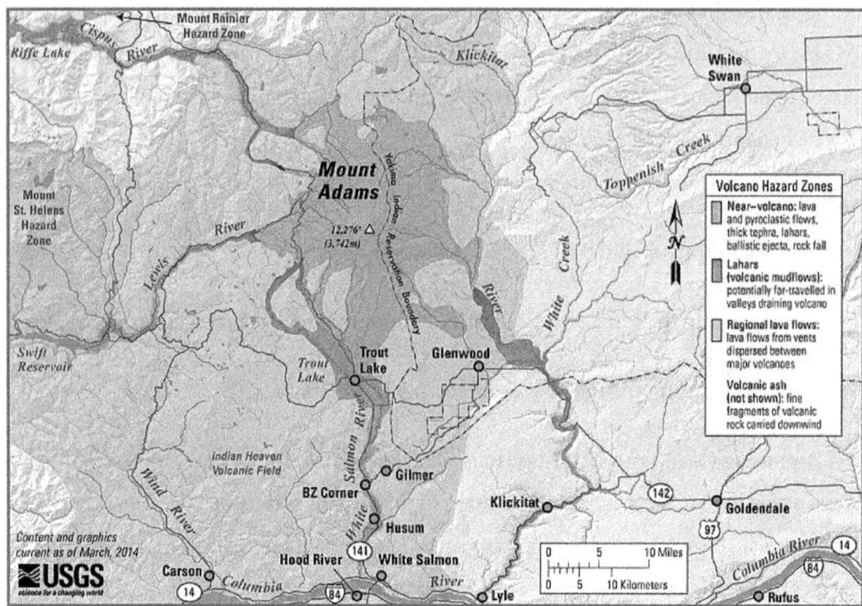

Figure 25: Mount Adams, Washington simplified hazards map showing potential impact area for ground-based hazards during a volcanic event. Lisa Faust, USGS, Public domain, via Wikimedia Commons.

Creating a hazard map involves several steps to gather, analyse, and visualize data related to hazards and their spatial distribution. This includes:

1. Identify Hazards: Begin by identifying the hazards that are relevant to the area of interest. These may include natural hazards such as floods, earthquakes, wildfires, landslides, hurricanes, or human-made hazards like industrial accidents, chemical spills, or terrorist threats.

2. Collect Data: Gather relevant data from various sources, including historical records, scientific studies, government reports, satellite imagery, topographic maps, and local knowledge. Data should include information on the frequency, intensity, and spatial distribution of hazards, as well as factors that may influence their occurrence or impact.

3. Assess Hazard Characteristics: Characterize each hazard by assessing its likelihood of occurrence, potential magnitude, duration, and spatial extent. Consider factors such as geological conditions, climatic patterns, human activities, and infrastructure vulnerabilities that may influence hazard characteristics.

4. Spatial Analysis: Utilize Geographic Information Systems (GIS) technology to analyse and visualize hazard data spatially. GIS software allows you to overlay different layers of information, such as hazard locations, vulnerability indicators, land use patterns, and infrastructure networks, to identify areas at risk.

5. Define Mapping Parameters: Determine the parameters and criteria for creating the hazard map, such as the scale, resolution, symbology, and colour scheme. Choose appropriate symbols and colours to represent different hazard types, severity levels, and areas of concern on the map.

6. Create Hazard Zones: Use GIS tools to delineate hazard zones based on the analysis of hazard data and spatial factors. Define boundaries for different hazard categories, such as high-risk zones, moderate-risk zones, and low-risk zones, considering the likelihood and potential consequences of hazards.

7. Incorporate Vulnerability Factors: Integrate vulnerability indicators into the hazard map to account for the susceptibility of exposed elements, such as population, infrastructure, environment, and economy, to the impacts of hazards. Overlay vulnerability layers to identify areas of heightened risk within the community.

8. Validate and Review: Validate the accuracy and reliability of the hazard map by comparing it with existing data, historical records, expert knowledge, and field observations. Review the map with relevant stakeholders, including local authorities, emergency managers, community members, and subject matter experts, to ensure its comprehensiveness and usability.

9. Document and Publish: Document the methodology, data sources, assumptions, and limitations used in creating the hazard map. Publish the map in accessible formats, such as digital files, interactive web platforms, or printed materials, to disseminate it to stakeholders and the wider community.

10. Update and Maintain: Regularly update and maintain the hazard map to reflect changes in hazard conditions, land use patterns, population dynamics, infrastructure development, and other factors. Continuously monitor and assess hazards to ensure the map remains accurate and relevant for emergency planning and decision-making.

Continuing with the preciously used example scenario, creating a hazard map for the Coastal City of Bayview, could include:

- **Identify Hazards**:
  - Begin by identifying hazards relevant to Bayview. These include natural hazards like hurricanes, coastal erosion, and storm surges due to its location by the sea. Human-made hazards such as industrial accidents from nearby chemical plants and potential terrorist threats targeting the port are also considered.
- **Collect Data**:
  - Gather data from various sources including historical records, scientific studies, government reports, and satellite imagery. Collaborate with local agencies and experts to collect information on hazard frequency, intensity, and spatial distribution, as well as factors influencing their occurrence.
- **Assess Hazard Characteristics**:
  - Characterize each hazard by assessing its likelihood of occurrence, potential magnitude, duration, and spatial extent. Analyse geological conditions, climatic patterns, and vulnerability of critical infrastructure like ports and chemical plants to understand hazard characteristics.
- **Spatial Analysis**:
  - Utilize GIS technology to analyse and visualize hazard data spatially. Overlay different layers of information such as hazard locations, vulnerability indicators, and infrastructure networks to identify areas at risk along the coastline and within the city.
- **Define Mapping Parameters**:
  - Determine mapping parameters including scale, resolution, symbology, and colour scheme. Choose symbols and colours to represent different hazard types and severity levels effectively on the map.
- **Create Hazard Zones**:

  - Use GIS tools to delineate hazard zones based on hazard data and spatial factors. Define boundaries for high-risk, moderate-risk, and low-risk zones considering likelihood and potential consequences of hazards on coastal infrastructure and communities.

- **Incorporate Vulnerability Factors**:

  - Integrate vulnerability indicators into the hazard map to account for susceptibility of exposed elements such as population density, critical infrastructure, environmental sensitivity, and socioeconomic factors. Overlay vulnerability layers to identify areas of heightened risk within Bayview.

- **Validate and Review**:

  - Validate map accuracy by comparing with existing data and expert opinions. Review the map with local authorities, emergency managers, and community members to ensure completeness and usability, incorporating feedback to refine the map.

- **Document and Publish**:

  - Document methodology, data sources, assumptions, and limitations used in creating the hazard map. Publish the map digitally and in print format to disseminate to stakeholders, city officials, emergency responders, and the wider community.

- **Update and Maintain**:

  - Establish a plan to regularly update and maintain the hazard map to reflect changes in hazard conditions, land use, population dynamics, and infrastructure development. Continuously monitor and assess hazards to ensure the map remains accurate and relevant for emergency planning and decision-making in Bayview.

Mapping techniques and tools encompass various methods for gathering information related to hazards and vulnerabilities within a community [224]:

1. **Community Knowledge**: Utilizing local knowledge is a fundamental approach to mapping hazards. Techniques such as Participatory Rural Appraisal

(PRA) and Rapid Rural Appraisal (RRA) are invaluable in rural development activities. These methods are cost-effective and capture the local perception of hazards. The information collected through community knowledge can be overlaid onto local contour maps, providing a comprehensive understanding of the terrain.

2. **Surveys on Historic Events**: Historical reports compiled on past events offer insights into previous occurrences of hazards. While these reports may have been created for different purposes, they often contain valuable information that can contribute to hazard mapping efforts. Analysing historic events helps in understanding patterns, trends, and the severity of past hazards.

3. **Scientific Investigation and Research**: Scientific investigation involves collaborative efforts among experts from various disciplines. For instance, mapping landslide hazards requires the expertise of geologists, geo-technical engineers, geomorphologists, and topographers. These multidisciplinary studies collect data over large areas and extended time periods, employing sophisticated tools and techniques that evolve with time. The advancement of computer modelling has further enhanced hazard prediction capabilities. Geographic Information Systems (GIS) modelling, coupled with remotely sensed data, has revolutionized hazard assessment by providing detailed spatial analyses and predictive modelling.

In India, hazard monitoring is conducted by several key organizations nationwide:

- The India Meteorological Department (IMD) monitors seismic activity and cyclone hazards.
- The Central Water Commission is responsible for flood monitoring.
- The Geological Survey of India and the Department of Earthquake Engineering at IIT Roorkee also play significant roles in hazard assessment.
- India has developed state-wise hazard maps for earthquakes, wind and cyclones, and floods. These maps, available on the Building Materials and Technology Promotion Council (BMTPC) website, provide valuable information for disaster preparedness and mitigation efforts.

Community Vulnerability Assessments

A vulnerability assessment lays the groundwork for formulating strategies aimed at mitigating disaster risks. By conducting such an assessment, a community can gauge the extent of vulnerability among its populace, including individuals with specific requirements. It facilitates the identification of vulnerable structures, including essential facilities like hospitals and schools, along with their precise locations. Moreover, the assessment scrutinizes communication channels and networks susceptible to disruption in the event of a disaster, encompassing informal communication avenues like community organizations such as churches.

Community vulnerability assessments are crucial tools for understanding and addressing the susceptibility of communities to the impacts of hazards. Here's a detailed breakdown of how these assessments work:

1. Data Collection: The process begins with gathering data on various factors that contribute to vulnerability. This includes collecting information on demographics, socio-economic indicators (like income levels and employment rates), infrastructure (such as housing quality and transportation networks), healthcare facilities, environmental conditions (like exposure to pollution or susceptibility to natural disasters), and governance structures (including the effectiveness of local government agencies).

2. Vulnerability Identification: Once data is collected, qualitative and quantitative methods are used to identify and analyse vulnerabilities within the community. This may involve assessing factors such as poverty levels, housing conditions (including vulnerability to damage from hazards like floods or earthquakes), access to healthcare and education, social cohesion within the community, and the effectiveness of local institutions and governance in managing disaster risks.

3. Vulnerability Mapping: Similar to hazard mapping, vulnerability assessments may involve spatial analysis to map vulnerable areas within the community. Geographic Information System (GIS) technology can be utilized to overlay vulnerability indicators with hazard maps, helping to identify areas that are at high risk of experiencing negative impacts from disasters.

4. Stakeholder Engagement: Community vulnerability assessments often involve collaboration with local stakeholders, including community members, government agen-

cies, non-profit organizations, and academic institutions. Engaging stakeholders ensures that the assessment process reflects the perspectives and priorities of those most affected by hazards, and helps to build ownership and support for the assessment findings and subsequent actions.

Purpose:

1. Risk Reduction and Resilience Building: By providing insights into the underlying drivers of vulnerability, vulnerability assessments inform strategies for reducing risk and enhancing community resilience. Addressing root causes of vulnerability, such as poverty, inequality, and inadequate infrastructure, enables communities to better prepare for and recover from disasters.

2. Targeted Interventions: Vulnerability assessments help identify priority areas and populations in need of assistance. This enables policymakers, humanitarian organizations, and other stakeholders to target interventions and allocate resources effectively to support the most vulnerable communities, maximizing the impact of limited resources.

3. Advocacy and Policy Change: By highlighting the social, economic, and environmental factors that contribute to vulnerability, vulnerability assessments can inform advocacy efforts and policy change. They provide evidence to support calls for investment in poverty reduction, social protection, and sustainable development initiatives that can strengthen community resilience over the long term, ultimately leading to more resilient and sustainable communities.

Community vulnerability assessments play a crucial role in understanding, mitigating, and responding to the risks posed by hazards within a community. They are utilized in various ways to achieve these objectives.

One primary use of vulnerability assessments is for risk identification and prioritization. By analysing factors such as demographics, socio-economic conditions, infrastructure, and environmental factors, these assessments help identify key hazards and vulnerabilities faced by a community. This information enables policymakers and stakeholders to prioritize resources and interventions effectively, focusing on areas and populations most at risk.

Another important application of vulnerability assessments is in resilience building. By understanding the underlying drivers of vulnerability, communities can develop strategies to enhance their ability to withstand and recover from disasters. Addressing root causes such as poverty, inadequate infrastructure, and social inequalities, vulnerability assessments inform the development of resilience-building initiatives tailored to the specific needs of the community.

Vulnerability assessments also assist in resource allocation by identifying priority areas and populations in need of assistance. By targeting interventions based on vulnerability profiles, policymakers and humanitarian organizations can ensure that resources are allocated effectively to support the most vulnerable communities. This targeted approach maximizes the impact of interventions and enhances community resilience.

Furthermore, vulnerability assessments provide evidence to support advocacy efforts and policy change. By highlighting the social, economic, and environmental factors contributing to vulnerability, these assessments inform policymakers and stakeholders about the need for investment in disaster risk reduction, poverty alleviation, social protection, and sustainable development initiatives. They play a crucial role in shaping policies that strengthen community resilience and reduce disaster risk over the long term.

Additionally, community vulnerability assessments often involve collaboration with local stakeholders, including community members, government agencies, non-profit organizations, and academia. By engaging stakeholders throughout the assessment process, assessments ensure that local knowledge and perspectives are incorporated into vulnerability analysis and response planning. This participatory approach fosters community ownership of resilience-building efforts and enhances the effectiveness of interventions.

Finally, vulnerability assessments provide baseline data for monitoring and evaluating the effectiveness of resilience-building initiatives over time. By periodically assessing changes in vulnerability profiles, communities can track progress towards reducing risk and enhancing resilience. Monitoring and evaluation help identify gaps in current strategies and inform adjustments to ensure that interventions remain relevant and impactful.

Conducting community vulnerability assessments involves a systematic process to understand and analyse the susceptibility of a community to the impacts of hazards. This includes:

1. Define the Scope and Objectives: Start by clearly defining the scope and objectives of the vulnerability assessment. Determine the hazards to be assessed and the geographic area of focus. Identify the key objectives, such as understanding vulnerability factors, identifying at-risk populations, and informing resilience-building strategies.

2. Gather Data: Collect relevant data on various factors that contribute to vulnerability. This may include demographics, socio-economic indicators, infrastruc-

ture, healthcare facilities, environmental conditions, and governance structures. Use a combination of existing data sources, surveys, interviews, and community consultations to gather comprehensive information.

3. Vulnerability Identification: Analyse the data collected to identify vulnerabilities within the community. Use both qualitative and quantitative methods to assess factors such as poverty, housing conditions, access to healthcare and education, social cohesion, and the effectiveness of local institutions and governance. Identify vulnerable populations and areas at high risk of hazard impact.

4. Vulnerability Mapping: Utilize spatial analysis techniques to map vulnerable areas within the community. Geographic Information Systems (GIS) technology can be particularly useful for overlaying vulnerability indicators with hazard maps to identify high-risk areas. Generate maps that visualize the spatial distribution of vulnerability factors and highlight areas of concern.

5. Stakeholder Engagement: Foster collaboration with local stakeholders throughout the assessment process. Engage community members, government agencies, non-profit organizations, academia, and other relevant stakeholders. Conduct stakeholder meetings, workshops, and focus groups to gather input, share findings, and ensure that the assessment reflects diverse perspectives.

6. Risk Assessment: Assess the potential impact of hazards on the community based on the identified vulnerabilities. Evaluate the likelihood and severity of various hazard scenarios and their potential consequences. Consider both immediate impacts and long-term consequences, including social, economic, and environmental effects.

7. Report and Communication: Compile the findings of the vulnerability assessment into a comprehensive report. Clearly communicate the results, including maps, data analysis, and key findings, to stakeholders and decision-makers. Use accessible language and visuals to ensure that the information is understandable to a wide audience.

8. Inform Resilience Strategies: Use the findings of the vulnerability assessment to inform the development of resilience-building strategies and interventions. Identify priority areas for action, including measures to address root causes of

vulnerability, enhance preparedness, improve response capacity, and promote community resilience. Engage stakeholders in the development and implementation of these strategies.

9. Monitor and Evaluate: Continuously monitor and evaluate the effectiveness of resilience strategies over time. Track changes in vulnerability indicators, assess the impact of interventions, and adjust strategies as needed. Maintain ongoing engagement with stakeholders to ensure that resilience efforts remain responsive to evolving community needs and priorities.

For an example, imagine a coastal community, Oceanview Town, situated in a region prone to hurricanes and storm surges. With the onset of hurricane season approaching, the local government decides to conduct a community vulnerability assessment to better understand the town's susceptibility to these hazards and develop effective resilience strategies.

1. Define the Scope and Objectives: The mayor convenes a meeting with key stakeholders, including town council members, emergency management officials, and community leaders, to outline the scope and objectives of the vulnerability assessment. They agree to focus on assessing the vulnerability of residential areas, critical infrastructure such as hospitals and schools, and vulnerable populations such as the elderly and low-income households.

2. Gather Data: The town forms a task force comprising local government staff, researchers, and volunteers to gather data for the assessment. They collect demographic information, socio-economic indicators, infrastructure data, healthcare facility locations, environmental conditions, and records of past disaster impacts. They conduct surveys, interviews with residents, and consultations with community groups to gather comprehensive information.

3. Vulnerability Identification: Using the collected data, the task force analyses vulnerability factors within Oceanview Town. They identify areas prone to flooding, inadequate infrastructure, lack of access to healthcare and education, and social disparities. Vulnerable populations, such as elderly residents living in flood-prone areas and low-income families without transportation, are also identified.

4. Vulnerability Mapping: The task force utilizes GIS technology to map vulnerable areas within Oceanview Town. They overlay vulnerability indicators with hazard maps to visualize high-risk zones prone to storm surges and flooding. The resulting maps highlight areas requiring immediate attention and intervention.

5. Stakeholder Engagement: Throughout the assessment process, the task force engages with local stakeholders, including residents, businesses, community organizations, and government agencies. They hold town hall meetings, workshops, and focus groups to gather input, share findings, and ensure community participation in the assessment.

6. Risk Assessment: The task force assesses the potential impact of hurricanes and storm surges on Oceanview Town based on the identified vulnerabilities. They evaluate the likelihood and severity of various hazard scenarios, considering both immediate impacts and long-term consequences on the community's social, economic, and environmental well-being.

7. Report and Communication: The task force compiles the findings of the vulnerability assessment into a comprehensive report. They include maps, data analysis, and key findings to clearly communicate the results to stakeholders and decision-makers. The report is disseminated through town meetings, online platforms, and local media to ensure broad accessibility.

8. Inform Resilience Strategies: Using the findings of the vulnerability assessment, the task force develops resilience-building strategies tailored to Oceanview Town's needs. They prioritize actions to address root causes of vulnerability, enhance preparedness, improve response capacity, and promote community resilience. Stakeholders are actively involved in the development and implementation of these strategies.

9. Monitor and Evaluate: The task force establishes mechanisms to monitor and evaluate the effectiveness of resilience strategies over time. They track changes in vulnerability indicators, assess the impact of interventions, and adjust strategies as needed. Regular engagement with stakeholders ensures that resilience efforts remain adaptive and responsive to evolving community needs and priorities.

6

Community-Based Disaster Preparedness

Community-Based Disaster Preparedness (CBDP) is an approach to disaster management that emphasizes the active participation of community members in all stages of disaster preparedness, response, and recovery. CBDP recognizes that communities are often the first to respond to disasters and possess valuable local knowledge, resources, and capacities that can enhance overall resilience.

Key components of Community-Based Disaster Preparedness include:

1. Community Participation: CBDP encourages active involvement of community members, including residents, local leaders, civil society organizations, and other stakeholders, in decision-making processes related to disaster preparedness. Communities are empowered to identify their own vulnerabilities, strengths, and priorities and to contribute to the development of preparedness plans and strategies.

2. Capacity Building: CBDP focuses on building the capacity of communities to prepare for, respond to, and recover from disasters. This includes training community members in first aid, search and rescue techniques, disaster response coordination, and other relevant skills. Capacity building efforts also aim to strengthen local institutions, networks, and infrastructure to enhance overall resilience.

3. Risk Assessment and Planning: CBDP involves conducting risk assessments at the community level to identify hazards, vulnerabilities, and capacities. Based on these assessments, communities develop disaster preparedness plans and strategies that outline specific actions to mitigate risks, enhance preparedness, and improve response and recovery efforts. These plans are often tailored to the unique needs and characteristics of each community.

4. Early Warning Systems: CBDP promotes the establishment of early warning systems that provide timely and accurate information to communities about impending disasters. This may include systems for monitoring weather patterns, river levels, seismic activity, or other potential hazards, as well as mechanisms for disseminating warnings to community members through various communication channels.

5. Community-Based Response and Recovery: CBDP emphasizes the importance of local resources and capacities in disaster response and recovery efforts. Communities are encouraged to develop local response teams, stockpile emergency supplies, establish evacuation routes and shelters, and engage in mutual aid and support networks to assist those affected by disasters. CBDP also emphasizes the importance of linking community-based efforts with formal disaster management systems and agencies to ensure coordinated and effective response and recovery efforts.

Overall, Community-Based Disaster Preparedness aims to empower communities to take proactive measures to reduce their vulnerability to disasters, enhance their resilience, and effectively respond to and recover from disasters when they occur. By fostering collaboration, participation, and capacity building at the local level, CBDP contributes to more sustainable and inclusive approaches to disaster management.

Community-Based Disaster Preparedness (CBDP) underscores the importance of collective community action and the internal mobilization of resources to enhance community resilience to disasters. By fostering self-reliance and facilitating a more systematic and effective mobilization of external resources, CBDP aims to ensure that disaster preparedness efforts are relevant and impactful.

The process of CBDP encompasses several key objectives [225]:

- Awareness and Risk Recognition: It begins with raising awareness within the community about the risks they face from disasters. Communities are encouraged to recognize and understand the hazards they are exposed to, empowering them to take proactive measures to mitigate risks.

- Utilization of Local Knowledge and Resources: CBDP acknowledges the significance of local knowledge and resources in disaster management. Communities, especially those in high-risk areas, are encouraged to leverage their existing coping mechanisms and strategies. Strengthening local capacities enhances the community's ability to withstand disaster impacts.
- Empowerment and Ownership: CBDP emphasizes the importance of empowering local communities and ensuring that they retain ownership of disaster reduction efforts. Communities should not be rendered powerless in the absence of external interventions. Instead, they should be actively involved in decision-making processes and regarded as proactive partners in disaster management.
- Participatory Approaches: Disaster reduction activities should be participatory, with local communities considered as proactive rather than passive recipients of interventions. Involving communities in planning and decision-making fosters collective action and ensures that interventions are tailored to local needs and priorities.
- Community Leadership and Capacity Building: CBDP promotes the development of community leadership and the training of local volunteers to respond effectively to disasters. Building resilience at the community level involves harnessing the leadership and resourcefulness of community members through participatory approaches.
- Sustainability: Solutions derived from within the community are more sustainable in the long run. By empowering communities to take ownership of disaster preparedness initiatives, CBDP aims to ensure the sustainability of efforts beyond the duration of external support.

Community involvement in disaster risk reduction yields several important outcomes [225]:

- Enhanced Preparedness: Communities are better equipped to respond to disasters, saving lives and reducing the impact of hazards through local response teams and organized efforts.

- Efficient Recovery: Active community involvement facilitates a more efficient recovery process, addressing survival and health needs effectively in the aftermath of disasters.
- Sustainability of Initiatives: Community participation ensures the sustainability of disaster risk management efforts, reducing vulnerability and losses in the long term.
- Diverse Perspectives: Engaging various community members and groups enables a more comprehensive understanding of risks and vulnerabilities, leading to more effective risk reduction strategies.

By involving communities in decision-making processes and leveraging their local knowledge and resources, CBDP contributes to more resilient and sustainable disaster preparedness efforts at the grassroots level.

The goal of Community-Based Disaster Preparedness (CBDP) is to cultivate resilient individuals residing within safer, more resilient communities, nested within safer, more resilient environments, and ultimately, within safer, more resilient countries. This is achieved through various measures aimed at reducing the probability of failure, minimizing the consequences of failure, and expediting the recovery process. Additionally, CBDP involves recognizing patterns of vulnerability that may arise during reconstruction efforts [225].

Before a disaster strikes, resilient communities exhibit certain characteristics that enable them to mitigate disaster impacts. These include drawing upon traditional knowledge, preparing emergency supplies, developing disaster management plans, reinforcing infrastructure, organizing training sessions, planning evacuation routes, and potentially relocating away from hazardous areas.

Figure 26: FEMA Disability Integration Specialists along with Federal, State, public and community-based organizations, are making sure persons with disabilities and others with access and functional needs, are achieving full inclusion in disaster preparedness planning and community recovery activities. National Archives at College Park - Still Pictures, Public domain, via Wikimedia Commons.

During a disaster, resilient communities demonstrate adaptability by leveraging community support, assessing available resources, restoring communication channels, addressing immediate risks, and embracing the experience as a learning opportunity.

After a disaster, recovery efforts should focus on building more resilient communities by implementing comprehensive recovery plans that encompass social, physical, economic, and environmental aspects. This involves utilizing local labour and resources, promoting community engagement, reducing future vulnerabilities, and recognizing the value of preparedness.

Safer and resilient communities possess capacities across three phases: absorbing shocks to prevent hazards from escalating into disasters, bouncing back during and after disasters, and seizing opportunities for change and adaptation following a disaster. Indicators of resilient communities include strong community organization, disaster risk reduction and preparedness plans, early warning systems, trained personnel, physical infrastructure, relational connectivity, knowledge of risks, dedicated disaster reduction funds, resilient housing, and sustainable livelihoods [225].

Participants and Stakeholders

Community-Based Disaster Preparedness (CBDP) involves the active participation of various stakeholders at different levels. These can include:

1. Community Members: The primary stakeholders in CBDP are the members of the local community. Their active participation is essential for identifying vulnerabilities, assessing risks, and implementing preparedness measures. Community members contribute local knowledge, resources, and perspectives that are crucial for effective disaster planning and response.

2. Local Government Authorities: Local government authorities, including municipal governments, district administrations, and community leaders, play a central role in CBDP. They are responsible for coordinating disaster preparedness efforts, allocating resources, and implementing policies and regulations to enhance community resilience. Local government agencies often collaborate with community members and other stakeholders to develop and implement CBDP initiatives.

3. Non-Governmental Organizations (NGOs): NGOs and community-based organizations (CBOs) are important partners in CBDP. These organizations often have expertise in disaster risk reduction, community development, and humanitarian assistance. NGOs work closely with local communities to provide training, technical support, and resources for disaster preparedness and response activities. They also advocate for community needs and facilitate access to external support and funding.

4. Academic and Research Institutions: Academic and research institutions contribute to CBDP by conducting studies, collecting data, and analyzing local vulnerabilities and risks. They provide technical expertise, research findings, and best practices to inform the development of effective preparedness strategies. Collaboration between academia and communities fosters innovation and evidence-based decision-making in disaster management.

5. International Organizations: International organizations, such as the United Nations agencies, the Red Cross and Red Crescent Movement, and international development agencies, often support CBDP initiatives through fund-

ing, technical assistance, and capacity-building activities. These organizations provide global expertise, resources, and networks to strengthen local disaster preparedness and response capabilities.

6. Private Sector: The private sector, including businesses, industries, and corporations, can contribute to CBDP by investing in community resilience-building initiatives, providing financial support, and offering technical expertise and resources. Private sector involvement in CBDP may include developing business continuity plans, supporting infrastructure upgrades, and participating in public-private partnerships for disaster risk management.

7. Media and Communication Channels: Media outlets, communication networks, and social media platforms play a critical role in raising public awareness, disseminating emergency information, and facilitating community engagement in CBDP. Effective communication strategies ensure that community members are informed about potential hazards, preparedness measures, and response protocols.

Overall, CBDP is a collaborative effort that involves the active participation and coordination of diverse stakeholders at the local, national, and international levels. By working together, these stakeholders can build community resilience, reduce disaster risks, and enhance the ability of communities to prepare for and respond to disasters effectively.

The responsibility for managing Community-Based Disaster Preparedness (CBDP) typically falls upon a combination of entities working collaboratively at different levels. Here are the key stakeholders involved in managing CBDP:

1. Local Government Authorities: Local government authorities, including municipal governments, district administrations, and community leaders, are often at the forefront of managing CBDP. They play a central role in coordinating disaster preparedness efforts, implementing policies and regulations, and allocating resources to enhance community resilience. Local authorities are responsible for engaging with community members, facilitating training and capacity-building initiatives, and overseeing the development and implementation of CBDP plans and strategies tailored to the specific needs of the local area.

2. Community Members: Community members themselves are actively involved in managing CBDP. They contribute local knowledge, resources, and perspec-

tives that are essential for identifying vulnerabilities, assessing risks, and implementing preparedness measures. Community members participate in various activities, including hazard mapping, risk assessment, emergency drills, and community-based early warning systems. They also play a critical role in disseminating information, mobilizing resources, and supporting one another during disaster events.

3. Non-Governmental Organizations (NGOs): NGOs and community-based organizations (CBOs) are important partners in managing CBDP. These organizations often have expertise in disaster risk reduction, community development, and humanitarian assistance. NGOs work closely with local communities to provide technical support, training, and resources for disaster preparedness and response activities. They also advocate for community needs, facilitate access to external support and funding, and collaborate with local authorities to strengthen CBDP initiatives.

4. Academic and Research Institutions: Academic and research institutions contribute to managing CBDP by conducting studies, collecting data, and analyzing local vulnerabilities and risks. They provide technical expertise, research findings, and best practices to inform the development of effective preparedness strategies. Academic institutions may offer training programs, capacity-building workshops, and knowledge-sharing platforms to empower local communities and enhance their resilience to disasters.

5. International Organizations: International organizations, such as the United Nations agencies, the Red Cross and Red Crescent Movement, and international development agencies, often support CBDP initiatives through funding, technical assistance, and capacity-building activities. These organizations provide global expertise, resources, and networks to strengthen local disaster preparedness and response capabilities. They work in collaboration with local and national authorities, NGOs, and other stakeholders to promote CBDP as part of broader disaster risk reduction efforts.

6. Private Sector: The private sector, including businesses, industries, and corporations, can also contribute to managing CBDP. Private sector entities may invest in community resilience-building initiatives, provide financial support,

and offer technical expertise and resources to strengthen local disaster preparedness and response capacities. They may develop business continuity plans, support infrastructure upgrades, and participate in public-private partnerships for disaster risk management.

The implementation of Community-Based Disaster Preparedness (CBDP) relies on a diverse array of skills and knowledge to navigate the intricate landscape of disaster risk reduction and community resilience. Key areas essential for CBDP implementation include:

- Disaster Risk Management: CBDP necessitates a profound grasp of disaster risk management principles, frameworks, and strategies. This encompasses expertise in hazard identification, risk assessment, vulnerability analysis, and the implementation of risk reduction measures.

- Community Engagement and Facilitation: Effective CBDP hinges on robust interpersonal and communication skills to engage with community members. Facilitating participatory decision-making processes, fostering collaboration, and empowering community members are pivotal aspects of this skill set.

- Capacity Building: Equipping community members with the requisite knowledge and skills to prepare for, respond to, and recover from disasters demands proficiency in designing and delivering capacity-building programs, workshops, and training sessions. This includes instruction on disaster preparedness, first aid, search and rescue techniques, and emergency evacuation procedures.

- Data Collection and Analysis: CBDP implementation requires proficiency in various data collection methods, including participatory tools like hazard mapping, risk ranking, and vulnerability assessment. Analytical skills are indispensable for interpreting data and identifying priority areas for intervention.

- Project Management: Sound knowledge of project management principles and techniques is crucial for planning, executing, and monitoring CBDP initiatives. This encompasses setting goals and objectives, developing action plans, resource allocation, and evaluating project outcomes.

- Community Development: Understanding community development principles and practices is pivotal for fostering community ownership, building social cohesion, and promoting sustainable development in tandem with disaster risk reduction efforts. This includes expertise in community organizing, empowerment strategies, and participatory approaches to development.

- Crisis Communication: Effective CBDP necessitates adept crisis communication and public awareness skills to disseminate information, raise awareness about potential hazards, and advocate for proactive preparedness measures within the community. Clear and sensitive communication across diverse audiences is paramount.
- Collaboration and Networking: Strong networking skills and the ability to collaborate with various stakeholders, including government agencies, NGOs, academia, and the private sector, are essential for mobilizing resources, sharing knowledge, and coordinating CBDP efforts.
- Cultural Competency and Sensitivity: Cultural awareness is crucial to ensure that CBDP initiatives are culturally appropriate and inclusive. Understanding local norms, values, and practices enables practitioners to engage respectfully and effectively with diverse communities.
- Adaptability and Resilience: The dynamic nature of disaster situations demands adaptability and resilience. Skills in problem-solving, decision-making, and coping with stress are essential for responding effectively to evolving challenges in CBDP implementation.

Implementing Community-Based Disaster Preparedness

Community-Based Disaster Preparedness (CBDP) involves a systematic approach to enhancing a community's resilience to disasters. It comprises several interconnected stages aimed at effectively preparing for and responding to potential hazards. Implementation of CBDP involves:

1. Assessing Hazards and Vulnerabilities: The initial stage of CBDP involves recognizing and analysing potential threats and challenges confronting the community. Employing participatory tools like hazard mapping, risk ranking, vul-

nerability assessment, and historical timelines aids in gathering and visualizing data on hazard frequency, intensity, and location, as well as community exposure, sensitivity, and adaptive capacity. This process aids in prioritizing urgent risks and needs while considering equity issues, non-property damage assessments, neighbourhood disinvestment, and other factors influencing a community's ability to prepare for and respond to disasters.

2. Defining Goals and Objectives: The subsequent phase of CBDP entails establishing clear and achievable goals and objectives for the plan. Community members and stakeholders are involved in defining desired outcomes, progress measurement, and the selection of indicators and targets. Alignment with national and local disaster management policies, as well as Sustainable Development Goals (SDGs), is essential. Objectives should account for short, medium, and long-term temporal considerations, along with budgetary priorities for each phase of action.

3. Identifying Strategies and Actions: Selecting and designing suitable strategies and actions to address identified hazards and vulnerabilities comprise the third step of CBDP. Considering the disaster management cycle's four phases—prevention, preparedness, response, and recovery—is crucial. Principles of disaster risk reduction (DRR), such as prevention, mitigation, adaptation, resilience, and participation, are applied. Strategies encompass hazard-proofing infrastructure, establishing early warning systems, conducting drills, forming emergency committees, providing relief support, and raising awareness. An intersectional approach to strategy design is vital to ensure support for all community members during disaster events.

4. Mobilizing Resources and Partnerships: The subsequent stage involves securing the necessary resources and partnerships for plan implementation. Identifying and leveraging existing community assets and capacities, including human, financial, material, social, cultural, and natural resources, are essential. Partnerships with government agencies, NGOs, private sector entities, media, academia, and donors should be established. Coordination, collaboration, and communication among partners, along with accountability and transparency, are emphasized. Forecast-based financing can enhance resource mobilization efficiency by utilizing early warnings and forecasts to trigger financial support

before disasters occur.

5. Implementing and Monitoring the Plan: Execution and progress tracking constitute the fifth step, where the action plan is followed, and roles and responsibilities are assigned to community members and partners. Monitoring plan implementation using predetermined indicators and targets is crucial. Data collection, analysis, and reporting on plan outputs, outcomes, and impacts are undertaken, alongside documentation of challenges, lessons learned, and best practices.

6. Evaluating and Revising the Plan: The final stage involves reviewing and updating the plan through participatory evaluation with community members and partners. Assessment of plan relevance, effectiveness, efficiency, sustainability, and impact, considering agreed-upon criteria and methods, is conducted. Identification of gaps, strengths, weaknesses, opportunities, and threats informs plan revisions, integrating new information, knowledge, and experiences gained.

Assessing hazards and vulnerabilities in a community is a crucial step in disaster preparedness. This process involves understanding the risks and challenges faced by the community through various tools such as hazard mapping, risk ranking, vulnerability assessment, and historical timelines. By gathering data on hazard frequency, intensity, and location, as well as considering community exposure, sensitivity, and adaptive capacity, communities can prioritize urgent risks and needs while addressing equity issues and other factors to enhance their disaster preparedness [130, 226-229].

Community resilience plays a significant role in disaster readiness, with adaptive capacities like economic development, social capital, information and communication, and community competence contributing to a strategy for disaster preparedness [130]. Building community resilience involves the ability to adapt to environmental changes, respond to disasters, and recover quickly to reduce disaster shocks [91]. Integrating local capacity building and disseminating accurate disaster-related information are essential elements in developing community resilience and disaster adaptability [227].

Furthermore, the concept of community resilience emphasizes the importance of social capital in forming resilience and enhancing disaster risk reduction [230]. Strengthening community resilience involves various domains such as wellness, access, education, engagement, self-sufficiency, and partnership, which are crucial for effective disaster risk reduction efforts [228]. By reinforcing the capacities of communities and actively involving them in disaster risk management and climate change adaptation planning, vulnerabilities can be reduced, and disasters better managed [229].

Defining goals and objectives in Community-Based Disaster Preparedness (CBDP) involves establishing clear and achievable outcomes with the active involvement of community members and stakeholders. This phase includes defining desired results, measuring progress, selecting indicators and targets, and ensuring alignment with national and local disaster management policies and Sustainable Development Goals (SDGs) [231-233].

The process of defining goals and objectives should consider short, medium, and long-term temporal aspects, as well as budgetary priorities for each phase of action. It is crucial to integrate community-based disaster risk reduction strategies that enhance knowledge of natural disasters, increase community preparedness, and improve emergency response efficiency [231]. Additionally, the involvement of health system authorities in issuing strategic plans, standards, guidelines, and procedures is essential to enhance hospital disaster preparedness [233].

Community resilience and disaster preparedness are interconnected, emphasizing the importance of strengthening intra- and inter-sector collaboration, information management systems, and community-based initiatives [234]. Studies have shown that community-oriented approaches have been effective in enhancing preparedness and mitigating vulnerability, highlighting the significance of involving communities in disaster risk reduction efforts [232].

Identifying suitable strategies and actions in Community-Based Disaster Preparedness (CBDP) involves selecting approaches that address identified hazards and vulnerabilities while considering the four phases of the disaster management cycle: prevention, preparedness, response, and recovery. Principles of disaster risk reduction (DRR) such as prevention, mitigation, adaptation, resilience, and participation are crucial in this phase [232, 235-237].

Strategies in CBDP encompass various actions like hazard-proofing infrastructure, establishing early warning systems, conducting drills, forming emergency committees, providing relief support, and raising awareness [238]. An intersectional approach to strategy design is essential to ensure that all community members receive support during disaster events [237]. Community-based disaster preparedness approaches have become increasingly important in reducing vulnerabilities and managing disasters effectively [232].

Studies have shown that disaster preparedness is a vital preventive strategy for protecting health and mitigating adverse effects of unforeseen disasters [235]. Effective disaster governance involves addressing multiple problems, including environmental issues, and promoting sustainable development, which contributes to disaster risk reduction [236]. Embracing community-based approaches has been proven effective in equipping disaster-prone communities with adequate information on disaster preparedness, facilitating swift responses during disasters [232].

The selection and design of appropriate strategies and actions in CBDP are essential for enhancing disaster preparedness. By applying DRR principles, implementing various strategies, and ensuring community involvement, communities can better address hazards and vulnerabilities, ultimately improving their resilience and readiness in the face of disasters.

To effectively mobilize resources and establish partnerships for disaster risk reduction and management, it is crucial to leverage existing community assets and capacities across various sectors. Partnerships with government agencies, NGOs, private sector entities, media, academia, and donors play a vital role in enhancing disaster resilience [130]. These partnerships facilitate coordination, collaboration, and communication among stakeholders, emphasizing accountability and transparency in the process [154]. By engaging in cross-sector collaborations, including public-private partnerships (PPPs), communities can enhance their disaster preparedness and response capabilities [239].

Forecast-based financing is a strategy that can improve resource mobilization efficiency by utilizing early warnings and forecasts to trigger financial support before disasters occur [240]. This proactive approach aligns with the Sendai Framework for Disaster Risk Reduction, which advocates for an all-hazard, prevention-driven, evidence-based, multisectoral, and multidisciplinary approach to disaster risk reduction [241]. Additionally, the involvement of academic institutions in disaster risk management through partnerships can enhance community understanding of risk assessment, prevention, mitigation, preparedness, and response [242].

Leadership plays a crucial role in promoting emergency management practices and supporting preparedness efforts, providing new resources for sustainability and resilience [243]. Furthermore, the role of religious institutions in disaster risk management is significant, as they can contribute to preparedness, response, recovery, and collaboration with various stakeholders in disaster management efforts [244]. Public-private partnerships have been recognized as beneficial for accelerating and improving responses to disasters, enhancing the resilience of local communities.

Implementing and monitoring a community health plan involves executing the plan, assigning roles and responsibilities, and tracking progress. This process includes following the action plan, assigning roles and responsibilities to community members and partners, and monitoring the plan's implementation using specific indicators and targets [245]. Data collection, analysis, and reporting on the plan's outputs, outcomes, and impacts are essential components of this step. Additionally, documenting challenges, lessons learned, and best practices is vital for ongoing improvement and success [246].

Monitoring the progress of a health plan is crucial for ensuring its effectiveness and making informed decisions for adjustments. This monitoring process involves engaging the community in assessment and decision-making, utilizing data and information systems systematically, basing decisions on the best available evidence, applying program-planning frameworks, conducting thorough evaluations, and disseminating findings [246]. By systematically monitoring and evaluating the plan's implementation, stakeholders can identify areas of success, challenges, and opportunities for improvement.

Moreover, technology and health informatics play a significant role in tracking progress in chronic illness management. Shared health informatics models, such as the CoMSHI, provide detailed insights into tracking tools that support individuals in managing chronic illnesses more effectively [247]. These tools not only track progress but also empower individuals to take control of their health through informed decision-making and self-monitoring.

Implementing and monitoring a community health plan involves a comprehensive approach that includes executing the plan, assigning responsibilities, monitoring progress using indicators, collecting and analysing data, and documenting key findings. By engaging stakeholders, utilizing technology for tracking, and following evidence-based practices, communities can enhance their health outcomes and address challenges effectively.

The final stage of a plan involves evaluating and revising the plan through participatory evaluation with community members and partners. This process includes assessing the plan's relevance, effectiveness, efficiency, sustainability, and impact based on agreed-upon criteria and methods [248]. Identification of gaps, strengths, weaknesses, opportunities, and threats informs the revisions of the plan, integrating new information, knowledge, and experiences gained [248].

Evaluation and revision of a sustainability plan are crucial for ensuring its continued effectiveness and relevance. Developing performance indicators for each sustainability strategy is essential for assessing and monitoring the overall progress of the plan [249]. Additionally, utilizing tools like the Program Sustainability Assessment Tool can aid in evaluating the sustainability of public health programs and identifying areas for improvement [249].

Incorporating participatory evaluation approaches, such as participatory action research, can enhance the sustainability and effectiveness of community engagement efforts [250]. Assessing factors like environmental support, funding stability, partnerships, organizational capacity, program evaluation, and strategic planning is vital for sustaining programs over the long term [251].

Furthermore, the process of evaluating and revising sustainability plans extends beyond the health sector. It includes assessing sustainability capacity in various programs, such as HIV programs, to ensure long-term success and impact [251]. Evaluating sustainability planning under different contexts, such as urban planning and risk assessment of earthquake hazards, highlights the importance of integrating sustainability principles into diverse fields [252].

The preceding is exemplified in the following scenario example:

Scenario: Implementing Community-Based Disaster Preparedness (CBDP) in Springfield

1. Assessing Hazards and Vulnerabilities: In Springfield, a suburban community located in a region prone to severe weather events such as tornadoes and flooding, the initial stage of CBDP involves recognizing and analysing potential threats and challenges. Community leaders organize workshops and town hall meetings to engage residents in hazard mapping exercises, risk ranking discussions, and vulnerability assessments. Through these participatory tools, residents identify key hazards, including tornadoes, floods, and infrastructure vulnerabilities. They also consider factors such as socioeconomic disparities and neighbourhood disinvestment that affect their ability to prepare for and respond to disasters effectively.

2. Defining Goals and Objectives: Following the hazard assessment, community members and stakeholders come together to establish clear and achievable goals and objectives for the CBDP plan. They prioritize goals such as enhancing public safety, minimizing property damage, and ensuring equitable access to

resources and support services during disasters. Aligning with national and local disaster management policies and Sustainable Development Goals (SDGs), they set short-term objectives, such as improving emergency response protocols, medium-term objectives, such as strengthening infrastructure resilience, and long-term objectives, such as promoting community-wide disaster awareness and preparedness.

3. Identifying Strategies and Actions: With goals and objectives in place, Springfield residents and stakeholders collaborate to identify and design suitable strategies and actions to address identified hazards and vulnerabilities. They adopt an intersectional approach to strategy design, ensuring that all community members, including vulnerable populations, are considered. Strategies include investing in hazard-proofing infrastructure, establishing a community-wide early warning system, conducting regular emergency drills, forming neighbourhood emergency committees, and providing targeted relief and support services. Additionally, they prioritize raising awareness and fostering community participation in disaster preparedness efforts.

4. Mobilizing Resources and Partnerships: Springfield's CBDP efforts require mobilizing necessary resources and partnerships for plan implementation. Community leaders work closely with local government agencies, NGOs, businesses, schools, and faith-based organizations to leverage existing assets and capacities. They secure funding through grants, donations, and collaborative initiatives, ensuring transparency and accountability in resource allocation. Partnerships are established to facilitate coordination, collaboration, and communication among stakeholders, with a focus on enhancing community resilience through collective action.

5. Implementing and Monitoring the Plan: Once resources and partnerships are in place, Springfield begins implementing the CBDP plan. Community members take on active roles, with responsibilities assigned based on expertise and interest. They monitor plan implementation using predetermined indicators and targets, tracking progress and adjusting strategies as needed. Data collection, analysis, and reporting are conducted regularly to assess plan outputs, outcomes, and impacts. Challenges, lessons learned, and best practices are documented to inform future decision-making.

6. Evaluating and Revising the Plan: As Springfield's CBDP efforts progress, community members and partners conduct participatory evaluations to review and update the plan. They assess plan relevance, effectiveness, efficiency, sustainability, and impact, identifying gaps, strengths, weaknesses, opportunities, and threats. Feedback and recommendations are provided to inform plan revisions, incorporating new information, knowledge, and experiences gained throughout the implementation process. By continuously evaluating and revising the plan, Springfield aims to enhance its resilience to disasters and promote the well-being of its residents.

Building Local Capacities and Public Awareness

Building local capacities and public awareness in Community-Based Disaster Preparedness (CBDP) involves a multifaceted approach aimed at equipping individuals and communities with the necessary knowledge, skills, and resources to effectively prepare for, respond to, and recover from disasters. The following is a breakdown of the key strategies involved:

- Education and Training Programs: Tailored education and training initiatives are crucial in addressing the specific needs and vulnerabilities of the community. Workshops, seminars, and training sessions focusing on disaster preparedness, first aid, search and rescue techniques, and evacuation procedures offer practical skills and empower community members to take decisive action during emergencies.

- Community Engagement and Participation: Actively involving community members in disaster preparedness activities fosters a sense of ownership and collective responsibility. Encouraging participation in decision-making processes, planning sessions, and emergency drills cultivates a culture of mutual support and cooperation. Establishing community-based organizations and volunteer groups dedicated to disaster preparedness and response further strengthens community resilience.

- Information Dissemination and Communication: Effective communication channels play a vital role in disseminating critical information and raising public awareness about potential hazards and preparedness measures. Leveraging various communication platforms such as social media, community newsletters, public announcements, and meetings ensures that information reaches diverse populations in accessible and culturally appropriate formats.

- Community-Based Early Warning Systems: Early warning systems tailored to local needs and context are essential for alerting residents to imminent threats and hazards. Installing sirens, warning signs, and other alert mechanisms in high-risk areas enhances community awareness and preparedness. Training community members to recognize warning signs and respond appropriately, along with forging partnerships with relevant stakeholders, strengthens the effectiveness of early warning systems.

- Capacity Building for Local Leaders and Institutions: Strengthening the capacity of local leaders, government agencies, and community-based organizations is fundamental to effective disaster preparedness. Providing training and resources equips local leaders with the necessary skills to develop and implement robust disaster management plans. Fostering collaboration and networking among local institutions maximizes the collective expertise and resources available for disaster response and recovery.

- Risk Communication and Behavioural Change: Promoting risk communication strategies is key to fostering behavioural change and resilience-building actions within the community. Emphasizing the importance of proactive preparedness measures and utilizing storytelling and real-life examples effectively communicate the potential impact of disasters, motivating individuals to take proactive steps to protect themselves and their communities.

- Community-Based Participatory Research: Conducting community-based participatory research allows for a comprehensive assessment of local vulnerabilities, strengths, and resilience capacities. Involving community members in data collection, analysis, and interpretation ensures that interventions are informed by local knowledge and priorities. Tailoring disaster preparedness initiatives based on research findings enables communities to address specific needs and characteristics effectively.

Education and training programs are crucial in equipping communities with the necessary knowledge and skills to effectively respond to disasters. Tailored initiatives are essential to address the unique needs and vulnerabilities of each community [253]. These programs encompass workshops, seminars, and training sessions focusing on various aspects of disaster preparedness, such as first aid, search and rescue techniques, and evacuation procedures [253]. By engaging in these initiatives, community members acquire practical skills and knowledge that empower them to take decisive action during emergencies, potentially saving lives and reducing property damage [253].

Research emphasizes the significance of long-term formal training, including undergraduate and postgraduate programs, in disaster medicine and public health preparedness [254]. Tailored preparedness programs aimed at specific communities are crucial for those lacking preparedness [255]. Moreover, the evaluation of disaster preparedness curricula on medical students' views underscores the importance of preparedness education requirements for health professionals [256].

Studies have shown that prior disaster education and training experience are significantly associated with higher levels of perceived competence in disaster preparedness among nurses [257]. Similarly, tailored community-based disaster risk reduction programs are essential to enhance villagers' knowledge and skills in disaster preparedness [258]. Furthermore, disaster preparedness education and training for child care teachers are vital to ensure effective responses to disasters [259].

The role of local wisdom-based disaster education and training through different education levels in disaster-prone areas is highlighted as a critical factor in enhancing preparedness [260]. Factors affecting the disaster response competency of emergency medical technicians underscore the need for a national-level campaign to encourage active participation in personal disaster preparedness activities [261]. Disaster preparedness knowledge among hospital and pre-hospital emergency nurses is crucial for effective triage decision-making during disasters [262].

As such, education and training programs tailored to specific communities play a crucial role in enhancing disaster preparedness, fostering a culture of proactive response, and building resilience within communities. These initiatives are essential for empowering individuals to respond promptly and effectively during emergencies, ultimately contributing to saving lives and minimizing damage to property.

Community engagement and participation are crucial in enhancing disaster preparedness and fostering resilience within communities. Actively involving community members in disaster preparedness activities creates a sense of ownership and collective responsibility [263]. Encouraging participation in decision-making processes, planning sessions, and emergency drills cultivates a culture of mutual support and cooperation [99]. Establishing community-based organizations and volunteer groups dedicated to disaster preparedness and response further strengthens community resilience [264].

Research indicates that community engagement for disaster risk reduction and management brings significant benefits in terms of ownership and direct savings in losses from disasters [263]. Social participation plays a crucial role in disaster risk reduction actions by broadening social connections, facilitating information exchange, and increasing peer support [99]. Moreover, community-oriented approaches have been effective in enhancing preparedness and mitigating vulnerability [232].

Studies emphasize that community resilience is a key factor influencing household disaster preparedness, highlighting the importance of programs that promote such resilience [104]. Community-based solutions to disaster preparedness are increasingly vital components of policies aimed at mitigating risk and managing disasters [265]. Disaster management authorities should implement projects and activities at the local level to empower communities for disaster preparedness and risk reduction [264].

Effective communication channels are crucial for disseminating critical information and increasing public awareness of potential hazards and preparedness measures. Leveraging various platforms such as social media, community newsletters, public announcements, and meetings ensures that information reaches diverse populations in accessible formats [266]. Information dissemination through leaflets, newsletters, posters, websites, and events has been shown to be effective in reaching the public [266]. Additionally, public health detailing, which involves one-on-one educational sessions with providers, has been successful in raising awareness and implementing evidence-based clinical practices [267].

Furthermore, the use of mass media campaigns has long been recognized as a tool for promoting public health and disseminating important information [268]. It is crucial to recognize the role of communication in facilitating understanding and improving outcomes in various fields, including medicine and public health [269]. For instance, in the context of mental health, building community connections to reduce stigma and foster inclusion requires increased public understanding and awareness, emphasizing the collective social responsibility in addressing such issues [270].

Moreover, public participation plays a significant role in information dissemination and empowerment [271]. Adequate public health funding, coupled with the right workforce mix, is essential to meet evolving public health needs effectively [272]. Recognizing the importance of surgical care as a public health issue and advocating for its role in achieving universal health coverage is crucial for effective healthcare delivery [273].

Community-based early warning systems are crucial for alerting residents to imminent threats and hazards, enhancing community awareness, and strengthening preparedness [274]. These systems typically involve installing sirens, warning signs, and other alert mechanisms in high-risk areas, training community members to recognize warning signs and respond appropriately, and establishing partnerships with relevant stakeholders [274]. Community-based disaster preparedness (CBDP) approaches are increasingly recognized as vital components of vulnerability reduction and disaster management strategies, emphasizing the importance of community participation in identifying issues and understanding root causes [274].

Research has demonstrated that community awareness campaigns, such as Health Education Based Interventions (HEBI), can significantly enhance disaster preparedness among communities [275]. Moreover, involving social and community groups in disseminating preparedness information can facilitate the delivery and processing of preparedness action messages, thereby improving the effectiveness of early warning systems [276]. Continuous public education and campaigns are also essential for boosting public awareness of household disaster preparedness and enhancing the public's ability to prepare for potential disasters [104].

Additionally, enhancing community awareness and understanding of risk factors, such as in the case of cystic echinococcosis, is crucial for disease control and eradication [277]. Community-based assessments of behaviour and awareness play a critical role in addressing health issues and improving public health outcomes [277]. Furthermore, the significance of sense of place, community, and confidence in government has been underscored as essential factors in disaster readiness and preparedness [278].

Strengthening the capacity of local leaders, government agencies, and community-based organizations is essential for effective disaster preparedness. Training and providing resources to local leaders equip them with the necessary skills to develop and implement robust disaster management plans. Fostering collaboration and networking among local institutions maximizes the collective expertise and resources available for disaster response and recovery [274]. Community-based disaster preparedness is increasingly recognized as a crucial component of disaster management, enhancing community resilience through local-level capacity building [279].

Research emphasizes the urgent need for building capacities of healthcare providers in disaster management to protect populations, decrease injuries and deaths, and maintain overall community health [280]. Furthermore, the capacity of government administrations to implement effective disaster preparedness and response measures relies on engaging local stakeholders as legitimate partners in planning, leveraging local resources, and utilizing existing social infrastructure to build resilience [281].

Institutional capacities need to be developed to prevent, prepare for, and respond to disasters effectively [282]. Capacity building programs play a vital role in enhancing disaster preparedness by improving coordination, communication, management, and tracking of incidents following outbreaks [283]. Additionally, building adaptive capacity through social development, community competencies, and robust communication systems is crucial for enhancing resilience in the face of disasters [284].

Risk communication and disaster education are considered crucial aspects of disaster preparedness. However, the extent to which these strategies influence children's behaviour during natural disasters and their coping mechanisms post-disaster remains unclear [238]. Research on community disaster awareness training programs has shown that they can impact hazard-related cognitions and preparedness behaviours, which can lead to sustainable behavioural changes and potentially reduce the impact of future disasters [285]. Empirical studies have indicated that income, education, and previous disaster experience significantly influence subjective disaster preparedness behaviours in communities that have undergone disaster awareness training [286].

Efforts in disaster and emergency preparedness predominantly focus on human behaviours influenced by various factors, such as risk perception and past experiences of disasters and emergencies [287]. Public education and awareness are crucial components of disaster risk reduction, emphasizing the need to strengthen these aspects to enhance community knowledge and intentional behaviour in areas at risk of hurricanes [288]. Psychological preparedness for disasters has been found to be correlated with resilience, highlighting the importance of including psychological preparedness in disaster risk reduction policy frameworks [289]. Recent studies suggest that children possess a unique perception of disaster risks, combining external information with personal experiences, and have the ability to communicate these perceptions effectively to influence behavioural changes that can mitigate risks and vulnerabilities [290]. Disaster preparedness measures encompass disaster management, resource maintenance, personnel training, and disaster management arrangements, emphasizing the importance of education in increasing earthquake disaster preparedness [291].

Conducting community-based participatory research is a vital process that allows for a thorough examination of the vulnerabilities, strengths, and resilience capacities within a local community. This approach involves actively engaging community members in every stage of the research process, including data collection, analysis, and interpretation. By involving community members directly, researchers can gain a deeper understanding of the unique challenges and opportunities present within the community.

One of the key benefits of community-based participatory research is that it ensures that interventions are informed by local knowledge and priorities. Community members possess invaluable insights into their own experiences, needs, and concerns, which may not be fully captured through traditional research methods. By actively involving community members in the research process, researchers can access this local knowledge and ensure that interventions are tailored to address the specific needs and characteristics of the community.

Through community-based participatory research, researchers can gather rich and nuanced data that reflects the complexities of the community's social, economic, and environmental context. This data can provide valuable insights into the root causes of vulnerability within the community, as well as the existing strengths and assets that can be leveraged to enhance resilience.

Once the data has been collected, community members play a crucial role in the analysis and interpretation process. By actively participating in these activities, community members can help identify patterns, trends, and insights that may not be immediately apparent to external researchers. This collaborative approach ensures that the research findings accurately reflect the community's perspectives and priorities.

Based on the findings of the research, tailored disaster preparedness initiatives can be developed to address the specific needs and characteristics of the community. These initiatives may include targeted interventions aimed at strengthening existing community assets, addressing systemic vulnerabilities, and building capacity for disaster response and recovery. By aligning interventions with the priorities identified through community-based participatory research, communities can maximize the effectiveness and impact of their disaster preparedness efforts.

Conducting community-based participatory research is essential for gaining a comprehensive understanding of local vulnerabilities, strengths, and resilience capacities. By actively involving community members in the research process, researchers can ensure that interventions are informed by local knowledge and priorities, leading to more effective and sustainable disaster preparedness initiatives.

7

Emergency Response Plans and Procedures

Disaster emergency planning is a comprehensive process that involves developing and implementing strategies to effectively respond to various emergencies or disasters. It aims to minimize the impact of emergencies by ensuring a coordinated and efficient response to safeguard lives, property, and essential services. Key components of disaster emergency planning include risk assessment, preparedness measures, response planning, recovery and continuity planning, communication and coordination, as well as evaluation and revision of plans based on lessons learned [292].

Research has shown that factors such as confidence in government, information dissemination, risk perception, and sense of place influence disaster preparedness [293, 294]. Effective communication and coordination among stakeholders are crucial for a timely and cohesive response [295, 296]. Studies have highlighted the importance of continuous improvement through evaluation and revision of disaster plans to ensure their relevance and effectiveness [292, 297].

Collaborative networks and effective communication between institutions are essential for successful disaster management [298]. Training personnel, conducting drills, and establishing coordination mechanisms with external stakeholders are vital aspects of response planning [292, 299]. Furthermore, the involvement of paediatric leadership in disaster planning is crucial to meet the specific needs of children during emergencies [300].

Household preparedness plays a significant role in disaster management, and previous disaster exposure has been found to increase preparedness levels [295, 297]. Education and awareness programs have been shown to enhance disaster preparedness and reduce vulnerability [301]. Additionally, the quality of emergency response plans and the readiness of organizations in deploying resources are critical for effective disaster preparedness [302, 303].

Sendai Framework for Disaster Risk Reduction

The Sendai Framework for Disaster Risk Reduction 2015-2030, established during the Third UN World Conference on Disaster Risk Reduction in Sendai, Japan, serves as a critical global policy framework for reducing disaster risk and enhancing resilience over a 15-year period [304]. This framework emphasizes the importance of understanding disaster risks, managing disaster risk, and investing in disaster risk reduction to enhance resilience [305]. It also highlights the need for integrated and inclusive measures across various sectors to reduce vulnerability and strengthen resilience at all levels [306].

The Sendai Framework is closely linked to other international agreements such as the sustainable development goals and the Paris Agreement on Climate Change [307]. It prioritizes the understanding of disaster risk as a key aspect of disaster risk reduction efforts [305]. Furthermore, the framework underscores the significance of local government involvement in disaster risk reduction activities [306].

Incorporating Indigenous knowledge and practices is advocated within the Sendai Framework to complement scientific knowledge for more effective emergency and disaster management [308]. The framework also addresses the implications of climate change within the context of disaster risk reduction, emphasizing the need to deal with climate change to reduce disaster risks [309].

The Sendai Framework aims to address the growing challenges posed by natural and human-induced hazards by shifting the focus from managing disasters after they occur to preventing and mitigating their impacts before they happen. It emphasizes the importance of proactive risk reduction measures, sustainable development practices, and multi-stakeholder collaboration to build resilience at local, national, regional, and global levels.

Key priorities and guiding principles of the Sendai Framework include:

1. Understanding Disaster Risk: Enhancing understanding of disaster risk by assessing hazards, vulnerabilities, and exposure in order to inform risk reduction policies and strategies.

2. Strengthening Governance: Promoting strong leadership, governance structures, and institutional mechanisms for disaster risk reduction at all levels of government and society.

3. Investing in Risk Reduction: Increasing investment in risk reduction measures, including infrastructure development, land-use planning, early warning systems, and social safety nets.

4. Enhancing Disaster Preparedness: Strengthening disaster preparedness and response capacities, including early warning systems, emergency response mechanisms, and community-based disaster management initiatives.

5. Building Back Better: Promoting the concept of "building back better" to ensure that post-disaster recovery and reconstruction efforts contribute to long-term resilience-building and sustainable development.

6. Integrating Risk Reduction into Development: Mainstreaming disaster risk reduction into development policies, plans, and programs to ensure that risk considerations are integrated across all sectors and activities.

7. Empowering Communities: Recognizing the importance of empowering communities, including women, children, and vulnerable groups, to participate in decision-making processes and take ownership of risk reduction initiatives.

8. Enhancing International Cooperation: Strengthening international cooperation and collaboration on disaster risk reduction, including sharing knowledge, technology, and resources to support global resilience-building efforts.

The Sendai Framework is structured around four priority areas of action:

1. Understanding disaster risk.

2. Strengthening disaster risk governance to manage disaster risk.

3. Investing in disaster risk reduction for resilience.

4. Enhancing disaster preparedness for effective response, and to "Build Back Better" in recovery, rehabilitation and reconstruction.

Overall, the Sendai Framework provides a comprehensive and holistic approach to disaster risk reduction, emphasizing the importance of proactive risk management, sustainable development, and community resilience-building to create a safer and more resilient world for present and future generations.

The Sendai Framework for Disaster Risk Reduction 2015-2030 is closely linked to Emergency Response Plans and Procedures as it provides a strategic framework for reducing disaster risk and enhancing resilience to disasters. While Emergency Response Plans and Procedures primarily focus on how to respond effectively to disasters when they occur, the Sendai Framework emphasizes the importance of proactive risk reduction measures and preparedness actions to prevent or mitigate the impacts of disasters before they happen.

Here's how the Sendai Framework intersects with Emergency Response Plans and Procedures:

1. Risk Understanding and Assessment: The Sendai Framework highlights the importance of understanding disaster risk by assessing hazards, vulnerabilities, and exposure. This information informs the development of Emergency Response Plans by identifying potential risks and vulnerabilities that need to be addressed in preparedness and response activities.

2. Strengthening Governance and Institutional Mechanisms: The Sendai Framework promotes the establishment of strong governance structures and institutional mechanisms for disaster risk reduction. This includes developing policies, laws, and regulations that support effective emergency response and coordination during disasters.

3. Investing in Disaster Risk Reduction: The Sendai Framework calls for increased investment in disaster risk reduction measures, including infrastructure development, early warning systems, and community-based preparedness initiatives. These investments contribute to the development and implementation of

Emergency Response Plans and Procedures by building capacities and enhancing resources for effective response.

4. Enhancing Preparedness and Response Capacities: The Sendai Framework emphasizes the importance of enhancing preparedness and response capacities to ensure an effective response to disasters. This includes developing Emergency Response Plans and Procedures that outline roles, responsibilities, and protocols for different stakeholders involved in disaster response.

5. Integrating Risk Reduction into Development: The Sendai Framework advocates for mainstreaming disaster risk reduction into development policies, plans, and programs. This integration ensures that risk considerations are incorporated into Emergency Response Plans and Procedures, allowing for a more comprehensive and coordinated approach to disaster management.

Emergency Planning Principles

Emergency planning principles serve as foundational guidelines for the development and implementation of effective emergency plans aimed at mitigating risks and enhancing preparedness and response capabilities. These principles are essential for ensuring that emergency plans are robust, comprehensive, and inclusive, addressing the complexities of various hazards and their potential impacts on communities [310]. The principles are outlined as follows [310]:

1. Risk Informed: Emergency planning begins with a thorough understanding of risks through a comprehensive risk management study. By identifying and analysing potential hazards, vulnerabilities, and exposure, planners can develop strategies and interventions to mitigate risks effectively.

2. Reduces Unknowns: Effective emergency planning aims to reduce uncertainties by increasing understanding of risks, vulnerabilities, and treatment options across social, built, economic, and natural environments. This comprehensive understanding enables planners to anticipate and address potential challenges more effectively.

3. Collaborative and Inclusive: Emergency planning involves consultation and engagement with stakeholders and communities affected by the plan. By incorporating diverse perspectives and involving all relevant parties in the planning process, plans can better reflect the needs, priorities, and capacities of those impacted by emergencies.

4. Strategic: Emergency planning develops strategic objectives, relationships, and networks to guide preparedness, response, and recovery efforts. By setting clear goals and priorities, planners can allocate resources efficiently and coordinate actions effectively during emergencies.

5. Solutions Oriented: Emergency planning focuses on developing agreed-upon approaches to managing risks and consequences. By identifying practical solutions and interventions, planners can ensure that emergency response efforts are well-coordinated and tailored to specific hazards and contexts.

6. Iterative: Emergency planning is an iterative process that involves learning from each step to inform subsequent actions. By continuously reviewing and updating plans based on new information, changing circumstances, and lessons learned from past experiences, planners can improve the effectiveness and relevance of emergency preparedness efforts over time.

7. Enables Adaptive Capacity: Emergency planning develops frameworks that provide a base for building flexible and adaptive solutions. By promoting adaptability and resilience, plans can better withstand unexpected events and changing conditions, ensuring a more effective response to emergencies.

8. Shared Responsibility: Emergency planning documents actions to be undertaken by a wide range of people and entities, emphasizing that emergency preparedness is a shared responsibility. By clearly defining roles, responsibilities, and expectations, planners can foster collaboration and coordination among various stakeholders, maximizing the collective capacity to respond to emergencies.

These principles guide the development of emergency plans that are comprehensive, inclusive, and adaptable, ensuring that communities are better prepared to mitigate, respond to, and recover from a range of emergencies and disasters.

Emergency Planning Process

The process of emergency planning follows a series of steps to prepare, implement, and continuously evaluate an emergency plan. This process also plays a role in enhancing the knowledge of those involved and fostering stronger relationships and networks among them. The scale of the planning process can be adjusted to match the size of the project, with the size of the project team and the scope of work varying based on the size of the community group or entity involved. In smaller entities, the responsibilities of the project team may be undertaken by a single individual.

Outlined in Figure 27, the emergency planning process includes several key steps:

1. Establishing a project plan.

2. Confirming the plan sponsor, who is responsible for providing the necessary resources and ensuring plan approval.

3. Establishing formal authority for the project, which could be derived from legislation, entity direction, or community agreement, to lend credibility and recognition to the plan.

4. Appointing a project manager, who will organize administrative support, lead the project team, and ensure effective communication and consultation with stakeholders.

5. Developing a comprehensive project plan that outlines the project audience, purpose, scope, objectives, deliverables, timeline, responsibilities, required resources, administrative arrangements, risk management strategies, and community/stakeholder engagement plans.

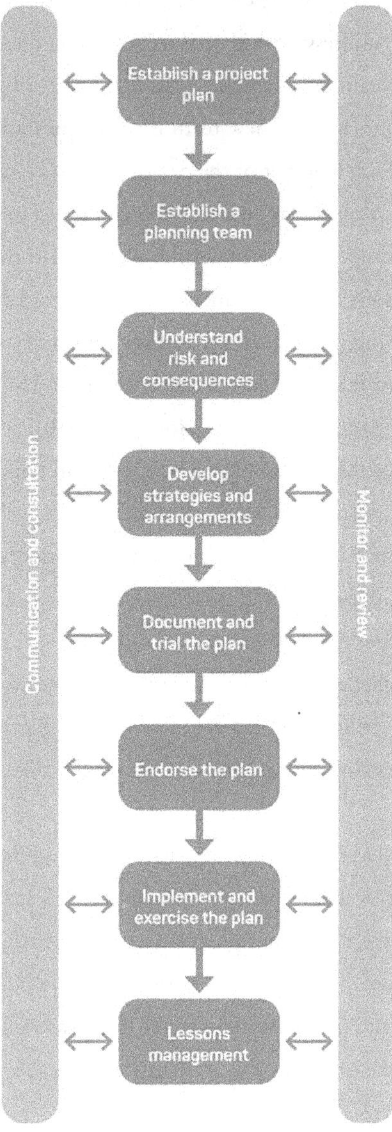

Figure 27: The emergency planning process. Source: Emergency Planning (AIDR 2020), CC BY-NC 4.0, via Australian Institute for Disaster Resilience.

The project plan serves as a roadmap for the development and implementation of the emergency plan, providing clarity on roles, responsibilities, timelines, and resource requirements. Through effective planning, communication, and collaboration, emergency planners can ensure that the resulting emergency plan is well-prepared, widely accepted, and capable of effectively addressing potential risks and emergencies.

Establishing a project team for emergency planning can involve either an existing emergency management committee or a new team formed specifically for the development of the emergency plan. Each member of the project team has individual responsibilities, including endorsing the project plan, providing input for plan development, reviewing documents, and organizing endorsement of the plan within their entity. Effective project teams require members who are sufficiently empowered to represent their entity, committed to the planning process, and maintain continuity throughout the project. Careful selection of team members ensures representation from relevant communities and entities while keeping the team at a functional size [310].

Communication and consultation play a crucial role in tailoring emergency plans to meet the specific characteristics and needs of communities and entities. Engaging with stakeholders impacted by the plan allows for a deeper understanding of their demographics, vulnerabilities, capacities, and previous experiences. Effective communication and consultation help identify risk factors, community values, and opportunities to enhance community resilience [310]. The scale and complexity of communication and consultation processes depend on the nature of the planning project, with methods such as workshops, newsletters, and community forums being utilized to engage stakeholders effectively.

Understanding the risks and consequences forms the foundation of emergency planning, typically informed by a risk management study. This study provides essential information on hazards, risks, risk reduction options, and potential consequences, guiding the development of the emergency plan. Considerations include the demographics, vulnerabilities, and capabilities of the community or entity, as well as relevant stakeholders and objectives to be met. Regulatory requirements and collaboration with other entities also influence risk treatments and emergency planning.

Developing strategies and arrangements involves research and a literature review to establish best practices and integrate relevant plans. The level of detail in the emergency plan depends on the clarity of the problem and solution, with more uncertainty requiring a strategic, principles-based approach. The range of strategies developed aligns with the project's aims, objectives, and scope, ensuring the plan remains adaptable to changing circumstances [310].

Documenting and trailing the plan involves producing the plan in a format suitable for users and conducting trials or reviews to ensure effectiveness. Assurance tools and review guides help confirm compliance with higher-level policies and requirements. Endorsement of the plan is essential, typically requiring approval from relevant entities involved in plan development and execution.

Implementing and exercising the plan involves ensuring accessibility, communicating with stakeholders, developing procedures, educating staff, and conducting exercises to test the plan's effectiveness. Monitoring and reviewing the plan occur regularly to account for changes in risk, incorporate lessons learned, and address emerging risks, ensuring the plan remains current and effective over time [310].

Documenting an Emergency Plan

Documenting the emergency plan involves creating a detailed and comprehensive document that outlines all necessary information and procedures to effectively respond to emergencies. Here's an explanation of what this entails:

- **Suitable Format**: The emergency plan should be produced in a format that is accessible and user-friendly for all stakeholders. This may include electronic formats such as digital documents or online platforms, as well as traditional paper-based options. The choice of format should consider the preferences and needs of the users.

- **Essential Elements**: The plan should include several essential elements to provide a clear understanding of its purpose, scope, and implementation. These elements typically include:

    - **Project Audience**: Identify the intended audience or users of the emergency plan, such as emergency response teams, staff members, or community members.

    - **Purpose**: Clearly state the purpose or objectives of the emergency plan, outlining its intended outcomes and goals.

    - **Scope**: Define the scope of the plan by specifying the types of emergencies it covers, the geographic areas it applies to, and the organizational units or stakeholders involved.

- **Objectives**: Outline specific objectives or targets that the plan aims to achieve, such as minimizing risks, protecting lives and property, or maintaining business continuity.
- **Deliverables**: Describe the tangible outputs or outcomes expected from the implementation of the plan, including actions, procedures, and resources.
- **Timeline**: Establish a timeline or schedule for various activities and milestones related to plan development, implementation, and review.
- **Responsibilities**: Clearly define the roles and responsibilities of individuals or entities involved in the emergency response process, including decision-makers, coordinators, and responders.
- **Resources**: Identify the resources required to support plan implementation, including personnel, equipment, facilities, and financial resources.
- **Administrative Arrangements**: Specify administrative procedures and arrangements for plan maintenance, updates, and distribution, as well as document control and version management.

By including these essential elements in the emergency plan, organizations can ensure clarity, consistency, and effectiveness in responding to emergencies and mitigating risks.

Tailoring the emergency plan to meet the needs of its users is paramount for its effectiveness. This includes:

Writing for the Plan Users: The project manager is tasked with formatting the emergency plan in a user-friendly manner. This involves structuring the plan into segments that allow users to easily locate the information they need. To achieve this, the plan should:

- Have logically labelled sections.
- Be written in plain English to enhance readability.
- Be easily searchable to facilitate quick access to relevant information.
- Utilize annexures for checklists and stand-alone parts, streamlining the presen-

tation of supplementary materials.

Plan Administration: Regular review and updating of the emergency plan are essential for its efficacy. To ensure all parties have access to the current version, the plan can be stored electronically on a server or in the cloud. Regardless of the format, procedures for updating the plan should be established. Version control mechanisms, including version numbers and dates on every page, aid users in identifying the latest version.

Plan Elements: The structure of the emergency plan is contingent upon its purpose and may include various elements:

- Contents, Abbreviations, and Glossary: Provide a table of contents and explanations of abbreviations and unfamiliar terms used in the plan.
- Authority: Specify the authority under which the plan is prepared and endorsed by relevant entities.
- Security Rating: Determine if certain information in the plan requires restricted access and outline measures for maintaining security.
- Review Schedule: Define the schedule for regular plan reviews and designate responsible parties.
- Amendment Register: Record changes made to the plan, including the date and personnel responsible.
- Distribution List: Document entities to whom the plan is distributed.
- Plan Aim and Objectives: Clearly state the goal and objectives of the emergency plan.
- Legislative and Policy Context: Describe relevant legislative and policy frameworks guiding the plan's development and implementation.

Plan Context and Scope: Detail the hazard, event, or entity to which the emergency plan applies. This includes specifying geographic areas, interfaces with other plans, planning limitations, and assumptions. Concisely outline the scope, including inclusions, exclusions, and limitations of the plan.

Leadership and Network Structures: Identify the leadership and network structures necessary to achieve the plan's aim and objectives. This involves delineating entities with authority, reporting chains, committee roles, governance arrangements, collaboration networks, and liaison requirements.

Roles and Responsibilities: Document the roles and responsibilities of entities involved in the plan. This encompasses leadership roles, functional responsibilities, prevention and mitigation strategies, preparedness programs, service provision, and community engagement.

Financial Management: Establish financial arrangements, including cost-sharing mechanisms between entities and levels of government. Consider all costs associated with prevention, preparedness, response, and recovery phases.

Communication Systems: Detail communication systems to be used during emergencies, including various modes such as radio, telephone, social media, websites, and video conferencing. Contingency communication methods should also be identified.

Information Management: Describe arrangements for sharing information between entities to build shared situational awareness. This includes strategies for collecting, collating, analysing, storing, and disseminating information while ensuring compliance with privacy legislation.

Resource Capability and Capacity Requirements: Identify resources and services required for plan implementation, addressing considerations such as resource shortfalls, mutual aid agreements, emergent groups, and surge capacity.

This thorough documentation ensures that the emergency plan is well-structured, accessible, and equipped to guide effective response and recovery efforts during emergencies.

Emergency Plan Development Guidelines

Guidance for Plan Design for Users

The project manager is tasked with designing the emergency plan to cater to the diverse needs of its users. The plan should be organized into clearly defined sections that enhance user accessibility to pertinent information. The emergency plan must feature:

- Clearly labelled sections for intuitive navigation.
- Language that is straightforward and understandable.
- A format that supports easy searching.

- Appendices that include checklists and autonomous components for comprehensive coverage.

Plan Management Procedures

Regular reviews and updates are crucial for the effectiveness of an emergency plan. All stakeholders must have access to the most recent version. The plan can be digitally stored on servers or cloud services for easy access. It's vital that both electronic and printed versions of the plan include procedures for timely updates. To ensure clarity, each page should display version control details like the version number and date, aiding users in verifying they are working with the correct version.

Structural Components of the Plan

The design of an emergency plan is dictated by its intended purpose, encompassing various elements such as:

- **Contents, Abbreviations, and Glossary:** A comprehensive table of contents and explanations for all abbreviations and terms used, with a glossary for unfamiliar terms.

- **Authority and Compliance:** This section outlines the legal and organizational authority under which the plan was developed, including endorsements from various entities committed to adhering to the plan's directives.

- **Security Considerations:** Depending on the sensitivity of the information, certain parts of the plan may need a security rating to restrict access, while ensuring less sensitive parts remain accessible.

- **Review and Amendments:** Outlines the review schedule, responsibilities for the review process, and maintains an amendment register documenting changes, who made them, and when.

- **Distribution Strategy:** Lists the entities that receive the plan, which may include organizations involved in planning, those needed for implementation, entities affected by the plan, and public resources like libraries or websites.

Plan Goals and Regulatory Context

- **Objectives and Aims:** Clearly states the primary goal and detailed objectives that the emergency plan aims to achieve.

- **Legislative Framework:** Describes the legislative and policy context that necessitates the plan.

- **Scope and Context of the Plan:** Details the specific hazards, events, or entities the plan addresses, including geographical and temporal scope, planning limitations, and assumptions.

Operational and Management Structures

- **Leadership and Network Requirements:** Identifies the required leadership structures and networks for achieving the plan's objectives. This includes the hierarchy of command, roles of committees, and interconnectivity with other plans and organizations.

Resource Management and Communication Protocols

- **Resource Requirements:** Specifies the resources and services essential for the plan's implementation, addressing potential gaps and contractual needs for private and community sectors.

- **Communication Channels:** Details the various communication systems to be used, such as radio frequencies, telephone systems, and digital platforms, along with contingency plans for communication failures.

Preventative Measures and Community Preparedness

- **Prevention and Mitigation Strategies:** Outlines strategies to reduce risks and enhance resilience through community planning, building regulations, and environmental management.

- **Community Preparedness and Engagement:** Establishes measures to prepare and educate the community about risks and emergency procedures, highlighting the importance of continuous engagement and education across diverse community sectors.

Response and Recovery Frameworks

- **Emergency Response and Coordination:** Defines the setup for emergency response, including location of coordination centres and operational procedures.

- **Recovery Strategies:** Focuses on long-term recovery efforts, emphasizing the importance of collaborative approaches for effective rebuilding and resilience enhancement.

Documentation and Evaluation

- **Public Information and Evacuation Protocols:** Sets out the protocols for disseminating information and managing evacuations effectively to ensure community safety.

- **Continuous Evaluation and Improvement:** Incorporates an exercise schedule to regularly test and refine emergency procedures and strategies.

A basic template to address each of these components follows:

Plan Implementation

Accessing the Plan

Ensuring the availability of the emergency plan is paramount. While online access may not always be feasible during infrastructure disruptions, alternate measures such as local file storage, thumb drives, or hard copies can ensure accessibility. Additionally, all related plans, procedures, and complementary documents must also be readily available and accessible during plan activation.

Establishing the Structure

It's important to note that the authority responsible for plan implementation may differ from the one leading its development. Therefore, the documented authorities and structure in the plan must be established to facilitate seamless implementation.

Notifications

Communication arrangements may be necessary to inform stakeholders of plan activation.

Undertaking Responsibilities

During plan implementation, it's imperative to fulfill the identified responsibilities and tasks to effectively mitigate, manage, or resolve risks. Conducting plan exercises can help clarify and reinforce roles and responsibilities. The successful execution of a plan relies on all individuals and entities with designated responsibilities fulfilling them effectively.

Developing Supporting Documentation

The emergency plan may necessitate supporting documents such as sub-plans, mutual aid plans, contracts, agreements, procedures, checklists, and action cards. Reviewing other plans may be required to ensure consistency and interoperability.

Implementing Risk Controls

Implementing risk controls for prevention and preparedness may involve various community resilience initiatives. Examples include land use planning policies, property buyback schemes, construction of levee banks, community education programs, warning sign erection, regulatory changes, property maintenance, training, relationship building, immunization programs, and staff education and exercises.

Exercising the Plan

Exercises play a vital role in educating staff and community members about the emergency plan's content and intent and strengthening relationships among entities. They are necessary when the plan has not been implemented recently, significant changes have occurred in the plan, people or entities required for plan implementation, or for low likelihood and/or high consequence events. Regular exercises maintain the currency and workability of plans, ensuring preparedness and effective collaboration among stakeholders. Therefore, an exercise schedule should be integrated into the emergency plan.

Monitoring and reviewing the emergency plan

Emergency planning relies on the knowledge and assumptions gathered during the planning phase, which are inherently time-sensitive. Continuous monitoring and review of emergency plans are essential due to various factors, including changes in the planning context, risks, community vulnerabilities and strengths, evolving expectations, advancements in technology, emergence of new entities, legislative changes, shifts in entity staffing and resources, as well as insights gained from exercises or previous emergency events. The responsibility for overseeing the review process should be clearly outlined in the emergency plan, with any modifications documented in an amendment register. Previous versions of the emergency plan should be archived by the authorizing entity.

Exercises

Exercises play a crucial role in:

- Validating the efficacy of the emergency plan.
- Identifying areas for improvement.
- Ensuring that the emergency plan remains relevant and responsive to stakeholders' evolving needs.

- Assessing the capabilities and capacities of individuals and entities involved in the plan.

Debriefs

Effective debriefing sessions are essential for pinpointing improvement opportunities. Through debriefs or after-action reviews, valuable insights are gathered to inform the ongoing refinement of the emergency plan. The emergency plan should articulate how these lessons are incorporated into the review process to enhance its effectiveness.

Specific Scenario Example - Flood

In developing an emergency management plan for floods, several key components need to be considered based on the available literature. Firstly, flood risk perception plays a crucial role in the effectiveness of such plans [311]. Therefore, it is essential to incorporate measures that enhance flood awareness and preparedness to ensure the community's perception of flood risk is accurate.

Secondly, sustainable flood management strategies should be integrated into the plan, focusing on prevention, protection, and preparedness [312]. This includes heightened awareness through improved warning systems, community engagement, land use planning, and the implementation of both structural (e.g., flood defences) and non-structural (e.g., insurance, emergency response) measures.

Furthermore, flood hazard mapping is vital for flood management plans, providing essential information such as flood extent, water levels, and flow velocity [313]. These maps serve as the foundation for identifying areas at risk and formulating appropriate risk management strategies.

Additionally, the incorporation of sustainability analysis mechanisms, including dynamic sustainability concepts, is recommended in flood management planning [314]. This ensures that the plan considers long-term environmental and social impacts while effectively mitigating flood risks.

Moreover, improved forecasting of heavy rainfall events is crucial for flood planning and management [315]. Enhanced weather and seasonal climate prediction enable communities to undertake proactive emergency measures, such as evacuation plans, levee reinforcement, and riverbed dredging.

An emergency management plan for a flood then, should include comprehensive strategies and procedures to effectively prepare for, respond to, and recover from flooding events, such as:

1. Risk Assessment and Hazard Identification: Identify flood-prone areas, poten-

tial causes of flooding (such as heavy rainfall, storm surges, or river overflow), and vulnerable infrastructure, communities, and populations.

2. Early Warning Systems: Establish systems for monitoring weather forecasts, river levels, and other relevant data to provide early warnings to residents and stakeholders.

3. Evacuation Plans: Develop clear evacuation routes, assembly points, and procedures for safely evacuating residents from flood-prone areas. Consider special needs populations and animals in evacuation plans.

4. Emergency Communication: Establish communication protocols for disseminating warnings, evacuation orders, and critical information to residents, emergency responders, and relevant authorities.

5. Emergency Sheltering: Identify and prepare emergency shelters capable of accommodating displaced residents. Ensure these shelters are accessible, equipped with necessary supplies, and staffed with trained personnel.

6. Search and Rescue Operations: Outline procedures for conducting search and rescue operations to assist individuals trapped or stranded by floodwaters.

7. Infrastructure Protection: Implement measures to protect critical infrastructure, such as levees, dams, utilities, and transportation networks, from flood damage.

8. Health and Safety Measures: Provide guidance on maintaining public health and safety during flooding, including sanitation, hygiene, disease prevention, and the provision of medical care.

9. Resource Management: Identify and allocate resources, including personnel, equipment, and supplies, needed to support flood response and recovery efforts.

10. Community Engagement and Education: Develop outreach initiatives to educate residents about flood risks, preparedness measures, evacuation procedures, and post-flood recovery resources.

11. Coordination with Stakeholders: Establish coordination mechanisms with lo-

cal government agencies, emergency services, community organizations, and neighbouring jurisdictions to facilitate a unified response to flooding events.

12. Post-Flood Recovery: Develop plans for assessing damage, restoring essential services, providing assistance to affected residents, and rebuilding infrastructure in the aftermath of a flood.
13. Training and Exercises: Conduct training exercises and drills to ensure that emergency responders and community members are familiar with their roles and responsibilities during flood emergencies.
14. Plan Review and Revision: Regularly review and update the emergency management plan to reflect changes in flood risks, community demographics, infrastructure, technology, and best practices in emergency management.

Coordination Among Emergency Services and Stakeholders

In disaster management, collaboration and coordination play pivotal roles. Collaboration involves collective efforts towards a shared objective, while coordination entails organizing and aligning actions to achieve that objective [316]. These elements are crucial for effective planning, resource distribution, implementation, and evaluation of response activities. To achieve successful collaboration and coordination, it's imperative to engage a diverse range of stakeholders, including government agencies, non-governmental organizations (NGOs), community-based organizations (CBOs), private sector entities, volunteers, among others. Each stakeholder contributes unique strengths, perspectives, and resources, which are instrumental in bolstering resilience in the face of disasters.

However, meaningful collaboration and coordination can be hindered by various challenges, such as disparities in organizational cultures and values, power differentials among stakeholders, and insufficient communication channels. Therefore, understanding the dynamics of these factors and adopting measures to foster effective collaboration and coordination are paramount in ensuring successful emergency response and disaster management [316].

Stakeholders encompass individuals, groups, organizations, and institutions affected by, interested in, or involved in the addressed issue. In emergencies, a broad spectrum of stakeholders must be engaged. While the specific stakeholders may vary based on the emergency type, certain key categories of organizations and institutions require involvement in communication efforts irrespective of the outbreak nature.

Ideally, identification of existing and potential stakeholders should occur during the preparedness phase. This allows for swift mobilization of existing structures and coordination mechanisms at the outbreak onset. Leveraging existing structures also promotes the development of activities likely to be embraced, owned, and sustained by governments and communities.

During an outbreak, there's often a need to swiftly assemble structures to address the emergency, leaving little time to review existing mechanisms for capitalization. Therefore, it's crucial to identify stakeholders in advance and define their roles in emergency response during the preparedness phase. Identifying coordination mechanisms, technical working groups, and other pertinent structures in advance facilitates swift mobilization through these existing setups.

Frequently, lists and maps of potential stakeholders already exist in countries. Coordinating with relevant agencies like the United Nations Office for the Coordination of Humanitarian Affairs (UNOCHA) and ministries helps obtain existing lists and identify suitable partners for SBCC (Social and Behavioural Change Communication).

The following list serves as an overview, providing descriptions of different stakeholder categories supporting communication efforts and outlining their significance [317]:

Government Institutions: Government and policymakers' buy-in and support are crucial for communication efforts' success. Engaging with the government ensures alignment with national priorities and facilitates a coordinated approach nationally. Understanding existing coordination mechanisms at national and local levels, including communities, is pivotal to ensuring participation and buy-in for all communication interventions.

Service Delivery: Numerous personnel within the service delivery system contribute to or support the emergency communication response. This includes service providers, frontline health workers, and their managers, both paid staff and volunteers. Mapping out different types of facilities, their operational levels, and personnel involved in emergency service delivery allows for a nationally coordinated approach and harmonization of practices, procedures, and messages.

United Nations Agencies and Bilateral Organizations: UN agencies often partner with government ministries to enhance capacity. Identifying active UN agencies in communication, social mobilization, and related areas sustains government support, streamlines activities, and prevents duplication. Bilateral organizations should also be considered for their contributions to government capacity building and communication-related domains.

Non-Governmental and Local Organizations: International and local NGOs, community-based organizations (CBOs), and faith-based organizations (FBOs) often work closely with communities, earning their trust. They serve as effective entry points into communities and may possess resources and infrastructure to support communication responses.

Media and Communication Agencies: Government, private, or non-profit media and communication agencies play crucial roles in disseminating information. This includes radio, television, social media, advertising agencies, and individual professionals like journalists and PR specialists. Community radio stations, particularly, can reach remote areas effectively.

Research Institutions and Universities: These institutions provide essential epidemiological and social data for developing communication strategies and continuously assessing interventions.

Private Sector: Some private sector entities may have interests in emergencies and related issues. For instance, soap manufacturers may donate products for brand visibility. Additionally, private organizations can support emergency responses through logistical or operational infrastructure.

Individuals and Community Members: Community-level actors' buy-in and support are as critical as government endorsement. Understanding local health service governance, traditional leadership systems, and established community groups aids in effective community engagement and acceptance of SBCC activities. Ultimately, individual community members' perspectives and concerns shape appropriate messaging and activities.

Coordination among emergency services and stakeholders is essential for effective emergency response and management. It involves collaboration, communication, and mutual support among various agencies, organizations, and individuals involved in emergency response efforts. This can include:

1. Collaboration: Coordination requires different emergency services, such as fire departments, law enforcement agencies, medical services, and public works departments, to work together seamlessly. This collaboration ensures that resources are pooled, efforts are synchronized, and response activities are coordi-

nated to maximize effectiveness.

2. Communication: Effective communication is critical during emergencies to ensure that information flows smoothly among all involved parties. Coordination efforts often include establishing communication protocols, such as radio channels, phone lines, and digital platforms, to facilitate timely and accurate exchange of information.

3. Resource Sharing: Coordination involves sharing resources, including personnel, equipment, and supplies, among emergency services and stakeholders based on the needs of the situation. This may involve mutual aid agreements, where neighbouring jurisdictions agree to assist each other during emergencies.

4. Unified Command Structure: In large-scale emergencies, a unified command structure may be established to coordinate response efforts across multiple agencies and jurisdictions. Under this structure, representatives from different organizations come together to make joint decisions and coordinate response activities.

5. Role Clarification: Coordination efforts clarify the roles and responsibilities of each agency and stakeholder involved in the response. This ensures that everyone knows their duties and can work together efficiently without duplicating efforts or creating confusion.

6. Training and Exercises: Regular training exercises and drills are conducted to enhance coordination among emergency services and stakeholders. These exercises allow responders to practice working together in simulated emergency scenarios, identify areas for improvement, and refine coordination protocols.

7. Community Engagement: Coordination extends beyond emergency services to include engagement with community stakeholders, such as local government officials, community organizations, businesses, and residents. Engaging the community ensures that response efforts are aligned with community needs and priorities.

8. Information Sharing: Coordination efforts involve sharing relevant information, such as incident updates, resource availability, and situational assessments,

among all stakeholders. This shared understanding of the situation enables informed decision-making and coordinated action.

Coordination among emergency services and stakeholders fosters a collaborative and integrated approach to emergency response, enhancing the ability to effectively mitigate, prepare for, respond to, and recover from emergencies and disasters [316].

Effective disaster management relies heavily on collaboration and coordination. When stakeholders, including emergency responders, government agencies, and community members, collaborate towards a common goal, the benefits are manifold. One significant advantage is enhanced decision-making. By pooling resources and expertise, stakeholders can make informed decisions that optimize the impact of response efforts, leading to more efficient resource utilization and reduced duplication of activities.

Furthermore, collaboration and coordination contribute to increased effectiveness in response endeavours. Ensuring comprehensive coverage of all aspects of disaster management prevents critical needs from being overlooked or neglected. Coordination also ensures alignment in executing plans and responding to emergencies, fostering seamless cooperation and timely assistance to affected populations.

Another benefit is the establishment of trust among stakeholders involved in disaster management. Through joint efforts towards shared objectives, mutual respect for each other's capabilities and contributions is cultivated, laying the groundwork for stronger partnerships in future endeavours. Ultimately, this fosters ongoing success in disaster response and other collaborative endeavours across diverse interests and perspectives [316].

While collaboration and coordination are vital in disaster management, several barriers impede their realization. One major challenge is the lack of trust among stakeholders, leading to rivalry and competition rather than cooperation during crises. Inadequate communication exacerbates this issue, resulting in misunderstandings, delays, and overlooked information critical for effective response.

Resource constraints pose significant hurdles to collaboration and coordination efforts in disaster management. Undefined roles and responsibilities, limited funding allocation, and skewed resource distribution among agencies contribute to inefficiencies in sharing resources, such as equipment and personnel.

Overcoming these barriers necessitates concerted efforts from all stakeholders. Building trust through transparency, establishing open communication channels with clear objectives, and improving funding allocation mechanisms are essential steps towards promoting effective collaboration and coordination practices, ultimately leading to successful disaster management outcomes.

Effective collaboration and coordination in disaster management rely on well-established foundational elements. Firstly, a clearly defined leadership structure with assigned roles and responsibilities for each stakeholder is essential. This ensures that everyone understands their duties and can contribute efficiently towards a shared objective. Secondly, robust communication channels, both formal and informal, such as regular meetings, conferences, email updates, and social media platforms, are vital for seamless collaboration and coordination during disaster response efforts.

Thirdly, adequate resources are crucial to support the response effort, including essential supplies, personnel with relevant expertise, and up-to-date technology. Lastly, comprehensive plans and protocols should be developed and implemented before a disaster occurs to ensure stakeholders have a clear understanding of their response procedures. By establishing these building blocks in advance, stakeholders can respond promptly and effectively during emergencies [316].

The significance of these foundational elements cannot be overstated in facilitating effective collaboration and coordination during disaster management efforts. They provide a solid groundwork for stakeholders to work together towards a common goal while ensuring essential resources are available when needed.

Stakeholders in collaborative disaster management play crucial roles in ensuring a coordinated and effective response to disasters. Government agencies, non-governmental organizations, community leaders, and private sector organizations all have unique responsibilities to ensure successful collaboration. For instance, government agencies coordinate emergency response efforts and provide necessary resources such as funds and manpower. Non-governmental organizations offer essential services like medical care, shelter, and food provision. Community leaders mobilize people within their jurisdiction, while private sector organizations can provide financial support.

Active involvement of all stakeholders in collaborative disaster management planning is crucial to define roles clearly and establish communication channels beforehand. It is essential for stakeholders to align efforts with the common goal of saving lives and property during a disaster event. The collective effort of all stakeholders ultimately determines the success of the response to a disaster event.

Collaboration and coordination are essential components of disaster management, and several effective tools are available to facilitate these processes. The Incident Command System (ICS) is widely used by emergency response agencies worldwide, providing a standardized organizational structure, terminology, and procedures to manage emergencies of any size or type. Geographic Information Systems (GIS) enable stakeholders to visualize disaster-related data on maps, facilitating quick identification of areas in need of assistance or resources. Social media platforms like Twitter and Facebook provide real-time updates and opportunities for individuals affected by disasters to connect with first responders or aid organizations quickly [316].

These tools demonstrate how technology can play a crucial role in ensuring effective collaboration and coordination during disaster management efforts. By leveraging these technologies effectively, stakeholders can work together seamlessly towards achieving common goals, ultimately saving lives and reducing damage caused by disasters.

Developing an Emergency Services and Stakeholders Coordination Plan

Developing an effective coordination plan for emergency services and stakeholders is essential for efficient crisis management. To develop such a plan:

- **Identify Stakeholders**
    - Begin by identifying all potential stakeholders involved in emergency responses, including emergency services (fire, police, EMS), government agencies, non-governmental organizations (NGOs), utility companies, hospitals, and community groups.
    - Determine the roles and responsibilities of each stakeholder in various types of emergencies.
- **Assess Risks and Needs**
    - Conduct a risk assessment to identify potential emergencies specific to the region, such as natural disasters, industrial accidents, or terrorist attacks.
    - Evaluate the resources, capabilities, and limitations of each stakeholder to address these risks.

- **Establish Communication Protocols**
  - Define clear lines of communication and information-sharing protocols. Decide on communication tools and systems to be used during emergencies (e.g., radios, emergency alert systems, mobile apps).
  - Ensure redundancy in communication systems to maintain connectivity even if primary systems fail.
- **Develop Standard Operating Procedures (SOPs)**
  - Create detailed SOPs that outline steps for response activities for various scenarios.
  - Include activation criteria for the coordination plan, command structure, roles and responsibilities, logistical details, and the integration of resources.
- **Set Up a Command Structure**
  - Decide on a unified command system or a similar framework that allows agencies to collaborate under a single command point during emergencies.
  - Define the hierarchy and the command chain, ensuring clarity in leadership and decision-making authority.
- **Plan for Resource Allocation**
  - Map out resource allocation strategies to ensure optimal use of available resources. This includes personnel, equipment, and facilities.
  - Develop mutual aid agreements and memorandums of understanding (MOUs) with neighbouring regions and agencies.
- **Conduct Training and Drills**
  - Organize regular training sessions and simulation exercises to prepare all stakeholders for actual emergency scenarios.
  - These drills should be designed to test and refine the coordination plan, communication, and operational capabilities.

- **Establish Public Information Systems**
    - Plan how information will be disseminated to the public during emergencies, including which platforms will be used (e.g., social media, local news).
    - Determine who is authorized to release information to avoid misinformation and ensure consistent messaging.
- **Review and Revise the Plan**
    - Regularly review and update the coordination plan to incorporate new technologies, changes in stakeholder capabilities, and lessons learned from recent emergency situations.
    - Include feedback from all stakeholders in the review process to ensure the plan remains relevant and effective.
- **Legal and Regulatory Compliance**
    - Ensure the plan complies with local, state, and federal laws and regulations.
    - Consider legal aspects such as data sharing agreements and privacy concerns when designing communication and information-sharing protocols.

A well-developed coordination plan not only prepares emergency services and stakeholders for an efficient response but also enhances community resilience and minimizes the impact of disasters.

Operationalise a Coordination System

Developing an effective, sustainable, and well-coordinated emergency response and recovery procedure for site-induced emergencies with potential off-site impacts requires input from key external stakeholders. These stakeholders encompass those who could be affected by such emergencies and those responsible for response and recovery planning and implementation [318].

The objective of engaging and coordinating with external stakeholders is multifaceted [318]:

- Identifying, mapping, and comprehending external stakeholders impacted by or involved in responding to emergency scenarios, including recovery planning.
- Understanding the regulatory mandates and capacities of external stakeholders to support response and recovery efforts.
- Reviewing and updating emergency scenario assessments, off-site impact assessments, response and recovery planning, and existing controls.
- Ensuring compliance with the site's legal obligations concerning emergency preparedness, response, and recovery.
- Establishing sustainable relationships fostering transparent communication, trust-building, and knowledge exchange.
- Forming partnerships to delineate clear responsibilities, accountabilities, and resource allocations.
- Formalizing relationships through a Memorandum of Understanding (MoU).

External stakeholders involved in co-developing and implementing the site's Emergency Management Plan (EMP) and associated procedures may vary based on context and the type of emergency. Typically, government agencies and state organizations bear statutory accountability and legal responsibility for responding to off-site impacts. International organizations, NGOs, other mining companies, industrial facilities, hospitals, transport authorities, local businesses, volunteer agencies, academic institutions, and affected communities are also key stakeholders.

Understanding the legal obligations and mandates of government agencies and state organizations is crucial, as these may vary by country. These entities often have their own EMPs and response plans, which should be assessed for alignment with the site-induced emergency and off-site impact scenarios.

In the event of challenges in engaging external stakeholders or significant gaps in emergency planning, escalation to internal stakeholders, including the General Manager and crisis management teams, is necessary. Documenting all engagement efforts is imperative.

The communication process with key external stakeholders is essential for effective emergency response and recovery. Establishing an emergency coordination group aids in managing local community expectations and ensures regular discussions on preparedness, response, and recovery planning.

When managing emergencies resulting from on-site incidents with potential off-site repercussions, involving and securing support from government entities, the private sector, or community-based organizations may be necessary. In such cases, a Memorandum of Understanding (MoU) acts as a formal agreement to institutionalize and formalize these relationships and their roles in emergency response and recovery [318]. According to the EMS guidelines, contracts or MoUs with external parties involved in emergency response and recovery must be formalized and documented during the emergency management planning phase. This ensures mutual understanding, alignment, and facilitates timely and coordinated action during emergencies. The MoU should outline responsibilities, mandates, and agreements regarding support provision (personnel and equipment), chain of command, jurisdiction, and triggers for decision-making escalation. The existence of such contracts or MoUs enhances the effectiveness and resilience of emergency response and recovery efforts.

During the Knysna Fires in South Africa in 2017, local authorities collaborated with an unexpected stakeholder, resulting in an effective emergency response and recovery effort [318].

The generous outpouring of support from individuals and businesses led to a significant influx of material donations, such as clothing and blankets, from across the country. However, distributing these donations to affected communities posed a challenge.

Through stakeholder mapping conducted as part of emergency management planning, the government had established a strong relationship with DHL, a global leader in transportation and logistics. DHL, equipped with a global disaster response system, swiftly offered assistance when the fires erupted. They bridged the logistical gap by promptly and freely transporting the donations directly to the disaster zone.

This scenario underscores the importance of recognizing that vital stakeholders may not always be those legally obligated to participate in response and recovery efforts. Being aware of alternative potential partners can be crucial, especially when local authorities face capacity limitations.

To ensure seamless integration of communication within the overarching national response mechanism and effective coordination of SBCC (Social and Behavioural Change Communication) activities, establishing a communication response committee comprising relevant stakeholders is highly recommended [316].

Ideally, this committee should stem from existing communication technical working group (TWG) structures, which already serve as networks for pertinent stakeholders. This coordination entity would oversee all communication preparedness activities, including mapping, formative research, community mobilization, and message development.

Below are recommendations for forming and coordinating a communication response pillar, categorized into three areas: composition, role, and effective functioning.

Composition of the Communication Pillar [316]:

- Designate an organization to chair the subcommittee, with co-chairing by an international agency and a government partner.
- Include various organizations dealing with communication, social mobilization, health promotion, health advocacy, civil society/peacebuilding, SBCC, or communication-related issues pertinent to emergencies.
- Incorporate representatives from local media and community, such as selected spokespeople, religious or local leaders.

Role of the Communication Pillar [316]:

- Facilitate coordination by regularly assessing and identifying relevant stakeholders, engaging credible spokespeople, and appointing media focal persons.
- Coordinate research and assessments addressing cultural practices and behaviours affecting the emergency, and oversee all SBCC initiatives for maximum impact.
- Mobilize communities by advocating policy changes, developing action plans, and engaging individuals through various channels and media.
- Develop, pretest, and disseminate messages and materials, authorize materials developed by partners, and distribute educational resources.
- Assess SBCC training needs, organize training sessions, and monitor ongoing developments to respond to rumours or new situations.
- Implement and coordinate an M&E plan, reassess activities, and adjust the action plan as necessary.

Effective Functioning of the Communication Pillar [316]:

- Ensure each agency appoints a focal point and maintains updated contact details.
- Develop TOR and SOP to guide the pillar's functioning, assigning clear responsibilities and reporting lines.
- Schedule regular but minimal meetings, providing alternative information-sharing systems like email to keep members updated.
- Foster regular communication with the national emergency response mechanism and ensure representation within related pillars.
- Integrate at least one representative from the national emergency response mechanism into the communication pillar to ensure a coordinated approach.

8

Disaster Response

Effective Disaster Response Strategies

Disaster response strategies encompass a range of approaches aimed at effectively managing and mitigating the impact of disasters. One key strategy involves enhancing medical surge capacity, which is crucial in responding to disasters that strain healthcare systems [319]. Community disaster resilience plays a vital role in disaster response, emphasizing the importance of preparedness across all stages of the disaster life cycle [320]. Providing accurate information on disasters and focusing on prevention and practical response strategies can help alleviate stress, anxiety, and depression in affected populations [321].

Well-designed emergency preparedness and response plans not only safeguard lives and property but also play a crucial role in bolstering resilience and facilitating post-disaster recovery by mitigating the impact of emergencies [322]. Through proactive preparedness measures, early warning systems, and effective communication channels, cities, communities, and individuals facing natural or man-made hazards can take timely and appropriate actions to minimize casualties, property damage, and environmental harm. Sustainability hinges upon fostering a shared understanding of the importance and necessity of local emergency preparedness and response among community members and local authorities.

This is achieved through [322]:

Enhance Preparedness Plans:

- Develop and regularly update comprehensive contingency and preparedness plans, ensuring dissemination to all stakeholders. These plans should encompass various aspects such as maintaining law and order, providing essential supplies (e.g., food, water, medical aid, shelter) to vulnerable populations, and securing staple goods.

- Conduct routine training sessions, drills, and exercises to ensure readiness across all components of the broader emergency response framework, including community groups and volunteers.

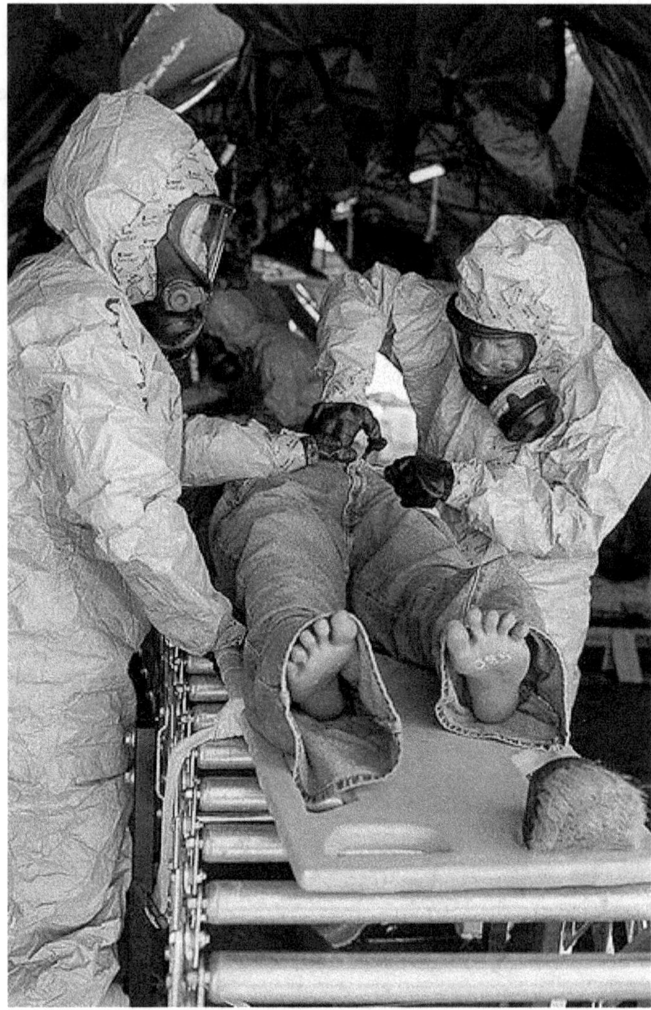

Figure 28: Soldiers of the 323rd Chemical Company, out of Sioux Falls, S.D., simulate the removal of chemical agents from a realistic dummy during Vibrant Response 11.1 a large-scale multi-agency training exercise. U.S. Army photo by Spc. Kayla F. Benson, Public domain, via Wikimedia Commons.

Fortify Early Warning Systems:

- Establish and deploy detection and monitoring equipment, alongside robust early warning systems, and ensure effective communication networks reach all stakeholders and community groups.

- Foster interoperability among emergency response systems within neighbouring countries, between different agencies, and with adjacent cities to streamline communication and coordination.

Enhance City's Emergency Response Services:

- Integrate risk reduction and emergency response efforts with relevant stakeholders such as engineers, contractors, etc., enabling effective engagement in preparedness, response, and recovery operations.

- Establish a reliable mechanism for the swift, transparent, and equitable allocation of funds post-disaster to facilitate efficient response and recovery efforts.

- Allocate sufficient financial resources for post-event response and recovery activities to ensure timely and effective assistance to affected communities.

Figure 29: Colorado National Guard Soldiers and Airman with the CONG Chemical, Biological, Radiological and Nuclear Enhanced Response Force Package work with simulated injured role-players, in Lakewood, Colo., June 3, 2017. Master Sgt. Wolfram M. Stumpf, Public domain, via Wikimedia Commons.

Effective disaster response strategies are crucial for mitigating the impact of disasters on communities, infrastructure, and the environment. These strategies encompass a range of actions and measures aimed at preparing for, responding to, and recovering from disasters in a timely and coordinated manner. Here's an in-depth exploration of key elements and principles that contribute to effective disaster response strategies:

- Preparedness:
    - Preparedness involves activities and measures undertaken in advance to enhance the ability to respond effectively to disasters. This includes developing emergency response plans, conducting risk assessments, and establishing communication and coordination mechanisms.
    - Preparedness also encompasses training and capacity-building initiatives for emergency responders, community members, and relevant stakeholders. This ensures that individuals and organizations understand their roles and responsibilities during a disaster and are equipped with the necessary skills and resources to respond effectively.
- Early Warning Systems:
    - Early warning systems are essential for providing timely and accurate information about impending disasters, such as hurricanes, floods, or earthquakes. These systems utilize various technologies, including meteorological sensors, seismic monitors, and communication networks, to detect and alert authorities and communities about potential threats.
    - Effective early warning systems not only save lives by enabling timely evacuations but also facilitate preparedness actions, such as securing infrastructure and mobilizing resources, before a disaster strikes.
- Coordination and Collaboration:
    - Coordination and collaboration among government agencies, emergency responders, non-governmental organizations (NGOs), and other stakeholders are fundamental to effective disaster response. Clear lines of communication, established protocols, and joint planning efforts ensure a cohesive and synchronized response.
    - Interagency coordination centres, such as emergency operations centres (EOCs), serve as hubs for information sharing, decision-making, and re-

source allocation during disasters. These centres facilitate collaboration among diverse stakeholders and streamline response efforts.

  - Effective disaster management strategies often involve civil-military coordination to strengthen response efforts [323]. Lessons learned from the COVID-19 pandemic underscore the importance of disaster risk knowledge and technology in engaging communities and enhancing response operations [324]. Disaster research can inform evidence-based practices, identify knowledge gaps, and evaluate response strategies to improve overall disaster preparedness and response [325].

- Rapid Deployment of Resources:
  - The timely deployment of resources, including personnel, equipment, and supplies, is critical for addressing immediate needs and mitigating the impact of disasters. Pre-positioning of assets, such as medical teams, search and rescue teams, and relief supplies, enhances response capacity and reduces response times.
  - Effective logistics and supply chain management systems ensure the efficient transportation, distribution, and utilization of resources in disaster-affected areas. This requires coordination between government agencies, humanitarian organizations, and private sector partners.
- Community Engagement and Empowerment:
  - Engaging and empowering communities is essential for building resilience and fostering effective disaster response at the local level. Community-based disaster preparedness initiatives, such as training programs, hazard mapping exercises, and neighbourhood disaster committees, enable residents to take proactive measures to protect themselves and their communities.
  - Community participation in decision-making processes, risk reduction activities, and post-disaster recovery efforts promotes ownership and sustainability. By harnessing local knowledge, resources, and capacities, communities can contribute significantly to disaster resilience and recovery.

- Adaptive Management and Learning:
    - Disaster response strategies should embrace adaptive management approaches that allow for flexibility, innovation, and continuous learning. As disasters are dynamic and unpredictable, response efforts must adapt to changing circumstances and emerging challenges.
    - Post-event evaluations, lessons learned exercises, and after-action reviews provide opportunities for reflection and improvement. By identifying strengths, weaknesses, and areas for enhancement, organizations and agencies can refine their response strategies and enhance their readiness for future disasters.

Effective disaster response strategies integrate preparedness, early warning systems, coordination, resource management, community engagement, and adaptive management principles. By adopting a comprehensive and proactive approach to disaster response, governments, organizations, and communities can minimize the impact of disasters and enhance resilience in the face of adversity.

As examples of effective disaster response strategies, Jakarta, Indonesia, a coastal metropolis and the outlet of 13 rivers, faces significant flood risks. Approximately 40% of Jakarta sits below sea level, encompassing 110 islands within the provincial authority area [322]. Hydrometeorological hazards have inflicted substantial damage in coastal and riverside residential areas. Annual and five-year floods have resulted in substantial financial losses, amounting to billions of dollars in investments in infrastructure and construction. Enhancing Jakarta's flood early warning system has been a collaborative effort involving various local authorities and partners. Through effective management of stakeholders' interests and roles, as well as improved coordination, the early warning system underwent comprehensive upgrades. Technical enhancements have enabled the issuance of earlier flood warnings. Moreover, the capacity for preparedness has been bolstered and streamlined. Key coordination hubs and standard operating procedures have been established and tested through comprehensive drills, enhancing the readiness of institutions and communities to respond to warnings [322].

Makati City, Philippines, situated in the heart of the National Capital Region, hosts a vibrant central business district, serving as the financial hub of the country and housing top corporations. Recognizing the need for improved services to ensure the safety and security of its residents, then Mayor, now Vice President, Jejomar C. Binay, established the

Makati Command, Control, and Communication (Makati C3) as the city's Emergency Operations Center in 2006 [322]. Tasked with monitoring, coordinating, and integrating services and resources during disasters and emergencies, Makati C3 was placed under the leadership of then Councillor, now City Mayor, Jejomar Erwin S. Binay, Jr. to enhance operational capabilities and standards. Through the adoption of an emergency 3-digit access number (168) and the upgrade of technical equipment such as Geographic Information Systems and video surveillance, Makati C3 improved its service delivery [322].

The centre also engaged with international organizations such as ASEAN, INSARAG, and UNDAC to enhance staff capabilities and standards. Strong linkages were forged with national, regional, local, and non-governmental organizations, as well as with the private and business sectors. Within the city, Makati C3 actively participates in risk-sensitive land use planning and community-based disaster risk reduction programs, aiming to create safer and disaster-resilient communities. Additionally, Makati extends its support to other cities and municipalities through its services and endeavours to establish a national training centre, furthering its commitment to disaster preparedness and response [322].

There are several different disaster response strategies that can be employed depending on the nature of the disaster and its impact. Some of these strategies include:

1. Preparedness and Mitigation: This involves taking proactive measures to reduce the risk of disasters and minimize their impact. It includes activities such as risk assessment, community education, infrastructure improvements, and land use planning.

2. Early Warning Systems: Implementing systems to provide timely and accurate warnings to communities about impending disasters, such as floods, storms, or tsunamis. Early warning systems help people take appropriate actions to protect themselves and their property.

3. Emergency Response Planning: Developing comprehensive plans and protocols for responding to disasters, including the allocation of resources, coordination of agencies, and communication strategies. These plans ensure a coordinated and effective response when a disaster occurs.

4. Search and Rescue Operations: Mobilizing teams to locate and rescue people who are trapped or injured as a result of a disaster. Search and rescue operations often involve specialized teams, equipment, and techniques to access affected

areas and provide assistance to survivors.

5. Medical Care and Humanitarian Assistance: Providing medical care, shelter, food, water, and other essential services to people affected by disasters. Humanitarian assistance may be provided by governments, non-governmental organizations, and international agencies to meet the immediate needs of affected populations.

6. Recovery and Reconstruction: After the immediate response phase, efforts shift towards long-term recovery and reconstruction. This involves rebuilding infrastructure, restoring essential services, and supporting communities to recover and rebuild their lives after a disaster.

7. Community Engagement and Capacity Building: Engaging communities in disaster preparedness and response efforts, including training programs, community-based organizations, and volunteer networks. Building local capacity empowers communities to take an active role in responding to disasters and reduces their vulnerability to future events.

8. International Cooperation and Assistance: Collaborating with other countries, international organizations, and humanitarian agencies to provide support and assistance during large-scale disasters. International cooperation helps mobilize resources, expertise, and funding to address complex emergencies and humanitarian crises.

These are just a few examples of disaster response strategies, and effective response often requires a combination of approaches tailored to the specific context and needs of each disaster situation.

Search and Rescue Operations

Search and rescue operations are essential in disaster response efforts to locate and rescue individuals in distress, ultimately saving lives and reducing the impact of disasters on affected communities. Prompt mobilization of specialized search and rescue teams is crucial for reaching survivors quickly and providing necessary assistance [326, 327]. These teams possess specific skills and resources to navigate hazardous environments and access hard-to-reach areas where survivors may be located [328, 329].

Efficient allocation of search and rescue personnel is key to optimizing disaster emergency response. Technologies such as fuzzy logic and artificial intelligence can aid in this process by utilizing data and knowledge from disaster management experts and experienced practitioners in the field [330, 331]. Additionally, the use of drones, robots, and wireless sensor networks has become increasingly prevalent in search and rescue missions, enhancing the safety of rescue team personnel in dangerous disaster scenarios [327, 332, 333].

Advanced algorithms and scheduling techniques are employed to streamline search and rescue operations, aiming to minimize response times and maximize the number of lives saved within set time limits [334]. Furthermore, the integration of various technologies such as unmanned aerial vehicles (UAVs) and mobile sensor networks enables the collection of critical information from disaster areas, facilitating immediate rescue operations [331, 332].

In the aftermath of disasters like earthquakes, floods, or building collapses, individuals are often at risk of becoming trapped under debris or in precarious situations, highlighting the urgent need for swift deployment of search and rescue teams. These teams play a critical role in responding to such emergencies by assessing the situation, prioritizing rescue efforts, and employing specialized techniques and equipment to extricate survivors safely from the rubble or hazardous environments.

Search and rescue teams undergo extensive training to prepare for various disaster scenarios. They are equipped with the knowledge and skills necessary to navigate through unstable structures and debris, assess structural integrity, and determine the safest approach for rescue operations. Upon arrival at the disaster site, these teams quickly evaluate the situation to identify areas where survivors may be trapped and prioritize rescue efforts based on factors such as the likelihood of survival and accessibility of the location.

Specialized equipment is a crucial aspect of search and rescue operations. Teams often carry a range of tools and gear designed specifically for extricating individuals from confined spaces or collapsed structures. This equipment may include cutting tools such as hydraulic shears, jackhammers, or saws capable of slicing through metal or concrete debris. Additionally, shoring materials such as timber, metal struts, or inflatable airbags are used to stabilize unstable structures and create safe working environments for rescue personnel.

Medical supplies are another essential component of search and rescue operations. Teams are equipped with basic medical kits containing supplies like bandages, splints, and pain relief medication to provide immediate aid to survivors until they can be transferred to medical facilities for further treatment. In situations where individuals are trapped for an extended period, search and rescue teams may also provide medical interventions such as intravenous fluids or pain management to ensure the well-being of survivors during the rescue process.

Moreover, search and rescue operations may leverage advanced technological tools to enhance their effectiveness in locating survivors. This may include the use of search dogs trained to detect human scent amidst debris or rubble, drones equipped with cameras to survey inaccessible areas from above, and seismic or acoustic sensors to detect signs of life beneath collapsed structures. These technological advancements complement the skills and efforts of search and rescue teams, enabling them to cover larger areas more efficiently and increase the chances of locating survivors in a timely manner.

Search and rescue operations are complex endeavours that require a combination of specialized training, equipment, and coordination to respond effectively to disasters. By deploying skilled teams equipped with the necessary tools and resources, communities can minimize casualties and expedite the rescue and recovery process in the aftermath of catastrophic events.

Figure 30: A member of the Fairfax County Urban Search and Rescue Team searches under debris in a downtown business following an 8.9-magnitude earthquake, which triggered a devastating tsunami through this Japanese coastal city. DVIDSHUB, CC BY 2.0, via Wikimedia Commons.

Search and rescue operations are typically conducted in environments characterized by challenging conditions, including unstable structures, limited access to resources, and adverse weather conditions. These factors significantly impact the complexity and difficulty of rescue efforts, underscoring the critical importance of coordination among various response agencies and organizations involved in disaster response.

Effective coordination is essential to ensure the optimal deployment of resources and personnel during search and rescue operations. This coordination involves bringing together a diverse range of stakeholders, including local authorities, emergency services such as fire departments and medical teams, volunteer groups such as community emergency response teams (CERTs), and international aid organizations [335].

Meticulous planning is a cornerstone of successful search and rescue operations. This planning process entails assessing the scale and scope of the disaster, identifying priority areas for search and rescue efforts, and determining the allocation of resources and personnel accordingly. Clear communication channels must be established to facilitate real-time information sharing and coordination among all involved parties.

Collaboration among different agencies and organizations is crucial for maximizing the effectiveness of rescue efforts. Each entity brings unique capabilities, expertise, and resources to the table, and by working together, they can leverage their strengths to address various aspects of the operation comprehensively. For example, local authorities may provide logistical support and coordination, while emergency services deploy specialized equipment and personnel for rescue operations. Volunteer groups can assist with crowd control, communication, and providing aid to survivors, while international aid organizations may contribute additional resources, technical expertise, and funding.

Effective coordination also involves establishing command structures and protocols to streamline decision-making processes and ensure efficient utilization of resources. Clear lines of authority and responsibility are established to facilitate effective leadership and decision-making during fast-paced and dynamic rescue operations.

Furthermore, coordination efforts extend beyond the immediate response phase and into the recovery and rebuilding stages of disaster management. Collaborative efforts among stakeholders continue as communities work to recover from the impact of the disaster, rebuild infrastructure, and support affected individuals and families in their recovery process.

Search and rescue operations encompass a broad spectrum of activities that go beyond the initial task of locating and extricating survivors from disaster scenarios. Once survivors are located, the focus shifts to providing them with immediate medical care to address any injuries they may have sustained. This often involves deploying medical personnel equipped with necessary supplies and equipment to administer first aid and stabilize survivors until they can be transported to more advanced medical facilities.

In the chaotic aftermath of a disaster, it is crucial to prioritize patients based on the severity of their injuries through a process known as triage. Triage helps medical personnel allocate limited resources effectively by identifying those in critical condition who require immediate attention, as well as those with less severe injuries who can wait longer for treatment. This systematic approach ensures that medical interventions are directed where they are most urgently needed, maximizing the chances of saving lives.

Facilitating the evacuation of survivors to medical facilities for further treatment is another key aspect of search and rescue operations. This may involve coordinating with transportation services, such as ambulances or helicopters, to safely transport patients to hospitals or triage centres equipped to handle their medical needs. Ensuring timely and efficient evacuation is essential for providing survivors with the best possible chance of recovery and minimizing the risk of further complications.

In addition to addressing physical injuries, search and rescue teams recognize the importance of providing psychological support to survivors who may be experiencing trauma as a result of their ordeal. Disasters can have a profound impact on mental well-being, leading to feelings of fear, anxiety, and distress among survivors. Therefore, search and rescue personnel may include mental health professionals or counsellors trained to offer emotional support and counselling to survivors in need. Providing this type of support is integral to promoting the overall well-being of survivors and helping them cope with the psychological effects of the disaster.

A comprehensive approach to disaster response acknowledges the interconnectedness of physical and emotional needs and seeks to address both aspects effectively. By providing immediate medical care, triaging patients, facilitating evacuation to medical facilities, and offering psychological support, search and rescue operations strive to meet the diverse needs of survivors and ensure their recovery and resilience in the aftermath of a disaster.

Disaster search and rescue techniques encompass a variety of methods and strategies designed to locate and extricate individuals who are trapped or injured in the aftermath of a disaster. These techniques are tailored to the specific circumstances of each situation and may involve specialized equipment, personnel training, and coordination among various response agencies. Here are some common search and rescue techniques:

1. Visual and Auditory Search: Search teams often begin by visually scanning the affected area for signs of survivors, such as movement or sounds indicating someone in distress. This may involve using binoculars, flashlights, or thermal imaging cameras to enhance visibility, especially in low-light conditions or debris-covered environments.

2. Canine Search Teams: Specially trained search dogs, or search and rescue dogs, play a crucial role in locating survivors by using their keen sense of smell to detect human scent. These dogs can cover large areas quickly and are trained to alert their handlers when they find a person buried under rubble or debris.

3. Technical Search and Rescue: In situations where survivors are trapped in confined spaces or inaccessible locations, technical search and rescue techniques are employed. This may involve using specialized equipment such as cameras, probes, and listening devices to locate survivors and assess their condition before

attempting extrication.

4. Urban Search and Rescue (USAR): USAR teams are specialized units trained to respond to disasters in urban environments, such as building collapses or structural failures. These teams are equipped with tools and equipment for breaching walls, shoring up unstable structures, and performing confined space rescues to reach survivors trapped in collapsed buildings.

5. Heavy Machinery and Equipment: In some cases, heavy machinery such as cranes, excavators, and bulldozers may be used to remove debris and clear pathways to reach trapped individuals. However, caution must be exercised to avoid causing further harm to survivors or destabilizing the rescue site.

6. Medical Triage and Treatment: Once survivors are located, medical personnel assess their injuries and provide immediate medical care, including first aid, wound management, and stabilization. Triage systems help prioritize patients based on the severity of their injuries and ensure that critical cases receive prompt attention.

7. Aerial Search and Rescue: Helicopters and drones equipped with cameras and sensors can provide aerial reconnaissance of disaster-affected areas, allowing responders to survey large areas quickly and identify survivors who may be difficult to spot from the ground. Helicopters may also be used for aerial evacuation of injured survivors to medical facilities.

8. Water Search and Rescue: In flood or water-related disasters, specialized water rescue teams may be deployed to locate and rescue individuals stranded in flooded areas or submerged vehicles. These teams use boats, life rafts, and other watercraft to access and evacuate survivors from hazardous water environments.

9. Collaborative Efforts: Effective search and rescue operations rely on collaboration and coordination among multiple agencies, including fire departments, law enforcement, emergency medical services, and volunteer organizations. Interagency communication and cooperation are essential for maximizing resources and optimizing rescue efforts.

By employing a combination of these techniques and leveraging the expertise of trained responders, search and rescue teams can effectively locate, extricate, and provide assistance to individuals in distress during and after disasters, ultimately saving lives and mitigating the impact of emergencies.

Figure 31: Search and rescue personnel are deployed across multiple villages that have been affected by the eruption of Mount Semeru. Indonesian National Board for Disaster Management, Public domain, via Wikimedia Commons.

Visual and auditory search is a fundamental technique utilized by search and rescue teams to locate survivors amidst the chaos of disaster scenarios. This method relies on the keen senses of sight and hearing to identify signs of life in disaster-affected areas. Here's a detailed explanation of how visual and auditory search works:

Search teams begin by systematically scanning the disaster site, carefully observing the surroundings for any visual cues that may indicate the presence of survivors. This involves looking for movement, gestures, or signals from individuals who may be trapped or injured. Visual scanning is typically conducted from vantage points that offer a broad view of the area, such as elevated positions or perimeter boundaries.

Binoculars are commonly employed by search teams to enhance visual acuity and magnify distant objects or areas of interest. This allows responders to survey the disaster site more effectively, particularly when searching large or expansive areas. Binoculars are especially useful for detecting subtle movements or signals that may not be visible to the naked eye.

In low-light conditions or during night time operations, flashlights become essential tools for illuminating dark or obscured areas of the disaster site. Search teams use powerful handheld or mounted flashlights to enhance visibility and search for survivors in dimly lit environments. Flashlights also aid rescuers in navigating through debris and obstacles safely.

Thermal imaging cameras detect heat signatures emitted by living organisms, making them valuable tools for locating survivors, especially in scenarios where visibility is limited or obstructed. These cameras can identify body heat through smoke, dust, or rubble, allowing search teams to pinpoint the precise location of trapped individuals even in challenging conditions.

In addition to visual cues, search teams listen for auditory signals that may indicate the presence of survivors, such as cries for help, tapping or knocking sounds, or calls for assistance. Rescuers use their acute hearing to detect these sounds amidst the background noise of the disaster site and focus their efforts on areas where such signals are heard.

Visual and auditory search operations often involve coordinated teamwork among search and rescue personnel, who work together to cover designated sectors of the disaster site. By sharing information, communicating effectively, and supporting one another, search teams maximize their chances of detecting and rescuing survivors efficiently.

Figure 32: LA County USAR, part of USAID Disaster Assistance Response Team, searches for earthquake survivors in Christchurch, NZ. USAID U.S. Agency for International Development, Public domain, via Wikimedia Commons.

Canine search teams, comprising specially trained search dogs, are indispensable assets in disaster response efforts, contributing significantly to locating survivors in various emergency situations. These search and rescue dogs are equipped with a remarkable sense of smell, allowing them to detect human scent even amidst the chaos of disaster sites. Their acute olfactory senses enable them to cover large areas swiftly, far more efficiently than human responders could accomplish alone.

Trained to recognize the scent of humans, search dogs meticulously comb through rubble, debris, and other disaster-affected areas, guided by their handlers. They are taught to indicate to their handlers when they detect the presence of a person buried under the wreckage. This indication could be in the form of barking, scratching, or other distinct behaviours that signify a potential discovery.

Figure 33: Urban Search and Rescue canine assists with response efforts after 2013 Colorado floods. Photo by Michael Rieger/FEMA, Public domain, via Wikimedia Commons.

One of the key advantages of utilizing search dogs is their ability to penetrate areas that may be inaccessible or challenging for human responders to navigate. Their agility and mobility enable them to manoeuvre through tight spaces and debris piles, increasing the likelihood of locating survivors who may be trapped or in need of assistance.

Moreover, search dogs are trained to remain focused on their task despite the surrounding distractions and noise typical of disaster environments. Their unwavering dedication and commitment to their training make them invaluable assets in search and rescue operations, offering hope to victims and their loved ones awaiting news of their whereabouts.

Technical search and rescue operations represent a critical component of disaster response efforts, especially in scenarios where survivors are trapped in confined spaces or inaccessible locations. These specialized techniques rely on the deployment of advanced equipment and tools designed to navigate challenging environments and locate individuals in need of assistance. Here's an in-depth explanation of how technical search and rescue works:

In confined or hard-to-reach areas, traditional search methods may be insufficient to locate survivors effectively. In such situations, technical search and rescue teams utilize specialized equipment to augment their search capabilities. This equipment includes cameras, probes, listening devices, and other cutting-edge technologies designed to penetrate debris, rubble, and other obstacles obstructing access to survivors.

Camera systems, such as fibre-optic cameras or miniature cameras mounted on robotic devices, are deployed to visually inspect confined spaces and remote areas where human access is limited. These cameras provide real-time video feeds, allowing rescuers to assess the condition of survivors and determine the best approach for extrication. By remotely surveying the area, responders can identify potential hazards and obstacles that may impede rescue efforts.

Probes and sensors are used to probe voids, cavities, and rubble piles, providing valuable information about the presence and location of survivors. These devices can detect signs of life, such as movement, heat signatures, or sound, helping rescuers pinpoint the exact position of individuals trapped beneath the debris. Probes equipped with sensors and imaging technology enable responders to gather data about the structural integrity of collapsed buildings or unstable environments, ensuring the safety of both survivors and rescue personnel.

Listening devices, such as microphones and acoustic sensors, are employed to detect faint sounds or signals emitted by survivors trapped in confined spaces. These devices amplify sounds and vibrations, enabling rescuers to identify and localize the source of noise, such as cries for help or tapping sounds. By precisely pinpointing the location of survivors, listening devices assist search teams in focusing their rescue efforts and maximizing the chances of successful extrication.

Figure 34: The use of Rescue Radar with Ground Penetrating Radar (GPR) technology to locate buried victims. Mvfra, CC BY-SA 4.0, via Wikimedia Commons.

Technical search and rescue operations leverage advanced equipment and innovative technologies to overcome the challenges of locating survivors in confined or inaccessible areas. By employing cameras, probes, listening devices, and other specialized tools, search teams can conduct thorough assessments, gather crucial information, and execute precise rescue missions, ultimately saving lives and providing aid to those in distress.

Urban Search and Rescue (USAR) teams represent highly specialized units dedicated to responding to disasters occurring in urban environments, particularly incidents involving building collapses or structural failures. These teams undergo rigorous training and are equipped with a wide array of tools and equipment tailored to the unique challenges posed by urban disasters.

Figure 35: A Japanese urban search and rescue team at the ruins of the CTV building, Christchurch. Gabriel, CC BY 2.0, via Wikimedia Commons.

In densely populated urban areas, disasters such as earthquakes, explosions, or building collapses can result in numerous casualties and extensive damage to infrastructure. USAR teams are specifically trained to navigate these complex and hazardous environments, employing specialized techniques and equipment to locate and rescue survivors trapped in collapsed structures.

One of the primary functions of USAR teams is breaching walls and accessing confined spaces within collapsed buildings. Using tools such as hydraulic cutters, concrete breakers, and pneumatic drills, rescuers can create openings in debris to reach survivors trapped beneath the rubble. These breaching operations require precision and expertise to ensure the safety of both rescuers and survivors.

Additionally, USAR teams are trained in shoring techniques to stabilize unstable structures and prevent further collapse during rescue operations. This may involve the installation of temporary support structures, such as shoring towers, timber beams, or metal props, to reinforce weakened or compromised building components. By shoring up unstable structures, rescuers create a safer environment for extricating survivors and conducting search operations.

Figure 36: Member of the French Urban Search and Rescue Task Force works with his Alsatian to uncover survivors at the site of the collapsed World Trade Center after the 9/11 attacks. Andrea Booher/ FEMA News Photo, Public domain, via Wikimedia Commons.

Confined space rescues represent another critical aspect of USAR operations in urban environments. Rescuers are trained to navigate tight or obstructed spaces within collapsed buildings, using specialized equipment such as ropes, harnesses, and rigging systems to access areas where survivors may be trapped. These confined space rescues require careful planning and execution to ensure the safety and well-being of both rescuers and survivors.

Heavy machinery and equipment play a crucial role in disaster response efforts, particularly in situations where large quantities of debris hinder access to trapped individuals. The use of machinery such as cranes, excavators, and bulldozers can expedite the removal of rubble and clear pathways for search and rescue teams to reach survivors. Here's a detailed explanation of the role and considerations associated with the use of heavy machinery in disaster response:

During disasters such as earthquakes, building collapses, or large-scale emergencies, structures may collapse, resulting in the entrapment of individuals beneath debris and rubble. In such scenarios, heavy machinery becomes indispensable for clearing the site and creating access points for rescue operations. Cranes are commonly employed to lift and remove heavy debris, while excavators and bulldozers are used to break apart and shift large chunks of rubble.

However, the use of heavy machinery in disaster zones presents inherent challenges and risks that must be carefully managed. First and foremost, rescuers must exercise caution to prevent inadvertently causing harm to survivors who may be trapped beneath the debris. Careful coordination between machinery operators and search and rescue teams is essential to ensure that operations are conducted safely and with minimal risk to survivors.

Figure 37: Members of the Fairfax County Search and Rescue team continue to dig through the rubble of what used to be the Hotel Montana in Port-au-Prince. U.S. Navy photo by Mass Communication Specialist 2nd Class Laura A. Moore, Public domain, via Wikimedia Commons.

Furthermore, the use of heavy machinery must be conducted in a manner that does not destabilize the rescue site or compromise the structural integrity of any remaining buildings or structures. Operators must assess the stability of the surrounding area and take precautions to prevent additional collapses or hazards during the clearance process. Additionally, specialized equipment and attachments may be utilized to delicately manoeuvre through confined spaces and tight quarters without causing further damage.

Incorporating heavy machinery into disaster response operations requires meticulous planning, coordination, and expertise to ensure the safety of both rescuers and survivors. Rescue teams must assess the specific needs of the situation, including the type and scale of the disaster, the condition of the debris, and the presence of any hazards or obstacles.

By leveraging heavy machinery effectively and responsibly, responders can enhance their capabilities and expedite rescue efforts, ultimately saving lives in critical situations.

Medical triage and treatment are critical components of disaster response efforts, aimed at providing timely and appropriate medical care to survivors who have been located by search and rescue teams. Here's a detailed explanation of how medical triage and treatment work in disaster scenarios:

Upon locating survivors, trained medical personnel quickly assess their injuries and medical needs to determine the most urgent cases requiring immediate attention. This process, known as triage, involves categorizing patients into different priority levels based on the severity of their injuries and the urgency of medical intervention required. Triage systems typically use color-coded tags or identifiers to designate patients as immediate, delayed, or minor cases, allowing medical teams to prioritize care accordingly.

Immediate medical attention is provided to patients with life-threatening injuries or conditions that require immediate intervention to stabilize their condition and prevent further deterioration. This may include administering first aid, controlling bleeding, managing airway and breathing, and addressing other critical medical needs to ensure the patient's survival.

For patients with less severe injuries or conditions that are not immediately life-threatening, medical personnel may provide intermediate care while awaiting further assessment and treatment. These patients are categorized as delayed and receive medical attention based on the availability of resources and the severity of their injuries relative to other patients.

Patients with minor injuries or conditions that do not require urgent medical attention are classified as minor cases and may receive basic first aid or symptomatic treatment as needed. These patients are typically managed with lower priority to focus resources on more critical cases.

Medical triage and treatment in disaster scenarios require efficient coordination and collaboration among medical personnel, emergency responders, and support staff to ensure that patients receive timely and appropriate care. This may involve setting up medical treatment areas or field hospitals near the disaster site, deploying medical supplies and equipment, and coordinating patient transport to healthcare facilities for further treatment.

Aerial search and rescue operations utilize helicopters and drones equipped with advanced cameras and sensors to conduct reconnaissance and surveillance of disaster-affected areas from the air. This aerial perspective enables responders to cover large areas swiftly and efficiently, providing crucial visibility over terrain that may be inaccessible or challenging to navigate on the ground. By flying over disaster zones, helicopters and drones can survey the extent of damage, identify hazards, and locate survivors who may be stranded or in need of assistance.

Helicopters are particularly versatile assets in aerial search and rescue operations, capable of manoeuvring into remote or hard-to-reach areas with ease. Equipped with high-resolution cameras and thermal imaging sensors, helicopters can capture detailed imagery and detect heat signatures indicative of human presence, even in adverse conditions such as darkness or inclement weather. This aerial reconnaissance provides valuable situational awareness to responders on the ground, guiding their efforts to prioritize search areas and deploy resources effectively.

Figure 38: Pararescue jumpers and combat rescue officers conduct a search and rescue response exercise during a Katrina-like flood March 8, 2015, in Perry, Ga. U.S. Air Force photo by Staff Sgt. Kelly Goonan/Released, Public domain, via Wikimedia Commons.

In addition to reconnaissance, helicopters play a crucial role in aerial evacuation of injured survivors from disaster sites to medical facilities for urgent medical care. Equipped with hoists or rescue winches, helicopters can perform swift extractions of survivors from inaccessible locations, such as rooftops, mountainsides, or debris piles. This capability significantly reduces the time taken to transport injured individuals to hospitals or trauma centres, increasing their chances of survival and recovery.

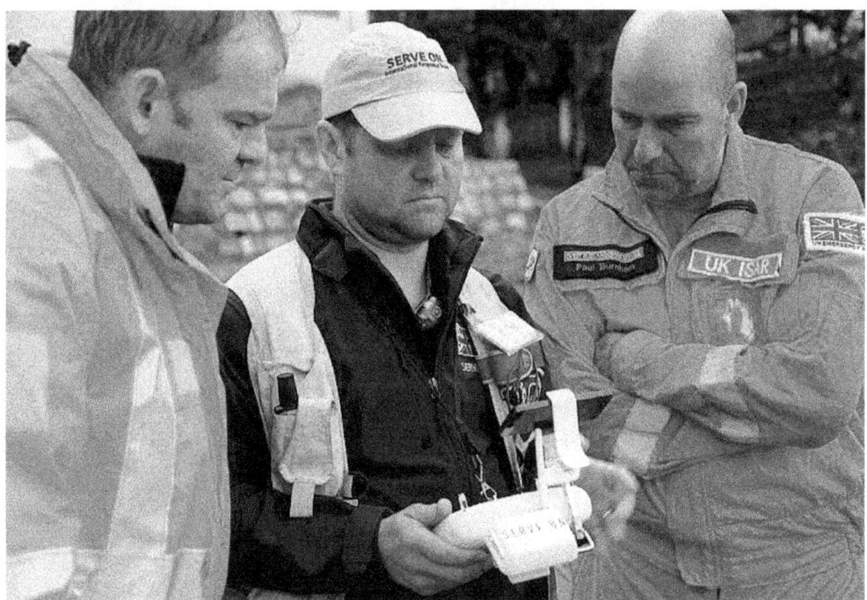

Figure 39: A member of "Serve On" holds up a drone control - used to help identify areas that are worst-hit by the earthquake in Nepal. DFID - UK Department for International Development, CC BY 2.0, via Wikimedia Commons.

Drones, or unmanned aerial vehicles (UAVs), have also become valuable assets in aerial search and rescue operations due to their agility, versatility, and ability to access tight or hazardous spaces. Equipped with cameras, thermal sensors, and other specialized payloads, drones can provide real-time aerial footage and thermal imaging of disaster zones, assisting responders in locating survivors and assessing the extent of damage. Furthermore, drones can cover large areas rapidly and autonomously, enhancing the efficiency and effectiveness of search and rescue efforts.

Figure 40: An FAA certified drone operator is tied in with rope and looks up at the edge of the canyon. Grand Canyon National Park, CC BY 2.0, via Wikimedia Commons.

Overall, aerial search and rescue operations, facilitated by helicopters and drones, play a critical role in disaster response by providing rapid reconnaissance, surveillance, and evacuation capabilities. By leveraging aerial assets, responders can maximize their situational awareness, optimize resource allocation, and expedite the rescue and evacuation of survivors, ultimately saving lives and mitigating the impact of disasters.

Water search and rescue operations are vital in flood or water-related disasters, where individuals may become stranded or trapped in submerged areas, vehicles, or structures. Specialized water rescue teams are trained and equipped to navigate through flooded environments and conduct rescue missions in challenging water conditions. These teams play a crucial role in locating and extricating individuals who are in distress, ensuring their safety and well-being amidst the hazards posed by rising waters.

Boats, life rafts, and other watercraft are essential tools utilized by water rescue teams to access flooded areas and reach survivors who may be isolated or stranded. These vessels are designed to manoeuvre through swift currents, debris-laden waters, and other obstacles commonly encountered during flood emergencies. Equipped with rescue equipment such as life jackets, throw ropes, and flotation devices, water rescue teams can provide immediate assistance to individuals in need and facilitate their evacuation to safer locations.

Water search and rescue operations require specialized training, expertise, and coordination among team members to effectively respond to dynamic and hazardous water environments. Rescuers must be skilled in swiftwater rescue techniques, navigation, and risk assessment to ensure their own safety while conducting rescue missions. Additionally, communication and coordination with other response agencies, such as fire departments, emergency medical services, and law enforcement, are essential to coordinate rescue efforts and optimize resource allocation.

During water search and rescue operations, responders face various challenges, including swift currents, submerged hazards, limited visibility, and unpredictable weather conditions. These challenges necessitate careful planning, situational awareness, and adherence to safety protocols to minimize risks to both rescuers and survivors. Training exercises, simulations, and ongoing proficiency assessments are conducted to maintain readiness and enhance the effectiveness of water rescue teams in responding to emergencies.

Figure 41: Sheriff and water rescue teams searching for a reported missing person on the flooded Red River. Mike Moore, Public domain, via Wikimedia Commons.

Water search and rescue operations play a critical role in saving lives and mitigating the impact of flood or water-related disasters. Specialized water rescue teams utilize boats, life rafts, and advanced rescue techniques to locate, assist, and evacuate individuals in distress, ensuring their safety and well-being amidst hazardous water environments. Through effective training, coordination, and preparedness, water rescue teams contribute to the overall effectiveness of disaster response efforts and help communities recover from the devastating effects of water-related emergencies.

Collaborative efforts are essential for the success of search and rescue operations, requiring coordination among various agencies and organizations to respond to emergencies. These collaborations involve stakeholders such as fire departments, law enforcement, EMS, volunteer groups, and governmental bodies [336]. Interagency communication serves as the cornerstone of collaborative search and rescue operations, enabling seamless coordination and information sharing among participating organizations [337]. Effective communication channels, including radio systems and digital platforms, facilitate real-time exchange of critical information and resource coordination [337].

Partnerships with community-based organizations and volunteer groups significantly supplement professional response agencies by providing additional resources and expertise [336]. Clear delineation of roles and responsibilities among agencies is crucial for the seamless integration of efforts [336]. Regular interagency training exercises enhance teamwork and refine coordination mechanisms among organizations [336].

Collaborative efforts extend beyond interagency cooperation to include joint training initiatives, fostering mutual understanding and effective working relationships among responders [336]. By promoting interagency communication, partnership building, and joint training, collaborative search and rescue initiatives enhance the overall effectiveness, efficiency, and resilience of disaster response efforts [336]. These initiatives ensure a coordinated and comprehensive response to emergencies, ultimately saving lives and effectively addressing disasters.

Coordinating a Search and Rescue Team

Coordinating a search and rescue (SAR) team involves effectively managing resources, personnel, and operations to conduct systematic searches, locate missing individuals, and facilitate their safe recovery. This includes:

1. Establish Command Structure: Designate a competent incident commander (IC) responsible for overseeing the SAR operation. The IC should have authority to make decisions, allocate resources, and coordinate activities throughout the mission.

2. Develop Action Plans: Collaborate with SAR team leaders and stakeholders to develop comprehensive action plans outlining objectives, search strategies, resource requirements, and deployment schedules. Action plans should address factors such as terrain, weather conditions, and potential hazards.

3. Assign Roles and Responsibilities: Assign specific roles and responsibilities to SAR team members based on their expertise, training, and capabilities. Clearly define duties such as search management, field operations, logistics support, medical care, and communications.

4. Establish Communication Protocols: Implement effective communication protocols to ensure seamless coordination and information sharing among SAR team members, command staff, support personnel, and external agencies. Utilize radio systems, mobile phones, or satellite communication devices to maintain contact in remote or inaccessible areas.

5. Conduct Briefings and Debriefings: Conduct pre-mission briefings to communicate objectives, operational plans, safety protocols, and assignment details to SAR team members. Encourage open dialogue, clarify expectations, and address any concerns or questions raised by team members. After completing the mission, conduct debriefings to review performance, identify lessons learned, and make recommendations for improvement.

6. Utilize Search Techniques: Deploy SAR teams to conduct systematic searches using a variety of techniques, including visual scanning, canine search, technical search, and aerial reconnaissance. Implement search grids, assign search sectors, and coordinate search efforts to ensure thorough coverage of the designated area.

7. Leverage Technology and Equipment: Equip SAR teams with advanced technology, specialized equipment, and personal protective gear to enhance search capabilities and ensure responder safety. Utilize GPS devices, drones, thermal imaging cameras, and other tools to facilitate navigation, detection, and identi-

fication of targets.

8. Monitor Progress and Adjust Strategies: Continuously monitor SAR operations, track progress, and evaluate search outcomes to assess effectiveness and identify areas for improvement. Remain flexible and adaptive, and be prepared to adjust search strategies, resource allocations, and priorities based on evolving circumstances and new information.

9. Coordinate with External Agencies: Collaborate with external agencies, such as law enforcement, fire departments, emergency medical services, and volunteer organizations, to leverage additional resources, expertise, and support. Maintain regular communication and coordination with incident command centres, dispatch centres, and other stakeholders involved in the SAR operation.

10. Ensure Safety and Welfare: Prioritize the safety and welfare of SAR team members by adhering to established safety protocols, conducting risk assessments, and providing adequate training, supervision, and support. Monitor environmental conditions, address fatigue and stress among responders, and implement measures to mitigate potential hazards and injuries.

Establishing a command structure is fundamental to the effective coordination of search and rescue (SAR) operations. At the core of this structure is the appointment of a competent incident commander (IC) who assumes overall responsibility for the SAR mission. The IC serves as the central authority figure, entrusted with the authority to make critical decisions, allocate resources, and coordinate activities among SAR team members.

The role of the incident commander encompasses various key responsibilities, including strategic planning, risk assessment, and tactical decision-making. The IC must possess strong leadership qualities, effective communication skills, and a comprehensive understanding of SAR protocols and procedures. Additionally, the IC should be capable of adapting to dynamic and challenging environments, where unforeseen circumstances may arise.

Figure 42: FEMA workers at the Alamo Command Center in Texas. Patsy Lynch, Public domain, via Wikimedia Commons.

In SAR operations, the incident commander acts as the focal point for information dissemination, ensuring that all team members are well-informed and aligned with the mission objectives. Through clear and concise communication channels, the IC coordinates the efforts of SAR personnel, directs search activities, and monitors progress towards achieving mission goals.

Moreover, the incident commander plays a vital role in resource management, ensuring that equipment, personnel, and logistical support are efficiently utilized to maximize operational effectiveness. This involves assessing the needs of the SAR mission, identifying available resources, and allocating them accordingly to address operational requirements.

The establishment of a command structure with a competent incident commander at its helm is essential for maintaining organizational coherence, optimizing decision-making processes, and enhancing overall operational efficiency in SAR missions. Through effective leadership and strategic direction, the incident commander guides SAR teams towards successful outcomes while prioritizing the safety and welfare of all personnel involved.

Developing action plans is a crucial step in coordinating search and rescue (SAR) operations effectively. These plans serve as roadmaps that outline the objectives, strategies, and logistical requirements necessary to conduct SAR missions successfully. Collaboration among SAR team leaders, stakeholders, and subject matter experts is essential in formulating comprehensive action plans that address various operational considerations.

The process of developing action plans begins with a thorough assessment of the mission objectives and the specific challenges posed by the operational environment. SAR team leaders work closely with stakeholders to identify key priorities, define search areas, and establish clear objectives that align with the overarching mission goals.

One of the central components of an action plan is the formulation of search strategies tailored to the unique characteristics of the terrain, weather conditions, and potential hazards encountered during the operation. SAR teams must consider factors such as topography, vegetation, and accessibility when devising search tactics to maximize efficiency and effectiveness.

Resource allocation is another critical aspect addressed within action plans. SAR coordinators collaborate with stakeholders to identify the necessary equipment, personnel, and logistical support required to execute the mission successfully. This includes assessing available resources, estimating deployment schedules, and coordinating the mobilization of assets to ensure timely and effective response capabilities.

Additionally, action plans incorporate risk management strategies aimed at mitigating potential hazards and ensuring the safety of SAR personnel. Contingency measures and emergency protocols are established to address unforeseen challenges and facilitate adaptive decision-making throughout the operation.

The development of action plans provides SAR teams with a structured framework for organizing their efforts, optimizing resource utilization, and adapting to evolving circumstances during search and rescue missions. By fostering collaboration, strategic planning, and proactive risk management, action plans enhance the overall effectiveness and efficiency of SAR operations, ultimately increasing the likelihood of successful outcomes and the safe recovery of individuals in distress.

Assigning roles and responsibilities is a foundational aspect of coordinating a search and rescue (SAR) team, ensuring that each member contributes effectively to the mission's success. This process involves identifying the unique skills, expertise, and training of team members and allocating them to tasks that align with their capabilities. Clear definition of roles and responsibilities fosters efficient teamwork, minimizes confusion, and enhances overall operational effectiveness.

The first step in assigning roles and responsibilities is to assess the composition of the SAR team and the diverse skill sets available among its members. Team leaders collaborate with SAR coordinators and stakeholders to identify individuals with expertise in various domains, such as search management, field operations, logistics, medical care, and communications.

Once team members' capabilities have been identified, specific roles and responsibilities are assigned based on their qualifications and training. For example, individuals with experience in search management may be tasked with overseeing search operations, coordinating search teams, and developing search strategies. Field operators are responsible for conducting ground searches, navigating terrain, and identifying potential targets for rescue.

Logistics support personnel play a crucial role in ensuring that SAR teams have access to essential resources, equipment, and supplies needed to sustain operations. They may be responsible for inventory management, equipment maintenance, and logistical coordination with external support agencies.

Medical care providers are assigned roles related to providing emergency medical treatment and first aid to survivors. They assess the medical needs of rescued individuals, administer immediate care, and facilitate their evacuation to medical facilities for further treatment.

Effective communication is essential for coordinating SAR efforts and maintaining situational awareness throughout the operation. Communication specialists are tasked with establishing and maintaining communication channels between SAR teams, command centres, and other stakeholders. They may operate radios, satellite phones, or other communication devices to facilitate real-time information exchange.

By clearly defining roles and responsibilities within the SAR team, each member understands their duties and contributions to the mission's objectives. This fosters a sense of accountability, enhances coordination, and optimizes resource utilization, ultimately improving the team's overall performance and increasing the likelihood of a successful outcome.

Conducting briefings and debriefings is integral to the effectiveness and efficiency of search and rescue (SAR) operations, providing a structured framework for communication, planning, and learning throughout the mission lifecycle.

Pre-mission briefings serve as a critical starting point, allowing SAR team leaders to communicate essential information to team members before deploying into the field.

During these briefings, objectives, operational plans, safety protocols, and assignment details are clearly outlined to ensure that every team member understands their role and responsibilities. By fostering open dialogue and encouraging questions, pre-mission briefings create a shared understanding among team members, enhance situational awareness, and mitigate the risk of misunderstandings or errors during the operation.

Additionally, pre-mission briefings provide an opportunity to address any concerns or questions raised by team members, allowing leaders to address potential challenges proactively and adapt plans accordingly. This collaborative approach promotes a sense of trust and cohesion within the team, fostering a positive working environment conducive to effective teamwork and problem-solving.

Following the completion of the mission, debriefings are conducted to review performance, assess outcomes, and capture lessons learned. Debriefings provide a structured forum for SAR team members to reflect on their experiences, share observations, and identify areas for improvement. By systematically reviewing the mission's successes, challenges, and opportunities, debriefings enable teams to extract valuable insights and make recommendations for enhancing future operations.

During debriefings, team leaders facilitate discussions to encourage honest feedback, constructive criticism, and self-reflection among team members. By analyzing strengths and weaknesses, identifying operational gaps, and exploring opportunities for innovation, debriefings support continuous improvement and promote a culture of learning within the SAR team.

Moreover, debriefings offer an opportunity to recognize and celebrate achievements, acknowledge individual contributions, and express appreciation for the collective efforts of the team. This reinforces a sense of camaraderie, fosters morale, and motivates team members to remain dedicated to their mission of saving lives and serving their communities.

To effectively locate missing persons or survivors, search and rescue (SAR) teams utilize various search techniques. These techniques include visual scanning, canine search, technical search, and aerial reconnaissance. SAR teams conduct systematic searches by implementing search grids, assigning search sectors, and coordinating efforts to ensure comprehensive coverage of the designated area. By deploying these techniques strategically, SAR teams maximize their chances of locating individuals in need of assistance during a search operation.

In the dynamic environment of search and rescue (SAR) operations, it's imperative to continuously monitor progress and adapt strategies accordingly. This ongoing evaluation ensures that SAR efforts remain effective and responsive to changing conditions throughout the mission. SAR teams employ a range of monitoring techniques to track their progress and assess the outcomes of search activities.

One key aspect of monitoring is tracking the movement and coverage of search teams within the designated search area. This may involve maintaining communication with field teams via radio or GPS tracking systems to monitor their locations and progress in real-time. By tracking team movements, incident commanders can ensure that search efforts are comprehensive and that all areas of the designated search area are thoroughly covered.

In addition to monitoring team movements, SAR operations also involve evaluating the effectiveness of search techniques and strategies employed. This may include assessing the success rates of different search methods, such as visual scanning, canine search, or aerial reconnaissance, and identifying which approaches yield the best results in specific circumstances. By analysing the effectiveness of different strategies, SAR teams can optimize their search efforts and allocate resources more efficiently.

Furthermore, SAR operations require constant vigilance to adapt to changing conditions and new information as they arise. This necessitates a flexible approach that allows SAR teams to adjust their strategies, resource allocations, and priorities in real-time based on evolving circumstances. For example, if new information suggests a shift in the location of survivors or changes in terrain conditions, SAR teams may need to modify their search patterns or deploy additional resources to address emerging challenges.

In the complex landscape of search and rescue (SAR) operations, effective coordination with external agencies is paramount to ensure the success of the mission. SAR teams often collaborate closely with a range of external entities, including law enforcement agencies, fire departments, emergency medical services (EMS), and various volunteer organizations. Each of these entities brings unique resources, expertise, and capabilities to the table, making collaboration essential for maximizing the effectiveness of SAR efforts.

One of the key aspects of coordinating with external agencies is maintaining regular communication and information sharing. SAR teams establish channels of communication with incident command centres, dispatch centres, and other relevant stakeholders to exchange critical information, coordinate activities, and make strategic decisions. This real-time communication allows SAR teams to stay informed about developments on the ground, coordinate resource allocations, and address emerging challenges effectively.

Collaboration with external agencies also enables SAR teams to leverage additional resources and expertise that may not be available internally. For example, law enforcement agencies may provide support in crowd control or perimeter security, while fire departments can offer specialized equipment for structural stabilization or extrication. By tapping into the resources and capabilities of external agencies, SAR teams can enhance their operational capacity and improve their ability to respond to complex or large-scale incidents.

Furthermore, coordination with external agencies facilitates a unified and integrated approach to SAR operations. By working closely together, SAR teams and external agencies can align their efforts, streamline processes, and avoid duplication of resources or efforts. This coordinated approach ensures that SAR operations are conducted efficiently, effectively, and in accordance with established protocols and best practices.

Ensuring the safety and welfare of search and rescue (SAR) team members is a foundational principle that underpins the entire operation. SAR missions often involve working in hazardous environments, unpredictable conditions, and high-stress situations, making safety protocols and precautions critical to the well-being of responders. To achieve this, SAR teams prioritize several key strategies to safeguard the health and safety of their personnel.

First and foremost, SAR teams adhere to rigorous safety protocols and guidelines established by relevant authorities or governing bodies. These protocols outline standard operating procedures, safety measures, and best practices for conducting SAR operations in various environments and scenarios. Team leaders and members are trained to follow these protocols meticulously, ensuring consistency and uniformity in safety practices across all aspects of the operation.

Conducting thorough risk assessments is another essential component of ensuring safety during SAR missions. Before deploying into the field, SAR teams assess potential hazards, evaluate environmental conditions, and identify any factors that may pose risks to team members. By proactively identifying hazards and assessing risks, SAR teams can implement appropriate control measures to mitigate potential dangers and minimize the likelihood of accidents or injuries.

Adequate training, supervision, and support are also crucial elements of ensuring the safety and welfare of SAR team members. SAR personnel undergo comprehensive training programs that equip them with the knowledge, skills, and competencies needed to perform their roles effectively and safely. Additionally, team leaders provide ongoing supervision and guidance to ensure that team members adhere to safety protocols, follow established procedures, and make informed decisions in the field.

Monitoring environmental conditions and addressing factors that may impact the well-being of SAR responders are vital considerations during SAR operations. SAR teams remain vigilant of changing weather patterns, terrain conditions, and other environmental factors that could affect the safety of team members. Additionally, measures are implemented to address fatigue, stress, and physical exertion among responders, such as rotating personnel, providing rest breaks, and offering psychological support services as needed.

Medical Care and Humanitarian Assistance

Disaster response knowledge, which involves equipping the general public with basic disaster response skills, is highlighted as a fundamental and effective strategy in disaster management [338]. Shifting towards proactive strategies focused on disaster mitigation and preparedness is essential to improve response outcomes [339]. Integrating health research into disaster response efforts is crucial, with local community organizations playing a significant role in resilience-building and preparedness planning [340].

Medical care and humanitarian assistance are critical components of disaster response efforts aimed at addressing the immediate needs of individuals and communities affected by disasters. In the aftermath of a disaster, such as earthquakes, hurricanes, or floods, the provision of medical care and humanitarian assistance becomes paramount in saving lives, alleviating suffering, and restoring stability to affected areas.

One of the primary objectives of medical care in disaster response is to provide timely and effective treatment to individuals who have been injured or are suffering from medical emergencies as a result of the disaster. This includes administering first aid, stabilizing critical patients, and providing emergency medical interventions to address life-threatening conditions. Medical teams deployed to disaster-affected areas are equipped with essential medical supplies, equipment, and personnel trained to respond to a wide range of medical emergencies.

In addition to addressing immediate medical needs, humanitarian assistance encompasses a broader range of support services aimed at meeting the basic needs of disaster-affected populations. This includes providing shelter, food, clean water, sanitation facilities, and essential household items to individuals who have been displaced or are unable to access basic necessities due to the disaster. Humanitarian assistance may also include psychosocial support services to help individuals cope with trauma, grief, and emotional distress caused by the disaster.

The provision of medical care and humanitarian assistance involves collaboration among various actors, including governments, non-governmental organizations (NGOs), humanitarian agencies, and local communities. Governments play a central role in coordinating the overall response effort, mobilizing resources, and ensuring that affected populations receive the necessary support and services. NGOs and humanitarian agencies often provide specialized expertise, logistical support, and personnel to complement government-led efforts and deliver assistance directly to affected communities.

International agencies, such as the United Nations Office for the Coordination of Humanitarian Affairs (OCHA) and the International Committee of the Red Cross (ICRC), play a crucial role in coordinating humanitarian assistance on a global scale, mobilizing resources, and providing support to countries facing large-scale disasters. These agencies work closely with governments, NGOs, and other stakeholders to ensure a coordinated and effective response to humanitarian crises worldwide.

Coordinating and managing medical care and humanitarian assistance in disaster response requires a comprehensive approach that involves various stakeholders, resources, and logistical considerations. The process begins with a thorough needs assessment to identify the specific requirements of the affected population. This assessment entails gathering information about the scale and severity of the disaster, the number and location of affected individuals, and the nature of their needs, such as medical care, shelter, food, and water.

Once the needs are identified, coordination mechanisms, such as coordination centres or clusters, are established to facilitate communication, collaboration, and resource-sharing among the different actors involved in the response. These mechanisms ensure that efforts are well-coordinated, resources are efficiently allocated, and duplication of services is minimized. Government agencies, NGOs, humanitarian organizations, and other stakeholders actively participate in these coordination mechanisms.

Efforts are then made to mobilize the necessary resources, including medical supplies, food, water, shelter materials, and personnel. This may involve procurement, donation drives, international assistance, and partnerships with private sector entities, philanthropic organizations, and other stakeholders. Medical teams comprising doctors, nurses, paramedics, and other healthcare professionals are deployed to disaster-affected areas to provide medical care to those in need. These teams operate from field hospitals, mobile clinics, or temporary medical facilities established near the affected communities.

Simultaneously, humanitarian aid, including shelter materials, food, water, hygiene kits, and other essential items, is distributed to affected populations to meet their immediate needs. Distribution points are strategically set up in accessible locations, and distribution processes are organized to ensure fairness, efficiency, and dignity for recipients. Local community leaders, volunteers, and aid workers play crucial roles in assisting with the distribution process.

Continuous monitoring and evaluation of medical care and humanitarian assistance activities are essential to assess their effectiveness, identify gaps or challenges, and make necessary adjustments to improve the response. Monitoring involves tracking the distribution of aid, the delivery of medical services, and the overall well-being of affected populations. Evaluation entails assessing the impact of assistance efforts on the health, safety, and welfare of beneficiaries.

Close coordination with local authorities, community leaders, and affected communities is vital to ensure that assistance efforts are culturally appropriate, responsive to local needs, and well-received by the affected population. Engagement with community members helps build trust, gather feedback, and ensure that assistance is tailored to the unique needs and preferences of the community.

In cases where disasters overwhelm local capacities, coordination with international partners, including governments, UN agencies, and international NGOs, may be necessary to provide additional support and resources. International coordination mechanisms, such as the United Nations Office for the Coordination of Humanitarian Affairs (OCHA), facilitate collaboration and resource-sharing among international actors involved in the response, ensuring a more comprehensive and effective disaster response effort.

Examples of Both Successful and Failed Disaster Responses

Successful Disaster Response Case Study

Hurricane Katrina in 2005 had a profound impact on the Gulf Coast, particularly in New Orleans. However, amidst the devastation, there were instances of successful community resilience, notably in Biloxi, Mississippi. The response in Biloxi showcased effective disaster management strategies, including well-coordinated evacuation plans and response efforts led by the city's emergency management team and community leaders [126].

Local organizations such as churches and community centres played a crucial role by serving as shelters and distribution centres for essential supplies like food, water, and medical aid. Moreover, volunteers from neighbouring areas and national organizations swiftly mobilized to provide additional support, emphasizing the significance of strong community partnerships in disaster response [126].

The success of the response efforts in Biloxi highlighted the importance of proactive planning and swift action in mitigating the impact of a disaster. This underscores the value of community resilience in facing catastrophic events like Hurricane Katrina. By leveraging partnerships, effective communication, and coordinated efforts, communities can enhance their ability to withstand and recover from adversity [126].

The 2011 Great East Japan Earthquake and Tsunami triggered a series of responses from the government to address the crisis. The government swiftly implemented evacuation measures, conducted efficient search and rescue operations, and set up emergency shelters to assist the affected population [341]. The coordination between local authorities, the military, and international aid agencies played a crucial role in facilitating the delivery of humanitarian assistance and medical care to those impacted by the disaster [342].

Figure 43: Scene after Tōhoku earthquake of Japan. sbiding, CC BY-SA 3.0, via Wikimedia Commons.

The earthquake, known as the 2011 Great East Japan Earthquake, had a magnitude of 9.0 and occurred off the Pacific coast of Japan on March 11, 2011 [343]. The seismic event resulted in significant displacement above the hypocenter and was one of the largest earthquakes in recorded history [344]. The earthquake and subsequent tsunami caused substantial damage, claiming the lives of over 15,000 people and leading to a meltdown at the Fukushima Daiichi nuclear power plant [345].

The response to the 2011 Tohoku Earthquake and Tsunami in Japan was marked by several key factors that collectively contributed to its success.

Firstly, Japan's advanced earthquake early warning systems played a pivotal role by providing residents with crucial seconds to minutes of advance notice before the tsunami struck. This allowed individuals to take protective actions, such as seeking cover or evacuating to higher ground, thereby minimizing loss of life.

Moreover, Japan's comprehensive disaster preparedness measures, including stringent building codes, infrastructure designs, and public education campaigns, ensured that the population was well-prepared to respond to seismic events. This heightened awareness facilitated a swift and orderly evacuation process, further reducing casualties.

The effective deployment of highly trained search and rescue teams immediately after the disaster was instrumental in locating and extricating survivors trapped under debris. These teams worked tirelessly in challenging conditions, providing critical medical care and assistance to those in need.

Additionally, strong government leadership, exemplified by Prime Minister Naoto Kan's proactive approach, played a crucial role in coordinating response efforts, mobilizing resources, and ensuring clear communication with the public. This streamlined decision-making and resource allocation, enhancing the overall effectiveness of the response.

Japan also benefited from significant support from the international community, including search and rescue teams, medical personnel, and humanitarian aid. This international collaboration facilitated the rapid deployment of assistance and expertise to areas most in need, further bolstering the response efforts.

Furthermore, the resilience and solidarity demonstrated by local communities in Japan were paramount. Residents supported each other, shared resources, and collectively worked towards rebuilding their communities in the aftermath of the disaster. This community cohesion not only fostered a sense of unity but also contributed significantly to the overall success of the response and recovery efforts.

The disaster prompted a re-evaluation of earthquake and tsunami recurrence on subduction zones globally, with a focus on the intervals between great earthquakes near Sendai [346]. Furthermore, insights from interviews with survivors have provided valuable information on the fatalities inflicted by the earthquake and tsunami, shedding light on evacuation behaviour and fatality rates during the disaster [347].

During the 2018 Kerala floods in India, a collaborative effort involving community-based organizations, volunteers, and government agencies was instrumental in conducting rescue operations, providing relief supplies, and offering medical assistance to the affected communities. The government's effective use of social media and mobile applications played a crucial role in coordinating rescue efforts and disseminating information, contributing to the success of the response [348].

The floods in Kerala were a result of heavy rainfall, with the state experiencing 36% excess rainfall than normal levels during the period from 1 June to 29 August 2018, leading to widespread floods, landslides, and significant loss of life [349]. The use of satellite-based assessments and space-borne synthetic aperture radar data helped in mapping and understanding the extent of the flood event in Kerala [350, 351]. Additionally, the combined impact of extreme rainfall and reservoir storage was identified as a significant factor contributing to the large-scale flooding that affected millions of people in Kerala [352].

Figure 44: NDRF teams carrying out rescue and relief operations in flood-affected areas of Kerala on August 11, 2018. Ministry of Home Affairs (GODL-India), GODL-India, via Wikimedia Commons.

The Kerala floods of 2018 provided valuable lessons on risk governance and climate policies, emphasizing the importance of effective disaster response strategies [353]. The government's ability to react rapidly to emergencies, developed through experiences with previous disasters like the Ockhi cyclone and Nipah virus outbreak, enabled a well-coordinated response during the floods [354]. Furthermore, the utilization of open/crowd-sourcing platforms through citizen-led initiatives and social media played a crucial role in coordinating rescue missions and response efforts during the floods [355].

The international humanitarian response to the 2010 Haiti earthquake was marked by the rapid deployment of search and rescue teams, medical personnel, and relief supplies despite significant challenges such as limited infrastructure and resources. This response involved coordination between government agencies, non-governmental organizations (NGOs), and international partners to facilitate the delivery of emergency aid and medical care to earthquake survivors [356-358].

The earthquake caused catastrophic physical damage, resulting in a significant loss of life, injuries, displacement, and destruction of homes in the greater Port-au-Prince area

[359]. The disaster brought about a complete spectrum of risk factors for psychological distress and psychopathology for those directly affected by the earthquake in Haiti [360]. Furthermore, the earthquake led to a surge in international solidarity and aid efforts, although the effectiveness of the aid and the ongoing needs of the Haitian population remained areas of concern [361].

Figure 45: Haitian men, women and children operate heavy equipment, pick up trash and remove debris in Port-au-Prince, Haiti, March 17, 2010, in the aftermath of a 7.0-magn itude earthquake that struck the Caribbean nation Jan. 12, 2010. MCC Spike Call, Public domain, via Wikimedia Commons.

The response to the earthquake highlighted the importance of collaboration between various organizations involved in disaster assistance. Studies have analysed the collaboration between international NGOs, local NGOs, faith-based organizations, and other entities in providing aid in the aftermath of the earthquake. Additionally, the earthquake underscored the need for effective coordination in humanitarian supply chain management to overcome the challenges posed by the disaster .

The 2010 Haiti earthquake triggered a massive international humanitarian response that showcased the importance of swift action, coordination, and collaboration among diverse entities to provide aid and support to those affected by the disaster. Despite the immense challenges faced, the response efforts demonstrated the resilience and commitment of the global community to assist in times of crisis.

Failed Disaster Response Case Study

Hurricane Maria (2017) - Failed Government Response in Puerto Rico: The aftermath of Hurricane Maria in Puerto Rico revealed significant failures in disaster response, particularly at the government level. The island's infrastructure suffered extensive damage, leading to widespread power outages, disrupted communication networks, and limited access to essential services such as clean water and medical care. However, the federal and local government's response was widely criticized for its slow and inadequate efforts to provide assistance and support to affected communities. Delays in deploying emergency supplies, inadequate distribution channels, and bureaucratic hurdles hindered relief efforts, exacerbating the suffering of residents [362]. The response to Hurricane Maria underscored the importance of timely and effective government intervention, adequate resource allocation, and transparent communication in disaster response and recovery efforts.

Although some aspects of the response to Katrina are identified above as a success, the response to Hurricane Katrina in New Orleans in 2005 was characterized by delays, inadequate planning, and insufficient coordination among federal, state, and local authorities. Failures in evacuation procedures, communication breakdowns, and delays in providing emergency assistance led to significant loss of life and widespread suffering among residents [363-368]. The flooding in New Orleans, primarily caused by the hurricane, resulted in two-thirds of the analysed fatalities, mainly due to drowning [18]. The storm's impact was so severe that it forced the evacuation of over one million people from the US Gulf Coast, with extensive flooding exacerbating the damage in the New Orleans metropolitan area [369].

The aftermath of Hurricane Katrina highlighted the disproportionate impact on vulnerable populations, such as people with disabilities, dialysis patients, and marginalized communities [370-373]. The response to the disaster also underscored the importance of effective disaster planning in healthcare services, as evidenced by the challenges faced in providing medical care during and after the hurricane [374-376]. Furthermore, the failure of FEMA and other governmental agencies to provide adequate disaster relief post-Katrina was analysed through a public choice theory perspective [366].

Figure 46: Damage and destruction to houses in Biloxi, Mississippi by hurricane Katrina. FEMA/Mark Wolfe, Public domain, via Wikimedia Commons.

The catastrophe of Hurricane Katrina also shed light on social and racial disparities, with African Americans being disproportionately affected by the storm and its aftermath [377]. The event prompted a re-evaluation of disaster recovery policies and highlighted the need for improved coordination among various relief organizations and government agencies [367, 378]. The response to Hurricane Katrina was a wake-up call regarding the necessity for better communication, coordination, and preparedness in the face of catastrophic disasters [363, 368].

The response to Typhoon Haiyan in the Philippines in 2013 faced significant criticism due to delays in delivering aid to affected communities. The slow and fragmented efforts were attributed to challenges in mobilizing relief supplies, logistical issues, and coordination problems among government agencies and humanitarian organizations [379, 380]. The aftermath of Typhoon Haiyan caused massive damage, affecting around 16 million people in the central part of the Philippines [183]. The typhoon, known as Yolanda locally, was one of the strongest to hit the Philippines, resulting in over 6,000 fatalities upon landfall [183]. The humanitarian crisis exacerbated by the delays in aid delivery highlighted the importance of effective disaster response and coordination mechanisms.

The devastation caused by Typhoon Haiyan also impacted hospital resilience in the affected areas, emphasizing the need for preparedness and resilience-building measures in the healthcare sector [381, 382]. Furthermore, the disaster prompted studies on the recovery and resilience of mangrove forests in the region, showcasing the long-term environmental impacts of such extreme weather events [383, 384]. The typhoon's effects on health staff in hospitals underscored the challenges faced by frontline workers during and after natural disasters, shedding light on the importance of supporting healthcare professionals in such crises [382].

Moreover, the use of social media and citizen aid played a significant role in the post-disaster recovery efforts following Typhoon Haiyan (Chandra & Paras, 2020). Social media platforms were instrumental in disseminating information, coordinating relief efforts, and providing support to affected communities. The study of social entrepreneurship in the disaster recovery context highlighted the role of public value creation in rebuilding efforts after the super typhoon.

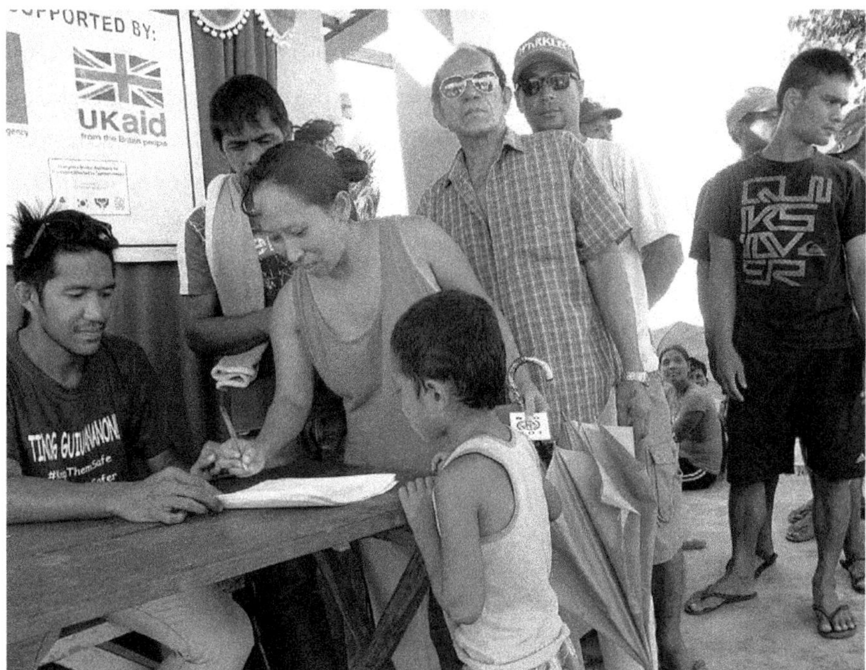

Figure 47: Filipinos displaced from their homes by Typhoon Haiyan register at a aid distribution point run by the International Organisation for Migration (IOM). DFID - UK Department for International Development, CC BY 2.0, via Wikimedia Commons.

The response to Typhoon Haiyan in the Philippines in 2013 revealed critical gaps in disaster preparedness, response coordination, and aid delivery. The lessons learned from this event emphasized the importance of efficient logistics, inter-agency collaboration, and community resilience in mitigating the impact of such catastrophic events in the future.

The 2020 Beirut explosion in Lebanon exposed critical weaknesses in the country's disaster management infrastructure. The Lebanese government faced criticism for its lack of transparency, accountability, and coordination in response to the explosion at the port. Failures in emergency preparedness, delays in providing assistance to affected residents, and inadequate medical response underscored systemic weaknesses [385]. The explosion, caused by a massive chemical detonation, resulted in extensive damage and casualties [385]. Estimates suggest the explosion had a yield between 0.50 kt TNT and 1.12 kt TNT [386].

The aftermath of the Beirut explosion exacerbated existing crises in Lebanon, including the COVID-19 pandemic and economic challenges [387]. The explosion strained the healthcare sector, highlighting the lack of formal preparedness and a clear chain of command [388]. Hospitals faced challenges in emergency preparedness, with the explosion leading to a surge in casualties and overwhelming healthcare facilities [389]. The blast also resulted in a significant number of injuries, including ophthalmic injuries, further stressing the healthcare system [390].

Figure 48: Damage after the Beirut explosion. Mehr News Agency, CC BY 4.0, via Wikimedia Commons.

The explosion's impact extended beyond immediate casualties, affecting the healthcare system's ability to respond to other crises like the COVID-19 pandemic [391]. The incident highlighted the need for resilience and adaptability in disaster response, emphasizing the importance of organizational learning and preparedness for hospitals [392]. The experiences of healthcare professionals, including pharmacists and nurses, underscored the challenges faced in managing multiple crises simultaneously [393-395].

The 2020 Beirut explosion exposed critical weaknesses in Lebanon's disaster management infrastructure and emergency response capabilities. The incident not only resulted in immediate casualties and damage but also strained an already fragile healthcare system, further compounded by existing crises in the country. Addressing the deficiencies highlighted by this disaster is crucial to enhancing Lebanon's resilience and preparedness for future emergencies.

These case studies illustrate the critical factors that contribute to both successful and failed disaster responses, including preparedness, coordination, leadership, community resilience, and government responsiveness. Learning from past experiences, both positive and negative, is essential for improving future disaster response efforts and enhancing the resilience of communities facing natural disasters.

From the successful disaster response case studies, several key lessons can be gleaned:

1. Importance of Proactive Planning and Swift Action: The successful responses in Biloxi, Mississippi, and Japan's Tohoku region underscore the significance of proactive planning and swift action in mitigating the impact of disasters. Early warning systems, comprehensive disaster preparedness measures, and effective deployment of resources played crucial roles in saving lives and minimizing damage.

2. Community Resilience and Partnerships: Strong community resilience and partnerships were evident in both Biloxi and Japan, where local organizations, volunteers, and government agencies worked collaboratively to provide assistance and support. These partnerships enhanced the effectiveness of response efforts and facilitated rapid recovery.

3. Government Leadership and Coordination: Effective government leadership and coordination were instrumental in Japan's response to the Tohoku earthquake and tsunami. Swift mobilization of resources, clear communication, and coordination among various agencies and stakeholders contributed to the success of the response efforts.

4. International Collaboration: International collaboration and support were crucial components of Japan's disaster response, highlighting the importance of global solidarity in times of crisis. The assistance provided by international partners further bolstered Japan's capacity to respond effectively to the disaster.

5. Utilization of Technology and Social Media: The successful responses in Japan and Kerala, India, demonstrated the effective use of technology, including early warning systems, social media, and satellite-based assessments, in coordinating response efforts and disseminating information. These technological innovations enhanced communication, coordination, and situational awareness during emergencies.

From the failed disaster response case studies, several critical lessons emerge:

1. Timely and Effective Government Intervention: The failed responses to Hurricane Maria in Puerto Rico and Hurricane Katrina in New Orleans underscore the importance of timely and effective government intervention in disaster response. Delays, inadequate planning, and insufficient coordination among gov-

ernment agencies led to significant shortcomings in relief efforts, exacerbating the suffering of affected communities.

2. Need for Improved Coordination and Communication: Ineffective coordination and communication among government agencies, humanitarian organizations, and relief efforts hampered the responses to disasters such as Typhoon Haiyan in the Philippines and the Beirut explosion in Lebanon. These failures highlight the critical need for improved coordination mechanisms, clear communication channels, and collaboration among diverse stakeholders in disaster response.

3. Enhanced Disaster Preparedness and Resilience: The failures in response efforts underscore the importance of enhanced disaster preparedness and resilience-building measures. Investing in infrastructure, strengthening healthcare systems, and prioritizing risk governance can help mitigate the impact of disasters and improve response capabilities.

4. Addressing Systemic Weaknesses: The responses to disasters like the Beirut explosion in Lebanon revealed systemic weaknesses in disaster management infrastructure and emergency response capabilities. Addressing these deficiencies requires comprehensive reforms, institutional capacity-building, and a commitment to organizational learning and adaptability.

Overall, the successful and failed disaster response case studies highlight the importance of proactive planning, effective leadership, coordination, and resilience-building in mitigating the impact of disasters and saving lives. Learning from both successes and failures is essential for improving disaster preparedness, response capabilities, and building more resilient communities and systems in the face of future emergencies.

9

Disaster Recovery

Recovery constitutes a vital segment of emergency management, encompassing prevention, preparedness, and response alongside broader considerations such as built, environmental, and economic facets, as well as social well-being [396]. It presents an opportunity to elevate these dimensions beyond pre-disaster conditions by enhancing social and natural environments, infrastructure, and economies, thereby fostering a more resilient community.

Emphasizing a community-centric approach to recovery is crucial. Disasters can profoundly disrupt people's lives and livelihoods, and aiding communities in their recovery can prove intricate and multifaceted. Each community possesses its own unique history, values, and experiences, thereby presenting distinct challenges that must be addressed [396].

Disaster recovery refers to the process of restoring normalcy and functionality in the aftermath of a disaster. It encompasses a range of activities aimed at rebuilding infrastructure, restoring essential services, and assisting affected individuals and communities in recovering from the impact of the disaster. Disaster recovery efforts typically begin once the immediate threat has passed and focus on long-term rehabilitation and reconstruction.

The key components of disaster recovery include:

1. Assessment and Planning: The first step in disaster recovery is to conduct a comprehensive assessment of the damage and needs of affected areas. This assessment helps identify priorities and formulate a recovery plan tailored to the specific circumstances of the disaster. Planning involves determining resource require-

ments, setting objectives, and establishing timelines for recovery activities.

2. Infrastructure Restoration: Disaster recovery involves repairing or rebuilding critical infrastructure such as roads, bridges, utilities, and communication networks that may have been damaged or destroyed during the disaster. This infrastructure restoration is essential for restoring essential services and enabling the resumption of normal activities.

3. Community Assistance and Support: Disaster recovery efforts include providing assistance and support to affected individuals and communities to help them rebuild their lives. This may involve providing temporary shelter, food, water, medical care, and psychosocial support to those in need. Assistance programs aim to address immediate needs and promote the long-term recovery and well-being of affected populations.

4. Economic Recovery: Disasters often have significant economic impacts, disrupting businesses, livelihoods, and local economies. Disaster recovery efforts include measures to support economic recovery, such as providing financial assistance to businesses, facilitating the reopening of businesses, and promoting job creation and economic development in affected areas.

5. Environmental Restoration: Some disasters, such as wildfires or oil spills, can cause environmental damage that requires restoration efforts. Disaster recovery may involve environmental cleanup and restoration activities to mitigate the impact of pollution, restore ecosystems, and preserve natural resources.

6. Resilience Building: Disaster recovery provides an opportunity to build resilience and better prepare for future disasters. This may involve implementing measures to reduce vulnerability, such as improving building codes, strengthening infrastructure, enhancing early warning systems, and increasing community preparedness and awareness.

7. Long-Term Recovery and Reconstruction: Disaster recovery is a long-term process that extends beyond the immediate aftermath of the disaster. It may take months or even years to fully recover and rebuild affected areas. Long-term recovery efforts focus on addressing ongoing challenges, supporting sustainable development, and fostering resilience in the face of future disasters.

Disaster recovery is a complex and multifaceted process that requires coordination, collaboration, and sustained effort from government agencies, humanitarian organizations, communities, businesses, and individuals. By investing in disaster recovery and resilience-building measures, societies can mitigate the impact of disasters, save lives, and build stronger, more resilient communities capable of withstanding future challenges.

Key elements of successful emergency disaster recovery include the establishment of a risk assessment framework to evaluate the effectiveness of pre-disaster deployment, emergency response, and post-disaster recovery capabilities [216]. Nonprofit organizations and non-governmental organizations (NGOs) play pivotal roles in disaster management, providing essential services for response and recovery, as recognized by agencies like FEMA [397].

Moreover, local health departments and public health administrations are integral in disaster recovery planning and implementation, focusing on building resilience and reducing vulnerabilities in communities [150]. Collaboration and coordination among various stakeholders, including governmental and international organizations, are crucial for effective disaster recovery [398, 399]. Lessons learned from past disasters highlight the significance of partnership and interorganizational cooperation in emergency response and recovery efforts [400].

Communities, governments, and recovery agencies can utilize the Australian National Principles for Disaster Recovery as an exemplar to steer our endeavours, methodologies, planning, and decision-making processes. Effective recovery hinges upon a thorough comprehension of the community context, recognizing that each locality possesses its own unique history, values, and social dynamics.

In this regard, recovery efforts should [396]:

- Acknowledge and leverage existing strengths and capacities within the community, drawing upon past experiences and resilience.

- Demonstrate an understanding of the risks and stressors confronting the community, addressing them in a proactive and responsive manner.

- Embrace and respect the cultural diversity present within the community, ensuring that recovery efforts are inclusive and sensitive to varying cultural norms and practices.

- Provide support and assistance to those who may be particularly vulnerable or marginalized within the community, prioritizing their needs and well-being.

- Acknowledge the intrinsic connection between the environment and the community's recovery process, recognizing the importance of environmental factors in fostering resilience and restoration.

- Be recognized as a prolonged and sustained endeavour, tailored to the specific needs and timelines of the community, and characterized by ongoing support and collaboration.

- Acknowledge that the impacts of the disaster may extend beyond the immediate geographical boundaries where the event occurred, necessitating a comprehensive and holistic approach to recovery that considers broader socio-economic and environmental factors.

Effective recovery efforts are attuned to the intricate and ever-changing dynamics inherent in both emergencies and the affected community.

In this context, recovery initiatives should acknowledge the following:

- Disasters generate a multitude of effects and consequences that necessitate diverse and adaptable approaches. Moreover, they can leave lasting legacies that shape the trajectory of recovery efforts. Initial information regarding the impacts of disasters is often limited and subject to change as the situation evolves over time.

- The needs, preferences, and expectations of affected individuals and communities are diverse and can evolve rapidly in response to unfolding circumstances. Responsive and flexible action is paramount to address immediate needs and effectively support recovery efforts.

- The knowledge and values embedded within the affected community may challenge the assumptions and perspectives of external stakeholders, highlighting the importance of engaging with local expertise and perspectives.

- Conflicting knowledge, values, and priorities among individuals, the community, and various organizations involved in the recovery process may give rise to tensions and complexities that require careful navigation.

- Emergencies create stressful environments wherein emotions such as grief and blame may influence the perceptions and behaviours of those involved in the recovery process.

- Over time, providing appropriate support to individuals and communities, both from within and outside, can foster hope and facilitate individual and collective growth amidst the challenges of recovery.

Successful recovery revolves around community-centric, responsive, and adaptable approaches, actively involving and supporting communities in their progression forward. In achieving this, recovery endeavours should [396]:

- Facilitate and empower individuals, families, and communities to actively engage in their own recovery journeys.
- Acknowledge that varying levels of support may be necessary for individuals and the community at different stages of the recovery process.
- Be guided by the priorities outlined by the community itself, respecting their unique needs and preferences.
- Utilize pre-existing community assets, including local knowledge, inherent strengths, and resilience, as key channels for recovery efforts.
- Foster collaborative partnerships between the community and stakeholders involved in the recovery process, enhancing synergy and effectiveness.
- Recognize the emergence of new community leaders during and post-disaster, who may not hold formal positions of authority but possess valuable insights and influence.
- Acknowledge that different communities may opt for diverse paths towards recovery, respecting their autonomy and decision-making processes.

Successful recovery necessitates a strategic, collaborative, and adaptable approach, forged through close coordination between the community and partner agencies, while continuously assessing impacts and needs. In achieving this, recovery initiatives should [396]:

- Establish clearly defined and mutually agreed-upon goals rooted in desired outcomes, fostering a shared vision among stakeholders.

- Demonstrate flexibility to accommodate shifts in community needs or stakeholder expectations, ensuring responsiveness to evolving circumstances.
- Rely on experienced and knowledgeable leadership, characterized by authenticity, skilfulness, and genuine engagement with the community.
- Progress at a pace aligned with the community's preferences, fostering collaboration and harmonization of diverse interests and timelines.
- Reflect comprehensive community planning and data collection efforts conducted before, during, and after the disaster, facilitating informed decision-making.
- Implement robust decision-making frameworks and transparent governance structures accessible to the community, promoting accountability and inclusivity.
- Exhibit a thorough understanding of the roles, responsibilities, and authorities of involved organizations, fostering seamless coordination across agencies to minimize service disruptions.
- Integrate with response operations as part of an overarching emergency management approach, contributing to both immediate relief efforts and long-term prevention and preparedness strategies.
- Embrace inclusivity by leveraging and nurturing relationships established before, during, and after the emergency, ensuring that all voices are heard and considered in the recovery process.

Successful recovery hinges on the establishment of robust communication channels between the affected community and its collaborators. To this end, recovery efforts should [396]:

- Emphasize the importance of two-way communication, fostering an environment where community input and feedback are actively encouraged and valued.
- Ensure that information is easily accessible to individuals in various circumstances, catering to diverse communication needs, and disseminated through a multitude of communication platforms and networks.

- Establish mechanisms for streamlined and harmonized communication among all stakeholders, including service providers, organizations, individuals, and the community at large.

- Prioritize the delivery of communication that is relevant, timely, clear, accurate, targeted, credible, and consistent, enhancing its efficacy and impact.

- Identify trusted sources of information and reinforce key recovery messages to instil greater confidence and receptivity within the community.

Successful recovery initiatives prioritize the identification, cultivation, and augmentation of individual, community, and organizational capacity and resilience. In line with this, recovery efforts should [396]:

- Conduct comprehensive assessments of capability and capacity requirements throughout all stages of a disaster, including before, during, and after the event.

- Foster the development of self-reliance, preparedness, and disaster mitigation strategies within the community.

- Swiftly identify and leverage community skills, strengths, and resources to bolster recovery efforts.

- Cultivate networks and partnerships aimed at enhancing capacity, capability, and resilience within the community.

- Facilitate opportunities for the sharing, transfer, and development of knowledge, skills, and training among community members.

- Acknowledge that resources may be sourced from a variety of partners and community networks.

- Recognize the potential strain on existing resources and actively seek additional support when necessary.

- Understand that supplementary resources may be available for a limited duration and address sustainability concerns accordingly.

- Recognize the appropriate timing and methodology for scaling back involvement while continuing to support individuals and the community in achieving greater self-sufficiency when they are prepared.

- Implement thorough evaluation processes to derive insights and lessons for future disaster response efforts and to enhance overall resilience.

This Australian National Principles for Disaster Recovery underscore the significance of disaster recovery as an integral component of emergency management, encompassing prevention, preparedness, and response. They emphasize the importance of planning for recovery alongside mitigation actions, often initiated during the recovery phase. Furthermore, they highlight how recovery efforts encompass various elements such as built, environmental, and economic factors, along with individual and social well-being. Recovery is seen as an opportunity to enhance these aspects, contributing to the overall resilience of the community.

The principles outlined in the Australian National Principles for Disaster Recovery serve as guidelines to steer recovery efforts, offering a structured approach to planning, decision-making, and implementation. They underscore the need to understand the unique context of each community, including its history, values, and dynamics. Additionally, they stress the importance of recognizing the complexity inherent in both emergencies and the affected community, requiring responsiveness and flexibility in recovery approaches.

Furthermore, the principles advocate for community-led approaches, emphasizing active participation, prioritization of community needs, and leveraging local assets and strengths. They also highlight the importance of coordination among various stakeholders and agencies involved in the recovery process, with a focus on shared goals, transparent governance, and inclusive decision-making.

Effective communication emerges as a critical element of successful recovery, emphasizing two-way communication, accessibility of information, consistency, and credibility. Lastly, the principles underscore the importance of capacity building and resilience at the individual, community, and organizational levels, emphasizing preparedness, resource mobilization, and sustainability in recovery efforts.

Successful disaster recovery efforts often involve citizen participation in planning, strong local leadership, and the establishment of clear recovery targets [401]. It is essential to consider the holistic nature of recovery, which goes beyond physical restoration to encompass social, economic, and environmental aspects [402]. By integrating health promotion, sustainable development goals, and intersectoral coordination, disaster recovery can contribute to building back "healthier" and more resilient communities [403].

Short-Term and Long-Term Recovery Processes

Short-term and long-term recovery processes are essential components of disaster management, aiming to address immediate needs and facilitate the restoration and rebuilding of communities affected by disasters over time.

Short-Term Recovery: Short-term recovery focuses on addressing immediate needs and stabilizing the situation in the aftermath of a disaster. This phase typically begins immediately after the disaster strikes and extends for several weeks or months, depending on the severity of the event. Key aspects of short-term recovery include:

1. Emergency Response: This involves search and rescue operations, medical assistance, evacuation of affected individuals, and the provision of temporary shelter, food, and water to survivors. The primary goal is to save lives and ensure the safety and well-being of affected populations.

2. Assessment of Damage: Assessments are conducted to evaluate the extent of damage to infrastructure, buildings, utilities, and other essential facilities. These assessments help prioritize recovery efforts and allocate resources effectively.

3. Immediate Relief: Short-term recovery efforts focus on providing immediate relief to affected communities, including the distribution of emergency supplies, medical care, and psychological support to survivors. This phase also involves the establishment of emergency shelters and temporary housing for displaced individuals.

4. Restoration of Basic Services: Efforts are made to restore essential services such as electricity, water supply, communication networks, and transportation infrastructure to facilitate the recovery process and improve living conditions for survivors.

5. Community Engagement: Short-term recovery efforts emphasize community engagement and participation, involving affected individuals and local stakeholders in decision-making processes and resource allocation to ensure that

recovery efforts are responsive to community needs.

Short-term recovery in the aftermath of a disaster is a critical phase that involves various key aspects. Emergency response is paramount, focusing on saving lives through search and rescue operations, medical aid, and providing temporary shelter, food, and water [404]. Assessing the damage helps in prioritizing recovery efforts efficiently [404]. Immediate relief efforts include distributing emergency supplies, medical care, and psychological support to survivors, along with setting up emergency shelters and temporary housing [404]. Restoring basic services like electricity, water, and transportation is crucial for improving living conditions [404]. Community engagement plays a vital role, ensuring that recovery efforts are community-responsive by involving affected individuals and local stakeholders in decision-making processes [404].

Studies emphasize the importance of risk reduction strategies to protect disaster responders from physical and mental health hazards during relief and recovery operations [404]. Engaging nursing students in volunteer relief activities can provide valuable expertise to support disaster-affected populations [404]. Non-governmental organizations (NGOs) are instrumental in providing immediate relief resources and long-term recovery support to communities post-disaster [404]. Wireless communication technologies are essential for coordinating rescue and relief activities, assessing damage, and facilitating recovery efforts [404].

In disaster recovery planning, community engagement is crucial for empowering disaster survivors and ensuring inclusivity and accessibility in all phases of disaster management [404]. Scholars highlight the need for distributive justice in disaster recovery processes, focusing on grassroots efforts and challenging neoliberal practices [404]. Engaging disaster survivors in planning and design stages enhances community empowerment and resilience [404].

Figure 49: Milwaukee, WI, September 23, 2010 -- Jessica Smith and her daughter Ameria meet with FEMA application specialist Maria Serbia in a Disaster Recovery Centerin Milwaukee. Disaster Recovery Centers provide an opportunity for applicants to meet with FEMA and SGA staffers who can help them. Ed Edahl, Public domain, via Wikimedia Commons.

Short-term recovery is a critical phase in the aftermath of a disaster, focusing on immediate needs and stabilization efforts to mitigate the impact of the event on affected communities. Typically initiated immediately after the disaster strikes, this phase extends over several weeks or months, depending on the severity and scale of the event. Several key aspects characterize short-term recovery, each playing a crucial role in addressing the immediate challenges faced by survivors and communities.

First and foremost, emergency response efforts take precedence during the short-term recovery phase. This involves swift and coordinated actions such as search and rescue operations, medical assistance, and evacuation procedures to save lives and ensure the safety and well-being of affected populations. Emergency responders, including first responders, medical personnel, and volunteers, work tirelessly to reach survivors, provide medical care, and evacuate individuals from danger zones.

Concurrently, assessments are conducted to evaluate the extent of damage caused by the disaster. These assessments cover various aspects, including damage to infrastructure, buildings, utilities, and other essential facilities. By assessing the scope and severity of damage, emergency management authorities can prioritize recovery efforts and allocate resources effectively to address the most urgent needs of affected communities.

Immediate relief efforts are another crucial component of short-term recovery. These efforts focus on providing essential supplies, including food, water, shelter, and medical assistance, to survivors who have been displaced or adversely impacted by the disaster. Emergency shelters and temporary housing facilities are established to accommodate displaced individuals and families, ensuring their safety and basic needs are met during this critical period.

Furthermore, short-term recovery initiatives aim to restore basic services that may have been disrupted or damaged during the disaster. This includes efforts to restore electricity, water supply, communication networks, and transportation infrastructure to facilitate the recovery process and improve living conditions for survivors. Restoring essential services is essential for ensuring the well-being and resilience of affected communities as they begin to rebuild and recover.

Community engagement is emphasized throughout the short-term recovery phase, with a focus on involving affected individuals and local stakeholders in decision-making processes and resource allocation. By engaging communities directly, recovery efforts can be tailored to meet the specific needs and priorities of each community, ensuring that assistance and support are provided where they are most needed. Community participation fosters ownership and resilience, empowering communities to actively contribute to their own recovery efforts.

On this basis, a broad short term recovery procedure should include:

I. Emergency Response:

A. Swift and coordinated actions by emergency responders, including:

1. Search and rescue operations to locate and extract survivors.

2. Provision of medical assistance to treat injuries and address immediate health concerns.

3. Implementation of evacuation procedures to move individuals away from danger zones.

4. Deployment of first responders, medical personnel, and volunteers to affected areas.

II. Damage Assessment:

A. Conduct assessments to evaluate the extent of damage to:

1. Infrastructure, including roads, bridges, and public facilities.

2. Buildings, both residential and commercial.

3. Utilities, such as water supply, electricity, and telecommunications.

B. Assessments inform prioritization of recovery efforts and resource allocation.

III. Immediate Relief Efforts:

A. Provide essential supplies to survivors, including:

1. Food and water to address immediate hunger and thirst.

2. Shelter and temporary housing for displaced individuals and families.

3. Medical assistance and psychological support for those affected by the disaster.

B. Establish emergency shelters and distribution centres for relief supplies.

IV. Restoration of Basic Services:

A. Restore essential services disrupted by the disaster, including:

1. Electricity to power homes, businesses, and critical infrastructure.

2. Water supply for drinking, sanitation, and hygiene purposes.

3. Communication networks to facilitate information dissemination and coordination.

4. Transportation infrastructure to enable movement of goods and people.

B. Prioritize restoration efforts based on critical needs and community impact.

V. Community Engagement:

A. Involve affected individuals and local stakeholders in decision-making processes.

B. Tailor recovery efforts to meet specific needs and priorities of each community.

C. Empower communities to actively participate in their own recovery efforts.

D. Foster ownership and resilience through community participation and engagement.

Overall, a well-coordinated approach to short-term recovery involves a combination of emergency response, damage assessment, immediate relief efforts, restoration of basic services, and community engagement. By addressing immediate needs and involving affected communities in the recovery process, short-term recovery efforts lay the foundation for long-term resilience and recovery.

In the short-term recovery procedure outlined above, various individuals play critical roles in ensuring the effective implementation of each phase. Here's a detailed breakdown of the roles of different people, including managers and coordinators:

I. Emergency Response:

A. Managers and Coordinators:

1. Emergency Managers: Oversee and coordinate all aspects of the emergency response, including resource allocation, communication, and decision-making.

2. Incident Commanders: Assume leadership roles at the scene of the disaster, directing response efforts and managing personnel.

3. Operations Managers: Coordinate specific response activities, such as search and rescue operations, medical triage, and evacuation procedures.

4. Logistics Coordinators: Manage the procurement, transportation, and distribution of essential resources and supplies to support response operations.

5. Communication Officers: Ensure effective communication between response teams, stakeholders, and the public, disseminating critical information and updates.

II. Damage Assessment:

A. Managers and Coordinators:

1. Assessment Team Leaders: Oversee assessment teams tasked with evaluating damage to infrastructure, buildings, and utilities.

2. Data Analysts: Analyse assessment data to identify trends, prioritize needs, and inform decision-making regarding resource allocation.

3. Liaison Officers: Coordinate with local authorities, government agencies, and external organizations to facilitate access for assessment teams and share information.

III. Immediate Relief Efforts:

A. Managers and Coordinators:

1. Relief Operations Managers: Coordinate the delivery of essential supplies, including food, water, shelter, and medical assistance, to affected populations.

2. Shelter Managers: Oversee the establishment and management of emergency shelters and distribution centres for relief supplies.

3. Medical Coordinators: Coordinate medical assistance and psychological support services for survivors, ensuring timely and appropriate care.

4. Volunteer Coordinators: Recruit, train, and deploy volunteers to support relief efforts, coordinating their activities and ensuring their safety.

IV. Restoration of Basic Services:

A. Managers and Coordinators:

1. Infrastructure Managers: Coordinate efforts to restore essential services such as electricity, water supply, communication networks, and transportation infrastructure.

2. Utilities Coordinators: Collaborate with utility providers and repair crews to prioritize and expedite repairs to critical infrastructure.

3. Technical Experts: Provide specialized knowledge and expertise in engineering, construction, and utility management to support restoration efforts.

V. Community Engagement:

A. Managers and Coordinators:

1. Community Liaisons: Serve as a bridge between response agencies and affected communities, facilitating communication, collaboration, and engagement.

2. Community Outreach Coordinators: Organize community meetings, focus groups, and information sessions to gather input, address concerns, and promote participation in recovery efforts.

3. Cultural Competency Trainers: Provide training and guidance to response personnel on cultural sensitivity and diversity awareness to ensure respectful and inclusive engagement with communities.

Effective coordination and leadership from managers and coordinators are essential for navigating the complexities of short-term recovery and ensuring that response efforts are timely, efficient, and responsive to the needs of affected communities.

Long-Term Recovery: Long-term recovery focuses on rebuilding and revitalizing communities affected by disasters, addressing the underlying vulnerabilities and promoting resilience to future hazards. This phase typically extends for several years and involves comprehensive planning and implementation strategies. Key aspects of long-term recovery include:

1. Reconstruction and Rehabilitation: Long-term recovery efforts focus on rebuilding damaged infrastructure, homes, businesses, and public facilities to restore communities to pre-disaster conditions or better. This may involve construction projects, housing programs, and infrastructure upgrades to enhance resilience.

2. Economic Recovery: Efforts are made to revitalize the local economy, including supporting small businesses, creating job opportunities, and attracting investment to stimulate economic growth and recovery. Economic development programs aim to build a more resilient economy that can withstand future shocks.

3. Psychosocial Support: Long-term recovery includes ongoing psychosocial support and mental health services for survivors, addressing trauma, grief, and emotional distress caused by the disaster. Counselling, support groups, and community resilience programs help individuals and communities cope with long-term effects.

4. Risk Reduction and Mitigation: Long-term recovery efforts prioritize risk re-

duction and mitigation strategies to minimize the impact of future disasters. This may involve land-use planning, zoning regulations, infrastructure improvements, and public awareness campaigns to build resilience and reduce vulnerabilities.

5. Capacity Building and Institutional Strengthening: Long-term recovery aims to strengthen local capacities and institutions to better prepare for and respond to future disasters. Training programs, education initiatives, and community empowerment activities enhance resilience and promote sustainable development.

Short-term and long-term recovery processes complement each other and form integral parts of the disaster management cycle, aiming to facilitate the holistic and sustainable recovery of communities affected by disasters.

Reconstruction and Rehabilitation represents a crucial phase in the long-term recovery process, focused on restoring communities to their pre-disaster condition or even elevating their resilience beyond previous levels. This phase unfolds following the initial emergency response and short-term recovery initiatives, spanning an extended period to address the extensive devastation left in the wake of the disaster .

During this phase, significant attention is directed towards rebuilding the infrastructure that has sustained severe damage. Efforts are channelled into repairing or reconstructing vital elements such as roads, bridges, schools, hospitals, utilities, and other essential facilities essential for community functioning [405]. Reconstruction projects vary widely in scale and complexity, ranging from minor repairs to comprehensive rebuilding endeavours.

Another critical aspect of long-term recovery involves the restoration of residential and commercial properties that have been impacted by the disaster. This entails repairing structural damages, ensuring safety compliance, and providing financial assistance or incentives to homeowners and businesses for reconstruction efforts. Housing programs are often implemented to support displaced individuals and families in securing suitable accommodation or rebuilding their homes.

Long-term recovery initiatives often include housing programs that offer financial aid and support for home reconstruction [406]. The ultimate objective of reconstruction and rehabilitation efforts is to rebuild communities in a resilient and sustainable manner, equipping them with the necessary tools to effectively withstand future disasters [407].

By integrating "build-back-better" principles into reconstruction projects, communities can enhance their resilience and sustainability [408, 409].

In addition to restoring physical infrastructure and properties, long-term recovery endeavours strive to enhance community resilience against future disasters. This entails integrating disaster-resistant design principles into reconstruction projects, utilizing durable materials, implementing effective land-use planning strategies, and reinforcing building codes and regulations. Infrastructure upgrades are also undertaken to mitigate the impact of potential hazards and bolster community resilience.

The reconstruction and rehabilitation phase also entail initiating various construction projects to address diverse community needs. These projects encompass the construction of new infrastructure to replace damaged or outdated facilities, including schools, hospitals, water treatment plants, and transportation networks. Additionally, efforts focus on constructing affordable housing, community centres, and other facilities to support the long-term recovery and revitalization of the community.

Furthermore, long-term recovery often involves the implementation of housing programs designed to assist individuals and families affected by the disaster. These programs may offer financial aid, grants, or low-interest loans to support home reconstruction or repair efforts. Housing initiatives may also encompass strategies to tackle homelessness, provide affordable housing options, and promote sustainable development practices.

Ultimately, the overarching goal of reconstruction and rehabilitation efforts during the long-term recovery phase is to rebuild communities in a resilient and sustainable manner. By fostering resilience and sustainability, these initiatives aim to equip communities with the necessary tools and infrastructure to withstand future disasters effectively and thrive in the face of adversity.

The following examples illustrate how reconstruction and rehabilitation efforts play a crucial role in the long-term recovery process, aiming to restore communities to their pre-disaster state while enhancing their resilience against future hazards. Through a combination of infrastructure rebuilding, housing programs, and community resilience initiatives, these endeavours contribute to the sustainable recovery and revitalization of affected areas.

1. Reconstruction of Infrastructure: After Hurricane Katrina devastated New Orleans in 2005, extensive efforts were made to rebuild the city's infrastructure. This included repairing damaged roads, bridges, and levees, as well as renovating schools, hospitals, and utilities. The reconstruction projects varied in scale, with

some involving minor repairs while others required comprehensive rebuilding to ensure the city's functionality and resilience against future disasters.

2. Restoration of Residential and Commercial Properties: Following the earthquake in Haiti in 2010, numerous residential and commercial properties were destroyed or severely damaged. International organizations and local authorities implemented housing programs to assist affected individuals and families in rebuilding their homes and businesses. Financial aid, grants, and low-interest loans were provided to support reconstruction efforts and help residents secure suitable accommodation.

3. Enhancing Community Resilience: In the aftermath of the 2011 Tohoku earthquake and tsunami in Japan, efforts were made to enhance community resilience against future disasters. Reconstruction projects integrated disaster-resistant design principles, such as building seawalls and elevated structures to mitigate the impact of tsunamis. Additionally, infrastructure upgrades were undertaken to improve warning systems, evacuation routes, and emergency response capabilities.

4. Construction of New Infrastructure: After the 2017 Hurricane Maria struck Puerto Rico, significant construction projects were initiated to replace damaged or outdated infrastructure. This included the construction of new schools, hospitals, water treatment plants, and transportation networks to meet the evolving needs of the affected communities. Efforts also focused on building affordable housing and community centres to support long-term recovery and revitalization.

5. Implementation of Housing Programs: In the aftermath of the 2019 wildfires in Australia, housing programs were implemented to assist individuals and families who lost their homes. Financial aid, grants, and government assistance programs were offered to support the reconstruction or repair of residential properties. Additionally, initiatives were launched to address homelessness, provide temporary accommodation, and promote sustainable development practices to prevent future disasters.

Economic recovery refers to the process of revitalizing and strengthening the local economy in the aftermath of a disaster or economic crisis. This phase focuses on implementing various strategies and initiatives aimed at restoring economic stability, creating job opportunities, and fostering sustainable growth within the affected community. Economic recovery includes:

1. Supporting Small Businesses: Small businesses often bear the brunt of disasters, facing significant disruptions to their operations and finances. Economic recovery efforts prioritize supporting these businesses by providing financial assistance, grants, or loans to help them recover and resume their operations. This support may include access to capital, technical assistance, and business counselling to rebuild damaged infrastructure, replenish inventory, and rehire employees.

2. Creating Job Opportunities: Job creation is a key component of economic recovery, as unemployment rates may spike following a disaster. Efforts are made to generate employment opportunities through public works projects, infrastructure development, and workforce training programs. By creating jobs, individuals are empowered to contribute to the recovery process while earning income to support themselves and their families.

3. Attracting Investment: Economic recovery initiatives aim to attract investment from both public and private sectors to stimulate economic growth and recovery. This may involve offering incentives such as tax breaks, grants, or subsidies to attract businesses and investors to the area. Investments in key sectors such as tourism, manufacturing, agriculture, and technology can contribute to job creation, infrastructure development, and overall economic revitalization.

4. Stimulating Economic Growth: Economic development programs are designed to foster sustainable growth and resilience within the local economy. This includes promoting entrepreneurship, innovation, and diversification of industries to reduce dependency on a single sector. By fostering a vibrant and diverse economic ecosystem, communities can better withstand future shocks and adapt to changing economic conditions.

Economic recovery efforts are aimed at building a more resilient and prosperous economy that can withstand future disasters and contribute to the long-term sustainability and well-being of the community. By supporting small businesses, creating job opportunities, attracting investment, and stimulating economic growth, communities can recover from adversity and thrive in the face of challenges.

Small businesses are particularly vulnerable to the impacts of disasters, often experiencing significant disruptions to their operations and finances. To aid in their recovery, economic efforts focus on providing financial assistance, grants, or loans to help these businesses resume their activities. This support encompasses access to capital, technical assistance, and business counselling to facilitate the rebuilding of infrastructure, restocking of inventory, and rehiring of employees.

Research indicates that small businesses face challenges in recovering from disasters due to their size, with studies highlighting that small size is a major source of vulnerability to negative outcomes [410]. Additionally, the availability of financial assistance, such as federal disaster aid, plays a crucial role in the survival and success of small family-owned businesses [411]. However, simply obtaining a loan or financial assistance post-disaster may not always lead to improved recovery outcomes and can potentially increase debt burdens [412].

Furthermore, the management strategies employed by small businesses significantly impact their survival and recovery post-disaster [413]. Factors such as business preparedness, including the purchase of business insurance and the development of continuity plans, are crucial for enhancing the resilience of small to medium-sized enterprises [414]. Additionally, the study of determinants of family business resilience post-disaster emphasizes the role of federal disaster assistance in contributing to firm-owning resilience [415].

Efforts to generate employment opportunities are essential for economic revitalization. Small and medium enterprises (SMEs) are often highlighted as significant contributors to job creation, with programs promoting SMEs under the premise that they are key in generating employment [416]. Additionally, studies have shown that green job opportunities, particularly in sectors like tourism, can play a vital role in sustainable recovery plans, offering new avenues for job creation while promoting environmental sustainability [417, 418].

Job creation is a dynamic process influenced by various factors such as firm size, industry dynamics, and economic policies. Research has indicated that younger firms tend to create and destroy more jobs, with job creation and destruction rates varying across different industries [419]. Moreover, the cyclical behaviour of job creation and destruction has been studied extensively, shedding light on the microeconomic evidence and macroeconomic implications of these processes [420].

Attracting investment is a crucial strategy for economic recovery, involving initiatives to entice both public and private sector investments to drive economic growth. This can be achieved through various incentives such as tax breaks, grants, or subsidies to attract businesses and investors to a particular area. Investments in key sectors like tourism, manufacturing, agriculture, and technology play a significant role in fostering job creation, infrastructure development, and overall economic revitalization [421].

Foreign direct investment (FDI) plays a vital role in economic development, especially during times of crisis. It is noted that attracting foreign investment can help in transforming transition economies into market economies and provide additional resources during economic downturns [421]. Additionally, the evaluation of investment attractiveness is a multifaceted concept that considers economic, legal, political, technological, geographical, and infrastructural factors that enable investors to gain a competitive advantage [422].

In the post-COVID-19 era, there is a heightened emphasis on reducing risks in businesses and enhancing resilience. This underscores the importance of revitalizing sectors like infrastructure to accelerate economic recovery [423]. Furthermore, the Economic Recovery and Growth Plan (ERGP) is a strategic initiative aimed at restoring growth, investing in people, and building a globally competitive economy, which is essential for economic recovery [424].

Economic development programs are essential for stimulating economic growth by fostering sustainable growth and resilience within local economies. These programs aim to promote entrepreneurship, innovation, and diversification of industries to reduce dependency on a single sector. By cultivating a vibrant and diverse economic ecosystem, communities can enhance their ability to withstand future shocks and adapt to changing economic conditions [425, 426].

Psychosocial support serves as a fundamental pillar in the continuum of long-term recovery efforts following a disaster or traumatic event. It encompasses a variety of interventions designed to attend to the psychological and emotional well-being of survivors who may be grappling with trauma, grief, or emotional distress stemming from the disaster. Here's a breakdown of the primary components that constitute psychosocial support:

- Counselling: One key aspect involves offering professional counselling services to individuals and families impacted by the disaster. These services aim to assist them in navigating emotional challenges, processing their experiences, and developing effective coping mechanisms [427]. Counsellors provide a supportive and non-judgmental environment where survivors can freely express their feelings, thoughts, and concerns [428].

- Support Groups: Another integral component entails the formation of support groups, which unite individuals who have undergone similar traumatic events. These groups offer a platform for participants to share their experiences, extend mutual support, and glean insights from one another's coping strategies. By fostering a sense of belonging and understanding, support groups help mitigate feelings of isolation and facilitate healing through peer support.

- Community Resilience Programs: Additionally, community resilience programs target the enhancement of collective resilience within disaster-affected communities. These initiatives encompass a spectrum of community-wide activities, workshops, and initiatives aimed at fostering social cohesion, nurturing supportive networks, and bolstering community resources and capacities to effectively navigate adversity.

- Mental Health Services: Access to mental health services forms a crucial component in addressing the enduring psychological ramifications of a disaster. Mental health professionals, including psychologists, psychiatrists, and social workers, play pivotal roles in providing comprehensive assessment, diagnosis, and treatment for individuals grappling with mental health challenges such as post-traumatic stress disorder (PTSD), depression, anxiety, and other trauma-related conditions.

In disaster situations, the overtaxing of material and psychological resources during the extended recovery period can lead to the deterioration of support networks, highlighting the need for ongoing counselling and assistance [199]. Additionally, utilizing pastoral counselling and religious resources has been recommended for survivors to address their spiritual and emotional needs during and after a disaster [429, 430]. Social support, including counselling services, has been identified as a key factor in promoting well-being and reducing psychopathology following disaster exposure [431, 432].

Figure 50: FEMA counselling desk at the Disaster Recover Center. John Ficara, Public domain, via Wikimedia Commons.

Furthermore, the emotional distress experienced during a disaster, such as feelings of helplessness, anxiety, and fear, can have lasting adverse effects if not addressed through appropriate support services like counselling [433]. It is essential for disaster-affected communities to have access to trauma-informed counselling to envision healthier futures and facilitate post-disaster recovery planning [434]. Overall, counselling services play a vital role in supporting individuals and communities in processing their experiences, fostering resilience, and promoting psychological well-being in the aftermath of a disaster.

Support groups serve as vital resources for individuals grappling with the aftermath of traumatic events, offering a supportive environment where they can find understanding and connection with others who share similar experiences. Their role and significance includes:

Platform for Sharing Experiences: Within support groups, participants find a safe haven to openly express their thoughts, emotions, and experiences stemming from the trauma they've endured. This environment fosters a sense of validation and understanding as individuals relate to one another's journeys.

Mutual Support: Participants in support groups extend empathy, encouragement, and validation to one another, forming a network of emotional support. This shared understanding cultivates a sense of camaraderie and solidarity, empowering individuals as they navigate their healing process.

Insights into Coping Strategies: Through the exchange of coping strategies and insights, support group members gain valuable tools for managing the aftermath of trauma. Learning from others' experiences allows individuals to explore different approaches and identify what resonates most with their unique circumstances.

Mitigating Feelings of Isolation: Trauma often induces feelings of isolation, but support groups provide a sense of belonging and connection. Knowing they're not alone in their struggles offers profound comfort and validation to participants, alleviating the sense of isolation that often accompanies trauma.

Facilitating Healing through Peer Support: The supportive atmosphere within support groups fosters healing through peer support. By sharing experiences, receiving validation, and offering encouragement, participants contribute to each other's healing journeys, fostering hope and resilience in the process.

Support groups offer a powerful avenue for individuals to connect with others, share their burdens, and find solace within a community of understanding peers. Through empathy, understanding, and mutual support, these groups play a crucial role in guiding individuals through the complexities of trauma toward a path of healing and recovery.

Long-term recovery efforts place significant emphasis on risk reduction and mitigation strategies aimed at lessening the impact of potential future disasters. This strategic approach recognizes the importance of proactive measures in safeguarding communities and infrastructure against similar or even more severe events. Here's a closer look at the key components of risk reduction and mitigation:

Land-Use Planning and Zoning Regulations: One crucial aspect of risk reduction involves implementing effective land-use planning and zoning regulations. By carefully designating areas for development, preservation, and potential hazard zones, communities can minimize exposure to risks such as floods, landslides, and wildfires. Zoning regulations help ensure that new construction adheres to safety standards and considers potential hazards, thus reducing vulnerability over the long term.

Infrastructure Improvements: Long-term recovery efforts also prioritize infrastructure improvements aimed at enhancing resilience and reducing vulnerability to future disasters. This may include retrofitting bridges, roads, and buildings to withstand seismic activity or extreme weather events. Additionally, investments in flood control measures, such as levees and stormwater management systems, can help mitigate the impact of flooding and minimize damage to communities.

Public Awareness Campaigns: Educating the public about potential hazards and effective risk reduction strategies is an integral part of long-term recovery. Public awareness campaigns aim to increase community preparedness and resilience by providing information on emergency procedures, evacuation routes, and disaster mitigation techniques. By empowering individuals with knowledge and resources, communities can better anticipate and respond to potential threats, ultimately reducing the overall risk of future disasters.

Building Resilience and Reducing Vulnerabilities: Overall, the goal of risk reduction and mitigation efforts is to build resilience and reduce vulnerabilities within communities. This involves not only addressing existing vulnerabilities but also proactively planning for future risks. By integrating risk reduction measures into community planning and development processes, communities can become more resilient to a wide range of hazards, ensuring their long-term sustainability and well-being.

Community resilience programs are comprehensive initiatives designed to strengthen the collective resilience of communities affected by disasters. These programs recognize that resilience is not just an individual trait but also a community-wide attribute that can be cultivated through concerted efforts. The key elements of community resilience programs include:

- Activities and Workshops: Community resilience programs encompass a variety of activities and workshops tailored to address the specific needs and challenges faced by disaster-affected communities. These activities may include training sessions, skill-building workshops, community meetings, and awareness campaigns focused on disaster preparedness, response, and recovery. By providing opportunities for learning and skill development, these programs empower community members to actively engage in resilience-building efforts.

- Fostering Social Cohesion: One of the primary goals of community resilience programs is to foster social cohesion within disaster-affected communities. Social cohesion refers to the sense of solidarity, trust, and mutual support among community members, which is essential for effectively responding to and recovering from disasters. Community resilience programs aim to strengthen social bonds by facilitating interactions, fostering relationships, and promoting a sense of belonging and connectedness among residents.

- Nurturing Supportive Networks: Building supportive networks is another key aspect of community resilience programs. These networks may include formal structures such as community organizations, neighbourhood associations, and volunteer groups, as well as informal support systems among friends, family members, and neighbours. Community resilience programs facilitate the establishment of these networks, providing opportunities for collaboration, cooperation, and mutual assistance among community members.

- Bolstering Community Resources: Community resilience programs work to bolster the resources and capacities available within disaster-affected communities. This may involve identifying and mobilizing local assets, such as human capital, physical infrastructure, natural resources, and cultural assets, to support resilience-building efforts. By leveraging existing resources and capacities, communities can enhance their ability to withstand and recover from disasters more effectively.

- Capacity Building: Capacity building is a central component of community resilience programs, focusing on enhancing the knowledge, skills, and capabilities of community members to address disaster-related challenges. This may include providing training in disaster preparedness and response, facilitating community-based planning and decision-making processes, and promoting sustainable practices that contribute to resilience. By building the capacity of individuals and organizations within the community, these programs empower communities to take proactive measures to reduce their vulnerability to disasters.

Figure 51: USAID Disaster Management Program. USAID Indonesia, Public domain, via Wikimedia Commons.

Capacity building and institutional strengthening represent integral components of long-term recovery efforts aimed at enhancing the ability of communities to prepare for and respond to future disasters effectively. This strategic approach recognizes the importance of investing in local capacities and institutions to build resilience and foster sustainable development. Here's a detailed explanation of the key elements involved:

Training Programs: Long-term recovery initiatives often include training programs designed to equip individuals and communities with the knowledge, skills, and resources necessary to mitigate risks and respond to emergencies. These programs may encompass various aspects of disaster preparedness, including first aid training, search and rescue techniques, emergency communication protocols, and community-based disaster management strategies. By providing training opportunities, communities can enhance their readiness and response capabilities, ultimately reducing the overall impact of disasters.

Education Initiatives: Education plays a vital role in promoting disaster resilience and fostering a culture of preparedness within communities. Long-term recovery efforts may include education initiatives aimed at raising awareness about potential hazards, disaster risk reduction strategies, and the importance of emergency preparedness. These initiatives may target diverse audiences, including school children, community members, local leaders, and vulnerable populations, to ensure widespread understanding and engagement in disaster resilience efforts.

Community Empowerment Activities: Empowering communities to take an active role in their own resilience-building process is fundamental to long-term recovery. Community empowerment activities may involve participatory decision-making processes, community-based planning and resource allocation, and the establishment of local emergency response teams or committees. By involving community members in decision-making and action, these activities promote ownership, resilience, and self-reliance, enabling communities to better withstand and recover from disasters.

Institutional Strengthening: In addition to building community capacities, long-term recovery efforts focus on strengthening local institutions and governance structures responsible for disaster management and response. This may involve improving coordination mechanisms among government agencies, enhancing disaster risk governance frameworks, and bolstering the capacity of local emergency management agencies. By investing in institutional strengthening, communities can ensure more efficient and effective responses to future disasters, as well as greater coordination and collaboration among stakeholders.

Promotion of Sustainable Development: Long-term recovery efforts are aligned with broader goals of sustainable development, emphasizing the importance of integrating disaster risk reduction into development planning and decision-making processes. By promoting sustainable development practices, such as eco-friendly infrastructure, green building standards, and natural resource conservation, communities can reduce their vulnerability to disasters while simultaneously advancing economic, social, and environmental sustainability.

Capacity building and institutional strengthening are essential components of long-term recovery efforts, enabling communities to build resilience, enhance preparedness, and foster sustainable development in the face of future disasters. By investing in training programs, education initiatives, community empowerment activities, and institutional strengthening measures, communities can better adapt to changing conditions and emerge stronger and more resilient in the aftermath of disasters.

The following highlights the human resource requirements for each aspect of long-term recovery:

- **Reconstruction and Rehabilitation:**
  - Civil engineers and architects for planning and designing reconstruction projects.
  - Construction workers, including carpenters, masons, electricians, and plumbers, for executing construction projects.
  - Project managers to oversee the progress of reconstruction efforts and ensure adherence to timelines and budgets.
  - Urban planners to assist in urban redevelopment and land-use planning initiatives.
  - Environmental specialists to assess environmental impacts and ensure compliance with regulations during reconstruction activities.
  - Community engagement specialists to involve local residents in decision-making processes and address their concerns.
- **Economic Recovery:**
  - Economic development specialists to devise strategies for revitalizing the local economy and attracting investment.
  - Small business advisors to provide guidance and support to entrepreneurs and small business owners.
  - Workforce development professionals to create job training programs and connect job seekers with employment opportunities.
  - Financial analysts to assess the economic impact of the disaster and identify opportunities for recovery.
  - Marketing and tourism experts to promote local businesses and attract visitors to the area.
  - Government officials and policymakers to implement supportive policies and regulations for economic recovery efforts.

- **Psychosocial Support:**
    - Clinical psychologists and counsellors to provide individual and group therapy sessions for survivors.
    - Support group facilitators to organize and lead support group meetings.
    - Social workers to connect survivors with social services and resources.
    - Community outreach workers to raise awareness about available psychosocial support services and programs.
    - Trained volunteers to provide emotional support and assistance to survivors.
    - Mental health professionals to conduct assessments and develop treatment plans for individuals experiencing mental health issues.
- **Risk Reduction and Mitigation:**
    - Urban planners and land-use specialists to develop zoning regulations and land-use plans that mitigate disaster risks.
    - Civil engineers and infrastructure specialists to design and implement infrastructure improvements aimed at reducing vulnerabilities.
    - Emergency management professionals to coordinate risk reduction efforts and develop emergency response plans.
    - Public outreach specialists to conduct public awareness campaigns on disaster preparedness and mitigation strategies.
    - Environmental scientists to assess environmental risks and develop strategies for environmental management and conservation.
    - Disaster risk management experts to assess risks and vulnerabilities and develop risk reduction strategies tailored to the local context.
- **Capacity Building and Institutional Strengthening:**
    - Trainers and educators to develop and deliver training programs on disaster

preparedness, response, and recovery.

- Community organizers to facilitate community empowerment activities and initiatives.
- Government officials and policymakers to enact legislation and policies that support capacity building and institutional strengthening.
- Nonprofit organizations and community-based organizations to collaborate on capacity-building initiatives and provide technical assistance.
- Subject matter experts to provide guidance and expertise on sustainable development practices and resilience-building strategies.
- Monitoring and evaluation specialists to assess the effectiveness of capacity-building efforts and identify areas for improvement.

Coordinators and managers play indispensable roles in each facet of long-term recovery:

- Reconstruction and Rehabilitation: Project Managers are pivotal in overseeing reconstruction projects, liaising with stakeholders, managing budgets and schedules, and ensuring compliance with regulations. Construction Managers supervise construction activities, ensuring quality control and coordinating subcontractors. Logistics Coordinators handle the procurement and delivery of materials and equipment. Community Engagement Managers facilitate communication between project teams and local communities, addressing concerns and fostering community participation.
- Economic Recovery: Economic Development Managers devise strategies for economic revitalization, identify growth opportunities, and coordinate development initiatives. Small Business Coordinators support small businesses, aiding in financing, planning, and development. Investment Managers attract investment, negotiate incentives, and promote economic opportunities. Workforce Development Managers design and implement job training programs, foster partnerships with employers, and connect job seekers with opportunities.
- Psychosocial Support: Clinical Directors oversee mental health programs, en-

sure adherence to guidelines, and supervise counsellors. Support Group Coordinators organize meetings, recruit facilitators, and provide guidance. Community Outreach Managers develop outreach strategies, coordinate events, and collaborate with organizations to raise awareness. Training and Education Managers develop training programs for mental health professionals and community members.

- Risk Reduction and Mitigation: Risk Managers assess risks, develop mitigation strategies, and coordinate efforts across sectors. Urban Planners create land-use plans and zoning regulations to minimize exposure to hazards. Emergency Management Coordinators implement response plans, coordinate with agencies, and ensure readiness. Public Awareness Managers design and execute awareness campaigns on disaster preparedness and risk reduction.

- Capacity Building and Institutional Strengthening: Training Managers design and deliver training for officials, leaders, and volunteers on disaster preparedness and recovery. Community Organizers facilitate empowerment activities, build partnerships, and mobilize resources. Policy Advisors offer guidance on policy development to strengthen disaster management and sustainable development. Monitoring and Evaluation Coordinators design frameworks, collect data, and provide feedback for improvement.

Emergency disaster recovery involves economic, infrastructural, and social aspects crucial for restoring communities post-disaster. The economic dimension includes activities aimed at rebuilding the economy, such as restoring businesses, employment opportunities, and financial stability [405]. Infrastructure plays a vital role in disaster recovery by providing essential services to the community and serving as the backbone for community functioning [435]. This includes restoring critical physical infrastructures like transportation networks, utilities, and communication systems [436].

On the social front, disaster recovery involves restoring social structures, community cohesion, and cultural activities [405]. It also entails awakening community participation in various aspects of social life and upholding law and order [405]. Social and economic recovery are intertwined, as rebuilding social networks and community ties can contribute to economic recovery by fostering a sense of normalcy and stability [405].

Effective emergency response and recovery capabilities are essential for disaster recovery. This includes maintaining social, economic, environmental, and physical components at a significant level to ensure a comprehensive recovery process [216]. Disaster recovery is a complex, nonlinear process that involves physical, social, economic, and institutional dimensions [402]. It requires coordination between governments, communities, and international organizations to restore critical infrastructures and socioeconomic environments [398].

In conclusion, emergency disaster recovery is a multifaceted process that involves addressing economic, infrastructural, and social aspects. Rebuilding the economy, restoring critical infrastructure, and enhancing social structures are all integral components of successful disaster recovery efforts. By focusing on these three dimensions, communities can work towards a comprehensive recovery that promotes resilience and sustainability in the face of disasters.

10

Sustainable Development and Disaster Mitigation

Integrating Disaster Risk Reduction with Sustainable Development

To effectively integrate disaster risk reduction with sustainable development, a comprehensive approach is essential. The Sendai Framework for Disaster Risk Reduction emphasizes the importance of linking disaster risk reduction efforts with sustainable development goals [437]. This integration is crucial as disaster risk reduction policies, such as those outlined in the Sendai Framework, provide a foundation for sustainable development by addressing risks that could hinder development progress [438]. Moreover, disaster risk reduction should not be isolated but rather embedded within broader development and sustainability agendas to ensure a cohesive approach [439].

Efforts to integrate disaster risk reduction with sustainable development involve various aspects such as incorporating disaster risk reduction measures into physical infrastructure, social systems, housing restoration, livelihoods, and environmental revitalization [440]. Additionally, public coordination plays a significant role in ensuring that sustainable development initiatives are implemented based on disaster risk reduction policies. The commitment to international frameworks like the 2030 Agenda for Sustainable Development, the Sendai Framework, and the Paris Agreement on Climate Change has spurred efforts to enhance policy coherence between climate change adaptation, disaster risk reduction, and sustainable development.

Integrating disaster risk reduction (DRR) with sustainable development involves incorporating measures to reduce the risk of disasters into policies, programs, and practices aimed at achieving sustainable development goals. This integration can be achieved through:

1. Policy Alignment: Ensure that DRR objectives are integrated into national and local development policies, strategies, and plans. This includes mainstreaming DRR considerations into development frameworks such as poverty reduction, environmental management, urban planning, and infrastructure development. Disaster risk reduction should be incorporated into national development programs to ensure risk-aware decision-making at all stages of disaster risk management [441]. The adoption of the Sendai Framework, the 2030 Agenda for Sustainable Development, and the Paris Agreement presents an opportunity to align policy agendas that impact the future of humanity [442]. Disaster risk reduction must be a priority in poverty alleviation and sustainable development efforts in developing countries [443].

2. Risk-Informed Decision Making: Incorporate risk assessments and analysis into decision-making processes across all sectors. This involves identifying and understanding existing and potential hazards, vulnerabilities, and exposure to risks, and using this information to inform development decisions.

3. Building Resilient Infrastructure: Develop infrastructure that is resilient to natural hazards and climate change impacts. This includes designing and constructing buildings, roads, bridges, and other critical infrastructure to withstand hazards such as earthquakes, floods, storms, and landslides.

4. Natural Resource Management: Promote sustainable management of natural resources to reduce environmental degradation and minimize the risk of disasters. This involves measures such as reforestation, soil conservation, watershed management, and coastal zone protection to enhance ecosystem resilience.

5. Community Engagement and Empowerment: Involve communities in disaster risk management processes and empower them to participate in decision-making. This includes raising awareness about disaster risks, building local capacities for response and recovery, and fostering community-led initiatives for risk reduction.

6. Education and Training: Incorporate DRR education and training into formal and informal education systems. This includes teaching students about disaster preparedness, response, and mitigation, as well as providing training for professionals and practitioners in DRR principles and practices.

7. Early Warning Systems: Establish and strengthen early warning systems to provide timely and accurate information about impending disasters. This includes investing in technology, communication networks, and community-based monitoring systems to ensure effective dissemination of warnings and enable prompt action.

8. Climate Change Adaptation: Address the interconnectedness between climate change and disaster risk by integrating DRR with climate change adaptation strategies. This involves identifying and addressing climate-related risks, such as sea-level rise, extreme weather events, and changing precipitation patterns, within the context of sustainable development planning.

9. Financial Mechanisms: Develop and implement financial mechanisms to support DRR and resilience-building efforts. This includes investing in risk financing instruments, such as insurance and contingency funds, as well as mobilizing resources for DRR projects and programs through public-private partnerships and international cooperation.

10. Monitoring and Evaluation: Establish monitoring and evaluation systems to assess progress in integrating DRR with sustainable development. This involves tracking key indicators related to disaster risk reduction, resilience building, and sustainable development outcomes, and using this information to inform policy adjustments and program improvements over time.

Policy alignment is a critical aspect of integrating disaster risk reduction (DRR) objectives into national and local development agendas. This entails ensuring that DRR considerations are seamlessly integrated into existing policies, strategies, and plans aimed at achieving sustainable development goals. By mainstreaming DRR into development frameworks such as poverty reduction, environmental management, urban planning, and infrastructure development, countries can adopt a holistic approach to disaster risk management.

Incorporating disaster risk reduction into national development programs is essential for promoting risk-aware decision-making across all stages of disaster risk management. This involves identifying, assessing, and addressing disaster risks in the design, implementation, and evaluation of development initiatives. By integrating DRR into policy agendas, governments can better anticipate and mitigate the impacts of disasters, thereby reducing the social, economic, and environmental costs associated with disasters.

The adoption of global frameworks such as the Sendai Framework for Disaster Risk Reduction, the 2030 Agenda for Sustainable Development, and the Paris Agreement on climate change presents an opportunity to align policy agendas that have a significant impact on the future of humanity. These frameworks provide a common roadmap for addressing interconnected challenges such as disaster risk, poverty, climate change, and sustainable development. By aligning policy agendas, countries can leverage synergies and maximize the effectiveness of their efforts to build resilience and achieve sustainable development outcomes.

In particular, disaster risk reduction must be prioritized in poverty alleviation and sustainable development efforts, especially in developing countries that are most vulnerable to the impacts of disasters. By integrating DRR into poverty reduction strategies and development programs, governments can address the root causes of vulnerability and promote inclusive and sustainable development pathways. This requires a multi-sectoral approach that engages stakeholders from government, civil society, academia, and the private sector to ensure that DRR objectives are integrated into all aspects of development planning and implementation.

Risk-informed decision making is a crucial component of disaster risk reduction, emphasizing the incorporation of risk assessments and analysis into decision-making processes across various sectors. By integrating risk assessments, decision makers can gain a comprehensive understanding of hazards, vulnerabilities, and exposure to risks, enabling them to quantify and prioritize risks and assess potential impacts on communities and infrastructure [444]. This approach allows for the identification and addressing of vulnerabilities, integration of risk reduction measures into infrastructure development, and promotion of sustainable land use practices [444].

Furthermore, risk-informed decision making facilitates the adoption of proactive measures to reduce risk and enhance resilience, leading to the minimization of disaster impacts and the building of resilience against future shocks [444]. It also fosters a culture of accountability and transparency by ensuring that decisions are evidence-based and involve stakeholders in risk assessment processes and decision-making forums [444]. This inclusive approach enhances local ownership, consensus building, and participatory governance, ultimately empowering communities to actively engage in disaster risk reduction efforts [444].

Moreover, the integration of risk information into planning, design, and implementation processes enables governments and organizations to make informed decisions based on robust evidence [444]. By involving stakeholders, governments can build trust, legitimacy, and resilience within communities, leading to more effective disaster risk reduction strategies [444].

Building resilient infrastructure is a crucial aspect of disaster risk reduction efforts, focusing on developing infrastructure capable of withstanding the impacts of natural disasters and climate change. This involves integrating engineering and design practices that enhance the resilience of buildings, roads, bridges, and other essential infrastructure to withstand various hazards such as earthquakes, floods, storms, and landslides [445].

Incorporating risk considerations into the design and construction process is vital for improving the resilience of infrastructure projects. Engineers and architects employ innovative techniques and technologies, including resilient materials, adherence to building codes, and retrofitting measures, to ensure that structures can endure the forces of nature [446]. Additionally, it is essential to assess the broader context of climate change and its potential effects on infrastructure systems. This includes evaluating infrastructure vulnerability to changing climate patterns like extreme weather events, rising sea levels, and altered precipitation patterns [447].

A comprehensive approach to constructing resilient infrastructure involves acknowledging the interconnectedness of infrastructure systems and their impacts on communities and ecosystems. By embracing nature-based solutions such as green infrastructure and ecosystem restoration, decision-makers can enhance resilience while providing additional benefits like improved water management, biodiversity conservation, and carbon sequestration [448]. Integrating nature-based approaches into infrastructure planning and design can lead to the development of more resilient and sustainable infrastructure systems that benefit both people and the environment.

Investing in resilient infrastructure is essential for reducing disaster risk, enhancing community resilience, and promoting sustainable development. By constructing infrastructure capable of enduring natural hazards and climate change impacts, decision-makers can protect lives, critical assets and services, and create more resilient and prosperous communities for the future [449].

Promoting sustainable management of natural resources is crucial for reducing the risk of disasters and safeguarding ecosystems. Reforestation initiatives are effective in restoring degraded landscapes and mitigating natural hazards like landslides and floods [14]. Soil conservation practices, including terracing and agroforestry, help preserve soil fertility and reduce the risk of erosion, landslides, and mudflows [450]. Watershed management plays a critical role in protecting water resources, enhancing water quality, and minimizing the risk of floods and droughts [143]. Coastal zone protection measures such as mangrove restoration and seawall construction are essential for safeguarding coastal communities from storms and sea-level rise [451].

Implementing these strategies is vital for reducing environmental degradation, enhancing ecosystem resilience, and minimizing disaster risks. By focusing on reforestation, soil conservation, watershed management, and coastal protection, communities can enhance their resilience to natural hazards and create more sustainable ecosystems [229]. These measures align with the global blueprint for disaster risk reduction efforts, emphasizing the importance of building resilience at the community level [452].

Community engagement and empowerment are fundamental principles in disaster risk management, emphasizing the active involvement of communities in decision-making processes and actions to reduce vulnerability and enhance resilience. This approach recognizes that communities possess valuable knowledge, resources, and capabilities that can contribute to effective disaster risk reduction efforts. Several key strategies are employed to promote community engagement and empowerment in disaster risk management.

Raising awareness about disaster risks is a crucial first step in empowering communities to take proactive measures to reduce their vulnerability. This involves providing information about the types of hazards that threaten the community, their potential impacts, and the actions that individuals and households can take to mitigate risks and protect themselves. By raising awareness, communities can become more informed and prepared to respond to disasters.

Building local capacities for response and recovery is crucial for enhancing community resilience in the face of disasters. By providing training and education programs to empower community members with the necessary skills and knowledge to effectively respond to emergencies, offer first aid, and contribute to recovery efforts, communities can enhance their self-reliance and ability to manage disasters [453]. Integrating local capacity building into community-based disaster risk management can foster community resilience and adaptability by ensuring the dissemination of accurate and credible disaster-related information [227]. Moreover, developing resilient communities involves equipping them with the capacity for mitigation, preparedness, response, and recovery across all types of hazards [454].

Efforts to strengthen community resilience should focus on enhancing individual self-efficacy and community advantage to promote disaster preparedness and overall resilience [455]. Strategies that facilitate bidirectional learning and engagement can aid in the adoption of resilience principles by communities [215]. Additionally, it is essential to invest in disaster risk governance, management, and preparedness to effectively respond to disasters and promote recovery [145]. The involvement of local governments in capacity development for disaster risk management is vital to ensure that communities are adequately prepared to handle disasters [456].

Fostering community-led initiatives for risk reduction empowers communities to take ownership of their safety and well-being. This involves supporting grassroots efforts to identify and address local hazards, develop risk reduction plans, and implement mitigation measures tailored to the community's specific needs and priorities. Community-led initiatives often leverage local knowledge, resources, and social networks to create innovative and sustainable solutions to reduce disaster risk.

Incorporating community engagement and empowerment into disaster risk management processes requires collaboration and partnership between government agencies, non-governmental organizations, and local community stakeholders. By working together, these stakeholders can create opportunities for meaningful participation, build trust and social cohesion, and ensure that disaster risk reduction efforts are inclusive, responsive, and sustainable.

Overall, community engagement and empowerment are essential components of effective disaster risk management, enabling communities to become active agents in their own resilience-building efforts. By involving communities in decision-making processes, raising awareness about disaster risks, building local capacities, and fostering community-led initiatives for risk reduction, stakeholders can empower communities to become more resilient and better prepared to face the challenges of disasters.

Education and training are pivotal in fostering disaster risk reduction (DRR) awareness and building the capacities necessary to mitigate risks and respond effectively to disasters. This involves integrating DRR education and training into both formal and informal education systems, reaching a broad spectrum of individuals across different age groups and professional sectors.

Within formal education systems, DRR principles and practices are incorporated into school curricula to educate students about disaster preparedness, response, and mitigation. This may involve integrating DRR topics into subjects such as geography, environmental studies, or civics, enabling students to understand the underlying causes of disasters, assess risks, and learn how to take appropriate actions to protect themselves and their communities.

Moreover, providing training for professionals and practitioners in DRR principles and practices ensures that those responsible for disaster management and response are equipped with the knowledge and skills needed to perform their roles effectively. This includes training for emergency responders, government officials, community leaders, and other stakeholders involved in disaster risk management. Training programs may cover various aspects of DRR, including risk assessment, early warning systems, emergency planning, and community engagement.

In addition to formal education systems, DRR education and training can also be delivered through informal channels, such as community workshops, public awareness campaigns, and online resources. These initiatives aim to reach a broader audience and raise awareness about disaster risks, preparedness measures, and resilience-building strategies. By engaging communities and providing accessible and relevant information, informal DRR education initiatives empower individuals to take proactive steps to reduce their vulnerability to disasters.

Integrating disaster risk reduction (DRR) education and training into formal and informal education systems is crucial for fostering proactive approaches to disaster risk reduction and building a culture of resilience. By incorporating DRR education into school curricula and providing professionals with the necessary knowledge and skills, stakeholders can enhance community preparedness, strengthen response capabilities, and reduce the impacts of disasters on lives and livelihoods.

Figure 52: FEMA Corps' team "Tundra 1" members, Nathan Krekelberg and team leader Chip Hennessy, show students what items families should include in an emergency preparedness kit. National Archives at College Park - Still Pictures, Public domain, via Wikimedia Commons.

Research has shown that integrating DRR education in schools can lead to positive outcomes [457]. Initiatives such as participatory child-centred DRR education programs have been developed to educate students effectively [458]. Furthermore, harnessing informal education can contribute to enhancing community resilience (Feng et al., 2018). Studies have also highlighted the importance of integrating DRR into formal education systems through appropriate learning strategies and methods [142].

It is essential to involve populations at risk in designing and implementing DRR policies, following an "all-of-society" approach as recommended by the Sendai Framework [459]. Additionally, partnerships between local governance structures and emergency services are crucial for implementing sustainable DRR activities [460].

Efforts to integrate DRR into education systems have been documented in various countries, including Indonesia [97], Nepal [461], and Ghana [462]. Recommendations include capacitating teachers to handle DRR subjects, using updated resource materials, and adopting an interdisciplinary approach to analyse natural disasters.

Establishing and enhancing early warning systems is paramount in mitigating the impacts of disasters by providing communities with timely and accurate information about impending threats. This proactive approach to disaster risk reduction involves investing in technology, communication networks, and community-based monitoring systems to ensure the effective dissemination of warnings and facilitate prompt action in response to potential hazards.

Modern early warning systems leverage a combination of technological advancements and community-based approaches to detect and forecast hazards such as floods, storms, tsunamis, earthquakes, and other natural disasters. These systems utilize a range of tools, including meteorological sensors, satellite imagery, weather radars, and seismic monitoring devices, to collect data and analyse trends that could indicate the onset of a hazardous event.

Effective communication networks are essential for delivering warnings to communities at risk in a timely manner. This may involve employing various communication channels such as radio, television, SMS alerts, mobile apps, social media platforms, and sirens to reach a diverse audience and ensure that warnings are accessible to all segments of the population, including those in remote or hard-to-reach areas.

Community-based monitoring systems complement technological solutions by engaging local residents in the monitoring and reporting of potential hazards. Community members, often trained as volunteers, observe changes in their environment, such as rising water levels, unusual weather patterns, or seismic activity, and relay this information to relevant authorities or local disaster management agencies.

Furthermore, early warning systems are not just about issuing alerts but also about enabling communities to take prompt and effective action in response to warnings. This requires robust preparedness and response plans that outline clear procedures for evacuation, sheltering, emergency communication, and coordination among stakeholders.

By establishing and strengthening early warning systems, communities can enhance their resilience to disasters by improving their ability to anticipate, prepare for, and respond to potential threats. Timely warnings enable individuals and communities to take proactive measures to protect lives, livelihoods, and assets, ultimately reducing the overall impact of disasters on society.

Integrating disaster risk reduction (DRR) with climate change adaptation strategies is essential for effectively managing climate-related risks and fostering sustainable development. This integration allows for a comprehensive approach to addressing challenges posed by climate change, such as sea-level rise, extreme weather events, and shifting precipitation patterns [463]. By recognizing the interconnectedness between climate change and disaster risk, policymakers and planners can identify areas of overlap and synergy between the two fields, maximizing resources and efforts to address shared challenges [463].

Sustainable development planning plays a crucial role in integrating DRR and climate change adaptation into broader development goals and policies [463]. This involves mainstreaming climate resilience considerations into various aspects of planning, including land-use planning, infrastructure development, natural resource management, and social welfare programs [463]. By embedding risk reduction and adaptation measures into development planning processes, policymakers can ensure that investments are sustainable and resilient in the face of climate-related threats [463].

Collaboration and partnership among stakeholders are fundamental for effective climate change adaptation and disaster risk reduction [464]. Engaging local communities, government agencies, civil society organizations, academia, and the private sector fosters collective action and ensures that interventions are context-specific, participatory, and socially inclusive [464]. This multi-stakeholder approach is crucial for developing and implementing strategies that promote resilience at local, national, and regional levels [464].

The integration of DRR with climate change adaptation represents a holistic approach to addressing complex challenges posed by climate change. By incorporating climate resilience considerations into sustainable development planning, policymakers can enhance resilience, promote sustainable development, and build a more secure future for communities worldwide [463].

Developing and implementing financial mechanisms stands as a critical aspect of disaster risk reduction (DRR) and resilience-building efforts. These mechanisms serve as crucial instruments in ensuring adequate resources are available to mitigate risks and respond effectively to disasters. One key component involves investing in risk financing instruments, such as insurance and contingency funds. By leveraging insurance mechanisms, communities and governments can transfer a portion of the financial burden associated with disaster losses to insurance providers, thus reducing the economic impact of disasters on affected populations.

Moreover, mobilizing resources for DRR projects and programs is essential for building resilience at various levels. This involves allocating funds for initiatives aimed at reducing vulnerability to disasters, enhancing preparedness and response capacities, and promoting sustainable development practices. Public-private partnerships play a significant role in this regard, as they facilitate collaboration between government entities, businesses, and non-profit organizations to pool resources, share expertise, and implement innovative solutions for DRR.

Additionally, international cooperation plays a vital role in strengthening financial mechanisms for DRR. Through partnerships with international organizations, donor agencies, and multilateral development banks, countries can access additional funding sources, technical assistance, and knowledge exchange opportunities. International cooperation also fosters solidarity among nations in addressing common challenges posed by disasters and climate change, promoting collective action and mutual support in resilience-building efforts.

Establishing monitoring and evaluation (M&E) systems is integral to assessing progress in integrating disaster risk reduction (DRR) with sustainable development. These systems are designed to track key indicators related to various aspects of DRR, resilience building, and sustainable development outcomes. By collecting and analysing data on these indicators, policymakers and stakeholders can gain insights into the effectiveness of interventions, identify areas for improvement, and make informed decisions to enhance the integration of DRR into sustainable development efforts.

Monitoring involves systematically collecting data on predetermined indicators to track progress towards specific goals and objectives. In the context of integrating DRR with sustainable development, monitoring efforts may focus on measuring changes in disaster risk levels, improvements in resilience capacities, and advancements in sustainable development outcomes. This data provides valuable information on the implementation of DRR initiatives, the effectiveness of interventions, and the overall trajectory of progress over time.

The first step in monitoring involves identifying relevant indicators that will be used to measure progress. These indicators should be specific, measurable, achievable, relevant, and time-bound (SMART). In the context of DRR and sustainable development integration, indicators may include metrics related to disaster risk reduction, resilience building, and sustainable development goals, such as the number of vulnerable populations reached with early warning messages, the percentage of infrastructure built to withstand natural hazards, or the improvement in livelihoods for communities in disaster-prone areas.

Once the indicators are identified, data collection methods and sources need to be determined. This may involve gathering data from various sources, including government agencies, non-governmental organizations, academic institutions, community-based organizations, and other stakeholders. Data collection methods may include surveys, interviews, focus group discussions, observations, and document reviews. It is essential to ensure that data collection is conducted consistently and systematically to maintain the reliability and validity of the data.

After collecting data, it needs to be analysed to identify trends, patterns, and areas of progress or challenges. Data analysis may involve statistical techniques, qualitative analysis methods, and data visualization tools to interpret the findings effectively. Through data analysis, stakeholders can gain insights into the effectiveness of DRR initiatives, the impact of interventions on disaster risk reduction and resilience building, and the contribution to sustainable development goals.

The next step is to interpret the findings and draw conclusions based on the data analysis. This involves synthesizing the information collected, identifying key findings, and assessing progress towards specific goals and objectives. Stakeholders can use this information to make informed decisions, prioritize areas for action, and adjust strategies or interventions as needed to improve outcomes.

Finally, monitoring involves communicating the findings to relevant stakeholders and using the information to inform decision-making processes. This may include presenting findings through reports, presentations, dashboards, or other communication channels to policymakers, government agencies, donors, community members, and other stakeholders. By sharing monitoring results, stakeholders can foster transparency, accountability, and learning, ultimately contributing to more effective and impactful DRR and sustainable development efforts.

The following provides an example scenario to demonstrate the monitoring process.

Scenario:

In a coastal city prone to hurricanes and flooding, the local government has implemented a comprehensive disaster risk reduction (DRR) program aimed at integrating DRR with sustainable development initiatives. The goal is to enhance the city's resilience to natural hazards while promoting sustainable growth and development.

As part of the program, a monitoring framework has been established to track progress towards achieving specific DRR and sustainable development objectives. Here's how the monitoring process unfolds:

1. Identification of Relevant Indicators: The city government, in collaboration with relevant stakeholders, identifies key indicators to measure progress. These indicators include metrics such as the number of resilient infrastructure projects completed, the percentage of vulnerable populations reached with early warning messages, and the reduction in disaster-related economic losses over time.

2. Data Collection Methods and Sources: Data collection methods are determined to gather information on the identified indicators. This involves collaborating with government agencies, NGOs, academic institutions, and community-based organizations to collect data through surveys, interviews, focus group discussions, and document reviews. For example, data on infrastructure projects are obtained from engineering reports, while information on early warning dissemination is gathered through community surveys and interviews.

3. Data Analysis: Collected data is analysed to identify trends, patterns, and areas of progress or challenges. Statistical analysis techniques and qualitative analysis methods are used to interpret the findings effectively. For instance, statistical analysis may reveal a decrease in the number of disaster-related fatalities, indicating improved resilience, while qualitative analysis may highlight community perceptions of early warning effectiveness.

4. Interpretation of Findings: Stakeholders interpret the findings to assess progress towards specific goals and objectives. Through synthesis of the information collected, key findings are identified, and progress is assessed. For instance, stakeholders may find that while infrastructure resilience has improved, there are still challenges in reaching vulnerable populations with early warning messages.

5. Communication of Findings: The monitoring results are communicated to relevant stakeholders through reports, presentations, and other communication channels. This includes sharing findings with policymakers, government agencies, donors, community members, and other stakeholders. The communication of findings fosters transparency, accountability, and learning, enabling stakeholders to make informed decisions and adjust strategies as needed.

In this scenario, the monitoring process plays a vital role in assessing the effectiveness of DRR initiatives, measuring progress towards sustainable development goals, and informing decision-making processes to enhance resilience and promote sustainable development in the coastal city.

Evaluation complements monitoring by providing an in-depth analysis of the outcomes and impacts of DRR interventions. Through evaluation, policymakers and stakeholders can assess the extent to which DRR efforts have contributed to sustainable development goals, identify lessons learned, and determine the effectiveness of different approaches and strategies. Evaluations also help stakeholders understand the reasons behind successes or failures, enabling them to make evidence-based decisions for future planning and programming.

The first step in conducting an evaluation is to define clear evaluation questions and objectives. These questions should be aligned with the goals of the DRR interventions and should focus on assessing the outcomes, impacts, and effectiveness of the interventions. For example, evaluation questions may include assessing the extent to which DRR efforts have reduced disaster risk levels, improved community resilience, enhanced livelihoods, or contributed to sustainable development outcomes.

Once the evaluation questions are defined, appropriate evaluation methodologies need to be selected. This may involve a combination of quantitative and qualitative methods, including surveys, interviews, focus group discussions, case studies, and participatory techniques. The choice of methodologies will depend on the nature of the DRR interventions, the available resources, and the specific context in which the evaluation is being conducted.

Data collection is a crucial component of the evaluation process. Data may be collected from various sources, including primary data collected directly from stakeholders and beneficiaries, secondary data from existing reports and studies, and qualitative data through interviews and observations. It is essential to ensure that data collection methods are rigorous, ethical, and culturally sensitive to obtain reliable and valid information.

Once the data is collected, it needs to be analysed to assess the outcomes and impacts of the DRR interventions. Data analysis may involve quantitative techniques such as statistical analysis and modelling to measure changes in disaster risk levels or community resilience indicators. Qualitative data may be analysed thematically to identify key themes, patterns, and insights from stakeholders' perspectives.

The next step is to interpret the findings and draw conclusions based on the evaluation results. This involves synthesizing the information collected, identifying key findings and trends, and assessing the overall effectiveness and impact of the DRR interventions.

Stakeholders should critically examine the evidence to understand the reasons behind successes or failures and identify lessons learned for future planning and programming.

Finally, the findings of the evaluation should be communicated to relevant stakeholders in a clear, concise, and accessible manner. This may involve preparing evaluation reports, presentations, or briefs summarizing the key findings, conclusions, and recommendations. By sharing the results of the evaluation, stakeholders can learn from past experiences, make informed decisions for future DRR efforts, and improve the overall effectiveness and impact of DRR interventions in contributing to sustainable development goals.

Role of Managers and Coordinators

Disaster managers and coordinators play a pivotal role in ensuring effective integration of disaster risk reduction (DRR) with sustainable development across various domains:

1. Policy Alignment: Disaster managers and coordinators advocate for the integration of DRR objectives into national and local development policies, strategies, and plans. They work closely with policymakers and stakeholders to mainstream DRR considerations into development frameworks such as poverty reduction, environmental management, urban planning, and infrastructure development. By ensuring that DRR is incorporated into national development programs, they promote risk-aware decision-making at all stages of disaster risk management, aligning with global frameworks such as the Sendai Framework, the 2030 Agenda for Sustainable Development, and the Paris Agreement.

2. Risk-Informed Decision Making: They incorporate risk assessments and analysis into decision-making processes across all sectors. Disaster managers and coordinators identify existing and potential hazards, vulnerabilities, and exposure to risks, and use this information to inform development decisions. By integrating risk-informed decision-making, they help prioritize investments, allocate resources effectively, and enhance the resilience of communities and infrastructure.

3. Building Resilient Infrastructure: Disaster managers and coordinators oversee the development of infrastructure that is resilient to natural hazards and climate

change impacts. They collaborate with engineers, urban planners, and other stakeholders to design and construct buildings, roads, bridges, and other critical infrastructure capable of withstanding hazards such as earthquakes, floods, storms, and landslides. By investing in resilient infrastructure, they reduce disaster risks and ensure the sustainability of development projects.

4. Natural Resource Management: They promote sustainable management of natural resources to reduce environmental degradation and minimize the risk of disasters. Disaster managers and coordinators implement measures such as reforestation, soil conservation, watershed management, and coastal zone protection to enhance ecosystem resilience. By safeguarding natural resources, they mitigate the impact of disasters and contribute to sustainable development goals.

5. Community Engagement and Empowerment: Disaster managers and coordinators involve communities in disaster risk management processes and empower them to participate in decision-making. They raise awareness about disaster risks, build local capacities for response and recovery, and foster community-led initiatives for risk reduction. By engaging communities, they promote ownership, resilience, and sustainability in disaster risk management efforts.

6. Education and Training: They incorporate DRR education and training into formal and informal education systems. Disaster managers and coordinators ensure that students are taught about disaster preparedness, response, and mitigation, while also providing training for professionals and practitioners in DRR principles and practices. By integrating education and training, they enhance awareness, knowledge, and skills necessary for effective disaster risk management.

7. Early Warning Systems: Disaster managers and coordinators establish and strengthen early warning systems to provide timely and accurate information about impending disasters. They invest in technology, communication networks, and community-based monitoring systems to ensure effective dissemination of warnings and enable prompt action. By enhancing early warning systems, they improve preparedness, response, and resilience to disasters.

8. Climate Change Adaptation: They address the interconnectedness between climate change and disaster risk by integrating DRR with climate change adaptation strategies. Disaster managers and coordinators identify and address climate-related risks within the context of sustainable development planning. By mainstreaming climate change adaptation, they enhance resilience to climate-related hazards and promote sustainable development.

9. Financial Mechanisms: Disaster managers and coordinators develop and implement financial mechanisms to support DRR and resilience-building efforts. They invest in risk financing instruments such as insurance and contingency funds, while also mobilizing resources for DRR projects and programs through public-private partnerships and international cooperation. By securing funding, they ensure the sustainability and effectiveness of disaster risk management initiatives.

10. Monitoring and Evaluation: Disaster managers and coordinators establish monitoring and evaluation systems to assess progress in integrating DRR with sustainable development. They track key indicators related to disaster risk reduction, resilience building, and sustainable development outcomes, using this information to inform policy adjustments and program improvements over time. By monitoring and evaluating progress, they enhance accountability, learning, and effectiveness in disaster risk management efforts.

Disaster managers and coordinators have access to various tools and techniques to facilitate the effective integration of disaster risk reduction (DRR) with sustainable development across different domains:

- Policy Alignment:
    - Policy analysis tools: These tools help managers and coordinators assess existing policies and identify opportunities to integrate DRR objectives into national and local development policies.
    - Stakeholder mapping: This technique helps identify key stakeholders involved in policy development and implementation, allowing managers to engage with them effectively to advocate for DRR integration.
    - Policy briefs: Managers can use concise policy briefs to communicate the

importance of DRR integration to policymakers and stakeholders, providing evidence-based recommendations for policy alignment.

- Risk-Informed Decision Making:
  - Risk assessment tools: These tools assist managers in conducting comprehensive risk assessments to identify hazards, vulnerabilities, and exposure to risks across different sectors.
  - Decision support systems: Decision support systems help managers analyse risk assessment data and make informed decisions about resource allocation, project prioritization, and infrastructure development.
  - Scenario planning: This technique allows managers to explore different future scenarios based on varying levels of risk, helping them anticipate potential challenges and develop adaptive strategies.
- Building Resilient Infrastructure:
  - Engineering design standards: Managers utilize engineering design standards that incorporate DRR principles to ensure infrastructure is resilient to natural hazards and climate change impacts.
  - Vulnerability mapping: Geographic Information Systems (GIS) and remote sensing technologies are used to map vulnerabilities and identify areas susceptible to hazards, guiding infrastructure planning and development.
  - Building codes and regulations: Managers enforce building codes and regulations that mandate resilient construction practices, such as earthquake-resistant building designs and flood-proofing measures.
- Natural Resource Management:
  - Environmental impact assessments: These assessments help managers evaluate the potential environmental impacts of development projects and identify measures to mitigate risks and enhance ecosystem resilience.
  - Participatory resource management approaches: Managers engage local communities in natural resource management processes, empowering them

to contribute local knowledge and traditional practices to enhance resilience.

    - Sustainable land-use planning: Managers employ land-use planning tools to promote sustainable land management practices, such as reforestation, soil conservation, and watershed management, to reduce disaster risks.

- Community Engagement and Empowerment:
    - Community risk assessments: Managers conduct participatory risk assessments with communities to identify local hazards, vulnerabilities, and capacities, fostering community ownership of risk reduction initiatives.
    - Community-based participatory approaches: These approaches empower communities to actively participate in decision-making processes, ensuring that DRR interventions are culturally appropriate and address local needs.
    - Information, education, and communication (IEC) materials: Managers develop IEC materials to raise awareness about disaster risks and resilience-building measures, facilitating community engagement and behaviour change.
- Education and Training:
    - Curriculum development tools: Managers use curriculum development tools to integrate DRR education into formal education systems, aligning educational materials with national curriculum standards.
    - Training needs assessments: These assessments help identify the training needs of professionals and practitioners involved in DRR, guiding the development of targeted training programs and capacity-building initiatives.
    - Participatory training methodologies: Managers employ participatory training methodologies that encourage active learning and skill-building, ensuring that training programs are engaging and effective.
- Early Warning Systems:
    - Technology platforms: Managers utilize technology platforms to collect,

analyse, and disseminate early warning information, ensuring timely and accurate communication of warnings to at-risk populations.

  - Community-based monitoring networks: Managers establish community-based monitoring networks that empower local communities to collect and share information about environmental conditions and early warning signs.
  - Public awareness campaigns: Managers conduct public awareness campaigns to educate communities about the importance of early warning systems and how to respond to warnings effectively, promoting community preparedness and resilience.

- Climate Change Adaptation:
  - Climate risk assessments: Managers conduct climate risk assessments to identify climate-related risks and vulnerabilities, informing adaptation planning and decision-making.
  - Adaptation mainstreaming tools: These tools help integrate climate change adaptation considerations into development planning processes, ensuring that DRR efforts are aligned with climate resilience goals.
  - Multi-stakeholder platforms: Managers facilitate multi-stakeholder platforms that bring together government agencies, civil society organizations, and other stakeholders to coordinate climate change adaptation efforts and share best practices.
- Financial Mechanisms:
  - Financial modelling tools: Managers use financial modelling tools to assess the financial viability of DRR and resilience-building projects and identify potential funding sources.
  - Public-private partnerships (PPPs): Managers leverage PPPs to mobilize private sector investment in DRR initiatives, pooling resources and expertise to support sustainable development goals.

- Grant management systems: Managers implement grant management systems to track funding allocations, monitor project progress, and ensure accountability and transparency in financial management.

- Monitoring and Evaluation:
  - Performance monitoring frameworks: Managers develop performance monitoring frameworks to track progress towards DRR and sustainable development goals, defining key performance indicators and data collection methods.
  - Impact evaluation methods: Managers use impact evaluation methods, such as randomized control trials and quasi-experimental designs, to assess the effectiveness of DRR interventions and identify lessons learned.
  - Participatory monitoring approaches: Managers employ participatory monitoring approaches that involve stakeholders in data collection and analysis, promoting ownership and accountability in monitoring and evaluation processes.

Environmental Considerations in Disaster Mitigation

Environmental considerations play a crucial role in disaster mitigation efforts by focusing on the protection, restoration, and sustainable management of natural ecosystems to reduce susceptibility to disasters. This strategy highlights the importance of utilizing ecosystems as "bioshields" in conjunction with early warning systems and disaster preparedness to decrease vulnerability to natural hazards [465, 466]. Implementing an ecosystem-based approach, such as sustainable forest management, can enhance ecosystem resilience, mitigate climate change impacts, and facilitate carbon sequestration [467]. Additionally, nature-based solutions, which aim to conserve and manage natural ecosystems to improve human well-being and lower disaster risks, are increasingly acknowledged [468].

Effective disaster mitigation necessitates a comprehensive and continuous approach to minimize risks and impacts, requiring efficient management strategies, operational planning, and education for vulnerable groups [100, 469]. Integrating risk management into development planning is also essential to mitigate the adverse effects of disasters [470]. Disaster mitigation encompasses various initiatives aimed at reducing disaster risks through physical development, raising awareness, and enhancing capacity to address potential threats [471].

Ecosystem resilience stands as a cornerstone in the realm of disaster mitigation, offering a natural buffer against the detrimental impacts of various hazards. Healthy ecosystems possess the innate capacity to absorb and alleviate the effects of disasters such as floods, landslides, and storm surges. This resilience is attributed to the intricate web of interactions between living organisms and their environment, which collectively contribute to ecosystem stability and functionality. Among the diverse array of ecosystems, wetlands, forests, and mangroves emerge as particularly vital in disaster mitigation efforts due to their unique characteristics and ecological services they provide.

Preservation and restoration of these ecosystems are pivotal strategies in bolstering their resilience and augmenting their ability to mitigate disasters. Wetlands, for instance, act as natural sponges, capable of absorbing excess water during floods and reducing the intensity of downstream flooding. Similarly, forests serve as natural barriers, intercepting rainfall, stabilizing slopes, and minimizing the risk of landslides. Mangroves, with their dense root systems and salt-tolerant vegetation, act as natural coastal defences, attenuating the impacts of storm surges and coastal erosion.

Furthermore, these ecosystems provide a multitude of ecological services that are indispensable for both human well-being and biodiversity conservation. Beyond disaster mitigation, wetlands, forests, and mangroves play critical roles in flood regulation, erosion control, carbon sequestration, water filtration, and habitat preservation. Preserving and restoring these ecosystems not only enhance their resilience but also safeguard the invaluable services they provide, thus contributing to the overall sustainability and resilience of ecosystems and communities alike.

Preserving and restoring wetlands, forests, and mangroves is crucial beyond disaster mitigation as these ecosystems play vital roles in flood regulation, erosion control, carbon sequestration, water filtration, and habitat preservation. Mangroves, in particular, are significant in carbon sequestration, with sediments underlying mangroves sequestering carbon and containing paleoenvironmental records of sea-level changes [472]. They sequester large amounts of carbon, which can become greenhouse gas sources if disturbed [473]. Despite their relatively small area, mangroves are disproportionately important for global carbon sequestration and storage [474]. Mangrove ecosystems' carbon sequestration potential depends on various factors such as wood production, microbial respiration, and sediment storage [475].

Wetlands also provide essential ecosystem services, including water filtration and flood mitigation. They can store water and release it slowly over time, reducing potential flood damage [476]. Additionally, wetlands are known for their water filtration function, which helps in sediment and phosphorus filtration [477]. These ecosystems are valuable for their natural functioning and provide crucial services to humans [478].

Furthermore, mangroves are crucial in decarbonizing the atmosphere, acting as significant carbon sinks and providing breeding grounds for various species [479]. The protection of mangroves is essential to reduce greenhouse gas emissions and support climate change mitigation [480]. Mangroves are recognized as blue carbon ecosystems that store large amounts of carbon for extended periods [480].

Land-use planning stands as a fundamental strategy in the endeavour to mitigate disaster risk while concurrently safeguarding ecosystems. It serves as a proactive approach to delineating how land is utilized, balancing human needs with environmental conservation and hazard mitigation considerations. Through strategic zoning, areas susceptible to natural hazards are identified and designated as protected or restricted zones. This designation aims to deter unsustainable development in high-risk regions, thereby curbing exposure to potential disasters and preserving the integrity of ecosystems.

By delineating protected or restricted zones, authorities can implement regulations and guidelines that steer development away from areas prone to natural hazards, such as floodplains, earthquake fault lines, or landslide-prone slopes. This proactive approach minimizes the likelihood of human settlements or critical infrastructure being located in harm's way, reducing vulnerability to disasters and averting potential loss of life and property. Moreover, it fosters the preservation of natural buffers, such as wetlands, forests, and coastal vegetation, which inherently contribute to ecosystem resilience and disaster mitigation efforts.

In parallel, sustainable land-use practices are promoted within designated zones to ensure that human activities harmonize with the surrounding environment and minimize adverse impacts on ecosystems. These practices may include measures such as afforestation, soil conservation, and sustainable agriculture, which not only mitigate disaster risk but also foster ecosystem health and resilience. Ultimately, effective land-use planning integrates disaster risk reduction objectives with ecosystem conservation priorities, striving for a harmonious coexistence between human development and environmental sustainability.

Implementing effective land-use planning requires a comprehensive approach that integrates disaster risk reduction and ecosystem conservation objectives. The process begins with a thorough assessment of the local environment, considering factors such as topography, hydrology, geology, and ecological characteristics. This assessment helps identify areas prone to natural hazards and ecological significance, forming the basis for strategic zoning decisions.

Once areas susceptible to natural hazards and ecosystems of importance are identified, authorities can delineate protected or restricted zones through the development of land-use plans and zoning regulations. These regulations specify permissible land uses, development standards, and restrictions within each designated zone, aiming to steer development away from high-risk areas and sensitive ecosystems.

To implement these regulations effectively, collaboration among various stakeholders is essential. This includes government agencies, local communities, environmental organizations, urban planners, and developers. Engaging stakeholders in the land-use planning process fosters consensus-building, ensures buy-in, and enhances the legitimacy and effectiveness of the regulations.

As part of the land-use planning process, authorities must also consider socioeconomic factors and community needs. Balancing human needs with environmental conservation and hazard mitigation considerations requires careful consideration of factors such as population density, infrastructure requirements, livelihood opportunities, and cultural heritage.

In addition to zoning regulations, land-use planning involves promoting sustainable land-use practices within designated zones. This may entail measures such as afforestation, soil conservation, sustainable agriculture, and green infrastructure development. These practices not only mitigate disaster risk but also enhance ecosystem health and resilience, contributing to long-term sustainability.

Regular monitoring and evaluation of land-use plans and zoning regulations are essential to ensure their effectiveness and adaptability to changing conditions. Periodic review and updates allow for adjustments based on new data, emerging threats, and evolving community needs, ensuring that land-use planning remains responsive and relevant over time.

In urban planning and infrastructure development, the incorporation of natural infrastructure emerges as a pivotal strategy for bolstering resilience and mitigating disaster risk. Natural infrastructure encompasses elements such as green spaces, urban forests, and permeable surfaces strategically integrated into urban landscapes. These components serve multifaceted roles in disaster risk reduction, particularly in mitigating the impacts of flooding, urban heat islands, and other climate-related hazards.

Figure 53: Tunnel with natural vegetation overhead in Despeñaperros Natural Park, Spain. T.R. Shankar Raman, CC BY-SA 4.0, via Wikimedia Commons.

One notable example of natural infrastructure is the implementation of green roofs, which involve the installation of vegetation atop buildings. Green roofs offer numerous benefits, including stormwater retention, reduction of runoff, and insulation against heat. By absorbing rainfall and slowing runoff, green roofs mitigate the risk of urban flooding during heavy precipitation events. Additionally, they contribute to cooling urban environments, thus helping alleviate the urban heat island effect and reducing the risk of heat-related disasters.

Permeable pavements represent another form of natural infrastructure that can be integrated into urban environments. These pavements are designed to allow rainwater to infiltrate the ground, reducing surface runoff and the likelihood of flooding. By promoting groundwater recharge and reducing the burden on stormwater drainage systems, permeable pavements help manage flood risk and enhance urban resilience to climate-related disasters.

Urban forests play a crucial role in natural infrastructure, offering a range of benefits for disaster risk reduction and community well-being. Trees within urban areas provide shade, absorb carbon dioxide, and regulate temperatures, thereby mitigating the urban heat island effect and reducing the risk of heat-related illnesses. Moreover, urban forests contribute to stormwater management by intercepting rainfall, reducing runoff, and enhancing soil infiltration rates, thus lowering the risk of flooding in urban areas.

Integrating natural infrastructure into urban planning and infrastructure development requires a holistic approach that considers multiple factors, including land use, hydrology, and ecological dynamics. Collaboration among urban planners, landscape architects, engineers, and environmental experts is essential to design and implement effective natural infrastructure solutions tailored to local contexts. By leveraging the ecological services provided by natural infrastructure, cities can enhance resilience, reduce disaster risk, and create more sustainable and liveable urban environments for present and future generations.

Integrating disaster mitigation efforts with sustainable development strategies is essential for fostering long-term resilience and environmental sustainability. By aligning these two objectives, communities can address immediate disaster risks while also promoting practices that support the well-being of both people and the planet.

Sustainable development principles emphasize the importance of balancing economic growth, social equity, and environmental protection. In the context of disaster mitigation, this involves implementing practices that minimize environmental degradation and enhance adaptive capacity to climate change and natural hazards. For example, promoting renewable energy sources such as solar and wind power reduces reliance on fossil fuels, mitigating greenhouse gas emissions and contributing to climate resilience.

Similarly, sustainable agriculture practices prioritize soil conservation, water management, and biodiversity conservation to ensure food security and environmental health. By adopting agroecological approaches that emphasize natural ecosystem processes, communities can enhance their resilience to droughts, floods, and other climate-related disasters while also promoting soil fertility and biodiversity.

In addition to energy and agriculture, sustainable infrastructure development plays a crucial role in disaster mitigation. Eco-friendly infrastructure designs, such as green buildings and low-impact development techniques, help minimize environmental impact while also enhancing resilience to natural hazards. Green infrastructure features, such as green roofs and permeable pavements, absorb stormwater, reduce urban heat island effects, and mitigate flood risks, contributing to both disaster resilience and environmental sustainability.

Integrating disaster mitigation efforts with sustainable development strategies requires a holistic approach that addresses the interconnectedness of social, economic, and environmental factors. By promoting sustainable practices across various sectors, communities can build resilience to disasters while also fostering environmental stewardship and ensuring a more sustainable future for generations to come.

Ecosystem-Based Adaptation (EbA) is a strategic approach that leverages the resilience of ecosystems to address the impacts of climate change and disasters. This approach acknowledges the intricate link between ecosystems and human well-being, highlighting the importance of healthy ecosystems in enhancing the resilience of communities facing environmental challenges. Research has demonstrated that EbA practices can assist smallholder farmers in adapting to climate change by identifying agricultural practices aligned with EbA principles [481]. The global collapse of ecosystems poses a threat to biodiversity, human health, and well-being, underscoring the significance of ecosystem resilience [482]. Studies have emphasized the role of ecosystem-based adaptation in promoting socio-ecological resilience to climate change impacts, recognizing the synergies and trade-offs involved in EbA implementation [483].

The concept of EbA has gained prominence as a climate change solution, focusing on enhancing ecosystem health to support human well-being [484]. By valuing ecosystem services and integrating human health with ecosystem services, practical tools can be developed to create healthier and more resilient communities [485]. Additionally, the connection between marine ecosystem services and human well-being highlights the importance of understanding how ecosystems contribute to the quality of life [485]. This holistic approach considers the interplay between nature and people, emphasizing the complex relationships between ecosystem services and human well-being.

Central to EbA is the utilization of biodiversity and ecosystem services as natural buffers against climate-related hazards and disasters. Rather than relying solely on engineered solutions, EbA emphasizes the conservation, restoration, and sustainable management of ecosystems to enhance adaptive capacity. By harnessing the protective functions of ecosystems—such as flood regulation, soil stabilization, and water purification—communities can bolster their resilience to extreme weather events, sea-level rise, and other climate-induced threats.

Moreover, EbA aligns with the principles of sustainable development by promoting ecosystem health and functionality alongside human development objectives. It recognizes that intact ecosystems not only provide critical services for human survival and well-being but also play a vital role in maintaining ecological balance and biodiversity. Therefore, integrating EbA into disaster risk reduction and adaptation strategies entails preserving and restoring ecosystems as a proactive measure to reduce vulnerability and enhance community resilience.

By incorporating EbA into planning and decision-making processes, stakeholders can unlock multiple benefits for both people and nature. Communities can become more resilient to climate change impacts, while simultaneously safeguarding biodiversity, enhancing ecosystem services, and promoting sustainable livelihoods. Ultimately, EbA offers a holistic and nature-based approach to adaptation that recognizes the interconnectedness of ecosystems and human societies, fostering resilience in the face of evolving environmental challenges.

Environmental Impact Assessment (EIA) is a systematic process employed to evaluate the potential environmental consequences of proposed projects or developments before they are undertaken. The primary objective of EIA is to identify, predict, and mitigate any adverse effects that the project may have on the environment, surrounding ecosystems, and local communities. By conducting EIAs, decision-makers can make informed choices about whether or how to proceed with a project, taking into account its potential environmental impacts [486].

The EIA process involves several key steps, including screening, scoping, assessment, and decision-making. During the screening phase, the project is evaluated to determine if it requires a full environmental assessment. If deemed necessary, the scope of the assessment is defined during the scoping phase, outlining the key environmental factors and potential impacts to be considered.

Subsequently, the environmental assessment is conducted, which involves gathering data, analysing potential impacts, and predicting the project's effects on various environmental components, such as air quality, water resources, biodiversity, and land use. Social and economic factors, including community health, livelihoods, and cultural heritage, are also assessed to understand the project's broader implications.

Based on the assessment findings, mitigation measures and alternatives are proposed to minimize or eliminate adverse impacts on the environment and local communities. These measures may include changes to project design, implementation of environmental management plans, or compensation for affected stakeholders. Decision-makers then use the results of the EIA to make informed choices about the project, considering its environmental, social, and economic implications.

Conducting an Environmental Impact Assessment (EIA) involves a systematic process to evaluate the potential environmental consequences of proposed projects or developments. The steps involved in conducting an EIA include:

- **Initiation and Screening**:
  - The process begins with the initiation of the EIA, where the need for an assessment is determined based on the nature, scale, and potential environmental significance of the project.
  - Screening involves identifying whether the project falls under the scope of activities that require a full environmental assessment. Projects with significant environmental impacts typically proceed to the next stage.
- **Scoping**:
  - Scoping defines the boundaries and key environmental factors to be considered during the assessment. It involves identifying the potential environmental impacts, stakeholders, and relevant regulatory requirements.
  - Stakeholder engagement is crucial during scoping to gather input from various parties, including government agencies, local communities, environmental organizations, and project proponents.
- **Baseline Data Collection**:
  - Baseline data collection involves gathering information about the existing environmental conditions in the project area. This includes data on air quality, water resources, biodiversity, land use, soil quality, cultural heritage, and socio-economic aspects.

  - Field surveys, site visits, literature reviews, and consultations with experts are common methods used to collect baseline data.

- **Impact Prediction and Assessment**:
  - Impact prediction involves assessing how the proposed project may affect the environment based on the collected baseline data and project plans.
  - Environmental impacts are identified, categorized, and assessed in terms of their magnitude, significance, duration, and spatial extent. Common impact categories include air quality, water quality, noise pollution, habitat loss, and socio-economic impacts.
  - Predictive tools, such as environmental modelling, simulation techniques, and Geographic Information Systems (GIS), may be used to assess and visualize potential impacts.

- **Alternatives Analysis**:
  - Alternatives analysis involves evaluating different project options or design alternatives to identify the most environmentally sustainable option.
  - This step explores alternative locations, designs, technologies, or operational practices that could minimize environmental impacts or achieve project objectives more effectively.

- **Mitigation and Enhancement Measures**:
  - Based on the identified impacts, mitigation measures are proposed to minimize, avoid, or compensate for adverse environmental effects.
  - Mitigation measures may include design modifications, pollution control measures, habitat restoration, compensation for affected communities, or development of environmental management plans.
  - Enhancement measures aim to maximize positive environmental outcomes and may include measures to enhance biodiversity, promote sustainable resource use, or improve environmental quality.

- **Reporting and Documentation**:
  - The findings of the EIA are compiled into a comprehensive report, which typically includes an executive summary, project description, baseline information, impact assessment, mitigation measures, and conclusions.
  - The report is submitted to regulatory authorities, decision-makers, and stakeholders for review and approval.
- **Decision-Making and Public Consultation**:
  - The EIA report is reviewed by regulatory authorities and decision-makers who consider the assessment findings when making decisions about the project's approval, modification, or rejection.
  - Public consultation and participation are integral parts of the decision-making process, allowing stakeholders to provide feedback, raise concerns, and contribute to the decision-making process.
- **Monitoring and Follow-Up**:
  - Monitoring and follow-up activities are conducted to ensure that the proposed mitigation measures are implemented as planned and to monitor the actual environmental impacts during project implementation.
  - Regular monitoring helps verify the effectiveness of mitigation measures, detect any unforeseen impacts, and inform adaptive management strategies.

Community participation and the integration of indigenous knowledge play a crucial role in enhancing the effectiveness of disaster mitigation efforts. By actively engaging local communities and incorporating indigenous wisdom and traditional practices, disaster managers can access a wealth of knowledge deeply rooted in centuries of environmental interaction [487]. Indigenous communities possess intricate systems of ecosystem management knowledge, passed down through generations, providing valuable insights into local ecosystems, weather patterns, and natural hazard dynamics [488]. This indigenous knowledge acts as a repository of wisdom, offering practical solutions for sustainable disaster risk reduction that align with cultural values [489].

Involving local communities not only taps into their knowledge but also fosters a sense of ownership and empowerment, ensuring that mitigation strategies address the specific needs and priorities of those directly impacted by disasters [490]. By engaging community members in decision-making processes, disaster managers can leverage local expertise and promote a collaborative approach to building resilience [491]. The Sendai Framework for Disaster Risk Reduction 2015-2030 advocates for the incorporation of indigenous knowledge and practices to complement scientific knowledge in emergency and disaster management [492].

Furthermore, the engagement of indigenous knowledge in disaster risk reduction is increasingly recognized as essential for enhancing resilience [493]. Indigenous knowledge systems are seen as critical elements in disaster resilience, as highlighted in frameworks like the Hyogo Framework for Action, emphasizing the importance of building the resilience of nations and communities to disasters [494]. The integration of indigenous and local knowledge, wisdom, and skills into policy frameworks is viewed as a wise decision to enhance disaster risk reduction efforts [495].

Incorporating indigenous knowledge into disaster mitigation efforts not only enhances the effectiveness of mitigation measures but also contributes to the preservation of indigenous cultures and ways of life. Indigenous communities possess valuable time-tested strategies for adapting to environmental changes and mitigating risks, deeply rooted in their cultural identities [308]. By acknowledging and integrating these traditional practices, disaster managers can develop more inclusive, sustainable, and culturally appropriate strategies for reducing disaster risks and building resilience in vulnerable areas [496].

Community participation plays a crucial role in strengthening social cohesion and resilience within local communities. Engagement initiatives foster networks of mutual support, cooperation, and solidarity, creating a robust foundation for collective action during disasters [497]. This social capital serves as a critical resource in times of crisis, enabling communities to mobilize effectively and recover swiftly from adverse events.

The Sendai Framework for Disaster Risk Reduction 2015-2030 advocates for the incorporation of Indigenous knowledge and practices to complement scientific knowledge for effective and inclusive emergency and disaster management [487]. There is a growing awareness of the value of indigenous knowledge within disaster risk reduction, prompting calls for its integration into disaster management plans [498].

Indigenous knowledge has been increasingly recognized as an important information source for reducing disaster risk in various parts of the world [499]. Studies have shown that indigenous knowledge remains integral to agricultural practices, drought risk reduction strategies, and resilience against disasters [500]. The integration of indigenous knowledge with existing scientific knowledge enhances the understanding of disaster causal factors and aids in the formulation of effective policy frameworks at different government levels.

Regulatory frameworks and stringent enforcement of environmental laws are essential components in safeguarding ecosystems and promoting sustainable development. Governments play a critical role in establishing and implementing policies that prioritize ecosystem conservation, disaster risk reduction, and sustainable land use practices. These frameworks are designed to minimize environmental degradation and mitigate disaster risks by regulating land use, pollution control, resource extraction, and infrastructure development [501].

Effective enforcement mechanisms are crucial for upholding environmental laws and ensuring accountability for violations. Governments need to invest in robust monitoring, enforcement, and compliance mechanisms to detect and deter environmental offenses effectively. By enforcing regulatory frameworks, governments signal that environmental protection is a priority and non-compliance will not be tolerated. Strong enforcement helps deter environmentally harmful practices, promote responsible behaviour, and safeguard ecosystems for future generations [501].

Regulatory frameworks help balance development interests with environmental conservation imperatives by creating clear rules and standards. Through strategic planning and zoning ordinances, governments can designate protected areas, restrict development in sensitive zones, and promote sustainable resource management. By enforcing these frameworks, governments contribute to the resilience and sustainability of communities and ecosystems, fostering a harmonious coexistence between human activities and the natural environment [501].

Robust regulatory frameworks and stringent enforcement of environmental laws are indispensable for sustainable development. Governments play a pivotal role in establishing policies that prioritize ecosystem conservation and disaster risk reduction. By enacting laws that set clear standards for environmental protection and investing in effective enforcement mechanisms, governments can ensure the preservation of natural resources, mitigate disaster risks, and promote responsible behaviour among individuals and businesses [501].

Capacity building and awareness initiatives are indispensable components of efforts to integrate environmental considerations into disaster mitigation strategies. These initiatives aim to empower a diverse range of stakeholders, including government agencies, civil society organizations, and local communities, with the knowledge, skills, and resources necessary to effectively address environmental challenges and reduce disaster risks.

Education lies at the core of capacity building efforts, providing stakeholders with a comprehensive understanding of the intricate linkages between ecosystems and disasters. Training programs and workshops offer opportunities for stakeholders to deepen their knowledge of environmental processes, ecosystem services, and the impacts of human activities on natural systems. By fostering a deeper understanding of these interconnections, stakeholders are better equipped to identify environmentally sustainable approaches to disaster mitigation and resilience building.

Awareness-raising campaigns play a crucial role in promoting a culture of environmental stewardship and disaster preparedness within communities. These campaigns aim to inform and engage individuals and communities about the importance of preserving ecosystems, reducing environmental risks, and adopting sustainable practices. Through targeted messaging, outreach activities, and community events, awareness-raising initiatives seek to foster a sense of collective responsibility for environmental conservation and disaster resilience.

Capacity building and awareness initiatives also facilitate the exchange of knowledge and best practices among stakeholders, enabling them to learn from each other's experiences and innovations. Collaborative learning platforms, knowledge-sharing networks, and peer-to-peer exchanges provide opportunities for stakeholders to share insights, lessons learned, and successful strategies for integrating environmental considerations into disaster mitigation efforts.

Moreover, capacity building efforts extend beyond traditional education and training programs to encompass the development of practical skills and tools for implementing environmental considerations in disaster risk reduction. This may include the development of guidelines, protocols, and decision-support tools tailored to the needs of different stakeholders. By equipping stakeholders with practical resources and tools, capacity building initiatives enable them to translate knowledge into action and implement effective environmental measures in their respective contexts.

In essence, capacity building and awareness initiatives serve as catalysts for fostering a culture of environmental resilience and sustainability within communities and institutions. By empowering stakeholders with the knowledge, skills, and resources needed to integrate environmental considerations into disaster mitigation strategies, these initiatives contribute to the development of more resilient and sustainable communities that are better equipped to address environmental challenges and reduce disaster risks.

International cooperation stands as a cornerstone in addressing the complex and interconnected environmental considerations inherent in disaster mitigation. Recognizing the transboundary nature of many environmental challenges and disasters, countries across the globe have increasingly turned to collaborative approaches to foster knowledge exchange, share best practices, and mobilize resources for effective mitigation efforts.

At the heart of international cooperation lies the sharing of knowledge and expertise, enabling countries to learn from each other's experiences and innovations in environmental management and disaster risk reduction. Through platforms such as international conferences, workshops, and knowledge-sharing networks, countries can exchange insights into successful strategies, emerging trends, and innovative technologies for integrating environmental considerations into disaster mitigation.

Moreover, international cooperation facilitates the pooling of resources and expertise to address common environmental challenges and build resilience to disasters. Collaborative initiatives, such as joint research projects, technical assistance programs, and capacity-building activities, allow countries to leverage their collective strengths and resources to tackle complex environmental issues that transcend national boundaries.

Multilateral frameworks and agreements play a pivotal role in facilitating international cooperation on environmental considerations in disaster mitigation. Treaties such as the Sendai Framework for Disaster Risk Reduction and the Paris Agreement on Climate Change provide frameworks for countries to coordinate their efforts, set common goals, and mobilize resources for disaster resilience and environmental sustainability.

Furthermore, international cooperation fosters solidarity and mutual support among nations, particularly in times of crisis. Countries often come together to provide humanitarian assistance, share expertise, and offer financial support to those affected by environmental disasters, underscoring the importance of global solidarity in addressing shared environmental challenges.

11

Technology and Innovation in Disaster Management

Use of Technology in Risk Assessment, Response, and Recovery

The integration of technology in risk assessment, response, and recovery stages significantly enhances the efficacy and efficiency of disaster management endeavours. In the phase of risk assessment, various technological tools such as remote sensing, satellite imagery, and sensor networks are employed. These systems provide real-time data on environmental conditions, infrastructure integrity, and natural phenomena like weather patterns and seismic activity. Additionally, Geographic Information Systems (GIS) technology integrates spatial data to analyse and visualize risk factors, enabling authorities to identify high-risk areas and prioritize mitigation efforts. Advanced predictive modelling techniques, including machine learning algorithms and simulation software, aid in forecasting the potential impact of disasters by simulating various scenarios.

During the response phase, technology facilitates rapid communication and coordination among emergency responders, government agencies, and affected communities. Mobile devices, radio systems, and emergency alert systems ensure timely dissemination of critical information and instructions. Information technology tools such as GIS, dashboards, and social media monitoring platforms provide real-time situational awareness, enabling responders to assess the evolving situation and allocate resources effectively. Additionally, drones, unmanned aerial vehicles (UAVs), and robotics are utilized for search and rescue operations in hazardous environments, enabling access to inaccessible areas and delivery of supplies to affected populations. Healthcare technologies, including telemedicine, mobile clinics, and medical drones, support healthcare delivery in disaster-affected areas, addressing medical needs especially in areas with limited access to traditional healthcare facilities.

In the recovery phase, technology aids in managing and analysing data related to damage assessment, resource allocation, and recovery progress. Information systems, cloud computing, and data analytics tools facilitate the collection, storage, and processing of large volumes of data. Construction technologies such as 3D printing, prefabrication, and modular construction expedite the restoration of critical infrastructure, enabling rapid deployment of temporary structures and expediting permanent repairs. Social media platforms, online forums, and mobile applications foster community engagement and participation in the recovery process, facilitating communication between residents, volunteers, and aid organizations. Furthermore, virtual reality (VR), augmented reality (AR), and teletherapy platforms offer innovative approaches to delivering psychosocial support services to disaster survivors, providing immersive experiences, remote counselling sessions, and mental health resources to address trauma and emotional distress.

Risk Reduction

Tools such as monitoring technology for buildings, unmanned aerial vehicles (UAVs), and sensor network systems aid local authorities in mitigating disaster risk. For instance, sensor networks deployed in critical infrastructure like bridges and roads monitor degradation and water level changes, providing valuable data for predicting and analysing river flooding [502]. Additionally, the use of open satellite imagery is increasingly popular for monitoring land use changes, which can inform hazard assessments in disaster planning. Information systems play a crucial role in recording information for disaster risk reduction, with recent advancements in AI enabling the analysis of recorded data to generate alerts, such as detecting water level rises from social media posts [502].

Preparedness

Information collected through sensor network systems enhances community-based disaster preparedness by identifying vulnerable areas. Information technologies facilitate scenario simulations and field exercises prior to disasters, with tools like Virtual Reality (VR) training systems offering immersive experiences to educate people on disaster survival techniques [502]. Messenger applications and online dashboards allow citizens to report their situations and requests, with specific algorithms categorizing critical information. These technologies also contribute to creating a knowledge repository based on past disaster experiences. Information systems support information exchange in disaster preparedness.

Response

During the initial response to disasters, information systems play a critical role in exchanging information essential for operations such as confirming the whereabouts and safety of residents, establishing and operating evacuation centres, managing relief goods, supporting evacuees, and issuing disaster victim certificates [502]. Social media has altered citizen response dynamics, enabling real-time reporting of situations, although challenges exist in verifying the credibility of such information. Initiatives like DISAster-information ANAlyzer (DISA ANA) aim to improve the trustworthiness of social media information. Collaboration with volunteers and IT professionals, as seen with initiatives like "shinsai.info" after the 2011 earthquake, addresses resource limitations in local governments during emergencies [502].

Recovery

Following the initial response, local governments focus on supporting residents in returning to normalcy. Effective operation and management of evacuation centres are crucial, highlighting the need for information systems to coordinate available resources. Systems like Sahana, designed for humanitarian assistance, aid in managing disaster response operations but face challenges in integrating with other recovery systems. Integration of data from various systems remains an unresolved issue [502]. Social media platforms facilitate situational awareness and collaboration between local communities and disaster relief agencies. While information systems are designed to aid in disaster recovery, the integration of data across different systems requires attention and resolution.

The field of emergency management relies heavily on technology and various tools for disaster recovery, encompassing a wide range of hardware, software, and resources. These technological tools are utilized by emergency responders, scientists, and analysts across different phases of disaster preparedness and response.

In the context of hardware, emergency management often involves the use of specialized equipment such as communication devices (e.g., radios, satellite phones), vehicles (e.g., ambulances, rescue boats), and protective gear (e.g., helmets, hazmat suits). These hardware resources enable responders to communicate effectively, navigate hazardous environments, and ensure their safety while carrying out rescue and recovery operations.

On the software front, there are various computer programs, applications, and platforms designed specifically for disaster management purposes. These software tools include geographic information systems (GIS) for mapping and spatial analysis, incident management systems for coordinating response efforts, simulation software for training and scenario planning, and data management systems for storing and analysing information related to disasters.

Additionally, there are numerous resources available to support disaster recovery efforts, ranging from databases and online repositories of information to educational materials and guidelines. These resources provide valuable insights, best practices, and reference materials for emergency managers, policymakers, and other stakeholders involved in disaster response and recovery.

Overall, the technology in emergency management and tools for disaster recovery form a comprehensive toolkit that enhances the capabilities of responders and enables effective coordination, decision-making, and resource allocation throughout all phases of disaster management. Some of these technologies and their applications will now be considered.

Seismographs

A seismograph serves as a crucial instrument in monitoring and recording ground motion during earthquakes, offering valuable insights into the behaviour and characteristics of seismic events. By detecting and measuring seismic waves generated by the movement of tectonic plates beneath the Earth's surface, seismographs provide scientists with essential data to analyse earthquake activity. Despite advancements in technology, accurately predicting earthquakes remains a significant challenge. Unlike some other natural phenomena, earthquakes cannot be reliably forecasted with precision. However, scientists utilize various methods, including data analysis, probabilistic models, and seismic activity monitoring, to estimate the likelihood of future earthquakes and their potential impact on affected regions. These predictions are often based on historical seismic data, geological studies, and mathematical algorithms, helping authorities and communities prepare for potential seismic events and mitigate their impact.

Figure 54: A seismometer, Mount Vesuvius, Italy. Jebulon, CC0, via Wikimedia Commons.

Emergency managers and coordinators can utilize seismograph data to enhance their preparedness and response strategies for earthquakes. By monitoring ground motion in real-time during seismic events, seismographs provide critical information about the intensity, duration, and location of earthquakes. Emergency managers can use this data to assess the severity of the earthquake and its potential impact on infrastructure, communities, and critical facilities.

Additionally, while earthquakes cannot be predicted with absolute certainty, seismograph data can help emergency managers forecast the likelihood of future seismic events based on historical patterns, regional seismic activity, and probabilistic models. By analysing this information, emergency managers can develop risk assessments, evacuation plans, and resource allocation strategies to mitigate the impact of future earthquakes.

Furthermore, seismograph data enables emergency managers to coordinate response efforts more effectively. By understanding the magnitude and distribution of ground motion, emergency managers can prioritize response activities, deploy resources to affected areas, and coordinate search and rescue operations. This real-time information also facilitates communication with other response agencies, government officials, and the public, enabling timely and informed decision-making during earthquake events.

Overall, seismograph data serves as a valuable tool for emergency managers and coordinators in assessing earthquake risk, planning response actions, and coordinating efforts to protect lives and property during seismic events.

Advanced Hurricane and Tropical Cyclone Forecasting

Preparing for and enduring hurricanes and tropical cyclones relies heavily on technology, forecasting tools, and observational methodologies. These resources play a crucial role in predicting various aspects of these weather events, including their size, structure, intensity, and projected landfall and path.

The National Hurricane Center (USA) employs a range of instruments and platforms to collect data for tracking and predicting hurricanes. These include buoys, radar systems, ships, reconnaissance aircraft, satellites, and land-based platforms. By gathering information from these sources, forecasters can monitor the development and movement of hurricanes, providing valuable insights into their potential impacts on coastal areas and inland regions.

In the case of tropical cyclones, ocean-based remote measurements using satellites are instrumental in tracking and predicting these weather phenomena. These satellites capture data on various atmospheric and oceanic parameters, enabling forecasters to monitor the formation and trajectory of tropical cyclones with greater accuracy.

The use of advanced warning technology allows individuals and communities to better prepare for impending hurricanes and tropical cyclones. By receiving timely and accurate forecasts, people can take proactive measures to secure their homes, protect their property, and, if necessary, evacuate to safer locations. This early warning system helps mitigate the risks associated with these hazardous weather events, ultimately saving lives and reducing the overall impact on affected areas.

Emergency managers and coordinators can utilize the information provided by technology, forecasting tools, and observational methodologies to enhance preparedness and response efforts for hurricanes and tropical cyclones. By leveraging these resources, emergency management teams can:

1. Monitor and Track Storm Development: Utilize data collected from buoys, radar systems, ships, reconnaissance aircraft, satellites, and land-based platforms to track the development and movement of hurricanes and tropical cyclones in real-time. This information allows emergency managers to assess the size, structure, intensity, and projected path of the storm, enabling them to make informed decisions about evacuation orders, resource allocation, and emergency response strategies.

2. Assess Potential Impacts: Analyze forecasted data to assess the potential impacts of hurricanes and tropical cyclones on coastal areas and inland regions. By understanding the projected landfall and path of the storm, emergency managers can identify high-risk areas, prioritize evacuation zones, and implement protective measures to mitigate damage to infrastructure and minimize the risk to human life.

3. Communicate Early Warnings: Use advanced warning technology to disseminate timely and accurate forecasts to individuals and communities in the path of the storm. By providing early warnings and actionable information, emergency managers can empower residents to take proactive measures to prepare for the impending weather event, such as securing their homes, stocking up on essential supplies, and making evacuation plans.

4. Coordinate Response Efforts: Coordinate response efforts among local, state, and federal agencies to ensure a swift and effective response to hurricanes and tropical cyclones. By sharing information and resources, emergency managers can streamline evacuation procedures, deploy emergency personnel and equipment, and establish emergency shelters to provide assistance to affected populations.

5. Evaluate and Adapt Plans: Continuously evaluate and adapt emergency pre-

paredness and response plans based on lessons learned from previous storms and evolving technology and forecasting capabilities. By incorporating new data and technologies into their planning processes, emergency managers can improve the effectiveness and efficiency of their response efforts, ultimately enhancing community resilience and reducing the impact of future storms.

Sensor Network System

Sensor network systems are instrumental in detecting activity and monitoring the condition of critical infrastructure such as bridges and roads. These systems consist of sensors strategically placed on the infrastructure and its surroundings to continuously collect data on various parameters. For example, they can detect vibrations, movements, or changes in temperature and humidity. Additionally, they can measure factors like water levels, which are particularly relevant in flood-prone areas.

Figure 55: Installing Alert Wildfire Camera Detection System. The Alert Wildfire detection camera project, which began over a decade ago, was developed in conjunction with the Bureau of Land Management (BLM) Oregon/Washington, BLM Idaho, BLM Nevada, and University of Oregon's Seismological Laboratories. BLM Oregon & Washington, CC BY 2.0, via Wikimedia Commons.

The data collected by sensor network systems provides valuable insights into the integrity of the infrastructure and any potential risks or vulnerabilities. By analysing this real-time data, authorities can assess the condition of sensor-equipped infrastructure and identify any anomalies or signs of damage. This proactive approach allows for early detection of issues, enabling prompt intervention to prevent further damage or potential disasters.

In the context of disaster recovery, sensor network systems serve as critical tools for assessing the impact of natural disasters on infrastructure. By providing data on compromised or damaged infrastructure, they help emergency responders and recovery teams prioritize their efforts and allocate resources effectively. This information is essential for determining which bridges and roads are safe to use and which may require immediate repair or reinforcement before they can be reopened to traffic. Overall, sensor network systems play a crucial role in disaster recovery efforts by providing timely and accurate data to support decision-making and facilitate the restoration of essential infrastructure.

Emergency managers and coordinators can leverage sensor network systems in several ways to enhance disaster preparedness, response, and recovery efforts. Firstly, these systems provide real-time data on critical infrastructure such as bridges and roads, allowing authorities to monitor their condition continuously. By detecting vibrations, movements, temperature fluctuations, and water levels, sensor networks offer valuable insights into potential risks or vulnerabilities, especially in flood-prone areas.

With access to this data, emergency managers can assess the integrity of infrastructure and identify any signs of damage or deterioration promptly. This proactive approach enables them to intervene early to mitigate further damage or potential disasters. For example, if sensors detect increased water levels near a bridge, emergency managers can issue warnings and take preventive measures to minimize the risk of flooding or structural failure.

Figure 56: CSIRO ScienceImage 3876 A remote sensing node part of CSIROs Fleck wireless sensor network technology. A solar-powered wireless sensor network at the CSIRO ICT Centre in Brisbane has had its second birthday, maintaining its position as the longest ad-hoc wireless sensor network in Australia. The Brisbane network measures environmental variables such as temperature, soil moisture, water quality, humidity and solar energy levels. CSIRO, CC BY 3.0, via Wikimedia Commons.

During disaster recovery efforts, sensor network systems play a crucial role in assessing the impact of natural disasters on infrastructure. By providing data on compromised or damaged infrastructure, these systems help prioritize response efforts and allocate resources effectively. Emergency responders can use this information to determine which bridges and roads are safe for use and which require immediate repair or reinforcement before reopening to traffic.

Overall, sensor network systems empower emergency managers and coordinators with timely and accurate data to make informed decisions and facilitate the restoration of essential infrastructure. By leveraging this technology, they can enhance the resilience of communities and minimize the disruption caused by natural disasters.

CAMEO

The Computer-Aided Management of Emergency Operations (CAMEO) software represents a sophisticated suite of environmental software tools designed to assist in both the preparation for and response to a wide range of chemical and oil-related emergencies. With its extensive capabilities, CAMEO is widely recognized as one of the most comprehensive pieces of emergency management technology available today. Developed to address the complex challenges posed by hazardous material incidents, CAMEO offers a suite of features and functionalities aimed at supporting emergency responders, environmental professionals, and decision-makers in effectively managing emergencies.

CAMEO, a comprehensive tool for emergency responders, integrates data from various sources and uses advanced algorithms to assist in managing chemical and oil spills effectively. It offers databases of hazardous substances, modelling capabilities for predicting chemical behaviour, and mapping functionalities to visualize contaminant spread, enabling emergency managers to make informed decisions and develop tailored response strategies [503].

Additionally, CAMEO supports emergency preparedness activities by facilitating scenario-based exercises, response plan development, and emergency scenario simulations. Its user-friendly interface and customizable features help organizations proactively identify risks, enhance readiness, and respond effectively to chemical and oil-related emergencies [504]. By emphasizing community resilience and integrating equity and social justice considerations in preparedness planning, CAMEO contributes significantly to public health, environmental protection, and community safety during emergencies [504].

CAMEO software is widely available and accessible to emergency management agencies, environmental professionals, and other relevant stakeholders worldwide. Developed by the United States Environmental Protection Agency (EPA) and the National Oceanic and Atmospheric Administration (NOAA), CAMEO is distributed free of charge and can be downloaded from the agencies' respective websites.

While CAMEO is primarily used in the United States, its tools and resources have been adopted by emergency responders and organizations in many countries around the globe. Additionally, the software is designed to be customizable and adaptable to different regulatory frameworks, emergency response protocols, and environmental conditions, making it suitable for use in diverse geographic regions and contexts.

However, the availability and use of CAMEO may vary depending on factors such as local regulations, resource constraints, and institutional capacity. Some regions or organizations may have limited awareness of CAMEO or may face challenges in implementing the software due to technical or logistical constraints. Nonetheless, efforts are continuously made to promote the adoption and utilization of CAMEO worldwide through training, outreach, and collaboration initiatives within the emergency management and environmental communities.

Emergency managers and coordinators can leverage the Computer-Aided Management of Emergency Operations (CAMEO) software to enhance their preparedness, response, and recovery efforts in handling chemical and oil-related emergencies. CAMEO offers a sophisticated suite of environmental software tools tailored to address the complex challenges posed by hazardous material incidents. One of its primary uses is aiding emergency responders in assessing and mitigating the impact of chemical and oil spills. By providing databases of hazardous substances, modelling capabilities to predict chemical behaviour, and mapping functionalities to visualize contaminant spread, CAMEO enables responders to make informed decisions and develop effective response strategies in real-time.

Moreover, CAMEO serves as a valuable resource for emergency preparedness activities. It allows users to conduct scenario-based exercises, develop response plans, and simulate emergency scenarios, empowering emergency managers to tailor their preparedness efforts to the specific needs and challenges of their communities. By proactively identifying potential risks and vulnerabilities, organizations can enhance their readiness to effectively respond to chemical and oil-related emergencies.

The user-friendly interface and customizable features of CAMEO make it accessible and adaptable for emergency management professionals. Its advanced capabilities facilitate collaboration among stakeholders and streamline communication during emergency response operations. Additionally, CAMEO's comprehensive support extends to the recovery phase, where it assists in assessing damages, managing resources, and facilitating the restoration of affected areas.

Overall, CAMEO represents an indispensable tool for emergency management professionals tasked with safeguarding public health, protecting the environment, and ensuring the safety and resilience of communities in the face of chemical and oil-related emergencies. Its advanced features, coupled with its user-friendly interface, make it a valuable asset for organizations striving to effectively prepare for and respond to hazardous material incidents.

GNOME, ALOHA, CAFE, ESI Maps, ROC

The General NOAA Operational Modelling Environment (GNOME) is software utilized during oil and toxic chemical spills to predict the movement and spread of pollutants on water. By employing intelligent modelling techniques, GNOME plays a crucial role in containing pollutants by providing accurate forecasts of their trajectory and dispersion.

Similarly, the Areal Locations of Hazardous Atmospheres (ALOHA) software tracks airborne pollutants and estimates their movement through the air after release. This information is essential for civilians in affected areas to prepare for potential exposure or evacuation, mitigating the risks associated with airborne toxins.

The Chemical Aquatic Fate and Effects (CAFE) software program enables responders and analysts to assess the potential harm to marine life resulting from oil or chemical spills. By evaluating the impact on aquatic ecosystems, CAFE aids in formulating effective response strategies and minimizing environmental damage.

Environmental Sensitivity Index (ESI) maps provide a summary of coastal resources at risk in the event of an oil or chemical spill. These maps help responders prioritize protective measures and allocate resources to areas most vulnerable to contamination, thereby enhancing the efficiency of response efforts.

Response Options Calculator (ROC) software predicts the degradation and transformation of spilled oil over time and evaluates options for recovery, treatment, or disposal. This critical tool informs decision-making by assessing the feasibility and effectiveness of various response strategies, guiding efforts to salvage resources and mitigate environmental harm.

Overall, these technologies, including GNOME, ALOHA, CAFE, ESI maps, and ROC, play essential roles in disaster recovery by providing accurate predictions, assessing environmental impacts, and guiding response efforts to minimize the consequences of oil and chemical spills.

GNOME, ALOHA, CAFE, ESI maps, and ROC are widely used tools and software programs developed by various governmental and environmental agencies, particularly in countries with significant coastlines or regions prone to environmental hazards such as oil spills or chemical releases. While these technologies may not be available in every single location globally, they are accessible to many emergency management and environmental response agencies worldwide.

The availability of these tools often depends on factors such as government funding, regional priorities, and the level of environmental risk in a given area. Developed countries with established emergency response infrastructure and regulatory frameworks are more likely to have access to these tools, as they are often supported and maintained by national or regional authorities.

In regions where environmental hazards are prevalent or where there is a high risk of oil spills or chemical releases, there is a greater likelihood of these tools being available and actively used by emergency responders and environmental agencies. However, even in areas with lower environmental risk, these tools may still be accessible through international collaborations, partnerships, or training programs aimed at enhancing preparedness and response capabilities.

Overall, while the availability of GNOME, ALOHA, CAFE, ESI maps, and ROC may vary depending on geographical location and local resources, they are important resources in disaster response and environmental management efforts worldwide.

Virtual Reality

Disaster preparedness involves ensuring that emergency responders are adequately trained to handle high-intensity situations effectively. Traditionally, training options have been somewhat limited, often relying on drills and simulated emergency scenarios to provide authentic learning experiences. However, recent advancements in technology, particularly the introduction of virtual reality (VR) training, have revolutionized disaster preparedness efforts.

Virtual reality training offers responders a highly immersive and realistic training environment, allowing them to experience lifelike simulations of various disaster scenarios. Unlike traditional methods, VR training provides a dynamic and interactive platform where responders can practice their skills in simulated disaster situations, ranging from natural disasters to industrial accidents. This technology enables responders to familiarize themselves with emergency procedures, assess different scenarios, and make critical decisions in a risk-free virtual setting.

In addition to virtual reality, augmented reality (AR) and virtual reality (VR) technologies have also emerged as valuable tools in disaster management. These technologies offer a range of applications beyond training, including education, disaster relief planning, donation drives, and information-sharing. AR and VR platforms can create virtual social spaces for remote meetings, allowing stakeholders to collaborate and coordinate response efforts effectively, even across vast distances.

Moreover, AR and VR technologies can aid search and rescue operations by providing real-time data and simulations. Responders can use AR overlays to visualize geographic information, structural damage, and other critical data, enhancing situational awareness and improving decision-making during rescue missions. By leveraging these innovative technologies, disaster management professionals can enhance disaster preparedness and response capabilities, ultimately improving outcomes and saving lives in times of crisis.

Telehealth

Amidst the onset of the COVID-19 pandemic, telehealth emerged as a crucial tool for healthcare facilities and hospitals to combat the spread of the virus. By allowing for the remote delivery of primary care services, telehealth enabled patients to consult with healthcare providers without the need for in-person visits, thereby reducing the risk of exposure to the virus. Additionally, intelligent chatbots were developed to provide initial diagnoses based on the symptoms reported by patients, offering a preliminary assessment of their health status.

Despite the subsequent introduction of COVID-19 vaccines and the subsequent decline in COVID cases, telehealth continues to play a valuable role in healthcare delivery, even in non-pandemic situations. Its benefits extend beyond mitigating virus transmission, offering a safe and convenient means of accessing healthcare services for patients. Telehealth allows individuals to consult with healthcare professionals remotely, eliminating the need for travel and reducing wait times for appointments. This accessibility makes healthcare more convenient and equitable, particularly for individuals with limited mobility or those residing in remote areas. Thus, telehealth has established itself as a sustainable and effective healthcare delivery model, poised to transform the way healthcare services are accessed and delivered in the future.

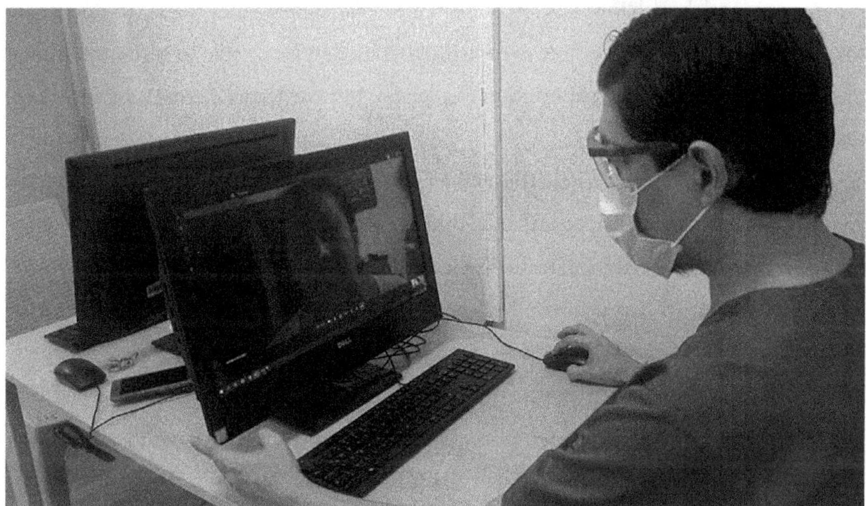

Figure 57: Doctor attending by teleconsultation. Ceibos, CC BY-SA 4.0, via Wikimedia Commons.

Emergency managers and coordinators can leverage telehealth as a valuable tool in disaster preparedness and response efforts. During public health emergencies like the COVID-19 pandemic, telehealth enables healthcare facilities to provide essential medical services while minimizing the risk of virus transmission. Emergency managers can collaborate with healthcare providers to incorporate telehealth into their disaster response plans, ensuring that medical care remains accessible to affected populations, even in situations where in-person visits are impractical or unsafe.

Intelligent chatbots, which offer initial diagnoses based on patient symptoms, can serve as triage tools during emergencies, helping emergency managers and healthcare professionals prioritize patient care. By providing a preliminary assessment of patients' health status, chatbots can assist in identifying individuals who require immediate medical attention, thus optimizing resource allocation and reducing strain on healthcare facilities.

Furthermore, telehealth offers a means of delivering healthcare services to remote or isolated areas during disasters when traditional medical infrastructure may be compromised. Emergency managers can establish telehealth networks to connect patients with healthcare providers remotely, facilitating timely medical consultations and interventions.

In non-pandemic scenarios, telehealth remains a valuable resource for emergency managers, offering a convenient and efficient means of accessing healthcare services. By incorporating telehealth into disaster preparedness plans, emergency managers can ensure that healthcare remains accessible to individuals who may be unable to access traditional medical facilities due to transportation challenges, infrastructure damage, or other barriers.

Telehealth represents a sustainable and effective healthcare delivery model that emergency managers can utilize to enhance disaster preparedness, response, and recovery efforts. By leveraging telehealth technologies and partnerships with healthcare providers, emergency managers can improve healthcare accessibility and resilience in the face of emergencies and disasters.

Telehealth availability varies depending on factors such as infrastructure, healthcare regulations, and technological adoption. While telehealth has seen significant growth and expansion, particularly during the COVID-19 pandemic, it may not be universally accessible in all regions or communities.

In some areas, telehealth services may be readily available, with healthcare providers offering remote consultations and virtual care options. These regions may have robust internet connectivity, supportive healthcare policies, and established telehealth infrastructure.

However, in other areas, especially rural or underserved communities, access to telehealth services may be limited due to challenges such as inadequate internet connectivity, technological barriers, or a lack of healthcare resources. In such cases, individuals may face difficulties accessing telehealth services and may need to rely on traditional in-person healthcare options.

Efforts are underway to expand telehealth access and address disparities in availability. Government initiatives, private sector investments, and community partnerships aim to improve internet infrastructure, increase technological literacy, and expand telehealth services to underserved populations.

While telehealth has the potential to improve healthcare access and outcomes, ensuring its widespread availability requires ongoing efforts to address barriers and promote equitable access to healthcare services for all individuals, regardless of location or socioeconomic status.

DEXTER

DEXTER, which stands for Detection of Explosives and Firearms to Counter Terrorism, represents an innovative approach to enhancing security measures in densely populated public spaces prone to terrorist threats. This technology is designed to detect both firearms and explosives, thereby bolstering security measures at locations such as subway stations, airports, and venues hosting large crowds [505]. Recently, the first successful testing of DEXTER technology was conducted in Rome, marking a significant milestone in its development and deployment.

The implementation of DEXTER technology is expected to play a pivotal role in NATO's counterterrorism efforts, with plans underway to roll out this tool as a primary method of enhancing security measures. By leveraging advanced detection capabilities, DEXTER aims to identify potential threats in high-traffic areas, enabling authorities to respond swiftly and effectively to mitigate security risks and safeguard public safety.

With its ability to detect both firearms and explosives, DEXTER offers a comprehensive solution for addressing diverse security threats in dynamic environments. By integrating cutting-edge technology with robust security protocols, DEXTER represents a proactive approach to combating terrorism and enhancing security measures in critical public spaces. As it continues to undergo testing and refinement, DEXTER holds the promise of significantly enhancing security infrastructure and strengthening defences against evolving threats posed by terrorism.

As of now, the availability of DEXTER is limited as it is still in the testing and development phase, with successful testing completed in specific locations like Rome. The future rollout of DEXTER technology on a broader scale will depend on various factors such as further testing, regulatory approvals, and deployment strategies by relevant authorities or organizations. Similar to other advanced security technologies, the adoption and deployment of DEXTER may vary regionally based on specific security needs, resource availability, and implementation timelines [506].

The successful implementation of advanced technologies like DEXTER often hinges on factors such as technological organizational readiness, availability of resources, and specialized human capital for adoption [507]. Additionally, the evolution of neuroprosthetic interfaces, although making significant strides, still requires substantial improvements to meet design goals and clinical requirements [508]. In the context of robotics, the review on human-like robot manipulation using dexterous hands emphasizes the importance of understanding the history, motivation, and learning-based methods for effectively manipulating dexterous hands [506].

Mobile Applications

Mobile applications have become integral tools in disaster emergency management and preparedness, offering a plethora of features to keep individuals informed and safe during critical situations. The American Red Cross stands at the forefront, providing a suite of free mobile apps tailored specifically for emergency alerts and response. These apps are meticulously designed to offer users a comprehensive array of resources, ensuring they are well-equipped to navigate various disaster scenarios.

To begin, users can download the American Red Cross apps from their respective app stores onto their smartphones or tablets. Once installed, these apps offer a wealth of customizable features and information to cater to diverse emergency needs. With over 30 customizable weather alerts, users can receive real-time notifications about severe weather conditions in their area, empowering them to take timely action and stay safe.

Moreover, the apps provide essential safety tips and guidance for 14 different types of disasters and emergencies, ranging from hurricanes and earthquakes to floods and wildfires. This curated information equips users with the knowledge and strategies needed to mitigate risks and respond effectively to different types of crises. For instance, users can access step-by-step instructions on how to prepare an emergency kit, create a family communication plan, and evacuate safely during a disaster.

In addition to the offerings from the American Red Cross, several other organizations contribute to the ecosystem of disaster preparedness apps. WeatherCaster, Storm Distance Tracker, QuakeFeed, and apps from authoritative bodies such as the National Oceanic Atmospheric Administration (NOAA), FEMA, and the Centers for Disease Control and Prevention (CDC) further augment the user's toolkit for disaster readiness.

Each of these apps serves a specific purpose, whether it's providing real-time updates on weather patterns, tracking the distance of storms, delivering earthquake alerts, or offering guidance on pandemic preparedness. By leveraging these diverse apps in conjunction with one another, users can access a comprehensive suite of tools to stay informed, plan effectively, and respond decisively in the face of emergencies.

The availability of these free disaster apps represents a significant advancement in leveraging technology for public safety. By harnessing the power of mobile applications, individuals can enhance their preparedness and resilience, ultimately contributing to safer and more resilient communities.

Emergency managers and coordinators can leverage mobile applications in several ways to enhance disaster emergency management and preparedness efforts. Firstly, they can encourage the adoption of these free disaster apps among the general public, promoting their availability and highlighting their usefulness in staying informed and safe during critical situations. By educating the community about the features and benefits of these apps, emergency managers can empower individuals to take proactive measures to prepare for and respond to disasters.

Furthermore, emergency managers can incorporate these mobile apps into their communication and outreach strategies. They can use these platforms to disseminate important information and updates to the public, such as evacuation orders, shelter locations, and safety tips. By leveraging the notification features of these apps, emergency managers can ensure that critical information reaches individuals quickly and efficiently, helping to minimize confusion and enhance response coordination.

Additionally, emergency managers can utilize the data and insights generated by these apps to inform their decision-making processes. For example, they can monitor real-time weather alerts and disaster reports to assess the evolving situation and allocate resources accordingly. By analysing trends and patterns in app usage, emergency managers can gain valuable insights into community preparedness levels and identify areas for improvement in their disaster response plans.

Moreover, emergency managers can collaborate with the developers of these apps and other relevant stakeholders to enhance their functionality and usability for disaster response purposes. They can provide feedback on features that would be beneficial for emergency responders and work towards integrating these capabilities into future updates of the apps. By fostering partnerships with app developers and leveraging their expertise, emergency managers can ensure that these tools remain relevant and effective in supporting disaster response efforts.

Mobile applications represent valuable resources for emergency managers and coordinators to enhance disaster emergency management and preparedness. By promoting their adoption, incorporating them into communication strategies, leveraging their data and insights, and collaborating with stakeholders, emergency managers can harness the power of technology to build safer and more resilient communities.

Social Media

Over the past decade, social media has emerged as a powerful tool in disaster monitoring, response, and recovery efforts, revolutionizing the way information is disseminated and assistance is provided during crises. Platforms like Facebook have played a particularly significant role in facilitating communication and support networks during disasters. For example, Facebook hosts dedicated pages for natural disasters, where users can access real-time information and updates on unfolding situations. These pages serve as centralized hubs for sharing critical updates, such as evacuation orders, shelter locations, and emergency contact information, helping affected individuals stay informed and connected.

Moreover, Facebook offers innovative features such as check-in pages, allowing users to quickly and easily indicate their safety status during emergencies. This functionality enables individuals to inform their friends and family members of their well-being with just a few clicks, providing reassurance and reducing anxiety during uncertain times. Additionally, the check-in feature helps emergency responders assess the scope and impact of disasters more efficiently, guiding their deployment of resources and assistance to areas of greatest need.

In addition to its communication and safety-check features, Facebook also serves as a platform for mobilizing support and resources for disaster relief efforts. Through fundraising initiatives and donation campaigns facilitated on the platform, individuals and organizations can contribute to the recovery and rebuilding efforts in affected communities. Facebook's extensive reach and user base make it a powerful tool for galvanizing support and solidarity in the aftermath of disasters, enabling people from around the world to offer assistance and solidarity to those in need.

Social media platforms like Facebook have become indispensable tools in disaster management, providing vital information, facilitating communication, and mobilizing resources to support affected communities. By harnessing the collective power of social networks, these platforms empower individuals to contribute to relief efforts, foster resilience, and strengthen community bonds in the face of adversity.

Emergency managers and coordinators can leverage social media platforms like Facebook as invaluable resources in disaster management and response strategies. Firstly, dedicated pages for natural disasters on Facebook serve as centralized hubs for disseminating real-time information and updates to users. Emergency managers can utilize these pages to share critical updates such as evacuation orders, shelter locations, and emergency contact information, ensuring that affected individuals remain informed and connected during crises.

The check-in feature on Facebook allows users to quickly indicate their safety status during emergencies, providing emergency managers with valuable insights into the scope and impact of disasters. By monitoring these check-ins, emergency responders can efficiently assess the areas of greatest need and deploy resources accordingly, optimizing response efforts and minimizing response times.

Furthermore, Facebook serves as a powerful platform for mobilizing support and resources for disaster relief efforts. Emergency managers can utilize fundraising initiatives and donation campaigns on the platform to solicit contributions from individuals and organizations worldwide. The extensive reach and user base of Facebook enable emergency managers to galvanize support and solidarity in the aftermath of disasters, facilitating the flow of resources to affected communities and accelerating the recovery process.

Disaster Database Management Systems

Disaster Database Management Systems (DDBMS) represent a sophisticated approach to handling the vast array of data generated during disaster events. These computer systems are specifically designed to manage, organize, and retrieve disaster-related information efficiently. With the ability to store diverse types of data, ranging from geographical information to demographic statistics, DDBMS serve as foundational tools for creating comprehensive disaster information networks and software applications. This structured repository of data serves as a crucial resource for emergency management agencies like FEMA, enabling them to make informed decisions and execute effective response strategies.

Disaster Database Management Systems (DDBMS) are recognized as a crucial element within contemporary disaster management infrastructure. By leveraging data and technology, these systems empower emergency management agencies to efficiently gather, analyse, and utilize information to mitigate risks, coordinate response efforts, and aid in recovery post-disaster [509]. The evolution of the field of disaster management highlights the increasing significance of DDBMS in bolstering resilience and preparedness against emerging threats and challenges.

One of the primary functions of DDBMS is to facilitate the dissemination of critical information to vulnerable regions and populations during disaster events. By centralizing data on hazard zones, population demographics, and infrastructure vulnerabilities, these systems empower emergency response professionals to issue timely warnings and advisories to at-risk communities. This proactive approach to communication is instrumental in mitigating the impact of disasters and saving lives by alerting individuals to potential threats and guiding them in taking appropriate protective measures.

Furthermore, DDBMS play a pivotal role in the allocation and distribution of relief funds following a disaster. By aggregating and analysing data on the extent of damage, population displacement, and resource needs, these systems enable authorities to accurately assess the financial requirements for recovery efforts in specific impacted areas. This data-driven approach ensures that relief funds are allocated efficiently and equitably, addressing the most pressing needs of affected communities and facilitating the recovery process.

One of the key advantages of DDBMS is their ability to visualize data in a variety of formats, including graphs, tables, and thematic maps. This visual representation enhances the understanding and interpretation of complex datasets, enabling stakeholders to identify patterns, trends, and spatial relationships within the data. By presenting information in a visually compelling manner, DDBMS facilitate decision-making processes and communication among stakeholders, fostering collaboration and synergy in disaster response and recovery efforts.

Research has shown that integrating eHealth technologies systematically throughout the disaster management cycle can significantly enhance efficiency and effectiveness in disaster scenarios [510]. Additionally, the utilization of Spatial Data Infrastructure (SDI) and web-based systems has been identified as instrumental in facilitating disaster management by addressing spatial data challenges [511]. Moreover, participatory mapping frameworks, such as Smart Web-GIS Disaster Monitoring systems, have been proven to expedite disaster information generation, thereby enhancing community disaster risk management capabilities [512].

Incorporating Internet of Things (IoT) and big data analytics into disaster risk management strategies has become a prevalent approach. This involves focusing on disaster risk reduction, resilience building, and minimizing disaster losses to enhance overall disaster risk management practices [513]. Furthermore, multinational SDI-based systems, like the Andean Information System for Disaster Prevention and Relief, have been developed to integrate spatial information across technical organizations in various countries to facilitate disaster risk management [514].

The role of open geographic data models and analysis tools, such as the Geospatial Data Infrastructure for Disaster Management (GDI4DM) project, has been pivotal in managing preparedness and response phases for disasters [515]. Additionally, the use of technology in disaster management, spanning the pre-disaster, disaster, and post-disaster phases, has been explored to predict, respond to, and analyse the impact of disasters effectively [516].

Management Information System (MIS)

A Management Information System (MIS) serves as a pivotal tool in establishing a Disaster Information Network and Disaster Support System, providing essential capabilities for managing and utilizing disaster-related data effectively. One of the primary functions of MIS in this context is to facilitate hazard mapping, which involves the creation of spatial representations of various hazards such as floods, cyclones, winds, and seismic activities. By integrating geographic information with relevant data sources, MIS enables the generation of hazard maps that identify vulnerable areas and assess the risks posed by different types of disasters.

In addition to hazard mapping, MIS plays a crucial role in providing detailed information on housing stock vulnerability across different districts and regions. Through the compilation and analysis of data on housing infrastructure, construction materials, and structural integrity, MIS generates vulnerability tables that quantify the susceptibility of housing stock to damage and destruction during disaster events. This information is invaluable for disaster preparedness and planning efforts, allowing authorities to prioritize mitigation measures, allocate resources effectively, and develop targeted interventions to enhance the resilience of communities.

Furthermore, MIS serves as a centralized platform for storing, managing, and disseminating disaster-related data to relevant stakeholders and decision-makers. By consolidating diverse datasets, including hazard maps, vulnerability assessments, demographic information, and resource inventories, MIS provides a comprehensive repository of information that supports informed decision-making and strategic planning in disaster management. This data-driven approach enhances the efficiency and effectiveness of disaster response and recovery efforts by ensuring that resources are deployed where they are most needed and that interventions are tailored to the specific needs of affected communities.

Emergency managers and coordinators leverage Management Information Systems (MIS) as a foundational tool in establishing comprehensive Disaster Information Networks and Disaster Support Systems. The primary utility of MIS lies in its ability to facilitate hazard mapping, a crucial aspect of disaster preparedness and response. By integrating geographic information with pertinent data sets, MIS enables the creation of hazard maps that identify vulnerable areas and assess the risks posed by various disasters such as floods, cyclones, winds, and seismic activities. These hazard maps serve as valuable decision support tools, guiding emergency managers in prioritizing mitigation efforts and resource allocation based on the identified risks.

Moreover, MIS provides vital insights into housing stock vulnerability across different districts and regions, offering detailed information on the susceptibility of housing infrastructure to damage during disaster events. Through the compilation and analysis of data on housing infrastructure, construction materials, and structural integrity, MIS generates vulnerability tables that inform disaster preparedness and planning efforts. This information empowers emergency managers to prioritize interventions, allocate resources efficiently, and develop targeted strategies to enhance community resilience.

In addition to facilitating hazard mapping and vulnerability assessments, MIS serves as a centralized platform for storing, managing, and disseminating disaster-related data to relevant stakeholders and decision-makers. By consolidating diverse datasets including hazard maps, vulnerability assessments, demographic information, and resource inventories, MIS provides a comprehensive repository of information that supports informed decision-making and strategic planning in disaster management. This data-driven approach enhances the efficiency and effectiveness of disaster response and recovery efforts by ensuring that resources are deployed where they are most needed and that interventions are tailored to the specific needs of affected communities.

Remote Sensing

Remote sensing is a scientific method used to gather information about the Earth's surface without the need for direct physical contact. Instead, it relies on sensors and recording devices to capture and measure the energy emitted or reflected by the Earth's surface and atmosphere. This collected data can then be analysed to gain valuable insights into various natural phenomena, including potential occurrences of natural disasters.

In remote sensing, sensors mounted on satellites, aircraft, or ground-based platforms detect and record electromagnetic radiation emitted or reflected by objects on the Earth's surface. Different objects and materials reflect and emit energy in unique ways, allowing remote sensing techniques to identify and distinguish between various features such as vegetation, water bodies, urban areas, and geological formations.

Figure 58: Remote sensing of coastal and marine environment. Badr El Mahrad, Alice Newton, John D. Icely, Ilias Kacimi, Samuel Abalansa and Maria Snoussi. Symbols courtesy of the University of Maryland Center for Environmental Science, credit: Badr El Mahrad., CC BY-SA 4.0, via Wikimedia Commons.

During natural disasters, remote sensing plays a crucial role in monitoring and assessing the extent and impact of the event. For example, satellite imagery can be used to track the progression of wildfires, monitor changes in sea surface temperatures during hurricanes, or assess the extent of flooding in affected areas. By analysing remote sensing data, scientists and emergency responders can gain valuable insights into the spatial distribution, magnitude, and severity of the disaster, enabling more effective decision-making and response efforts.

Remote sensing technology provides emergency managers and coordinators with invaluable tools for disaster monitoring, assessment, and response. By leveraging sensors mounted on satellites, aircraft, or ground-based platforms, remote sensing enables the collection of real-time data about the Earth's surface and atmosphere without the need for direct physical contact. This data can then be analysed to gain insights into various natural phenomena, including the occurrence and impact of natural disasters.

One key application of remote sensing in disaster management is monitoring and tracking the progression of disasters such as wildfires, hurricanes, and floods. Satellite imagery allows emergency managers to observe changes in the environment, such as the spread of flames during a wildfire or the expansion of floodwaters in a flooded area. By continuously monitoring these events from space, responders can assess the extent and severity of the disaster, identify areas at high risk, and prioritize resource allocation and response efforts accordingly.

Additionally, remote sensing technology provides valuable data for assessing damage and conducting post-disaster assessments. High-resolution satellite imagery can be used to survey affected areas and identify areas of infrastructure damage, such as collapsed buildings, roads, and bridges. This information is critical for guiding search and rescue operations, identifying areas in need of immediate assistance, and planning for long-term recovery and rebuilding efforts.

Furthermore, remote sensing facilitates the generation of hazard maps and risk assessments, which are essential for disaster preparedness and mitigation planning. By analysing remote sensing data, emergency managers can identify areas prone to natural hazards such as landslides, earthquakes, and tsunamis, and implement preventive measures to reduce vulnerability and enhance resilience.

Drones

Drone technology has emerged as a highly effective tool for conducting rapid damage assessments in areas affected by earthquakes and other disasters. By deploying drones, emergency response teams can efficiently survey large areas and assess the extent of damage without putting human responders at risk. Drones equipped with cameras and sensors provide invaluable aerial footage and imagery, enabling first responders to locate survivors, identify hazards, and plan their response efforts more effectively.

Figure 59: The unmanned submersible Deep Drone is ready for deployment from the fleet tug, USNS NARRAGANSETT (T-ATF 167) during search operations for Korean Airlines Flight 007. PH1 FEL BARBANTE, Public domain, via Wikimedia Commons.

One of the key advantages of using drones in disaster response is their ability to access hard-to-reach or hazardous areas that may be unsafe for human responders to enter. Drones can navigate through debris-filled streets, collapsed buildings, and unstable terrain, providing critical situational awareness to emergency teams on the ground. This aerial perspective allows responders to quickly identify areas of urgent need and prioritize their rescue and relief efforts accordingly.

Moreover, drones can be equipped with advanced imaging technology that allows them to create detailed 3D maps and renderings of damaged buildings and infrastructure. By capturing high-resolution images and data from multiple angles, drones can generate accurate digital models of disaster-affected areas, including structural damage and potential hazards. These 3D renderings provide valuable insights into the condition of buildings and help rescue teams assess the structural integrity of compromised structures before entering them.

Figure 60: A member of "Serve On" holds up a flying drone - used to help identify areas that are worst-hit by the earthquake in Nepal. DFID - UK Department for International Development, CC BY 2.0, via Wikimedia Commons.

In addition to damage assessment, drones can also play a crucial role in search and rescue operations by providing real-time aerial surveillance and monitoring. Thermal imaging cameras and other specialized sensors can be mounted on drones to detect heat signatures and signs of life in debris piles, helping responders locate survivors more quickly and efficiently.

Overall, drone technology has revolutionized disaster response by offering a safe, efficient, and cost-effective means of assessing damage, locating survivors, and planning rescue efforts. By leveraging the capabilities of drones, emergency response teams can enhance their situational awareness, improve coordination, and ultimately save lives in the aftermath of disasters.

GPS Tracking

GPS tracking technology has become an indispensable tool for disaster management, providing critical information to first responders and emergency personnel during crisis situations. By harnessing GPS tracking capabilities, responders can effectively navigate hazardous environments and avoid potential dangers, such as wildfires and other natural disasters.

One of the key advantages of GPS tracking is its ability to provide real-time information on the location and movement of emergency vehicles, ensuring that responders can make informed decisions about their routes and avoid entering the direct path of a disaster. GPS tracking systems installed in emergency vehicles enable authorities to monitor their positions and trajectories, allowing for timely adjustments to route planning based on evolving conditions on the ground.

In disaster scenarios such as wildfires, where road closures and compromised infrastructure are common, GPS tracking on vehicles plays a crucial role in identifying safe and accessible routes for first responders. By monitoring the status of roads and highways in real-time, GPS tracking systems can indicate which routes have been compromised and which remain passable, enabling responders to navigate around obstacles and reach affected areas more efficiently.

Furthermore, GPS tracking technology enhances coordination and communication among emergency personnel by providing a common operating picture of the disaster area. By sharing real-time location data via GPS tracking systems, responders can collaborate more effectively, allocate resources efficiently, and streamline response efforts to maximize effectiveness and minimize risks.

GPS tracking technology provides emergency managers and coordinators with invaluable tools for enhancing disaster response and management efforts. By leveraging GPS tracking capabilities, these professionals can effectively coordinate and deploy resources to areas affected by natural disasters, ensuring timely and efficient assistance to those in need.

One of the primary uses of GPS tracking technology is to monitor the location and movement of emergency vehicles in real-time. This allows responders to make informed decisions about route planning, ensuring that they avoid hazardous areas and reach affected areas safely and efficiently. By tracking the positions and trajectories of emergency vehicles, authorities can adjust route planning dynamically based on evolving conditions on the ground, such as road closures or changes in traffic patterns.

In scenarios like wildfires, where road closures and compromised infrastructure are common, GPS tracking on vehicles becomes particularly vital. GPS tracking systems provide up-to-date information on the status of roads and highways, indicating which routes are safe and passable for first responders. This enables emergency managers to identify alternative routes and navigate around obstacles, facilitating quicker access to affected areas and more effective response efforts.

Moreover, GPS tracking technology enhances coordination and communication among emergency personnel by providing a shared operating picture of the disaster area. By sharing real-time location data via GPS tracking systems, responders can collaborate more effectively, allocate resources efficiently, and streamline response efforts. This collaborative approach improves situational awareness, optimizes resource allocation, and minimizes risks, ultimately enhancing the overall effectiveness of response operations.

Short Message System (SMS)

The Short Message System (SMS), despite being an older technology, remains a vital tool in emergency communication due to its widespread availability and reliability. Unlike many modern messaging platforms that rely on internet connectivity, SMS is supported by every smartphone and cellular device by default, making it accessible to a vast majority of the population. This ubiquity ensures that emergency messages can reach a wide audience, even in areas with limited or disrupted internet service.

One of the key strengths of SMS is its ability to handle large volumes of messages, particularly when internet service is unavailable or unreliable. Unlike internet-based messaging platforms that may experience congestion or downtime during emergencies, SMS operates over cellular networks, which are designed to prioritize critical communications, ensuring that messages are delivered promptly and reliably. This resilience makes SMS the most effective and efficient method of sending out emergency-related mass communications, especially in situations where other communication channels may be compromised.

In disaster scenarios where infrastructure damage or network congestion may disrupt internet connectivity, SMS emerges as a lifeline for emergency responders and affected communities. Whether it's issuing evacuation orders, providing safety instructions, or disseminating critical updates, SMS enables authorities to reach individuals quickly and efficiently, helping to mitigate risks and save lives. Moreover, SMS can be used to coordinate response efforts, gather information from affected individuals, and facilitate two-way communication between responders and the public, enhancing situational awareness and response coordination.

Cybersecurity

Cybersecurity is a critical component of modern information technology infrastructure, safeguarding computer systems and networks from a variety of cyber threats and attacks orchestrated by malicious actors. These threats range from common malware and phishing scams to sophisticated cyber espionage and ransomware attacks. By implementing robust cybersecurity measures and response protocols, organizations can mitigate the risks associated with cyber threats and protect sensitive data and information from unauthorized access or manipulation.

One of the primary objectives of cybersecurity is to prevent cyber criminals from accessing, manipulating, or destroying sensitive data and information stored within computer systems and networks. This includes personal identifiable information (PII), financial data, intellectual property, and other proprietary information that could be exploited for malicious purposes. By deploying advanced security technologies such as firewalls, antivirus software, encryption protocols, and intrusion detection systems, organizations can establish multiple layers of defence to thwart cyber attacks and unauthorized access attempts.

Moreover, cybersecurity plays a crucial role in safeguarding the integrity and availability of information technology resources and infrastructure. Cyber attacks aimed at disrupting critical systems and services can result in significant damage and disruption to normal business operations. For instance, a successful ransomware attack could encrypt essential data and systems, rendering them inaccessible until a ransom is paid, leading to costly downtime and financial losses. By implementing proactive cybersecurity measures and response strategies, organizations can minimize the impact of cyber attacks and ensure the continuity of operations in the face of evolving threats.

In today's interconnected digital landscape, the absence of robust cybersecurity measures can expose organizations to a myriad of risks and vulnerabilities, including data breaches, financial losses, reputational damage, and regulatory penalties. As cyber threats continue to evolve and become increasingly sophisticated, organizations must remain vigilant and proactive in their cybersecurity efforts, continuously updating their defences and response capabilities to adapt to emerging threats and protect against potential cyber attacks. By prioritizing cybersecurity and investing in comprehensive security solutions, organizations can safeguard their assets, reputation, and competitive advantage in an ever-changing threat landscape.

Innovations that enhance community resilience

Innovations play a crucial role in enhancing community resilience by fostering adaptive capacities and promoting strategies for disaster readiness. Community resilience is built upon various pillars such as Economic Development, Social Capital, Information and Communication, and Community Competence [130]. Strengthening social infrastructure at the community level through initiatives like social learning, innovative adaptation, and knowledge sharing can significantly contribute to enhancing community resilience [165, 517-519]. Additionally, the role of public relations in understanding community cultures, communication, and networking skills can further enhance efforts to build community resilience to natural disasters [165].

In the context of disasters like the COVID-19 crisis, placing community building, social cohesion, and resilience at the forefront can align solutions that promote 'planetary health' and contribute to community well-being [520]. Furthermore, social innovation systems and social technologies are instrumental in building resilient communities by fostering engagement, practice, and ultimately enhancing community resilience [521]. The capacity to transform at different scales, drawing on resilience from multiple sources, can help navigate social-ecological transitions and promote innovation for resilience building [522].

Innovative technologies, such as off-grid solar renewable energy systems, have been identified as tools to promote local, community-based resilience to climate change and enhance livelihood security [523]. Moreover, social innovations that increase community resilience can lead to the development of more effective and innovative solutions, contributing to the overall resilience of communities [524]. By leveraging innovation capabilities, organizations can enhance their resilience and responsiveness to crises like the COVID-19 pandemic [525].

A combination of social innovation, knowledge sharing, adaptive capacities, and community engagement are essential elements in enhancing community resilience to disasters and crises. By fostering a culture of innovation, collaboration, and adaptability, communities can better prepare for and respond to challenges, ultimately increasing their resilience and ability to thrive in the face of adversity.

One key area of innovation in community resilience is technology, which offers powerful tools for improving disaster preparedness and response capabilities. For example, advanced early warning systems leverage real-time data and predictive analytics to alert communities to impending natural disasters, such as hurricanes, floods, or wildfires, allowing residents to take timely action to protect themselves and their property. Similarly, communication technologies, including social media platforms and mobile applications, enable rapid dissemination of critical information during emergencies, facilitating coordination among stakeholders and enhancing public awareness and preparedness.

Technology plays a pivotal role in advancing community resilience by providing powerful tools that enhance disaster preparedness and response capabilities. One key innovation in this regard is the development of advanced early warning systems, which leverage real-time data and predictive analytics to alert communities to impending natural disasters. These systems utilize a combination of sensors, satellite imagery, weather forecasting models, and machine learning algorithms to detect early signs of hazards such as hurricanes, floods, or wildfires. By analysing various environmental parameters and historical data, these systems can forecast the likelihood and severity of potential disasters, providing communities with valuable lead time to prepare and take preventive measures.

For instance, in flood-prone areas, early warning systems may monitor river levels, rainfall intensity, and soil moisture to anticipate flash floods and issue timely alerts to residents. Similarly, in regions prone to wildfires, remote sensing technologies and thermal imaging can detect heat signatures and smoke plumes, enabling authorities to issue evacuation orders and deploy firefighting resources before the situation escalates. By providing advance warning and actionable information, these early warning systems empower individuals, businesses, and governments to mitigate risks, protect lives, and minimize property damage.

In addition to early warning systems, communication technologies play a crucial role in enhancing community resilience by facilitating the rapid dissemination of critical information during emergencies. Social media platforms, mobile applications, and other digital communication channels serve as vital tools for sharing emergency alerts, evacuation orders, shelter locations, and safety tips with the public in real time. These platforms enable authorities to reach a wide audience quickly, regardless of geographic location, language, or socioeconomic status, thereby enhancing public awareness and preparedness.

During disasters, communication technologies also facilitate coordination among stakeholders, including emergency responders, government agencies, non-governmental organizations, and community groups. By providing a centralized platform for sharing information, coordinating response efforts, and mobilizing resources, these technologies improve the efficiency and effectiveness of disaster response operations. For example, emergency management agencies can use social media monitoring tools to gather situational awareness data, identify emerging needs, and engage with affected communities in meaningful ways. Similarly, mobile applications can enable citizens to report emergencies, request assistance, and access support services directly from their smartphones, streamlining the response process and ensuring timely assistance to those in need.

In addition to technology, innovative strategies for community engagement and empowerment are essential for building resilience. Community-based participatory approaches involve local residents in decision-making processes, empowering them to identify risks, prioritize needs, and develop solutions tailored to their unique circumstances. By fostering collaboration and ownership among community members, these approaches promote resilience from the ground up, strengthening social cohesion, trust, and collective action in the face of adversity.

Innovative strategies for community engagement and empowerment are crucial components of building resilience, complementing technological advancements with human-centric approaches that prioritize local knowledge, participation, and ownership. Community-based participatory approaches represent a paradigm shift in disaster resilience planning, emphasizing the active involvement of residents in decision-making processes and fostering collaborative partnerships between community members, organizations, and institutions.

At the heart of community-based participatory approaches is the recognition that local residents possess invaluable insights into their environments, experiences, and needs. By engaging community members as active participants rather than passive recipients of aid, these approaches empower individuals to contribute their knowledge, skills, and resources to the resilience-building process. Through dialogue, deliberation, and consensus-building, residents can collectively identify risks, vulnerabilities, and opportunities for improvement, ensuring that resilience strategies are informed by local realities and reflective of community priorities.

One key aspect of community-based participatory approaches is the promotion of social cohesion and trust within communities. By fostering inclusive decision-making processes and meaningful engagement opportunities, these approaches strengthen social bonds, mutual support networks, and collective solidarity among residents. As community members collaborate to address common challenges and work towards shared goals, they develop a sense of ownership and responsibility for their collective well-being, which in turn enhances their capacity to withstand and recover from disasters.

Moreover, community-based participatory approaches promote equity and social justice by prioritizing the voices and needs of marginalized and vulnerable populations.

By centring the perspectives of those most affected by disasters, including low-income households, minority communities, and individuals with disabilities, these approaches ensure that resilience-building efforts address systemic inequalities and promote inclusive, equitable outcomes for all residents. Through targeted outreach, capacity-building initiatives, and inclusive decision-making structures, community-based participatory approaches empower marginalized groups to actively participate in resilience planning and decision-making processes, thereby amplifying their voices and strengthening their resilience.

Ultimately, community-based participatory approaches contribute to the development of more resilient, adaptive, and sustainable communities by harnessing the collective wisdom, resources, and capacities of local residents. By engaging communities as active partners in resilience-building efforts, these approaches foster a culture of empowerment, collaboration, and solidarity that enables communities to effectively anticipate, respond to, and recover from disasters while promoting social cohesion, equity, and well-being.

Furthermore, innovations in infrastructure and urban planning contribute to community resilience by enhancing the built environment's ability to withstand and recover from disasters. Sustainable design principles, such as green infrastructure and resilient building materials, help mitigate the impact of extreme weather events and climate change, reducing vulnerability and enhancing long-term resilience. Similarly, smart city technologies, such as sensor networks and data analytics, enable more efficient resource management and infrastructure monitoring, improving resilience to environmental hazards and infrastructure failures.

Innovations in infrastructure and urban planning play a crucial role in bolstering community resilience by integrating sustainable design principles and leveraging cutting-edge technologies to enhance the built environment's ability to withstand and rebound from disasters. Sustainable design approaches prioritize resilience, durability, and adaptability, aiming to minimize environmental impacts while maximizing the capacity of infrastructure to withstand various hazards and stressors.

One key aspect of innovative infrastructure design is the incorporation of green infrastructure solutions, which mimic natural processes to manage stormwater, reduce flooding, and mitigate the urban heat island effect. Features such as green roofs, rain gardens, permeable pavements, and bioswales help absorb excess water, improve water quality, and enhance ecosystem services, thereby reducing the risk of flooding and water-related damage during extreme weather events. By integrating nature-based solutions into urban landscapes, communities can enhance their resilience to climate change impacts while promoting environmental sustainability and biodiversity conservation.

Resilient building materials and construction techniques also play a critical role in enhancing the resilience of infrastructure to disasters. Innovations such as earthquake-resistant structures, flood-resistant foundations, and fire-resistant materials help minimize damage and disruption during disasters, ensuring the safety and stability of buildings and critical infrastructure systems. Additionally, the use of modular construction methods and prefabricated components can expedite the rebuilding process after disasters, enabling communities to recover more quickly and cost-effectively.

Furthermore, the emergence of smart city technologies holds significant promise for enhancing resilience by enabling more efficient resource management and infrastructure monitoring. Sensor networks embedded in urban environments can provide real-time data on environmental conditions, infrastructure performance, and public safety indicators, allowing authorities to detect potential hazards and vulnerabilities before they escalate into disasters. Data analytics and predictive modelling techniques can analyse large datasets to identify patterns, trends, and potential risks, enabling proactive decision-making and targeted interventions to mitigate threats and enhance resilience.

By integrating these innovations into urban planning and infrastructure development processes, communities can create more resilient, adaptive, and sustainable built environments that are better equipped to withstand and recover from disasters. By embracing sustainable design principles, leveraging resilient building materials, and harnessing smart city technologies, communities can enhance their resilience to a wide range of hazards and challenges, ensuring the safety, well-being, and prosperity of residents now and in the future.

Moreover, innovations in education and capacity building play a crucial role in enhancing community resilience by equipping individuals and organizations with the knowledge, skills, and resources needed to prepare for and respond to emergencies effectively. Disaster preparedness training programs, community resilience workshops, and public awareness campaigns raise awareness about risks, promote proactive behaviours, and empower individuals to take responsibility for their safety and well-being.

Innovations in education and capacity building represent a cornerstone of efforts to enhance community resilience, as they empower individuals and organizations with the knowledge, skills, and resources necessary to prepare for, respond to, and recover from emergencies and disasters effectively. These initiatives aim to foster a culture of resilience by equipping community members with the information and tools they need to understand and mitigate risks, build social connections, and mobilize collective action in times of crisis.

One key innovation in this realm is the development of tailored disaster preparedness training programs that cater to the specific needs and vulnerabilities of different communities. These programs provide practical guidance on emergency planning, evacuation procedures, first aid techniques, and disaster response protocols, empowering individuals to take proactive steps to protect themselves, their families, and their communities in the event of a disaster. By imparting essential knowledge and skills, these training initiatives enable community members to respond effectively to emergencies, minimize risks, and enhance overall resilience.

Additionally, community resilience workshops and public awareness campaigns play a vital role in raising awareness about disaster risks and promoting proactive behaviours among community members. These initiatives utilize innovative educational strategies, such as interactive workshops, tabletop exercises, and multimedia campaigns, to engage participants and facilitate learning about disaster preparedness, response, and recovery. By fostering dialogue, collaboration, and knowledge-sharing, these workshops and campaigns empower individuals to make informed decisions, build social networks, and contribute to community resilience efforts.

Furthermore, capacity-building initiatives focus on strengthening the resilience of local organizations, institutions, and community groups by providing training, resources, and support to enhance their preparedness and response capabilities. These initiatives may include the establishment of community emergency response teams (CERTs), the development of community resilience hubs, and the provision of technical assistance and funding for resilience-building projects. By building the capacity of local stakeholders to coordinate and mobilize resources effectively, these initiatives strengthen the overall resilience of communities and enhance their ability to withstand and recover from disasters.

As examples of innovation projects focussed on building resilience, the Resilient Cities Program by 100 Resilient Cities (100RC), initiated by The Rockefeller Foundation, is a comprehensive effort aimed at aiding cities globally in enhancing their resilience to various challenges in the 21st century. Through this program, cities receive financial support, technical guidance, and access to a network of experts to develop and implement resilience strategies tailored to their specific circumstances. Cities such as New York,

Bangkok, and Rotterdam have utilized this program to create innovative solutions for climate adaptation, infrastructure resilience, and social cohesion.

The 100 Resilient Cities Program, established in 2013, is a crucial part of The Rockefeller Foundation's mission to promote global well-being by fostering resilience in cities worldwide [526]. Resilience has become increasingly important in sectors like social protection, disaster risk reduction, and climate change adaptation [527]. Various organizations, including federal and nongovernmental entities, have adopted resilience frameworks to steer disaster management efforts [528].

Figure 61: Mayor Garcetti delivers a speech on 100 Resilient Cities. Eric Garcetti, CC BY 2.0, via Wikimedia Commons.

The program underscores the significance of social equity in urban resilience planning, advocating for a framework that includes distributional, recognitional, and procedural dimensions of equity [529]. Additionally, the initiative collaborates with a variety of stakeholders, such as the World Bank, global consultants, NGOs, and private sector service providers, to facilitate the creation and dissemination of urban resilience assessment tools [530].

By engaging with frameworks like the City Resilience Index and partnering with organizations like the UN Office for Disaster Risk Reduction and UN-Habitat, the 100 Resilient Cities Program plays a crucial role in shaping resilience policies and practices globally [531, 532]. The initiative has also been instrumental in assisting cities like Rome and Athens in Southern Europe in enhancing their resilience capacities [533].

As another example, resilience hubs in San Francisco, as part of the Resilient City Initiative, are community centres established in vulnerable neighbourhoods to enhance community resilience during disasters by providing backup power, communication tools, emergency supplies, and trained staff. These hubs aim to strengthen social networks, improve resource access, and promote collaboration among residents, businesses, and local organizations [534].

Studies have shown that disaster preparedness is crucial for protecting health and mitigating adverse effects of disasters [235]. Enhancing flood resilience through improved risk communication has been recommended as an effective strategy for disaster management [535]. Additionally, factors such as previous disaster exposure, early warnings, evacuations, and awareness of risk contribute to improved preparedness and awareness [536].

Community resilience and disaster preparedness are influenced by various factors such as self-efficacy, family resilience sources, and levels of citizen public health emergency preparedness [537, 538]. Moreover, education for caregivers and the development of community support programs play a vital role in assisting vulnerable groups like older adults with long-term care needs [539].

In the context of disaster risk reduction, it has been highlighted that knowledge, income, resources, previous disaster experience, risk perception, vulnerability level, and cost-effectiveness of preparedness measures are significant factors affecting disaster preparedness [540]. Furthermore, place attachment, including house and neighbourhood attachment, is considered a relevant predictor of mitigative and community preparedness in at-risk communities [541].

In another approach, building resilient communities in Nepal post the 2015 earthquakes has been a critical focus for various organizations like Mercy Corps. One notable initiative involves constructing earthquake-resistant homes utilizing local materials and traditional building methods, not only ensuring structural integrity against seismic shocks but also fostering community empowerment through training and employment opportunities for local artisans and builders.

Efforts to enhance community resilience in Nepal have been significant, with international development organizations dedicating substantial resources to bolstering community resilience. This support aims to enable communities to better absorb shocks during adverse conditions and recover more swiftly towards resilience [169].

The earthquakes in Nepal have highlighted the importance of disaster resilience policies and frameworks. The adoption of acts like the Nepal Disaster Risk Reduction and Management Act in 2017 and the Post Disaster Recovery Framework in 2018, aligned with the Sendai Framework for Disaster Risk Reduction, emphasizes the necessity of building community resilience to mitigate the impact of disasters [542].

Moreover, the vulnerability of Nepal to climate change has prompted the revisitation of agroforestry practices to build climate-resilient communities. Implementing community-based agroforestry practices, combined with modern technology, is seen as a significant contribution to enhancing the resilience of vulnerable communities in Nepal [543].

As a further example, resilience-Based Urban Planning in Medellín, Colombia has been a transformative process that has significantly improved the city's liveability and sustainability. Through innovative initiatives such as the construction of cable car systems, escalators in hillside neighbourhoods, and public parks in former conflict zones, Medellín has enhanced social inclusion, reduced vulnerability to natural disasters and violence, and improved access to services [544]. These projects have not only contributed to the physical infrastructure of the city but have also fostered a sense of community and resilience among its residents [545].

One key aspect of urban resilience highlighted in the context of Medellín is the importance of long-term visioning and appropriate plans for mitigation, absorption, recovery, and adaptation to disruptive events [546]. This forward-thinking approach has been crucial in Medellín's transformation from a city plagued by violence to one that is now recognized for its innovative urban planning strategies [547].

Furthermore, the integration of green infrastructure, such as urban forests, has played a significant role in offsetting urban pollution and mitigating carbon dioxide emissions in Medellín [548]. Coordinating green infrastructure efforts with broader territorial policies has been emphasized as essential for the effectiveness of such initiatives [548].

In addition to physical infrastructure improvements, the involvement of grassroots movements, particularly women's grassroots movements, has been instrumental in shaping urban planning processes in Medellín (Rivera, 2020). These movements have actively participated in decision-making processes alongside government officials, contributing to more inclusive and community-driven urban development.

As a final example, Singapore is a leading proponent of smart resilient cities through initiatives like the Smart Nation program and the Resilience Lab. These projects utilize advanced technologies such as sensors, artificial intelligence, and predictive analytics to bolster disaster preparedness, monitor environmental risks, and optimize resource allocation during emergencies. The Smart Nation initiative, initiated in 2014, is designed to encourage the use of information and communications technologies (ICTs) to tackle intricate urban challenges and cultivate industries that support these solutions [549]. This initiative is in line with Singapore's goal to establish itself as an innovation hub, with the government actively promoting smart urbanism as a developmental strategy [550, 551].

The Smart Nation program in Singapore is a significant endeavour aimed at technologically revolutionizing urban living, working, and recreational spaces [552]. By integrating big data analytics and existing technology infrastructure, the program seeks to digitally connect entire communities, fostering a more efficient and sustainable urban environment [553]. Moreover, Singapore's Smart Nation initiative not only focuses on technological advancements but also on transforming the city-state into a premier location for technology-driven experiments geared towards business development [554].

In the realm of healthcare, the Smart Nation initiative extends to the digitalization of industries, including healthcare, as a pivotal element of Singapore's digitalization efforts [555]. This digital transformation is critical for enhancing healthcare services and safeguarding the well-being of the population. Additionally, Singapore's response to the COVID-19 pandemic, including the establishment of a national task force, underscores the country's commitment to leveraging technology and data-driven solutions to effectively address public health crises [556, 557].

Singapore's Smart Nation initiative serves as a blueprint for other cities in the region, with insights from projects like digital payments being shared with other Asian cities aspiring to be smart cities [558]. The strategic positioning of the city-state as a hub for knowledge exchange and policy transfer for smart city development within the ASEAN Smart Cities Network further cements its role as a leader in smart urbanism [556].

These examples illustrate how innovation projects are being implemented globally to enhance community resilience and address complex challenges such as climate change, urbanization, and social inequality. By investing in innovative solutions and partnerships, communities can build resilience, adapt to changing conditions, and thrive in the face of adversity.

12

Legal and Policy Frameworks

Legal Basis for Emergency Management

The legal basis for emergency management encompasses a complex web of laws, regulations, policies, and guidelines at the local, national, and international levels. At its core, the legal framework for emergency management provides the authority, structure, and procedures necessary to prevent, prepare for, respond to, and recover from disasters and emergencies of various scales and types.

At the national level, many countries have enacted legislation specifically addressing emergency management and disaster response. These laws typically define the roles and responsibilities of government agencies, establish coordination mechanisms, and allocate resources for disaster preparedness, response, and recovery efforts. For example, in the United States, the Robert T. Stafford Disaster Relief and Emergency Assistance Act serves as the primary legal authority for federal disaster response, outlining the conditions under which the federal government can provide assistance to state and local authorities during emergencies.

Disaster governance arrangements are influenced by various factors such as globalization, social inequality, and demographic trends, which shape the challenges and structures of disaster management [236]. Legislation plays a fundamental role in ensuring that records and archives are managed effectively for accountability and historical purposes, as seen in the case of Statistics South Africa [559]. Moreover, legislative and organizational structures form the foundation of public health emergency management systems, as demonstrated during the COVID-19 pandemic in Belgium [560].

National policies and legislation are essential for addressing disaster-induced displacement, as highlighted by the United Nations and the Sendai Framework for Disaster Risk Reduction [561]. Furthermore, restructuring administrative organizations, revising disaster-related laws, and enhancing inter-ministerial coordination are proposed measures to improve disaster response and management systems [562]. Legislation also plays a critical role in guaranteeing public health core competence, as recognized by international bodies like the World Health Organization [563].

In addition to national laws, many jurisdictions have adopted state or provincial legislation to govern emergency management activities within their borders. These laws often delegate authority to state or provincial emergency management agencies, establish emergency management plans and protocols, and outline the legal framework for coordinating response efforts among different levels of government and stakeholders. For instance, states in the U.S. may have their own emergency management acts that complement federal legislation and provide additional guidance on disaster preparedness and response.

At the local level, municipalities and local governments play a critical role in emergency management, often enacting ordinances and regulations tailored to their specific needs and circumstances. These local laws may address issues such as zoning, building codes, evacuation procedures, and emergency declarations, empowering local authorities to take swift and effective action to protect public safety and welfare during emergencies.

Internationally, various legal instruments and agreements govern disaster response and humanitarian assistance across borders. Treaties such as the Sendai Framework for Disaster Risk Reduction and the International Health Regulations provide a legal framework for international cooperation in disaster preparedness, response, and recovery. These agreements promote collaboration among countries, facilitate the sharing of resources and expertise, and establish standards and guidelines for effective disaster management on a global scale.

In addition to statutory law, the legal basis for emergency management may also encompass common law principles, court decisions, and legal precedents established through litigation and judicial proceedings. These legal doctrines may shape the interpretation and application of emergency management laws and regulations, providing further guidance on issues such as liability, negligence, and the protection of individual rights during emergencies.

Overall, the legal basis for emergency management is multifaceted and dynamic, evolving in response to changing threats, technologies, and societal needs. By establishing clear legal frameworks and mechanisms for coordination and cooperation, governments can enhance their capacity to mitigate risks, respond effectively to disasters, and protect the safety and well-being of their citizens.

Legal Basis in the United States of America

In the United States, the legal basis for emergency management is primarily established through federal legislation, supplemented by state and local laws, regulations, and policies. At the federal level, the Robert T. Stafford Disaster Relief and Emergency Assistance Act serves as the cornerstone of emergency management law. Enacted in 1988 and subsequently amended, this law provides the statutory authority for the federal government to coordinate disaster response and provide assistance to states, local governments, tribal nations, and certain private non-profit organizations during major disasters and emergencies.

The Stafford Act outlines the process for declaring a federal disaster or emergency, triggering the release of federal resources and assistance. It also delineates the roles and responsibilities of various federal agencies, such as the Federal Emergency Management Agency (FEMA), in coordinating disaster response efforts. Under the Stafford Act, eligible activities for federal assistance include debris removal, emergency protective measures, and public infrastructure repair and replacement.

In addition to the Stafford Act, other federal laws and regulations contribute to the legal framework for emergency management in the United States. These include the National Response Framework, which establishes the guiding principles and structures for coordinating federal, state, local, tribal, and territorial response efforts, and the Homeland Security Act of 2002, which created the Department of Homeland Security (DHS) to oversee and coordinate the nation's efforts to prevent and respond to terrorist attacks, natural disasters, and other emergencies.

At the state level, emergency management laws and regulations vary from state to state but generally delegate authority to state emergency management agencies to coordinate disaster preparedness, response, and recovery activities within their jurisdictions. Many states have enacted their own emergency management acts, which outline the powers and duties of state and local emergency management officials, establish emergency management plans and procedures, and provide mechanisms for requesting and receiving federal assistance during disasters.

Local governments, including counties, cities, and municipalities, also play a crucial role in emergency management and disaster response. Local emergency management ordinances and regulations govern issues such as emergency declarations, evacuation procedures, sheltering, and public safety measures. These local laws empower local authorities to take prompt and effective action to protect lives, property, and public welfare during emergencies.

In addition to statutory law, the legal basis for emergency management in the United States may also encompass court decisions, legal precedents, and executive orders issued by federal, state, and local authorities. These legal instruments further clarify the rights, responsibilities, and obligations of government agencies, private entities, and individuals involved in emergency management and disaster response activities.

Overall, the legal basis for emergency management in the United States reflects a complex and evolving framework that seeks to balance federal, state, and local authorities while promoting effective coordination, cooperation, and accountability in preparing for and responding to disasters and emergencies. By establishing clear legal authorities, procedures, and mechanisms for collaboration, the United States aims to enhance its resilience and capacity to protect communities and mitigate the impact of disasters.

Legal Basis in Australia

In Australia, the legal basis for emergency management is primarily established through a combination of federal, state, and territory legislation, as well as various regulations, policies, and frameworks. The legal framework for emergency management in Australia is designed to ensure effective coordination, response, and recovery efforts across all levels of government and with relevant stakeholders.

At the federal level, the primary legislation governing emergency management is the Disaster Recovery Funding Arrangements (DRFA). The DRFA outlines the financial assistance provided by the Commonwealth Government to states and territories following natural disasters and emergencies. It establishes the criteria for disaster declarations and the eligibility criteria for assistance, as well as the responsibilities of the Commonwealth, states, and territories in disaster recovery efforts.

Another key federal law is the Emergency Management Act 2005, which provides the legal basis for emergency management planning, coordination, and response at the national level. This act establishes the role of the Australian Government in coordinating emergency management activities, including the development of national policies, strategies, and frameworks for disaster preparedness and response.

Additionally, the Australian Government has enacted legislation to address specific types of emergencies, such as the Biosecurity Act 2015, which provides powers to manage biosecurity risks and respond to public health emergencies, including pandemics.

At the state and territory level, each jurisdiction has its own legislation governing emergency management. For example, in New South Wales, the State Emergency and Rescue Management Act 1989 establishes the legal framework for emergency management, including the roles and responsibilities of government agencies, emergency services, and other stakeholders. Similar legislation exists in other states and territories, providing the legal authority for emergency management activities within their respective jurisdictions.

In addition to legislation, emergency management in Australia is supported by a range of policies, plans, and frameworks developed by government agencies and emergency services organizations. These documents outline strategies for disaster prevention, preparedness, response, and recovery, as well as mechanisms for coordination and collaboration between government agencies, non-government organizations, and the private sector.

The legal basis for emergency management in Australia reflects a coordinated and multi-jurisdictional approach, with federal, state, and territory governments working together to address the diverse range of hazards and risks facing the country. By establishing clear legal frameworks and mechanisms for cooperation, Australia aims to enhance its resilience and ability to respond effectively to emergencies and disasters, thereby protecting the safety and well-being of its citizens.

Legal Basis in Asia

The legal basis for emergency management in Asia varies significantly across countries due to differences in governance structures, legal systems, and cultural contexts. However, several common themes and approaches can be observed across the region.

1. National Legislation: Many countries in Asia have enacted national legislation to establish the legal framework for emergency management. These laws typically define the roles and responsibilities of government agencies, emergency services, and other stakeholders in preparing for, responding to, and recovering from disasters. For example, Japan has the Disaster Countermeasures Basic Act, which provides the legal basis for disaster prevention, preparedness, and response efforts at the national and local levels.

2. Constitutional Provisions: Some countries incorporate provisions related to disaster management in their constitutions. These provisions may outline the

government's obligation to protect citizens from disasters and ensure their safety and well-being. For instance, the Constitution of India includes provisions directing the state to promote the welfare of the people and protect them from natural calamities.

3. Regional Cooperation: In addition to national legislation, there are efforts to enhance regional cooperation and collaboration in emergency management across Asia. Regional organizations such as the Association of Southeast Asian Nations (ASEAN) and the South Asian Association for Regional Cooperation (SAARC) have developed frameworks and agreements to facilitate joint disaster response and cooperation among member states.

4. Sector-Specific Regulations: Some countries have sector-specific regulations related to emergency management. For example, regulations may exist to govern disaster response activities in specific sectors such as healthcare, transportation, or telecommunications. These regulations ensure coordination and compliance with standards during emergencies.

5. Local Government Regulations: Local governments often play a significant role in disaster management, particularly in countries with decentralized governance structures. Local regulations and ordinances may complement national laws by addressing specific risks and vulnerabilities at the community level and outlining the responsibilities of local authorities and stakeholders.

6. International Agreements and Treaties: Many Asian countries are party to international agreements and treaties related to disaster management and humanitarian assistance. These agreements facilitate cooperation, information sharing, and resource mobilization during emergencies, contributing to a coordinated regional and global response to disasters.

The legal basis for emergency management in Asia reflects the diverse challenges and priorities of countries in the region. While there are common elements such as national legislation and regional cooperation frameworks, the specific legal arrangements vary depending on each country's context, including its political, social, and economic circumstances. Effective emergency management requires not only robust legal frameworks but also strong institutional capacities, community engagement, and international cooperation to address the complex and evolving nature of disaster risks.

Legal Basis in Africa

The legal basis for emergency management in Africa is shaped by various factors, including historical, political, and socio-economic contexts, as well as the diverse range of hazards and risks faced by countries across the continent. While there is significant variation in the legal frameworks among African nations, several common elements can be identified:

1. National Legislation: Many African countries have enacted national legislation to establish the legal framework for emergency management. These laws typically outline the roles and responsibilities of government agencies, emergency services, and other stakeholders in preparing for, responding to, and recovering from disasters. For example, South Africa has the Disaster Management Act, which provides the legal basis for disaster risk reduction, response, and recovery efforts at the national and provincial levels.

2. Constitutional Provisions: Some African constitutions include provisions related to disaster management and emergency response. These provisions may define the government's obligations to protect citizens from disasters and ensure their safety and well-being. For instance, the Constitution of Kenya includes provisions requiring the state to take measures to mitigate the impact of disasters and provide assistance to those affected.

3. Regional Cooperation: In addition to national legislation, there are efforts to enhance regional cooperation and collaboration in emergency management across Africa. Regional organizations such as the African Union (AU) and the Economic Community of West African States (ECOWAS) have developed frameworks and agreements to facilitate joint disaster response and cooperation among member states.

4. Sector-Specific Regulations: Some countries have sector-specific regulations governing emergency management in specific sectors such as healthcare, transportation, or telecommunications. These regulations ensure coordination and compliance with standards during emergencies and address the unique risks and vulnerabilities faced by each sector.

5. Local Government Regulations: Local governments often play a significant role in disaster management, particularly in countries with decentralized governance structures. Local regulations and ordinances may complement national laws by addressing specific risks and vulnerabilities at the community level and outlining the responsibilities of local authorities and stakeholders.

6. International Agreements and Treaties: African countries are party to various international agreements and treaties related to disaster management and humanitarian assistance. These agreements facilitate cooperation, information sharing, and resource mobilization during emergencies, contributing to a coordinated regional and global response to disasters.

The legal basis for emergency management in Africa reflects the continent's commitment to building resilience and addressing the complex challenges posed by natural and man-made disasters. Effective emergency management requires not only robust legal frameworks but also strong institutional capacities, community engagement, and international cooperation to address the diverse and evolving nature of disaster risks across the continent.

Legal Basis in Europe

The legal basis for emergency management in Europe varies across countries due to differences in governance structures, legal traditions, and historical contexts. However, there are several common elements that characterize the legal frameworks for emergency management in many European nations:

1. National Legislation: Most European countries have enacted national legislation to establish the legal framework for emergency management. These laws typically define the roles and responsibilities of government agencies, emergency services, and other stakeholders in preparing for, responding to, and recovering from disasters. For example, in Germany, the Civil Protection Act (Zivilschutzgesetz) provides the legal basis for civil protection measures and emergency response.

2. Constitutional Provisions: Some European constitutions include provisions related to emergency management and civil protection. These provisions may outline the government's obligations to protect citizens from disasters, ensure public safety, and safeguard fundamental rights during emergencies. For instance, the Italian Constitution includes provisions allowing the government to

declare a state of emergency and take extraordinary measures to address urgent situations.

3. European Union (EU) Legislation: The European Union has developed legislation and policies to enhance cooperation and coordination among member states in emergency management. The EU's Civil Protection Mechanism, established in 2001, facilitates cooperation, information sharing, and mutual assistance among EU countries during disasters. Additionally, the EU has adopted regulations and directives addressing specific aspects of emergency management, such as the management of major accidents involving hazardous substances.

4. International Agreements and Treaties: European countries are party to various international agreements and treaties related to emergency management and humanitarian assistance. These agreements, including the Sendai Framework for Disaster Risk Reduction and the International Civil Protection Convention (ICPC), promote cooperation, coordination, and mutual assistance among countries in disaster response and recovery efforts.

5. Local Government Regulations: In countries with decentralized governance structures, local governments often play a significant role in emergency management. Local regulations and ordinances may complement national laws by addressing specific risks and vulnerabilities at the community level and outlining the responsibilities of local authorities and stakeholders.

6. Sector-Specific Regulations: Some European countries have sector-specific regulations governing emergency management in areas such as healthcare, transportation, or energy. These regulations ensure coordination and compliance with standards during emergencies and address the unique risks and vulnerabilities faced by each sector.

Overall, the legal basis for emergency management in Europe reflects a commitment to building resilience, ensuring public safety, and fostering cooperation among countries to address the diverse and complex challenges posed by disasters and emergencies.

Impact of Legal Basis on Management and Coordination Activities

The legal basis for emergency management provides the framework within which disaster managers and coordinators operate, influencing their roles, responsibilities, and decision-making processes in several ways:

- Clarity of Authority: Clear legal provisions delineate the authority and jurisdiction of disaster managers and coordinators, specifying their powers and duties during emergencies. This clarity ensures that decision-makers understand their roles and responsibilities, enabling them to take prompt and effective action to mitigate risks, respond to disasters, and protect public safety.

- Resource Allocation: Legal frameworks often establish mechanisms for resource allocation and coordination among government agencies, emergency services, and other stakeholders. Disaster managers and coordinators rely on these provisions to mobilize resources, such as personnel, equipment, and funding, to support emergency response and recovery efforts. The legal basis may dictate procedures for requesting and deploying resources, ensuring a coordinated and efficient response to disasters.

- Interagency Cooperation: Many legal frameworks mandate interagency cooperation and collaboration in emergency management. Disaster managers and coordinators work closely with multiple agencies and organizations, including law enforcement, healthcare providers, public utilities, and non-governmental organizations, to coordinate response efforts and share information. The legal basis may establish mechanisms for interagency coordination, such as emergency operations centres or multi-agency task forces, facilitating communication and collaboration among stakeholders.

- Legal Protections and Liabilities: Legal frameworks establish protections and liabilities for disaster managers and coordinators, safeguarding them from legal risks associated with their roles and actions during emergencies. These provisions may include immunity from liability for decisions made in good faith during emergencies, as well as legal protections for volunteers and emergency responders. Conversely, the legal basis may also impose legal obligations, such as duty of care and compliance with relevant regulations, on disaster managers and coordinators, ensuring accountability and adherence to legal standards.

- Compliance with Regulations: Disaster managers and coordinators must ensure compliance with relevant laws, regulations, and standards governing emergency management. This includes adherence to protocols for declaring states of emergency, implementing evacuation orders, providing emergency services, and protecting vulnerable populations. Compliance with legal requirements is essential to maintaining public trust, ensuring transparency and accountability, and minimizing legal risks during emergencies.

- Coordination with International Partners: In cases where disasters cross national borders or require international assistance, disaster managers and coordinators must navigate legal frameworks at the national and international levels. Cooperation with international partners, including neighbouring countries, international organizations, and humanitarian agencies, requires adherence to applicable laws, treaties, and agreements governing cross-border cooperation, mutual assistance, and humanitarian response.

Clear legal provisions delineating the authority and jurisdiction of disaster managers and coordinators play a crucial role in ensuring effective disaster management. These provisions specify the powers and duties of decision-makers during emergencies, enabling them to understand their roles and responsibilities clearly and act promptly to mitigate risks, respond to disasters, and safeguard public safety [564]. Establishing a common disaster management language is essential for facilitating effective communication between first responders and governing authorities involved in disaster response [565]. Coordination is a key factor positively linked to disaster management, emphasizing the importance of coordination provisions to enhance trust among agencies involved in disaster relief operations [566, 567]. Furthermore, the involvement of communities in disaster-prone areas based on clear legal criteria contributes significantly to effective disaster management [568].

Resource allocation in disaster management is a crucial aspect that legal frameworks often address to ensure effective coordination and mobilization of resources for emergency response and recovery efforts. These provisions play a crucial role in guiding disaster managers and coordinators in requesting, deploying, and managing resources efficiently [569, 570]. Sustainable emergency resource allocation models have been developed to enhance the rational use of rescue-related resources while minimizing casualties [571].

Additionally, equitable allocation of resources is highlighted as essential alongside efficient allocation in emergency relief efforts [572].

Various studies have emphasized the importance of optimizing resource allocation in post-disaster scenarios to facilitate economic recovery and mitigate losses [573, 574]. The allocation of scarce medical resources, especially during crises like the COVID-19 pandemic, remains a significant challenge that requires fair distribution strategies [575]. Moreover, proactive risk assessment models have been proposed to optimize resource allocation and enhance disaster response effectiveness [576, 577].

Efficient resource allocation models have been developed to balance multiple objectives, such as efficiency and fairness, in emergency situations [578]. These models aim to ensure that resources are allocated effectively while considering the diverse needs and interests of stakeholders involved in disaster response and recovery [578]. Furthermore, decision support models have been designed to aid in the allocation and routing of search and rescue resources after disasters, focusing on maximizing demand coverage and effectiveness.

Interagency cooperation is a crucial aspect of effective emergency management, involving collaboration among various agencies and organizations to coordinate response efforts and share information [579]. This collaboration is essential for dealing with natural disasters, technological hazards, and the consequences of terrorism [579]. The interests driving interagency collaboration are often based on voluntary agreements that emerge from a political contracting process where benefits outweigh transaction costs [580].

Legal frameworks play a crucial role in establishing mechanisms for interagency coordination, such as emergency operations centres and multi-agency task forces, facilitating communication and collaboration among stakeholders [579]. The literature emphasizes the importance of partnerships in building collaborative relationships, especially in the recovery phase of disasters [399]. Furthermore, the legal basis for collaboration is essential for disaster governance to be more effective and efficient [581].

Various studies highlight the need for coordination and collaboration in disaster management, acknowledging the importance of multisector engagement and action [582]. Disaster governance involves complex relationships between the state, civil society, economic organizations, and societal transitions, all of which impact disaster management [236]. Additionally, legal frameworks are crucial for disaster resilience planning strategies, requiring well-defined mandates and plans for disaster resilience and sustainable development programs [583].

Legal frameworks are essential in disaster management to establish protections and liabilities for disaster managers and coordinators. These frameworks provide immunity from liability for decisions made in good faith during emergencies [584]. This protection allows disaster managers to act decisively without fear of personal legal repercussions. Legal frameworks also include protections for volunteers and emergency responders to ensure their safety and recognize their contributions [585].

Conversely, legal obligations within these frameworks aim to uphold accountability and adherence to legal standards among disaster managers and coordinators. These obligations may include the duty of care towards those affected by disasters and compliance with relevant regulations [586]. Such requirements are crucial to ensure that emergency management professionals act responsibly and ethically in their roles.

Legal preparedness is emphasized as a critical aspect of disaster management, highlighting the need for appropriate liability protections for team members acting in good faith during emergencies [584]. These protections are necessary to align the legal status of disaster response team members with that of domestic clinicians, ensuring fair treatment and support for those involved in emergency response efforts.

Disaster managers and coordinators play a crucial role in ensuring compliance with laws, regulations, and standards related to emergency management. This involves adhering to protocols for declaring states of emergency, implementing evacuation orders, providing emergency services, and safeguarding vulnerable populations. Compliance with legal requirements is vital for upholding public trust, ensuring transparency, accountability, and reducing legal risks during emergencies.

To achieve effective compliance, it is essential to have a robust legal framework in place. Legal, regulatory, and policy bases need to be continuously strengthened to support the assessment and management of public health emergencies [587]. Additionally, the evolution of legal changes has led to the creation of new legal classifications such as "public health emergencies," which redefine the roles and responsibilities of both public and private actors in emergency response efforts [588].

Compliance with regulations not only ensures legal adherence but also offers numerous benefits. Most business organizations recognize the advantages of complying with regulations and standards, which incentivize enterprises to adhere to statutory and private regulations. Moreover, by targeting enforcement efforts on specific segments of the regulated community, greater compliance with environmental regulations can be achieved [589].

In the context of emergency management, achieving public health legal preparedness involves several core elements, including laws, competencies of practitioners, critical information dissemination, and coordination across sectors and jurisdictions [590]. Furthermore, the clarification of legal authority mandates and the designation within laws of the scope of preparedness activities are crucial for enhancing emergency preparedness and response [591].

In cases where disasters transcend national borders, effective coordination with international partners is crucial. Disaster managers and coordinators must navigate legal frameworks at both national and international levels to ensure seamless cooperation with neighbouring countries, international organizations, and humanitarian agencies. This necessitates adherence to relevant laws, treaties, and agreements that govern cross-border cooperation, mutual assistance, and humanitarian response.

International collaboration in disaster management involves various aspects such as community organizing, disaster planning, and emergency response. Organizational learning theory can aid in understanding community coordination during disasters [592]. Challenges in disaster risk management include weak coordination among sectors, lack of skills in loss assessment, absence of consensus on terminology, and limited stakeholder coordination [593]. Legal relationships between sustainable development, climate change adaptation, and disaster risk reduction can be understood through a model emphasizing coherence, alignment, and integration at different levels [594].

Cross-regional emergency cooperation for natural disasters enhances coordination among response organizations, leading to complex interaction modes [595]. Effective NGO disaster relief networks in China demonstrate the influence of sustained coordination and cooperation on disaster relief operations [596]. The interface between science and policy for disaster risk reduction in Europe faces challenges related to knowledge transfer, disaster expertise, and risk awareness [597].

Collaborative processes during emergency response in China highlight the importance of building and maintaining effective coordination mechanisms [598]. Open borders and well-functioning cross-border cooperation, as seen in the European Union integration, emphasize the significance of international cooperation [599]. Sustainable cross-border cooperation relies on harmonization and understanding determinants that promote inter-organizational collaboration [600].

Cross-border entrepreneurship development models and cluster-based cooperation exemplify opportunities for enhancing cross-border cooperation [601]. International disaster governance frameworks, such as the UN Cluster Approach, aim to improve coordination among various disaster sectors [602]. Initiatives in cross-border cooperation in Eastern Europe and the Romanian-Hungarian border area underscore the importance of cross-border projects in securing funding for interventions [603].

Strengthening intergovernmental and interorganizational networks is essential for improving emergency management systems, emphasizing the need for enhanced coordination among emergency function groups [604]. Structural models can assess hidden factors influencing sustainable cross-border cooperation, aiding in identifying key determinants for successful collaboration [605]. Capacity development in disaster health management within ASEAN Member States and Japan highlights the importance of regional cooperation mechanisms in disaster risk reduction [606].

Emergency Management Policy Frameworks

Emergency Management Policy Frameworks provide the foundational principles, guidelines, and strategies for organizing, coordinating, and implementing emergency management activities at various levels of government and within organizations. These frameworks serve as comprehensive blueprints for disaster preparedness, response, recovery, and mitigation efforts, outlining roles, responsibilities, and protocols for stakeholders involved in emergency management.

Key components of Emergency Management Policy Frameworks typically include:

1. Risk Assessment and Planning: Policies within the framework emphasize the importance of conducting risk assessments to identify potential hazards, vulnerabilities, and risks within a given jurisdiction or organization. Based on these assessments, comprehensive emergency management plans are developed to outline strategies for preventing, preparing for, responding to, and recovering from various types of disasters.

2. Coordination and Collaboration: Effective emergency management requires collaboration and coordination among multiple agencies, organizations, and stakeholders. Policy frameworks establish mechanisms for interagency cooperation, information sharing, and coordination of resources to ensure a unified and coordinated response to emergencies.

3. Governance and Leadership: Emergency management policy frameworks define governance structures and leadership roles responsible for overseeing and coordinating emergency management activities. This may include the establishment of emergency management agencies or departments at the national, regional, or local levels, as well as the appointment of emergency management coordinators or directors to lead efforts within organizations or jurisdictions.

4. Resource Management: Policies within the framework address resource allocation, procurement, and management to ensure adequate resources are available to support emergency response and recovery operations. This includes provisions for funding, personnel, equipment, and supplies necessary to address various types of emergencies effectively.

5. Communication and Public Information: Effective communication is essential during emergencies to disseminate timely and accurate information to the public, media, and stakeholders. Policy frameworks establish communication protocols, systems, and channels for sharing emergency alerts, warnings, instructions, and updates to ensure public safety and facilitate informed decision-making.

6. Training and Exercises: Policies promote continuous training, education, and exercises to build and maintain the capacity and readiness of emergency management personnel and stakeholders. Training programs and exercises help enhance skills, test response plans, identify gaps, and improve coordination and collaboration among responders.

7. Evaluation and Continuous Improvement: Policy frameworks emphasize the importance of evaluating emergency management activities, identifying lessons learned, and implementing continuous improvement processes. This involves conducting after-action reviews, debriefings, and evaluations to assess the effectiveness of response efforts and identify areas for enhancement.

Emergency Management Policy Frameworks may vary in scope and complexity depending on the jurisdiction, organizational structure, and specific needs and risks of the community or organization. However, they serve as essential guiding documents for shaping and guiding emergency management efforts to enhance preparedness, resilience, and response capabilities in the face of disasters and emergencies.

Emergency Management Policy Frameworks vary significantly across different countries and regions, reflecting unique political, social, economic, and environmental contexts. Here are examples of Emergency Management Policy Frameworks from various parts of the world:

1. United States: The United States has several policy frameworks for emergency management, including the National Response Framework (NRF), the National Incident Management System (NIMS), and the Post-Katrina Emergency Management Reform Act (PKEMRA). These frameworks establish standardized approaches to emergency response, coordination, and recovery at the federal, state, tribal, and local levels.

2. Australia: In Australia, emergency management is guided by the National Disaster Risk Reduction Framework, which emphasizes a comprehensive and risk-based approach to disaster management. Each state and territory also has its own emergency management frameworks, such as the New South Wales State Emergency Management Plan and the Queensland Disaster Management Plan.

3. Canada: Canada's Emergency Management Framework includes the Emergency Management Act and the Federal Emergency Response Plan (FERP), which outlines roles, responsibilities, and coordination mechanisms for responding to emergencies and disasters at the federal level. Provinces and territories have their own emergency management legislation and frameworks, such as Ontario's Emergency Management and Civil Protection Act.

4. Japan: Japan's Disaster Management Framework includes the Basic Act on Disaster Management, which establishes the legal basis for disaster management activities. The framework emphasizes a comprehensive approach to disaster risk reduction, preparedness, response, and recovery, with specific attention to earthquake and tsunami hazards.

5. European Union (EU): The EU has various policy frameworks for disaster risk reduction and emergency management, including the EU Civil Protection Mechanism, the Sendai Framework for Disaster Risk Reduction, and the Disaster Risk Management Directive. These frameworks aim to enhance coopera-

tion, coordination, and capacity-building among EU member states in disaster response and risk reduction efforts.

6. United Kingdom: In the UK, emergency management is governed by the Civil Contingencies Act 2004, which sets out legal duties and responsibilities for emergency preparedness, response, and recovery. The National Resilience and Risk Agency (NRRA) coordinates emergency management activities across government departments and agencies.

7. New Zealand: New Zealand's emergency management framework is guided by the Civil Defence Emergency Management Act 2002 and the National Disaster Resilience Strategy. These frameworks promote a coordinated and collaborative approach to emergency management, with a focus on community resilience and risk reduction.

These examples illustrate the diversity of Emergency Management Policy Frameworks around the world, highlighting common principles and approaches while reflecting the specific needs and priorities of each country or region.

Frameworks in the USA

The National Response Framework (NRF) is a vital component of the United States' emergency management system, providing a comprehensive guide for how the nation responds to all types of disasters and emergencies. Developed by the Federal Emergency Management Agency (FEMA), the NRF outlines the roles, responsibilities, and coordination structures that federal, state, tribal, and local governments, as well as private-sector and non-profit organizations, should follow during disaster response efforts.

The National Response Framework (NRF) is a crucial document that delineates how the United States federal government responds to various emergencies, encompassing natural disasters and human-caused crises [607]. It serves as a blueprint for federal agencies to synchronize their actions in response to such events, highlighting the significance of collaboration and efficient communication [608]. The NRF places notable importance on the critical infrastructure, such as the transportation system, in emergency management and evacuation planning [609].

At its core, the NRF is built on the principle of a unified and coordinated response, emphasizing collaboration and cooperation among all levels of government and across various sectors. It establishes a framework for organizing response activities into five mission areas: Prevention, Protection, Mitigation, Response, and Recovery. Each mission area outlines specific objectives and actions to be taken before, during, and after disasters to minimize the impact on communities and expedite recovery efforts.

One of the key features of the NRF is the concept of the Emergency Operations Center (EOC), which serves as the focal point for coordinating response activities at all levels of government and with partner organizations. The NRF outlines the structure and functions of EOCs, including how they should be staffed, equipped, and operated to support effective decision-making and information sharing during emergencies.

Additionally, the NRF emphasizes the importance of a whole-community approach to emergency management, recognizing that disaster response and recovery efforts are most successful when they involve and engage all stakeholders, including government agencies, private-sector partners, community organizations, and individual citizens. By promoting collaboration and inclusivity, the NRF seeks to build resilience and enhance the nation's ability to prepare for, respond to, and recover from disasters of all types and sizes.

The National Response Framework serves as a cornerstone of the United States' emergency management system, providing a flexible and scalable framework for coordinating and managing disaster response efforts. By establishing clear roles, responsibilities, and coordination mechanisms, the NRF helps ensure a unified and effective response to emergencies, ultimately saving lives, protecting property, and supporting the nation's resilience in the face of disasters.

The National Incident Management System (NIMS) is a fundamental component of the United States' approach to incident management and emergency response. Established by the Department of Homeland Security (DHS), NIMS provides a standardized framework and set of principles for coordinating and managing incident response efforts across federal, state, tribal, and local agencies, as well as non-governmental organizations and the private sector.

NIMS is designed to promote interoperability, scalability, and flexibility in incident response operations. It establishes common terminology, organizational structures, and processes to ensure seamless communication and coordination among disparate entities involved in emergency response. By standardizing these elements, NIMS enhances the ability of responders to work together effectively, regardless of jurisdictional boundaries or organizational affiliations.

One of the key components of NIMS is the Incident Command System (ICS), which serves as the foundation for incident management at all levels. ICS provides a modular and scalable organizational structure that can adapt to the size, complexity, and nature of the incident. It delineates clear lines of authority and responsibility, ensuring efficient decision-making and resource allocation during response operations.

In addition to ICS, NIMS incorporates other essential elements, such as the Multiagency Coordination System (MACS) and the Joint Information System (JIS), to facilitate coordination and information sharing among response partners. MACS enables collaboration and resource sharing across agencies and jurisdictions, while JIS ensures the timely dissemination of accurate and consistent information to the public and the media.

Moreover, NIMS emphasizes the importance of preparedness, training, and exercises to ensure that responders are adequately trained and equipped to effectively manage incidents. It provides guidance on developing incident response plans, conducting training and drills, and evaluating performance to identify areas for improvement.

The Post-Katrina Emergency Management Reform Act (PKEMRA) represents a significant piece of legislation enacted by the United States Congress in response to the catastrophic Hurricane Katrina in 2005. This act was aimed at addressing the deficiencies and failures in the nation's emergency management and response systems exposed by the disaster, with the goal of enhancing preparedness, coordination, and effectiveness in future emergencies.

PKEMRA introduced several key reforms to the nation's emergency management framework, including the establishment of the Federal Emergency Management Agency (FEMA) as an independent agency within the Department of Homeland Security (DHS). Prior to PKEMRA, FEMA was an independent agency, but it was later absorbed into DHS in 2003. PKEMRA restored FEMA's autonomy, recognizing the need for a dedicated agency focused solely on emergency management and disaster response.

Furthermore, PKEMRA strengthened FEMA's authority and capabilities in several areas, including disaster response, recovery, and mitigation. The act clarified FEMA's role in coordinating federal assistance to states and localities during emergencies, streamlining the process for requesting and receiving aid, and providing resources to support disaster response and recovery efforts.

PKEMRA also emphasized the importance of emergency preparedness and planning at all levels of government. It required state and local governments to develop and maintain comprehensive emergency management plans and capabilities, ensuring that they were adequately prepared to respond to a wide range of hazards and threats.

Additionally, PKEMRA included provisions to enhance accountability and transparency in emergency management operations. It mandated regular assessments and evaluations of FEMA's programs and activities, as well as increased oversight by Congress and other federal agencies to ensure that taxpayer dollars were being spent effectively and efficiently.

Frameworks in Australia

The National Disaster Risk Reduction Framework serves as a comprehensive strategy and roadmap for countries to address the complexities of disaster risk reduction (DRR) effectively. It encompasses a range of policies, programs, and initiatives aimed at reducing vulnerabilities, enhancing resilience, and promoting sustainable development in the face of natural hazards and disasters.

At its core, the framework emphasizes a proactive and holistic approach to disaster risk reduction, recognizing that the impacts of disasters are shaped by a combination of hazards, vulnerabilities, and exposure. By integrating risk reduction considerations into various sectors and decision-making processes, the framework seeks to mainstream DRR across government agencies, civil society organizations, and the private sector.

One key aspect of the National Disaster Risk Reduction Framework is its focus on risk assessment and mapping. By conducting comprehensive risk assessments, countries can identify existing and emerging hazards, assess vulnerabilities and exposure, and prioritize areas for intervention. This data-driven approach enables policymakers and stakeholders to make informed decisions about resource allocation, land use planning, infrastructure development, and disaster preparedness measures.

Moreover, the framework emphasizes the importance of building resilience at all levels of society, from individual households to communities, regions, and nations. It promotes investments in resilient infrastructure, early warning systems, capacity-building initiatives, and community-based disaster management programs to enhance preparedness, response, and recovery capabilities.

Furthermore, the National Disaster Risk Reduction Framework underscores the need for multi-stakeholder collaboration and partnerships to address the complex and interconnected nature of disaster risks. It encourages cooperation among government agencies, international organizations, academia, the private sector, and civil society to leverage expertise, resources, and best practices in disaster risk reduction.

The key features of the framework comprise:

1. Risk Assessment and Mapping:

    - Conducting comprehensive risk assessments to identify hazards, vulnerabilities, and exposure.

   - Utilizing advanced technologies and data analytics for hazard mapping and risk modelling.
   - Incorporating climate change projections and socio-economic factors into risk assessments.

2. Prevention and Mitigation:
   - Implementing measures to prevent and mitigate the impacts of disasters, such as land-use planning regulations, building codes, and infrastructure improvements.
   - Promoting nature-based solutions and ecosystem-based approaches to enhance resilience to natural hazards.

3. Preparedness and Response:
   - Enhancing preparedness through community education, awareness campaigns, and training programs.
   - Establishing robust early warning systems and emergency response protocols to facilitate timely and effective responses to disasters.
   - Conducting regular drills, exercises, and simulations to test emergency response capabilities.

4. Recovery and Reconstruction:
   - Supporting affected communities in their recovery and reconstruction efforts following disasters.
   - Providing financial assistance, counselling services, and livelihood support to disaster-affected individuals and businesses.
   - Incorporating principles of sustainable recovery and building back better to reduce future risks.

5. Governance and Coordination:
   - Establishing clear roles, responsibilities, and coordination mechanisms

among government agencies, stakeholders, and communities.

- Enhancing collaboration and partnerships between different levels of government, non-governmental organizations, academia, and the private sector.
- Promoting a whole-of-society approach to disaster risk reduction, with active engagement from all sectors of society.

6. Monitoring and Evaluation:
   - Developing robust monitoring and evaluation frameworks to assess the effectiveness of disaster risk reduction efforts.
   - Collecting data on disaster impacts, response measures, and recovery outcomes to inform policy development and decision-making.
   - Conducting regular reviews and updates of the framework to ensure its relevance and effectiveness in addressing evolving risks and challenges.

Overall, the Australian National Disaster Risk Reduction Framework aims to build a resilient and adaptive society capable of minimizing the impacts of disasters and adapting to changing risk landscapes.

Frameworks in Canada

The Emergency Management Act in Canada serves as a legal framework that governs emergency management activities at the federal level. Enacted in 2007, the act provides a systematic approach to preparing for, mitigating, responding to, and recovering from emergencies and disasters. It outlines the roles, responsibilities, and authorities of various government agencies, departments, and stakeholders involved in emergency management across the country.

One of the key features of the Emergency Management Act is the establishment of Public Safety Canada as the lead federal department responsible for emergency management. Public Safety Canada coordinates and supports the efforts of federal, provincial, territorial, and municipal governments, as well as Indigenous organizations, non-governmental organizations, and other partners involved in emergency management.

The act outlines the principles and objectives of emergency management, emphasizing the importance of an all-hazards approach, collaboration, and cooperation among stakeholders, and the protection of life, property, and the environment. It also emphasizes the need for risk assessment, planning, training, and exercising to enhance preparedness and resilience to emergencies and disasters.

Under the Emergency Management Act, the Government of Canada has the authority to declare a national emergency when an urgent and critical situation threatens public safety, security, or well-being. Such declarations enable the government to mobilize resources, provide assistance to affected jurisdictions, and coordinate national response efforts.

The act also establishes the framework for the development and implementation of national emergency management plans, including the Federal Emergency Response Plan (FERP) and the National Emergency Response System (NERS). These plans outline the roles and responsibilities of federal departments and agencies in responding to various types of emergencies and provide guidance for coordinated and effective response operations.

The Emergency Management Act in Canada provides the legal basis for a coordinated and integrated approach to emergency management at the federal level. By establishing clear authorities, responsibilities, and mechanisms for collaboration, the act aims to enhance the country's resilience to emergencies and disasters and ensure a timely and effective response to protect Canadians and their communities.

The Federal Emergency Response Plan (FERP) in Canada serves as a comprehensive framework for coordinating the federal government's response to emergencies and disasters that exceed the capacity of provincial, territorial, or municipal authorities. Established under the Emergency Management Act, FERP outlines the roles, responsibilities, and procedures for federal departments and agencies involved in emergency response operations.

One of the key features of the FERP is its all-hazards approach, which recognizes that emergencies and disasters can take various forms, including natural events (such as floods, wildfires, and earthquakes), technological accidents, biological incidents, and security threats. By adopting an all-hazards approach, FERP ensures that response plans and procedures are flexible and adaptable to different types of emergencies.

FERP outlines the structure of the federal response system, including the roles and responsibilities of key federal departments and agencies, such as Public Safety Canada, Health Canada, Environment and Climate Change Canada, the Canadian Armed Forces, and the Royal Canadian Mounted Police (RCMP). Each department and agency has specific responsibilities based on its mandate and expertise, contributing to a coordinated and integrated response effort.

The plan also establishes the mechanisms for coordination and communication among federal, provincial, territorial, and municipal authorities, as well as Indigenous organizations, non-governmental organizations, and other partners involved in emergency response. This includes the establishment of Emergency Operations Centers (EOCs) at the federal, provincial, and territorial levels to facilitate coordination and information sharing during response operations.

FERP outlines the procedures for activating and deploying federal resources and assets in support of provincial, territorial, and municipal authorities affected by emergencies and disasters. This may include the provision of personnel, equipment, supplies, and technical expertise to assist with response and recovery efforts, as well as the coordination of financial assistance and logistical support.

Frameworks in Japan

The Basic Act on Disaster Management, often considered the cornerstone of Japan's disaster management framework, provides the legal foundation for the country's approach to disaster preparedness, response, and recovery. Enacted in 1961 and subsequently revised in response to evolving risks and challenges, the Act outlines the principles, objectives, and responsibilities for disaster management at the national, prefectural, and municipal levels.

At its core, the Basic Act on Disaster Management establishes the fundamental principles that guide Japan's approach to disaster risk reduction and resilience-building. These principles include prioritizing the safety and well-being of the public, fostering collaboration and coordination among relevant stakeholders, promoting comprehensive and integrated disaster management measures, and ensuring the effective utilization of resources and technology to enhance disaster preparedness and response capabilities.

One of the key features of the Basic Act is its emphasis on the importance of comprehensive disaster management planning and preparedness. The Act mandates the development of disaster management plans at the national, prefectural, and municipal levels, which outline the roles, responsibilities, and procedures for responding to various types of disasters, including earthquakes, tsunamis, typhoons, floods, and nuclear incidents. These plans serve as the blueprint for coordinated response efforts and ensure that all levels of government are prepared to address disasters effectively.

The Basic Act on Disaster Management also establishes the legal framework for disaster risk reduction and mitigation measures. It calls for the implementation of proactive measures to reduce the vulnerability of communities to disasters, including the construction of resilient infrastructure, the adoption of land-use planning and building codes to mitigate risks, and the promotion of public awareness and education on disaster preparedness and safety measures.

Furthermore, the Act mandates the establishment of disaster management organizations and mechanisms at the national, prefectural, and municipal levels to facilitate coordination and collaboration among government agencies, emergency responders, and relevant stakeholders. These organizations, such as the Central Disaster Management Council and the Disaster Management Councils at the local level, play a crucial role in planning, coordinating, and implementing disaster management activities.

The Basic Act on Disaster Management in Japan encompasses several key features that form the foundation of the country's approach to disaster preparedness, response, and recovery. These features include:

1. Legal Framework: The Basic Act serves as the primary legal framework for disaster management in Japan, outlining the fundamental principles, objectives, and responsibilities for disaster risk reduction and resilience-building. It provides the statutory basis for the development and implementation of disaster management policies, plans, and measures at the national, prefectural, and municipal levels.

2. Comprehensive Approach: The Act emphasizes a comprehensive and integrated approach to disaster management, recognizing that effective risk reduction requires coordination and collaboration across multiple sectors and levels of government. It calls for the involvement of various stakeholders, including government agencies, emergency responders, community organizations, businesses, and the public, in planning, implementing, and evaluating disaster management activities.

3. Risk Reduction and Mitigation: The Basic Act prioritizes proactive measures to reduce the vulnerability of communities to disasters and mitigate their impact. It mandates the implementation of strategies and measures to enhance disaster resilience, including the construction of resilient infrastructure, the adoption of land-use planning and building codes to mitigate risks, and the promotion of

public awareness and education on disaster preparedness and safety measures.

4. Disaster Management Planning: The Act requires the development of disaster management plans at the national, prefectural, and municipal levels, which outline the roles, responsibilities, and procedures for responding to various types of disasters. These plans serve as the basis for coordinated response efforts and ensure that all levels of government are prepared to address disasters effectively.

5. Establishment of Disaster Management Organizations: The Basic Act mandates the establishment of disaster management organizations and mechanisms at the national, prefectural, and municipal levels to facilitate coordination and collaboration among government agencies, emergency responders, and relevant stakeholders. These organizations, such as the Central Disaster Management Council and the Disaster Management Councils at the local level, play a crucial role in planning, coordinating, and implementing disaster management activities.

6. Public Participation and Awareness: The Act emphasizes the importance of public participation and awareness in disaster management. It encourages the active involvement of individuals, communities, and businesses in disaster preparedness, response, and recovery efforts. Additionally, the Act promotes public education and awareness campaigns to enhance understanding of disaster risks and encourage proactive measures to reduce vulnerability and enhance resilience.

Frameworks in the European Union

The EU Civil Protection Mechanism and the Sendai Framework for Disaster Risk Reduction represent two critical components of international efforts to enhance disaster preparedness, response, and resilience.

The EU Civil Protection Mechanism is a collaborative framework established by the European Union (EU) to facilitate cooperation among member states and other participating countries in disaster response and civil protection. Under this mechanism, participating countries pool their resources and expertise to provide assistance to disaster-affected countries both within and outside the EU. This includes deploying search and rescue teams, medical personnel, equipment, and other resources to support affected populations during emergencies. The EU Civil Protection Mechanism also coordinates information sharing, training, and capacity-building initiatives to strengthen disaster preparedness and response capabilities across Europe and beyond.

In contrast, the Sendai Framework for Disaster Risk Reduction is a global framework adopted by UN member states to guide efforts to reduce disaster risk and build resilience at the national, regional, and international levels. The framework, which was adopted in 2015 at the Third UN World Conference on Disaster Risk Reduction in Sendai, Japan, outlines seven global targets for reducing disaster risk and losses by 2030. These targets focus on areas such as understanding disaster risk, strengthening disaster governance, enhancing disaster preparedness, and building back better after disasters. The Sendai Framework emphasizes the importance of integrating disaster risk reduction into development policies and practices, promoting multi-stakeholder partnerships, and empowering communities to take proactive measures to reduce their vulnerability to disasters.

Both the EU Civil Protection Mechanism and the Sendai Framework play complementary roles in advancing the global agenda on disaster risk reduction and resilience-building. While the EU Civil Protection Mechanism focuses on facilitating rapid and effective response to disasters through international cooperation and coordination, the Sendai Framework provides a comprehensive framework for guiding long-term efforts to reduce disaster risk and build resilience at the national and international levels. Together, these initiatives contribute to strengthening the global community's capacity to prevent, prepare for, and respond to disasters, ultimately enhancing the safety, well-being, and resilience of populations around the world.

The Disaster Risk Management (DRM) Directive is a crucial piece of legislation established by the European Union (EU) to enhance disaster preparedness, response, and resilience across its member states. Adopted in 2019, the directive aims to strengthen the EU's capacity to prevent, prepare for, and respond to disasters by establishing common standards and procedures for disaster risk management.

The DRM Directive emphasizes a comprehensive and multi-dimensional approach to disaster risk management, recognizing that effective disaster risk reduction requires coordinated action across various sectors and levels of governance. The directive outlines key principles and objectives for disaster risk management, including risk assessment, prevention, preparedness, response, and recovery. By integrating these elements into a coherent framework, the directive seeks to enhance the EU's ability to anticipate, mitigate, and respond to a wide range of natural and man-made hazards.

One of the central features of the DRM Directive is its emphasis on risk assessment and mapping as fundamental tools for understanding and addressing disaster risk. Member states are required to conduct comprehensive risk assessments to identify and prioritize areas of vulnerability, as well as to develop risk maps that provide detailed information on hazards, exposure, and vulnerability. These assessments serve as the foundation for developing risk reduction strategies, allocating resources, and implementing targeted interventions to reduce disaster risk and enhance resilience.

Furthermore, the DRM Directive promotes a proactive approach to disaster risk management by emphasizing the importance of prevention and preparedness measures. Member states are encouraged to implement measures to prevent or mitigate the impact of disasters, such as land-use planning, building codes, and early warning systems. Additionally, the directive calls for the development of emergency response plans, the establishment of coordination mechanisms, and the provision of training and capacity-building initiatives to ensure effective response and recovery operations.

Frameworks in the United Kingdom

The Civil Contingencies Act 2004 is a pivotal piece of legislation in the United Kingdom designed to enhance the country's preparedness and response capabilities for emergencies and disasters. Enacted in the aftermath of several major incidents, including the 9/11 attacks and the 2001 foot-and-mouth disease outbreak, the act provides a comprehensive framework for managing emergencies across England, Wales, Scotland, and Northern Ireland.

The Act establishes a clear legal basis for emergency preparedness, response, and recovery at both the national and local levels. The act defines the roles and responsibilities of various authorities, including central government, local authorities, emergency services, and other relevant stakeholders, in coordinating and managing responses to emergencies of all kinds.

One of the key features of the Civil Contingencies Act is its emphasis on a risk-based approach to emergency planning and management. The act requires responsible authorities to assess and identify potential risks and threats, develop emergency plans and procedures to address those risks, and maintain readiness to respond effectively to a wide range of scenarios, from natural disasters to terrorist attacks.

Furthermore, the Civil Contingencies Act establishes a statutory framework for the creation of emergency plans and protocols, known as civil protection arrangements, at the local level. Local authorities, known as Category 1 responders, are required to develop and maintain emergency plans to address a range of specific risks and hazards within their jurisdictions. These plans outline procedures for coordinating response efforts, mobilizing resources, and ensuring the safety and well-being of residents in times of crisis.

Additionally, the Civil Contingencies Act (CCA) empowers the government to declare a state of emergency, known as a "serious and imminent threat to public health, national security, or the environment," in exceptional circumstances. This declaration grants authorities the necessary powers to take extraordinary measures to protect life, property, and public safety, including the deployment of emergency services, the imposition of restrictions on movement and gatherings, and the requisitioning of resources.

The following outlines the key features of the Act:

1. Definition of Responsibilities: The CCA defines the roles and responsibilities of various authorities, including central government, local authorities, emergency services, and other responders, in managing emergencies.

2. Risk Assessment and Planning: It requires responsible authorities to conduct risk assessments to identify potential hazards and threats. Based on these assessments, authorities develop emergency plans and procedures to address various scenarios, ensuring readiness to respond effectively.

3. Category 1 and Category 2 Responders: The CCA categorizes responders into two groups: Category 1 responders, which include local authorities, emergency services, and other designated organizations with key responsibilities for emergency planning and response; and Category 2 responders, which include organizations that support Category 1 responders in their roles.

4. Duty to Co-operate: The act establishes a duty to cooperate among responders at all levels to ensure effective coordination and collaboration in emergency management efforts.

5. Local Resilience Forums (LRFs): The CCA requires the establishment of Local Resilience Forums (LRFs) in each local area, comprising representatives from Category 1 and Category 2 responders, as well as other relevant stakeholders. LRFs facilitate joint emergency planning, information sharing, and coordination at the local level.

6. Emergency Plans: It mandates Category 1 responders to develop and maintain

emergency plans to address specific risks and hazards within their jurisdictions. These plans outline procedures for response, recovery, and public communication during emergencies.

7. Emergency Powers: The CCA grants the government powers to declare a state of emergency in exceptional circumstances, allowing for the implementation of extraordinary measures to protect life, property, and public safety.

8. Communication and Public Information: It emphasizes the importance of communication and public information in emergencies, requiring authorities to disseminate timely and accurate information to the public and stakeholders.

9. Training and Exercises: The act encourages regular training and exercises to test emergency plans, enhance preparedness, and identify areas for improvement.

10. Review and Evaluation: The CCA includes provisions for the regular review and evaluation of emergency plans and procedures to ensure their effectiveness and relevance.

Frameworks in New Zealand

The Civil Defence Emergency Management Act 2002 (CDEM Act) and the National Disaster Resilience Strategy (NDRS) are two significant components of New Zealand's emergency management framework, aimed at enhancing the country's resilience to disasters.

The CDEM Act provides the legal basis for civil defence emergency management in New Zealand, outlining the roles, responsibilities, and powers of various stakeholders involved in emergency management. It establishes a clear framework for risk assessment, emergency planning, response coordination, and recovery efforts. Under this act, local authorities are designated as the primary entities responsible for emergency management within their jurisdictions, working in collaboration with central government agencies, emergency services, and other key stakeholders.

One of the key features of the CDEM Act is the establishment of Civil Defence Emergency Management Groups (CDEM Groups) at the regional and local levels. These groups bring together representatives from local authorities, emergency services, lifeline utilities, and community organizations to coordinate emergency management activities and ensure a cohesive response to disasters. They are responsible for developing and implementing comprehensive emergency management plans tailored to the specific risks and hazards within their regions.

The National Disaster Resilience Strategy (NDRS) complements the CDEM Act by providing a strategic framework for building resilience across New Zealand. Adopted in 2019, the NDRS sets out a vision and priorities for enhancing the country's resilience to natural hazards and other disasters. It emphasizes a whole-of-society approach to disaster risk reduction, involving government agencies, businesses, communities, and individuals in collaborative efforts to reduce vulnerabilities and enhance preparedness.

Key components of the NDRS include risk identification and assessment, mitigation measures, preparedness initiatives, response capabilities, and recovery planning. The strategy emphasizes the importance of proactive risk management, community engagement, and investment in resilience-building measures to minimize the impact of disasters on lives, livelihoods, and infrastructure. It also highlights the need for adaptive governance structures, innovative approaches to risk reduction, and continuous learning and improvement in emergency management practices.

Use of Emergency Management Policy Frameworks

Emergency Management Policy Frameworks serve as essential guidelines and roadmaps for managers and coordinators in effectively preparing for, responding to, and recovering from disasters and emergencies. These frameworks typically outline the principles, objectives, roles, responsibilities, and procedures that govern emergency management activities at various levels of government and across different sectors. Managers and coordinators can use these frameworks in several ways to enhance their effectiveness in managing emergencies:

1. Guidance and Direction: Emergency Management Policy Frameworks provide clear guidance and direction on the overarching goals and priorities of emergency management efforts. By aligning their strategies and actions with the objectives outlined in these frameworks, managers and coordinators can ensure that their initiatives contribute to broader national or regional objectives for disaster risk reduction, preparedness, response, and recovery.

2. Standardization and Consistency: These frameworks help standardize practices and procedures across different agencies and organizations involved in emer-

gency management. By adhering to established protocols and guidelines, managers and coordinators can promote consistency and coherence in their operations, facilitating seamless coordination and collaboration during emergencies.

3. Risk Assessment and Planning: Emergency Management Policy Frameworks often include provisions for conducting risk assessments, developing emergency plans, and implementing risk reduction measures. Managers and coordinators can utilize these frameworks to assess the specific hazards and vulnerabilities faced by their communities or organizations, identify priority areas for action, and develop comprehensive emergency management plans tailored to their unique circumstances.

4. Resource Allocation and Coordination: Policy frameworks delineate the roles and responsibilities of different stakeholders in emergency management and specify mechanisms for resource allocation and coordination. Managers and coordinators can leverage these frameworks to allocate resources effectively, mobilize support from relevant agencies and partners, and ensure seamless coordination of activities across multiple sectors and jurisdictions.

5. Training and Capacity Building: Emergency Management Policy Frameworks often emphasize the importance of training, capacity building, and professional development for emergency responders and stakeholders. Managers and coordinators can use these frameworks to identify training needs, develop training programs and exercises, and enhance the skills and competencies of their teams to better prepare for and respond to emergencies.

6. Communication and Public Engagement: Effective communication and public engagement are critical components of emergency management. Policy frameworks typically include provisions for communication strategies, public awareness campaigns, and community engagement initiatives. Managers and coordinators can utilize these frameworks to develop communication plans, disseminate timely and accurate information to the public, and engage communities in preparedness and mitigation efforts.

7. Evaluation and Continuous Improvement: Finally, Emergency Management Policy Frameworks often emphasize the importance of evaluation, monitoring,

and continuous improvement in emergency management practices. Managers and coordinators can use these frameworks to establish mechanisms for evaluating the effectiveness of their emergency management programs, identifying lessons learned from past experiences, and implementing corrective actions to enhance resilience and preparedness over time.

13

Psychological Aspects of Disasters

Natural disasters can present overwhelming and potentially traumatic experiences for those directly affected. Individuals impacted by events like Hurricane Harvey may endure severe injuries, witness widespread devastation among their communities, and face the loss of possessions and property [610]. The immediate aftermath of such disasters is often disorienting, characterized by displacement, shock, and a strong urge to restore order. In the weeks and months following, individuals may grapple with the tasks involved in rebuilding their lives and adjusting to a "new normal," which may include relocating to new homes and acquiring new possessions. Consequently, the full impact of the disaster on mental health may not become apparent until weeks or even months later.

Disasters, whether stemming from natural phenomena or human activities, wield profound psychological repercussions on individuals, communities, and societies at large. Comprehensive comprehension of these psychological dimensions is indispensable for crafting effective strategies in disaster preparedness, response, and recovery endeavours. Among the prominent psychological facets of disasters are trauma and stress reactions. Exposure to or witnessing of catastrophic events often triggers trauma and acute stress reactions, manifesting as shock, disbelief, fear, anxiety, and sadness. These reactions vary in intensity and duration, potentially culminating in post-traumatic stress disorder (PTSD) or other mental health conditions for some individuals.

Grief and loss constitute another significant psychological aspect of disasters. The aftermath of such events frequently encompasses substantial loss of life, property, livelihoods, and communal infrastructure. Mourning the loss of loved ones, homes, possessions, and familiar environments is an inherent response to the devastation wrought by disasters. The psychological recovery process for individuals and communities hinges significantly on effectively managing grief and navigating through the complexities of loss.

Displacement and disruption represent additional psychological challenges encountered in the wake of disasters. Forced evacuations, temporary relocations to shelters, or prolonged displacement upend normal routines, amplifying stress and uncertainty. The resultant disorientation, feelings of helplessness, and loss of control can further exacerbate psychological distress among affected individuals and families.

Social support networks and community resilience emerge as critical factors in mitigating the psychological impacts of disasters. Strong social connections and supportive relationships serve as buffers against stress, fostering resilience in the face of adversity. Communities that unite to extend mutual aid, comfort, and solidarity showcase heightened resilience, aiding in the collective psychological recovery from disasters.

Moreover, certain segments of the population exhibit heightened vulnerability to the psychological ramifications of disasters. Children, older adults, individuals with pre-existing mental health conditions, and marginalized or disadvantaged groups are particularly susceptible. Addressing the distinct needs of these vulnerable populations necessitates tailored interventions and support services to safeguard their psychological well-being and facilitate recovery.

Individuals and communities employ diverse coping mechanisms and adaptive strategies to navigate the psychological aftermath of disasters. These strategies encompass seeking social support, engaging in religious or spiritual practices, practicing mindfulness or relaxation techniques, participating in community activities, and accessing mental health services.

Furthermore, understanding how individuals perceive and respond to disaster risks is pivotal for effective preparedness efforts. Factors such as past experiences, cultural beliefs, trust in authorities, and perceived efficacy of preparedness actions shape individuals' risk perceptions and preparedness behaviour. Accurate risk communication and promotion of proactive preparedness measures are instrumental in mitigating the psychological impacts of disasters.

Finally, it is crucial to recognize the enduring nature of the psychological effects of disasters. While immediate attention may be focused on addressing the acute impacts, the repercussions can persist long after the event has passed. Chronic stress, ongoing disruptions, loss of social support, and economic challenges can contribute to long-term mental health issues within disaster-affected populations. Providing sustained mental health support and resources is paramount for fostering long-term recovery and resilience in the aftermath of disasters.

Depending on the extent of their losses, individuals may experience a range of emotional responses, including grief, panic, fear, and sadness. Difficulty sleeping, anger, irritability, and feelings of guilt are common, with some individuals experiencing survivor's guilt if they were not severely affected [610]. Despite these challenges, most survivors ultimately recover without major mental health disturbances, even if they experience heightened symptoms in the immediate aftermath.

Maintaining social connections in the aftermath of a disaster is crucial for both individual and community healing. Avoiding isolation and seeking social support can bolster resilience. Additionally, engaging in self-care practices, such as maintaining regular eating, sleeping, and exercise routines, is essential for promoting overall well-being during challenging times. Techniques like deep breathing exercises, journaling, taking walks, and talking to supportive individuals can also help alleviate acute stress and anxiety [610].

While many individuals and communities demonstrate remarkable resilience following traumatic events, a minority may experience longer-term psychological disturbances. Conditions such as post-traumatic stress disorder (PTSD), depression, anxiety disorders, or substance use may develop, particularly among those who have endured extreme stress or trauma. Seeking counselling or additional mental health support may be beneficial for individuals experiencing symptoms such as nightmares, avoidance of reminders of the disaster, changes in thinking or mood, sleep disturbances, irritability, panic attacks, increased worry or fear, loss of interest in activities, changes in appetite, or increased substance use lasting for one month or more after the disaster.

Post-Traumatic Stress Disorder (PTSD) is a mental health condition triggered by experiencing or witnessing traumatic events. Symptoms of PTSD include flashbacks, nightmares, severe anxiety, and uncontrollable thoughts related to the traumatic event.

Research has shown that the prevalence of PTSD among directly impacted populations can range from 30% to 40% in the year following a disaster [611].

Studies have highlighted the features of trauma memories in PTSD, such as unintentional re-experiencing symptoms and intentional recall of trauma narratives [611]. Traumatic events like wars, terrorist attacks, and natural disasters have increased public interest in understanding the risk and protective factors for PTSD [612]. New technologies have been explored to improve the prediction and assessment of PTSD, including using computerized methods and machine learning [613].

PTSD is often associated with fear learning circuitry biases and generalization of fear associations, particularly in individuals with a history of trauma [614]. Additionally, PTSD symptoms can be triggered by reminders of traumatic events, leading to autonomic surges and physiological reactions like increased heart rate and blood pressure [615]. Individuals with PTSD may experience intrusive memories and emotional responses when faced with distressing reminders or triggers [616].

Furthermore, research has shown that prior exposure to traumatic events can sensitize individuals to develop PTSD following subsequent stressors, a phenomenon known as "stress sensitization" [617]. Women are at a higher risk of developing PTSD due to experiencing traumatic events like sexual assault, which carry a higher risk of precipitating PTSD [618].

Anxiety and depression are common responses among disaster survivors, characterized by persistent sadness, hopelessness, and elevated anxiety levels that can endure for years [619]. Studies indicate that rates of depression and anxiety are notably heightened in populations affected by disasters, impacting around 20% to 30% of individuals [619]. Post-traumatic stress disorder (PTSD) and depression rates have been found to significantly increase following disasters [619]. Symptoms of anxiety, depression, and insomnia are prevalent among post-disaster survivors, such as war veterans and Ebola survivors [620]. Additionally, comorbidity between PTSD, depression, and anxiety is observed in various groups, including children affected by extreme weather events [621].

Persistent mental health difficulties, including anxiety disorders, depressive disorders, and PTSD, are common among survivors of disasters and traumatic events [622]. Factors such as enduring disaster-related stressors, injuries, and physical adversities can increase the risk of mental illness among affected individuals [623]. Post-traumatic stress disorder (PTSD) is a prevalent psychological distress following natural disasters, persisting over time [624]. Longitudinal studies have shown that posttraumatic stress symptoms (PTSS) and depressive symptoms often persist among survivors of major disasters [625]. Furthermore, the loss of homes due to disasters has been linked to cognitive decline and increased risk of posttraumatic stress symptoms (PTSS) among older survivors [626].

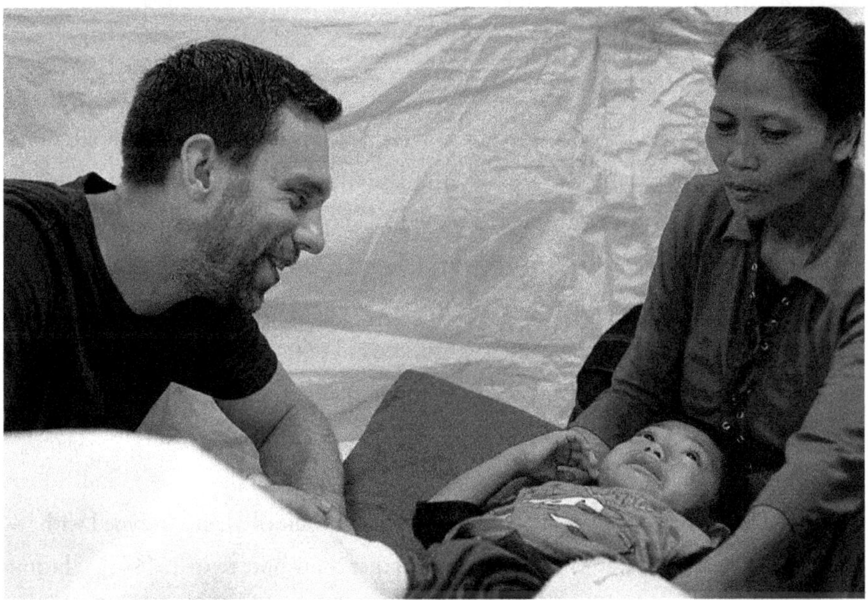

Figure 62: British physiotherapist Peter Skelton tries to make friends with five-year-old Angelo, who suffered severe, life-changing injuries when Typhoon Haiyan struck the Philippines on 8 November 2013. DFID - UK Department for International Development, CC BY 2.0, via Wikimedia Commons.*

Increased substance use or misuse as a coping mechanism following disasters can have detrimental effects on mental health and lead to various health and social issues. Research indicates that disasters often result in heightened rates of psychological distress and psychiatric disorders [627]. While disaster-specific factors play a significant role in this, better preparedness and community empowerment can help improve outcomes for vulnerable populations affected by disasters [7].

The aftermath of disasters can result in various mental health issues, ranging from temporary distress reactions to ongoing mental health problems and more severe conditions like PTSD and depression [628]. Disasters can also lead to negative mental health impacts among individuals who experience residential displacement or damage, with increased rates of alcohol and cigarette smoking observed post-disaster [629, 630].

In addressing the mental health impacts of disasters, it is crucial to consider the role of emergency departments in providing care during crises, emphasizing the need for experienced mental health staff [631]. Community mental health programs have been identified as effective interventions to enhance community mental health post-disasters [632]. Additionally, the presence of substance misuse in families can have intergenerational effects, highlighting the need for comprehensive approaches to address substance use issues in disaster-affected populations [633].

Chronic stress, resulting from various life challenges such as loss, displacement, and disruptions in daily routines, has been extensively linked to long-term health implications. Studies have shown that chronic stress can lead to accelerated telomere shortening [634], impact health and cognition through allostatic load biomarkers [635], and result in a dysregulated acute stress response [636]. Furthermore, chronic psychological stress and depression have been associated with negative effects on the immune system and overall health [637]. Lower socioeconomic status has been linked to chronic stress due to various environmental stressors [638], and the subjective experience of relative disadvantage can contribute to chronic stress [639].

Research has indicated that chronic stress can exacerbate health issues in individuals with chronic conditions [640], affect decision-making abilities when combined with social isolation [641], and lead to living conditions that contribute to stress [642]. Chronic stress has been proposed as a causal mechanism for various health problems, including hypertension, heart attack, stroke, diabetes, and obesity [643]. Additionally, chronic stress has been found to have direct, indirect, and interactive effects on mental and physical health outcomes in later life [644].

Moreover, chronic stress interacts with culture, socioeconomic status, and other psychosocial factors to influence health-related behaviour and physiological systems [645]. Exposure to prolonged psychological stress has been associated with alterations in physiological responses, contributing to morbidity and mortality [646]. Chronic stress can lead to brain alterations and physiological disruptions impacting health and developmental outcomes across the lifespan [647].

Case Studies on Disaster Impact

Case Study 1: Hurricane Katrina, 2005

Hurricane Katrina stands as one of the deadliest hurricanes in U.S. history, leaving a trail of destruction and flooding along the Gulf Coast. Beyond the physical devastation, the storm had profound psychological consequences, as revealed by a study conducted by the Columbia University Mailman School of Public Health [648]. Two years post-Katrina, the study found that approximately 21% of directly affected individuals suffered from post-traumatic stress disorder (PTSD), while 54% reported experiencing symptoms of depression [648]. Prolonged displacement exacerbated mental health issues, with many survivors grappling with stress and instability. Unfortunately, the lack of immediate and accessible mental health services impeded recovery efforts, prolonging the suffering of impacted communities.

In a follow-up study conducted five years after Hurricane Katrina, Columbia University researchers focused on the long-term impacts, particularly among children and adolescents [648]. Their findings were alarming, revealing that one-third of child survivors had developed mental health disorders. Shockingly, less than half of these children had access to professional mental health services, underscoring a concerning disparity. Furthermore, the study highlighted that children affected by the disaster were 4.5 times more likely to experience serious emotional disturbances compared to their unaffected peers.

Case Study 2: Fukushima Daiichi Nuclear Disaster, 2011

The Fukushima Daiichi nuclear disaster triggered significant psychological distress among the Japanese population, particularly among evacuees who faced sudden and indefinite displacement. A report from Fukushima Medical University revealed that years after the disaster, approximately 20% of evacuees still reported severe psychological distress [648]. The fear of radiation exposure and social stigma attached to being an evacuee compounded these mental health challenges. The prevalence of PTSD among evacuees was estimated to be around 14.6%, significantly higher than the general population [648]. Long-term mental health monitoring and support were recommended to address the persistent impacts.

The profound psychological toll of disasters exemplified by Hurricane Katrina and the Fukushima Daiichi nuclear disaster underscores the imperative of integrating mental health considerations into disaster preparedness and response frameworks. By prioritizing psychological well-being and establishing robust mechanisms for mental health support, communities can enhance their resilience and facilitate a more sustainable recovery process.

Psychological First Aid

Psychological first aid is a recommended and adaptable approach aimed at assisting individuals affected by trauma, helping to alleviate initial distress and support coping in the aftermath of traumatic events such as disasters, workplace accidents, or assaults. This approach is evidence-informed and can be applied across various situations to aid individuals, families, teams, and communities navigating potentially traumatic experiences [649, 650]. It serves as a psychosocial support activity designed to offer a humane and supportive response to those in distress, fostering feelings of safety, connection, calmness, and hopefulness while facilitating access to necessary physical, emotional, and social support . It aims to provide social, emotional, and practical support to mitigate distress and promote adaptive functioning [651].

Psychological first aid emphasizes promoting natural recovery and assisting individuals in feeling secure, connected, and equipped to cope with the challenges they face. It aims to mitigate initial distress, address immediate needs, foster adaptive coping strategies, and encourage adjustment to the new normal following a traumatic event. While commonly utilized in the immediate aftermath of a disaster, psychological first aid remains relevant in the long term, as individuals may experience stress triggers months or even years later, such as anniversaries of the event or encountering situations reminiscent of the traumatic experience [649].

Central to psychological first aid is the acknowledgment of the range of early reactions individuals may experience in response to trauma, including physical, psychological, emotional, and behavioural reactions. Recognizing these reactions as normal and understandable given the circumstances, psychological first aid seeks to facilitate recovery and resilience. While a minority of individuals may require more extensive mental health support, the majority are expected to recover well with the assistance of compassionate disaster responders, supportive networks, and caring loved ones.

Despite its long history, psychological first aid gained prominence following research highlighting the risks associated with critical incident stress debriefing. Since 2002, it has been recommended as a fundamental component of psychosocial support following disasters, emphasizing a proactive and supportive approach to aiding individuals in their recovery journey [649].

In disaster management, PFA plays a crucial role in addressing the mental health needs of individuals affected by disasters. It is considered a practical and early psychosocial intervention to reduce distress caused by disasters [652]. The National Preparedness and Response Science Board recommends training mental health professionals, first responders, and the general public in community-based psychological first aid to respond effectively to immediate mental health needs post-disaster [653]. PFA is also recognized as an effective way to guide psychological support activities for disaster mental health professionals, including nurses, in providing immediate psychological support to those in need [654].

Moreover, PFA training has been widely disseminated and adopted by various disaster response organizations and agencies internationally [655]. It is viewed as a critical component in disaster preparedness, equipping aid workers with the necessary skills for effective disaster response [656]. The Psychological First Aid Field Operations Guide provides evidence-informed guidance for workers responding to survivors of disasters, including children, reflecting best practices in disaster mental health [657].

Understanding how individuals react to difficult experiences is complex and multifaceted, influenced by various factors such as the nature of the event, individual resilience, age, personality, support systems, coping mechanisms, and past experiences. Despite this variability, there are common emotional and physical distress reactions that individuals may experience immediately during and in the aftermath of a crisis event. These reactions include feelings of guilt, sadness, relief, anger, fear, anxiety, confusion, uncertainty, and hopelessness, alongside physical symptoms like numbness, increased heartbeat, sweating, shaking, trembling, or shortness of breath.

It's essential to recognize that people react differently to crises, and not everyone may require or seek support. Witnesses to traumatic events may also experience strong emotional reactions and may need assistance coping. While some individuals may remain calm during the event but experience strong reactions later, others may exhibit immediate distress but manage their situation independently or with support from other sources. Stress is a common response to pressure or strain resulting from changes, whether positive or negative, and is a natural part of everyday life. However, prolonged stress can lead to distress, causing physical and emotional discomfort and suffering, which may result from a one-off crisis event or accumulated stress over time.

In more severe cases, individuals may exhibit complex reactions that necessitate specialized assistance or support. These reactions can manifest as panic attacks, overwhelming anxiety, anger, aggressive behaviour, self-harm, suicidal ideation, harmful coping methods like substance abuse or withdrawal, prolonged grief, sleeping problems, flashbacks, and intense or prolonged feelings of anxiety or anger. Certain factors, such as separation from family, perceived threat to life, high horror element in the situation, previous traumatic experiences, loss of loved ones, or underlying psychological disorders, can increase the risk of developing complex reactions.

While feelings of anxiety and anger are common reactions to crises, some individuals may experience intense or prolonged distress that requires more specialized support. It's crucial to be aware of these potential reactions and risk factors to provide appropriate support and assistance to individuals experiencing distress in the aftermath of a crisis event.

Psychosocial support encompasses five fundamental elements derived from research on risk and resilience, field experience, and expert consensus, which form the basis of the psychological first aid approach [649]. These elements guide individuals in providing effective psychological first aid to those affected by crises. The five elements of psychosocial support include ensuring safety, promoting calm, fostering connectedness, promoting self-efficacy and group efficacy, and instilling hope.

Ensuring safety is paramount as individuals may continue to experience negative psychological reactions while under threat or danger. Studies across cultures have shown that reintroducing safety gradually reduces negative reactions over time. Safety measures may involve removing individuals from harm's way, helping them meet basic needs, providing medical attention, offering physical and emotional comfort, and providing accurate information on obtaining necessities [649].

Promoting calm acknowledges that anxiety and distress are normal responses following traumatic events. While most people return to manageable emotional levels within days or weeks, ongoing negative symptoms may lead to long-term mental health issues. Normalizing stress reactions and providing stability, compassionate listening, accurate information, and reminders of available help can help promote calm.

Promoting connectedness recognizes the importance of social support in emotional well-being and recovery following mass trauma. Re-establishing connections with loved ones and fostering social networks post-crisis is vital for recovery. Activities such as facilitating contact with friends and family, keeping families together, and respecting cultural norms contribute to promoting connectedness.

Promoting self-efficacy involves empowering individuals to regain a sense of control over their lives. While crises may make individuals feel incompetent, reminding them of their capacity to cope and manage tasks can help restore self-efficacy. Engaging individuals in meeting their own needs, assisting with decision-making, and problem-solving are essential aspects of promoting self-efficacy.

Instilling hope is crucial as optimism can lead to favourable outcomes following trauma. Maintaining a reasonable degree of hope for the future is vital for resilience. Conveying an expectancy of recovery, being present and supportive, and reassuring individuals that their feelings are normal can help instil hope and facilitate the healing process.

Figure 63: Members of the National Crisis Response Canines and their handlers listen to the morning firefighter briefing for the McHugh Fire. Certified National Crisis Response Canines are specially trained in psychological first aid and to work effectively in crisis environments with people experiencing intense emotions in the aftermath of a critical incident. U.S. Department of AgricultureU.S. Forest Service/Alaska/USDA, Public domain, via Wikimedia Commons.

Providing Psychological First Aid

The abrupt and disruptive nature of emergencies exposes individuals to uncertainty and stress, eliciting varying degrees of distress among affected populations. Psychological first aid, accessible to any person experiencing distress, becomes crucial in these scenarios, extending its reach to adults, adolescents, children, disaster relief and recovery workers, and first responders alike. How individuals respond and cope hinges on several factors, including their direct experience of the emergency, their health status, personal history, and the availability of support networks [649].

Certain individuals may exhibit more complex reactions and face heightened risks of adverse consequences, such as those with previous traumatic experiences, underlying mental health conditions, exposure to high horror events, perceived imminent danger, traumatic bereavement, or significant losses in property and livelihoods. In complex situations where immediate specialized care is required, individuals such as those severely injured, survivors of sexual or gender-based violence, those unable to perform daily activities due to distress, or children experiencing abuse or neglect, need prompt referral to specialized support services.

It's essential to recognize that not everyone exposed to emergencies will experience emotional distress, and not all will require psychological first aid. Protective factors such as good functioning levels, social support, coping abilities, strong moral beliefs, returning to normal life, and minimizing disruption can mitigate the need for immediate psychological intervention. In instances where individuals require more support than psychological first aid can offer, helpers must acknowledge their limits and seek assistance from medical or other relevant professionals [649].

In large-scale disasters, psychological first aid should ideally be delivered by appropriate agencies as part of coordinated response mechanisms. This ensures a cohesive and organized approach to delivering psychosocial support as an integral component of emergency response efforts. In Australia, this coordinated response involves various stakeholders, including health professionals, educators, members of faith-based organizations, Red Cross volunteers, community responders, and local government personnel.

Psychological first aid (PFA) is a crucial intervention in disaster settings aimed at mitigating distress and promoting emotional recovery among individuals affected by traumatic events [658]. PFA is designed to stabilize individuals' mental and physical well-being, reduce stress, alleviate pain, and facilitate a return to normalcy [659]. It is an evidence-informed approach that draws on research, expert consensus, and practical experience to provide immediate psychological support to those in need [660]. PFA is recommended as an early intervention for all survivors in disaster situations [658].

Psychological first aid principles empower a broad spectrum of individuals in the community, from emergency personnel to volunteers, to offer humane, supportive, and practical assistance to those in distress [649]. These principles serve as a vital foundation for all emergency responders, emphasizing the importance of responding to the immediate crisis while promoting safe and effective recovery practices. Responsible helping, rooted in respect for survivors' dignity and capacity, serves to protect and enhance their mental health and psychosocial well-being.

PFA can be administered in diverse settings, ranging from evacuation centres and hospitals to schools, businesses, community centres, and even memorial services [661]. Its timing is flexible, proving beneficial both during the immediate aftermath of a crisis and in addressing distress that may arise weeks, months, or even years later. Acknowledging the enduring impact of traumatic events and the potential triggers that may evoke distress underscores the ongoing relevance of psychological first aid in facilitating recovery and resilience across diverse contexts and timeframes .

Training in PFA is crucial for frontline workers to effectively support distressed individuals and manage their own self-care during and after disasters [662]. The World Health Organization (WHO) recognizes PFA as an effective way to guide psychological support activities in disaster mental health, including for professionals like nurses [654]. Moreover, the dissemination of PFA training is increasing globally, highlighting the growing commitment to equipping individuals with the skills needed to provide psychological support in disaster settings [662].

PFA forms an integral part of the comprehensive response to significant humanitarian crises [663]. When hundreds or even thousands of individuals are impacted, a range of emergency response initiatives are mobilized, including search-and-rescue operations, urgent healthcare provisions, temporary shelter setups, food distribution efforts, and initiatives focusing on family tracing and child protection. However, aid workers and volunteers often face challenges in discerning the availability of specific services amidst such crises, particularly in scenarios of mass disasters or in areas lacking established infrastructures for healthcare and other essential services. It becomes crucial for them to proactively familiarize themselves with the available services and supports to effectively relay this information to those they are assisting, thereby facilitating access to practical assistance [663].

Effective communication with someone in distress is paramount. Individuals who have experienced a crisis event may be overwhelmed with emotions such as anxiety, confusion, or guilt. Remaining calm and demonstrating empathy can help them feel safe, understood, respected, and appropriately cared for during such challenging times [663].

It's common for someone who has gone through a distressing event to feel compelled to share their story. Listening attentively can provide significant support, but it's essential not to pressure them into divulging details if they're not ready. Some individuals may prefer silence or practical support like offering a meal or a glass of water. Creating a supportive atmosphere by being present without imposing conversation can encourage them to open up at their own pace.

Effective communication involves being mindful of both verbal and nonverbal cues, including facial expressions, eye contact, gestures, and body language. Recognizing and respecting cultural norms related to behaviour, age, gender, customs, and religion is crucial [663]. It's also advisable to choose a quiet environment for conversation and minimize distractions to facilitate meaningful communication.

When engaging in conversation, respecting privacy, maintaining an appropriate distance, and conveying active listening through nods or affirmations are essential. Providing factual information when available and expressing empathy towards their feelings and losses can help establish rapport. It's vital to acknowledge the person's strengths and avoid judgmental remarks or false reassurances.

However, there are also several things to avoid in communication. Pressuring someone to share their story, interrupting, rushing, or using technical terms can hinder effective communication. It's crucial not to touch someone without assurance of appropriateness or to discuss personal troubles or make false promises.

Maintaining good communication involves a balanced approach of active listening, empathy, and respect while refraining from imposing solutions or judgments. By being mindful of these principles, helpers can effectively support individuals in distress while adhering to cultural sensitivities and promoting a sense of empowerment and resilience [663].

Accounting for Culture

In times of crisis, the affected population often comprises individuals from diverse cultural backgrounds, including minority groups or those who may face marginalization. Cultural norms dictate how individuals interact and what behaviours are considered acceptable or inappropriate [663]. For instance, in some cultures, sharing emotions with someone outside of the family may not be customary, or there may be gender-specific protocols for communication. Additionally, certain dress codes or customs related to attire may hold significant importance.

As a helper, it's crucial to recognize and set aside one's own cultural biases to offer assistance in a manner that aligns with the preferences and comfort levels of those being supported [663]. Acknowledging and respecting cultural differences is paramount in providing effective aid. Each crisis situation presents unique challenges, necessitating adaptation of assistance strategies to local social and cultural norms.

In preparation for offering Psychological First Aid (PFA) in diverse cultural contexts, several questions can guide helpers in tailoring their approach [663]:

- Dress: Is there a specific attire required to demonstrate respect? Are there clothing items needed to preserve the dignity and customs of impacted individuals?

- Language: What is the customary greeting in this culture? What languages are spoken by the affected population?

- Gender, Age, and Power: Are there gender-specific norms dictating who should provide assistance to affected women? Who holds authority within the family or community?
- Touching and Behaviour: What are the cultural norms regarding physical contact? Is it acceptable to offer physical reassurance, such as holding hands or touching shoulders? Are there particular behavioural expectations concerning interactions with different demographics, such as the elderly or children?
- Beliefs and Religion: What are the ethnic and religious affiliations of the affected population? What beliefs or practices hold significance for them? How might their understanding or interpretation of the crisis event differ based on their cultural and religious perspectives?

By considering these questions and adapting their approach accordingly, helpers can ensure that their support is culturally sensitive and respectful, fostering effective communication and rapport with those in need [663].

Psychological First Aid Action Principles

When engaging in psychological first aid (PFA), helpers tailor their actions to suit the specific situation and the needs of those they're assisting. This approach is guided by three fundamental sets of actions: LOOK, LISTEN, and LINK, which serve as a framework for entering an emergency situation safely, identifying individuals requiring support (LOOK), understanding their needs (LISTEN), and connecting them with necessary information and practical assistance (LINK) [649]. It's important to acknowledge that helpers may need to adapt and repeat these actions based on evolving circumstances and the needs of affected individuals.

LOOK involves ensuring the safety of helpers and determining who may require immediate assistance. PFA helpers gather information about the situation, assessing factors such as who needs help, potential safety risks, physical injuries, immediate basic needs, and emotional reactions. This initial assessment is crucial for prioritizing assistance and effectively addressing urgent concerns [649].

LISTEN emphasizes the importance of effective communication and empathy when interacting with individuals in distress. PFA helpers consider various aspects of communication, including how they approach someone, introduce themselves, actively listen to others' concerns, acknowledge their feelings, and provide reassurance. By creating a supportive environment and encouraging open dialogue, helpers can help individuals express their needs and concerns, facilitating a sense of calm and trust [649].

Proper listening is a cornerstone of effective assistance, enabling helpers to comprehend the situation and needs of those they are aiding, fostering a sense of calm, and facilitating the provision of suitable support. Listening should encompass engagement with one's eyes, ears, and heart, signifying undivided attention, genuine hearing of concerns, and demonstrating care and respect [663].

Initiating contact with individuals who may require support involves approaching them respectfully, adhering to cultural norms, and introducing oneself with name and affiliation. Offering assistance should be done with sensitivity, finding a safe and tranquil space for conversation and ensuring the person feels at ease, perhaps by providing water. Prioritizing safety, especially by removing individuals from immediate danger and shielding them from media exposure for privacy, is imperative.

When inquiring about people's needs and concerns, it's essential to avoid assumptions and instead ask directly to ascertain their priorities. Actively listening to individuals without pressuring them to speak and being present for them during distressing moments fosters a supportive environment.

Some individuals experiencing a crisis may exhibit heightened anxiety or distress, accompanied by physical symptoms like trembling or difficulty breathing. Techniques to promote calmness include maintaining a soothing tone, culturally appropriate eye contact, and reassuring the person of their safety. Grounding exercises such as focusing on sensory experiences or breathing can help individuals reconnect with their surroundings and alleviate feelings of unreality or dissociation.

Encouraging individuals to focus on their breathing and engage in simple physical actions can further aid in restoring a sense of calmness. By employing these strategies, helpers can effectively assist individuals in managing distress and restoring a sense of stability during challenging circumstances [663].

LINK focuses on practical outcomes, with helpers providing information and assisting individuals in accessing essential resources to cope with their situation. This may involve guiding individuals to access relevant information, reconnect with loved ones and social support networks, address practical challenges, and access necessary services and assistance. By facilitating access to resources and support systems, helpers empower individuals to navigate their circumstances more effectively and regain a sense of control.

Assisting individuals in addressing basic needs and accessing essential services is crucial following a crisis event. This involves immediate provision of necessities such as food, water, shelter, and sanitation, as well as identifying and fulfilling specific needs like healthcare or childcare items. Ensuring marginalized individuals are not overlooked and maintaining promises of follow-up support are paramount considerations [663].

Helping individuals cope with their problems requires aiding them in prioritizing urgent needs and considering their support systems. This involves identifying sources of support, offering practical suggestions, affirming their coping abilities, and encouraging positive coping strategies while discouraging negative ones. Promoting activities that facilitate relaxation, engaging in physical exercise, and participating in community efforts are among the encouraged strategies.

Offering accurate information is vital for those affected by a crisis, covering aspects such as the event itself, safety, rights, and accessing necessary services. Despite challenges in obtaining accurate information amidst the chaos, efforts should be made to provide reliable updates, disseminate information about available services, and ensure vulnerable individuals are informed. Transparency, simplicity, and repetition in communication are key, with consideration given to the potential frustration and anger that may arise from unmet expectations.

Facilitating connections with loved ones and social support networks is integral to post-crisis coping. Keeping families together, assisting individuals in contacting friends and relatives for support, and facilitating spiritual or community connections contribute to individuals feeling supported and better able to cope. Encouraging mutual support among affected individuals and linking them to community resources further enhances resilience and recovery.

Figure 64: FEMA workers helping residents at Mobile Disaster Recovery Center in Ohio. John Ficara, Public domain, via Wikimedia Commons.

Overall, the action principles of psychological first aid underscore the importance of responsiveness, empathy, and practical assistance in supporting individuals experiencing distress. By following the LOOK, LISTEN, and LINK framework, helpers can provide timely and effective support to those in need, promoting resilience and facilitating recovery in the aftermath of emergencies and crises.

Preparing to Provide Psychological First Aid in the Field

Emergency situations can be highly stressful, demanding immediate action and effective response from those involved. The effectiveness of support provided in such situations is greatly enhanced when responders are well-informed about the crisis and adequately prepared psychologically. Before engaging in PFA in the field, helpers are advised to undertake several preparatory steps to ensure they can offer effective assistance [649].

Firstly, helpers should familiarize themselves with the specifics of the crisis event. This includes understanding what occurred, when and where it took place, the extent of its impact, and the demographics of those affected [649]. Additionally, gaining insights into the duration of the event and its potential ongoing effects is crucial for tailoring support interventions accordingly.

Furthermore, helpers need to acquaint themselves with available services and supports relevant to the crisis. This involves identifying the authorities responsible for managing the crisis, as well as organizations and agencies providing essential services such as emergency first aid, food, water, shelter, and material assistance. Understanding how affected individuals can access these services and the involvement of community members in the response effort is essential for effective coordination and collaboration [649].

Safety and security considerations are paramount before entering an emergency site. Helpers must assess whether the crisis event has concluded or is ongoing, including any potential hazards such as aftershocks, floods, or bushfire dangers. Identifying environmental dangers such as debris or damaged infrastructure is crucial for ensuring the safety of both helpers and those they aim to assist. Additionally, being aware of restricted areas or security risks that may prohibit entry is essential for personal safety and compliance with regulations.

Finally, helpers must evaluate their own physical and mental preparedness before providing PFA. Ensuring they have necessary items such as communication devices, personal belongings, and provisions is essential for sustained assistance in the field. Communicating plans with family members or friends, arranging care for dependents, and addressing emotional readiness to provide PFA are vital considerations to ensure helpers can effectively fulfill their role amidst challenging circumstances [649].

Psychological First Aid for Children

Psychological first aid for children adheres to the same foundational action principles as for adults, yet it requires additional considerations and tailored approaches to effectively support young individuals during crises. Recognizing the challenges inherent in providing care to children amidst distress, it becomes imperative to address the well-being of parents and caregivers first, enabling them to better support their children through the crisis [649].

The 'LOOK, LISTEN, LINK' framework for supporting children encompasses specific considerations and steps tailored to their unique needs. Under the 'LOOK' phase, additional attention is directed towards gathering information on the child's situation, including their whereabouts, any physical injuries, and their emotional state. Identifying safety risks and addressing immediate basic needs with a focus on protection are essential components of this phase [649].

During the 'LISTEN' phase, helpers are advised to approach children with sensitivity, avoiding physical contact without consent and offering reassurance to calm their distress. Actively listening to children, validating their emotions, and asking age-appropriate questions to understand their needs form the basis of effective support. Helping children identify solutions to their immediate concerns empowers them to regain a sense of control amidst uncertainty [649].

In the 'LINK' phase, additional considerations involve assessing the child's needs in collaboration with them whenever possible. Facilitating access to protection services and providing age-appropriate information are crucial steps in ensuring the child's safety and well-being. In cases where children are unaccompanied, linking them with trusted child protection networks or agencies becomes paramount, with strict adherence to safety protocols to prevent potential risks [649].

Further guidance for supporting children emphasizes the importance of keeping them together with loved ones whenever possible to provide a sense of security and familiarity. In instances where children are unaccompanied, it is imperative to connect them with trustworthy child protection networks and to avoid leaving them unattended. Any offers of assistance from unauthorized individuals should be declined, and any concerns regarding child protection should be promptly reported to the relevant authorities [649].

Figure 65: Young earthquake survivors live in a tent after their house was destroyed at Muzaffarabad, Pakistan, Nov. 11, 2005. U.S. Air Force photo by Airman 1st Class Barry Loo/Released, Public domain, via Wikimedia Commons.

Keeping Them Together with Loved Ones: Whenever feasible, prioritize keeping children together with their caregivers and family. Strive to prevent them from becoming separated during the crisis. In instances where children are unaccompanied, ensure they are connected with a reliable child protection network or agency to avoid leaving them unattended. If there are no available child protection services, take proactive measures to locate their caregivers or contact other family members who can provide care [663].

Ensuring Safety: Shield children from exposure to distressing scenes such as injured individuals or significant destruction. Likewise, protect them from hearing distressing narratives about the event. Limit their exposure to media coverage and interviews by individuals not involved in the emergency response to safeguard their emotional well-being.

Listening, Communicating, and Engaging in Play: Maintain a calm demeanour, speak softly, and exhibit kindness when interacting with children. Listen attentively to their perspectives on the situation, striving to communicate with them at eye level and using language they can comprehend. Introduce yourself by name, reassuring them of your presence to offer assistance. Gather information about their identity and background to facilitate efforts to locate their caregivers and family members.

When children are with their caregivers, support the caregivers in attending to their needs. Engage children in age-appropriate play activities or conversations about their interests to provide a sense of normalcy amidst the crisis.

Ensuring children are shielded from distressing scenes, upsetting stories, or intrusive media exposure is essential for protecting their emotional well-being. Engaging in active listening, age-appropriate communication, and encouraging play or conversation about their interests can help children cope with their experiences and regain a sense of normalcy amidst adversity. Supporting caregivers in attending to their own well-being further strengthens their capacity to provide effective care to children during crises.

Psychological First Aid for People with Physical or Mental Health Conditions or Intellectual Disabilities

When assisting individuals who may have physical, mental health conditions, or intellectual disabilities, certain considerations are crucial to ensure their safety and well-being. Firstly, helping these individuals find a safe space is paramount to mitigate any potential risks or hazards. Additionally, inquiring about their health conditions or medication regimen is essential to address any immediate medical needs and ensure access to necessary medications or medical services whenever available [649].

Staying with the person or arranging for someone to assist them if you need to leave is vital for continuity of support. Furthermore, linking them with relevant long-term support services can provide ongoing assistance beyond the immediate crisis. Individuals with disabilities, especially cognitive disabilities, may heavily rely on established routines in their lives, and disruption to these routines can induce significant anxiety.

When communicating with individuals with disabilities, it's crucial to address them directly rather than speaking through a companion, attendant, or interpreter who may be present. Utilizing 'Person-First' language is important, prioritizing the person over their disability to foster respect and dignity [649]. Avoiding assumptions about the individual's capacity and allowing them ample time to absorb information and respond autonomously is essential for effective communication.

Disability can manifest in various forms, ranging from obvious physical aids like walkers or wheelchairs to invisible impairments such as intellectual disabilities or sight impairments. It's imperative not to make assumptions about their abilities and instead let the individual guide the communication process, adjusting the volume and speed as needed.

Providing opportunities for short breaks can be beneficial for individuals who require extra time to process information. Additionally, offering multiple options for further contact, such as face-to-face interaction, telephone calls, or email correspondence, ensures that individuals can choose the mode of communication that they are most comfortable with.

It's crucial to recognize the resilience of individuals and acknowledge their ability to cope with appropriate support. Encouraging the use of familiar coping strategies and support systems empowers individuals to navigate through challenging situations effectively, promoting their overall well-being and recovery.

Self Care for People Working in the Field

Supporting individuals in the aftermath of an emergency can be both fulfilling and demanding for those involved in emergency response efforts. However, it's not uncommon for disaster workers to experience a range of stress-related emotions, including stress, distress, fatigue, overwhelm, and frustration during their work. Stress, as the body's response to operating outside of its normal comfort zone, can arise from internal factors such as thoughts and feelings or external factors like poor health or conflict. If not managed effectively, stress can accumulate, leading to chronic stress, not necessarily due to the difficulty of tasks but often due to the volume or continuity of work [649].

To mitigate stress and prevent its escalation, individuals must proactively identify stressors and implement strategies for stress reduction. This self-care approach becomes especially crucial when supporting others in times of crisis. Strategies may include reflecting on past coping mechanisms, prioritizing time for rest and relaxation, maintaining reasonable working hours, and distributing workload among helpers. It's essential to acknowledge that while there may be many problems arising from a crisis event, individuals should focus on what they can reasonably address and empower affected individuals to help themselves.

Minimizing the intake of substances like alcohol, caffeine, and nicotine, and seeking support from fellow helpers, friends, or trusted individuals are vital aspects of stress reduction and self-care. The principles of psychological first aid, specifically 'Look, Listen, Link,' can also guide individuals in recognizing risk factors for their own well-being, understanding personal limitations, and knowing when to seek support from others. Observing one's reactions to crisis situations, listening to inner thoughts and feelings about work, and engaging in self-care activities are fundamental steps in this process.

Figure 66: FEMA working with a resident at the Disaster Recovery Center. Ed Edahl, Public domain, via Wikimedia Commons.

Additionally, individuals can utilize psychological first aid principles to support their colleagues in managing stress and maintaining well-being. This may involve applying the 'Look, Listen, Link' framework to recognize signs of distress in colleagues, actively listening to their concerns, assisting in restoring calmness after distressing experiences, and referring them to appropriate support services when needed. By fostering a supportive work environment and prioritizing collective well-being, individuals can navigate the challenges of emergency response more effectively [649].

Concluding Your Assistance

The manner in which you conclude your assistance is contingent upon various factors including the crisis context, your role and situation, and the needs of those you are aiding. Employ your best judgment, considering the individual's needs as well as your own [663].

If deemed appropriate, inform the individual that you will be departing. If someone else will be assuming the role of assistance, endeavour to introduce them to the individual. In cases where you have facilitated connections with other services, ensure the individual is aware of what to anticipate and provide them with necessary follow-up details. Regardless of the nature of your interaction with the individual, bid them farewell in a positive manner by expressing well wishes.

14

Future Trends and Challenges in Disaster Management

Emerging threats and global climate change impacts have significantly influenced emergency and disaster management practices. The Sendai Framework for Disaster Risk Reduction emphasizes the importance of addressing climate change as a key driver of disaster risk [664]. Climate change is recognized as a factor that not only increases the frequency and intensity of disasters but also influences their impacts on communities and infrastructure [665]. The changing climate patterns have led to challenges such as extreme weather events, droughts, heatwaves, and alterations in the spread of infectious diseases, all of which contribute to the complexity of disaster management [664].

In light of these challenges, there is a growing recognition of the need for resilience-building and a shift towards a more proactive and holistic approach in disaster management [14, 666]. Resilience is crucial in enhancing the capacity of communities and organizations to withstand and recover from disasters, especially in the context of climate change [14, 666]. The concept of resilience highlights the importance of not only responding to disasters but also preparing and adapting to minimize their impacts [14, 666].

Furthermore, the era of big data and analytics presents new opportunities for disaster management by providing valuable insights for decision-making and response strategies [509]. Leveraging big data can enhance the effectiveness of emergency responses and improve preparedness efforts in the face of evolving threats posed by climate change [509].

Emerging threats and the impacts of global climate change pose significant challenges in the realm of emergency and disaster management. These phenomena introduce new complexities and exacerbate existing vulnerabilities, necessitating comprehensive strategies to mitigate risks and enhance resilience.

The increased frequency and intensity of disasters attributed to global climate change, such as hurricanes, floods, droughts, and wildfires, strain emergency response systems, overwhelm infrastructure, and escalate humanitarian crises.

Climate change alters the geographical distribution and patterns of hazards, leading to unexpected occurrences in regions previously unaffected. For example, rising sea levels increase the likelihood of coastal flooding and erosion, impacting communities unaccustomed to such risks.

Furthermore, climate change exacerbates existing vulnerabilities, often resulting in compound disasters where multiple hazards intersect. For instance, a hurricane may trigger landslides in areas destabilized by deforestation, compounding the impact on affected communities.

In essence, shifts in the global climate exacerbate climate-related hazards, heightening the risk of extreme weather disasters [667]. As air and water temperatures increase, they contribute to rising sea levels, intensified storms with higher wind speeds, extended periods of drought, more severe wildfire seasons, and heightened levels of precipitation leading to flooding. The evidence supporting these changes is overwhelming, and the consequences are profound [667]:

- The frequency of climate-related disasters has tripled over the past three decades.
- Between 2006 and 2016, the rate of global sea-level rise accelerated to 2.5 times faster than the majority of the 20th century.
- Each year, over 20 million individuals are displaced from their homes due to climate change.
- The United Nations Environment Programme projects that adapting to climate change and addressing associated damages will demand $140-300 billion annually from developing nations by 2030.

The recent surge in destructive climate disasters has been alarming, with various regions across the globe bearing the brunt of unprecedented environmental upheaval.

In March 2019, Cyclone Idai wreaked havoc across Zimbabwe, Malawi, and Mozambique in Southern Africa, claiming the lives of over 1000 individuals and leaving countless others displaced and deprived of essential resources. The lethal landslides caused widespread devastation, demolishing homes, ravaging land, and decimating crucial infrastructure. Shortly after, Cyclone Kenneth struck northern Mozambique, marking the first occurrence of a tropical cyclone in this region since the satellite era, compounding the region's plight with further destruction and suffering.

Figure 67: People in Chimanimani complain, March 22, 2019, to senior army officials in charge of a temporary camp set up after Cyclone Idai that food is not reaching them. Columbus Mavhunga/VOA, Public domain, via Wikimedia Commons.

Australia's bushfire crisis at the onset of 2020 plunged the country into its most severe bushfire season on record, exacerbated by soaring temperatures from the previous year. The raging fires, scorching over 10 million hectares of land, claimed numerous lives, razed entire communities, and displaced thousands of families. The aftermath left millions grappling with hazardous smoke haze, while the staggering loss of biodiversity continues to haunt the ecosystem.

Figure 68: A burned structure in the Tambo Complex north of Orbost, Victoria (Australia). National Interagency Fire Center, Public domain, via Wikimedia Commons.

In East Africa, escalating sea temperatures, attributed to climate change, have doubled the likelihood of drought in the Horn of Africa. Severe droughts in recent years have ravaged crops and livestock, leaving millions in Ethiopia, Kenya, and Somalia grappling with acute food and water shortages. Despite the dire need for assistance, the aid efforts remain critically underfunded, exacerbating the humanitarian crisis.

Figure 69: Oxfam distributing water in the Horn of Africa where in the period 2010-2011, experienced a severe drought. Oxfam, CC BY 2.0, via Wikimedia Commons.

Meanwhile, South Asia has been besieged by deadly floods and landslides, uprooting millions from their homes in India, Nepal, and Bangladesh. The intensification of monsoon rains, fuelled by rising sea surface temperatures, has exacerbated the flooding, with vast swathes of land submerged and communities devastated.

In Central America, the Dry Corridor has endured its sixth consecutive year of drought, exacerbated by the effects of the climate crisis. Countries like Guatemala, Honduras, El Salvador, and Nicaragua are grappling with prolonged dry seasons, leading to widespread crop failures and severe food insecurity for millions who rely on agriculture for sustenance.

Climate-induced disasters force populations to flee their homes, leading to internal displacement and cross-border migration, placing additional strain on resources, infrastructure, and social cohesion, thereby heightening the complexity of emergency response and management efforts.

Additionally, climate change influences the spread of vector-borne diseases, heat-related illnesses, and other health threats, amplifying public health challenges in disaster-affected areas, requiring emergency responders to contend with increased health risks and prioritize interventions to safeguard vulnerable populations.

Figure 70: Aftermath of the 2020 Hyderabad floods in a street. Strike Eagle, CC BY-SA 4.0, via Wikimedia Commons.

Climate-related disruptions to agricultural systems, water availability, and natural resources exacerbate food insecurity and resource scarcity in disaster-prone regions. Consequently, emergency management efforts must address these challenges to ensure access to essential resources for affected communities.

Moreover, climate change poses threats to critical infrastructure such as transportation networks, energy systems, and water supply facilities. Aging infrastructure and inadequate adaptation measures heighten vulnerability to climate-related hazards, necessitating investments in resilience-building initiatives.

Climate-induced disasters disproportionately affect marginalized and vulnerable populations, exacerbating social inequalities and economic disparities. Consequently, emergency management strategies must address these underlying vulnerabilities and prioritize equitable responses to ensure inclusive disaster preparedness and recovery efforts [668].

In response to these emerging threats and climate change impacts, effective emergency and disaster management strategies emphasize proactive risk reduction, community engagement, multi-sectoral collaboration, and adaptive capacity-building initiatives. By integrating climate resilience into emergency planning and response frameworks, stakeholders can enhance preparedness, mitigate risks, and promote sustainable development in the face of evolving challenges.

Public-private partnerships in disaster management are often lauded for their potential to harness the innovation inherent in the private sector and combine it with the resources and infrastructure of the public sector. While the perception of innovation being more natural in the private sector may be nuanced, the collaboration between government agencies and businesses in forming such partnerships yields tangible benefits, particularly in disaster management.

Advancements in modern technology provide invaluable advantages, enabling experts to swiftly analyse vast amounts of data and potentially develop predictive models to forecast the location and severity of natural disasters well in advance. Although some of these technological efforts serve proprietary business interests, they can also be leveraged to aid government agencies in disaster response efforts [668].

Guidance provided by the Federal Emergency Management Agency (FEMA) facilitates the sharing of information within public-private partnerships and lays the groundwork for their establishment. For instance, FEMA has documented a supply chain group in Houston comprising representatives from various sectors such as power, water, building supplies, telecommunications, transportation, and grocery stores. This collaborative group played a crucial role during the city's response to the COVID-19 pandemic, which was one of the most disruptive emergencies in recent memory.

The impact of climate change on the frequency and intensity of natural disasters is becoming increasingly evident and is a significant concern for emergency managers. As highlighted by the U.S. Geological Survey, rising global surface temperatures contribute to heightened drought risks, increased water vapor in the atmosphere fuels more powerful storms, warmer ocean surfaces lead to stronger storm winds, and rising sea levels expose elevated locations to erosive waves and currents.

Emergency managers can take proactive steps to address climate change by implementing strategies outlined by FEMA and other agencies. These strategies include providing information on climate-related risks, utilizing climate forecasting data for planning purposes, supporting risk reduction initiatives, promoting the use of disaster insurance, and fostering community adoption of resilience-building approaches.

Social media's pervasive presence in society has transformed emergency response practices by enabling the rapid dissemination of critical information to a wide audience. With over half of the global population actively using social media, emergency managers can leverage these platforms to communicate real-time updates and identify crisis situations promptly using social listening tools. However, the proliferation of social networks also presents challenges, such as the spread of misinformation and malicious content, exacerbated by the emergence of generative artificial intelligence tools. Therefore, emergency managers must remain vigilant and equipped to discern and address misinformation effectively.

The integration of advanced technology, including drones, artificial intelligence (AI), and satellite imagery, represents a significant transformation in the landscape of disaster response. These cutting-edge technologies offer unprecedented capabilities for real-time data collection, analysis, and decision-making, empowering disaster response teams to operate with greater efficiency and effectiveness.

Drones, often referred to as unmanned aerial vehicles (UAVs), play a crucial role in disaster response efforts. Equipped with high-resolution cameras and sensors, drones can capture detailed aerial imagery of disaster-affected areas, providing response teams with valuable situational awareness. This aerial surveillance enables responders to assess the extent of damage, identify hazards, and locate survivors in remote or inaccessible areas. Additionally, drones can be deployed for the rapid delivery of essential supplies, such as medical supplies, food, and water, to areas cut off by disaster-induced disruptions in transportation infrastructure. Furthermore, drones are invaluable tools for search and rescue operations, allowing responders to cover large areas quickly and efficiently while minimizing risks to human rescuers.

Artificial intelligence (AI) plays a complementary role in disaster response by leveraging machine learning algorithms to analyse vast volumes of data, including satellite imagery, weather forecasts, social media feeds, and emergency call data. By processing and interpreting this data in real-time, AI-powered tools can identify patterns, trends, and anomalies that may indicate areas most in need of aid or areas at high risk of further damage. For example, AI algorithms can analyse satellite imagery to detect changes in terrain, infrastructure damage, and population displacement following a disaster. This information enables response teams to prioritize resources and allocate assistance to where it is most urgently needed.

Satellite imagery is another essential technology utilized in disaster response and recovery efforts. High-resolution satellite images provide detailed insights into the extent and impact of a disaster, allowing response teams to assess damage, plan evacuation routes, and coordinate relief efforts. Satellite imagery can also be used to monitor environmental conditions, such as floodwaters, wildfires, and storm surges, in real-time, enabling proactive decision-making and early warning systems to mitigate risks to affected populations.

The integration of advanced technologies such as drones, AI, and satellite imagery is revolutionizing disaster response by enhancing situational awareness, enabling rapid decision-making, and optimizing resource allocation. These technologies enable response teams to respond more efficiently and effectively to disasters, ultimately saving lives and minimizing the impact of catastrophes on affected communities.

References

1.Friedt, F.L., *Natural Disasters, Aggregate Trade Resilience, and Local Disruptions: Evidence From Hurricane Katrina.* Review of International Economics, 2021. **29**(5): p. 1081-1120.

2.Tabari, H., et al., *Amplified Drought and Flood Risk Under Future Socioeconomic and Climatic Change.* Earth S Future, 2021. **9**(10).

3.Ghazanfari, M.J., S. Karkhah, and T. Yaghoubi, *Emergency Evacuation Related Challenges in Specialized Hospitals for Children and Neonates: A Narrative Review.* Journal of Pediatrics Review, 2022. **10**(2): p. 111-120.

4.Kessler, R.C., et al., *The Importance of Secondary Trauma Exposure for Post-Disaster Mental Disorder.* Epidemiology and Psychiatric Sciences, 2012. **21**(1): p. 35-45.

5.Sun, C., J.B. Sharma, and M. Maiti, *A Deep Learning Ensemble Framework for Off-Nadir Geocentric Pose Prediction.* 2022.

6.González, F.A.I., *Natural Disasters and Economic Growth: A Synthesis of Empirical Evidence.* Nóesis Revista De Ciencias Sociales Y Humanidades, 2022. **31**(1): p. 155-173.

7.Makwana, N., *Disaster and Its Impact on Mental Health: A Narrative Review.* Journal of Family Medicine and Primary Care, 2019. **8**(10): p. 3090.

8.Amatya, B., et al., *Medical Rehabilitation in Disaster Relief: Towards a New Perspective.* Journal of Rehabilitation Medicine, 2017. **49**(8): p. 620-628.

9.Khan, F. and B. Amatya, *Update in Disaster Rehabilitation.* American Journal of Physical Medicine & Rehabilitation, 2021. **100**(11): p. 1021-1026.

10.Zin, N.M. and F.Z. Ismail, *Cultural Heritage Protection From Disaster Impacts: A Review of Global Disaster Risk Reduction Frameworks.* Iop Conference Series Earth and Environmental Science, 2023. **1217**(1): p. 012004.

11.Tulane University, *What Is a Disaster Management Cycle?* 2023.

12.Bayraktar, N. and M. Yıldırım, *Senior Undergraduate Nursing Students' Perceptions of Disaster Preparedness: A Descriptive Study.* Disaster Medicine and Public Health Preparedness, 2016. **10**(4): p. 557-561.

13.Shaluf, I.M., *Disaster Types.* Disaster Prevention and Management an International Journal, 2007. **16**(5): p. 704-717.

14.Manyena, B., *The Concept of Resilience Revisited.* Disasters, 2006. **30**(4): p. 434-450.

15.Australian Government Department of Home Affairs, *Australian Disaster Resilience Community Recovery Handbook (AIDR 2018).* 2018: Australian Institute for Disaster Resilience.

16.Durant, T.J.S., *The Utility of Vulnerability and Social Capital Theories in Studying the Impact of Hurricane Katrina on the Elderly.* Journal of Family Issues, 2011. **32**(10): p. 1285-1302.

17.World Association for Disaster and Emergency Medicine, *Chapter Three: Overview and Concepts.* Prehospital and Disaster Medicine, 2002. **17**(S3): p. 31-55.

18.Jonkman, S.N., et al., *Loss of Life Caused by the Flooding of New Orleans After Hurricane Katrina: Analysis of the Relationship Between Flood Characteristics and Mortality.* Risk Analysis, 2009. **29**(5): p. 676-698.

19.Vigdor, J.L., *The Economic Aftermath of Hurricane Katrina.* Journal of Economic Perspectives, 2008. **22**(4): p. 135-154.

20.Youngman, N., *The Development of Manufactured Flood Risk: New Orleans' Mid-century Growth Machine and the Hurricane of 1947.* Disasters, 2015. **39**(s2).

21.Zahran, S., et al., *New Orleans Before and After Hurricanes Katrina/Rita: A Quasi-Experiment of the Association Between Soil Lead and Children's Blood Lead.* Environmental Science & Technology, 2010. **44**(12): p. 4433-4440.

22.Ide, S., A. Baltay, and G.C. Beroza, *Shallow Dynamic Overshoot and Energetic Deep Rupture in the 2011 <i>M</I> _w 9.0 Tohoku-Oki Earthquake.* Science, 2011. **332**(6036): p. 1426-1429.

23.Satake, K., et al., *Time and Space Distribution of Coseismic Slip of the 2011 Tohoku Earthquake as Inferred From Tsunami Waveform Data.* Bulletin of the Seismological Society of America, 2013. **103**(2B): p. 1473-1492.

24.Ikehara, K., et al., *Documenting Large Earthquakes Similar to the 2011 Tohoku-Oki Earthquake From Sediments Deposited in the Japan Trench Over the Past 1500 Years.* Earth and Planetary Science Letters, 2016. **445**: p. 48-56.

25.Minoura, K., et al., *Aftereffects of Subduction-Zone Earthquakes: Potential Tsunami Hazards Along the Japan Sea Coast.* The Tohoku Journal of Experimental Medicine, 2015. **237**(2): p. 91-102.

26.Fujii, Y., et al., *Tsunami Source of the 2011 Off the Pacific Coast of Tohoku Earthquake.* Earth Planets and Space, 2011. **63**(7): p. 815-820.

27.Zhu, N., et al., *A Novel Coronavirus From Patients With Pneumonia in China, 2019.* New England Journal of Medicine, 2020. **382**(8): p. 727-733.

28.Palem, S.P. and H.P. Palem, *The Effect of COVID-19 on Global Population and Its Fatality Rate: Retrospective Study by Online Database.* Indian Journal of Medical Sciences, 2020. **72**: p. 13-16.

29.Sadeghi, B., R.C.Y. Cheung, and M. Hanbury, *Using Hierarchical Clustering Analysis to Evaluate COVID-19 Pandemic Preparedness and Performance in 180 Countries in 2020.* BMJ Open, 2021. **11**(11): p. e049844.

30.Hartman, T.K., et al., *Different Conspiracy Theories Have Different Psychological and Social Determinants: Comparison of Three Theories About the Origins of the COVID-19 Virus in a Representative Sample of the UK Population.* Frontiers in Political Science, 2021. **3**.

31.Shereen, M.A., et al., *COVID-19 Infection: Emergence, Transmission, and Characteristics of Human Coronaviruses.* Journal of Advanced Research, 2020. **24**: p. 91-98.

32.Xiao, K., et al., *Isolation and Characterization of 2019-nCoV-Like Coronavirus From Malayan Pangolins.* 2020.

33.Guo, Y., et al., *The Origin, Transmission and Clinical Therapies on Coronavirus Disease 2019 (COVID-19) Outbreak – An Update on the Status.* Military Medical Research, 2020. **7**(1).

34.Yang, Z., X. Luo, and H. Jia, *Is It All a Conspiracy? Conspiracy Theories and People's Attitude to COVID-19 Vaccination.* Vaccines, 2021. **9**(10): p. 1051.

35.Li, X., et al., *Emergence of SARS-CoV-2 Through Recombination and Strong Purifying Selection.* Science Advances, 2020. **6**(27).

36.Wang, Y.-S., et al., *The Association Between COVID-19 and Asthma: A Systematic Review and Meta-analysis.* Clinical & Experimental Allergy, 2020. **50**(11): p. 1274-1277.

37.Li, H., et al., *Comparison and Impact of COVID-19 for Patients With Cancer: A Survival Analysis of Fatality Rate Controlling for Age, Sex and Cancer Type.* BMJ Health & Care Informatics, 2021. **28**(1): p. e100341.

38.Ullah, M., et al., *COVID-19 Infection in Vaccinated Healthcare Professionals.* Cureus, 2022.

39.Odriozola-González, P., et al., *Psychological Effects of the COVID-19 Outbreak and Lockdown Among Students and Workers of a Spanish University.* Psychiatry Research, 2020. **290**: p. 113108.

40.Ellis, W.E., T.M. Dumas, and L.M. Forbes, *Physically Isolated but Socially Connected: Psychological Adjustment and Stress Among Adolescents During the Initial COVID-19 Crisis.* Canadian Journal of Behavioural Science/Revue Canadienne Des Sciences Du Comportement, 2020. **52**(3): p. 177-187.

41.Joshi, H., et al., *Stability Analysis of a Non-Singular Fractional-Order Covid-19 Model With Nonlinear Incidence and Treatment Rate.* Physica Scripta, 2023. **98**(4): p. 045216.

42.Barry, C.T. and B.M. Halter, *Relations of Adolescent Knowledge of COVID-19, Social Media Engagement, and Experiences During Quarantine/Lockdown With Well-Being.* Journal of Child and Family Studies, 2022. **32**(1): p. 110-121.

43.Jiang, Y., J. Laranjo, and M. Thomas, *COVID-19 Lockdown Policy and Heterogeneous Responses of Urban Mobility: Evidence From the Philippines.* Plos One, 2022. **17**(6): p. e0270555.

44.Bežanović, V., et al., *Effects of the COVID-19 Quarantine Measures On PM_{2.5}, PM₁₀ And NO₂ Concentration Levels In Serbia.* Polish Journal of Environmental Studies, 2022. **31**(4): p. 3509-3521.

45.Alpers, S.E., et al., *Alcohol Consumption During a Pandemic Lockdown Period and Change in Alcohol Consumption Related to Worries and Pandemic Measures.* International Journal of Environmental Research and Public Health, 2021. **18**(3): p. 1220.

46.Muhaibes, A.M.H.A.M., *Knowledge, Practice and Attitude About the Detrimental Effect of Social Lockdown and Quarantine Due to Covid_19 Pandemic on Human Health Aspects.* Journal of Pharmaceutical Negative Results, 2022: p. 1729-1738.

47.Al-Ajlan, S.A., et al., *The Impact of Lockdown Strategies on the Basic Reproductive Number of Coronavirus (COVID-19) Cases in Saudi Arabia.* Saudi Journal of Biological Sciences, 2021. **28**(9): p. 4926-4930.

48.Stein, S. and E.A. Okal, *Speed and Size of the Sumatra Earthquake.* Nature, 2005. **434**(7033): p. 581-582.

49.Lay, T., et al., *The Great Sumatra-Andaman Earthquake of 26 December 2004.* Science, 2005. **308**(5725): p. 1127-1133.

50.Kolbe, A.R., et al., *Mortality, Crime and Access to Basic Needs Before and After the Haiti Earthquake: A Random Survey of Port-Au-Prince Households.* Medicine Conflict & Survival, 2010. **26**(4): p. 281-297.

51.Hough, S.E., T. Taniguchi, and J.R. Altidor, *Estimation of Peak Ground Acceleration From Horizontal Rigid Body Displacement: A Case Study in Port-Au-Prince, Haiti.* Bulletin of the Seismological Society of America, 2012. **102**(6): p. 2704-2713.

52.Eberhard, M.O., et al., *The MW 7.0 Haiti Earthquake of January 12, 2010: USGS/EERI Advance Reconnaissance Team Report.* 2010.

53.Rathje, E.M., et al., *Damage Patterns in Port-Au-Prince During the 2010 Haiti Earthquake.* Earthquake Spectra, 2011. **27**(1_suppl1): p. 117-136.

54.Borchers-Arriagada, N., et al., *Unprecedented Smoke-related Health Burden Associated With the 2019–20 Bushfires in Eastern Australia.* The Medical Journal of Australia, 2020. **213**(6): p. 282-283.

55.Godfree, R.C., et al., *Implications of the 2019–2020 Megafires for the Biogeography and Conservation of Australian Vegetation.* Nature Communications, 2021. **12**(1).

56.Tin, D., A. Hertelendy, and G.R. Ciottone, *What We Learned From the 2019–2020 Australian Bushfire Disaster: Making Counter-Terrorism Medicine a Strategic Preparedness Priority.* The American Journal of Emergency Medicine, 2021. **46**: p. 742-743.

57.Smith, E., et al., *Supporting Volunteer Firefighter Well-Being: Lessons From the Australian "Black Summer" Bushfires.* Prehospital and Disaster Medicine, 2022. **37**(2): p. 273-276.

58.Phillipson, M., R. Emmanuel, and P. Baker, *The Durability of Building Materials Under a Changing Climate.* Wiley Interdisciplinary Reviews Climate Change, 2016. 7(4): p. 590-599.

59.Anthonia, A.N., et al., *Review of Paradigm Shift in Building Consruction Occasioned by Climage Change.* Global Journal of Pure and Applied Sciences, 2021. **27**(2): p. 253-262.

60.Jayasinghe, A.D. and P. Stewart, *Level of Preparedness of the Residential Building Industry in Australia to Climate Change Adaptation: A Case of Residential Building*

Companies in Brisbane, Queensland. Mitigation and Adaptation Strategies for Global Change, 2022. **27**(4).

61.Seifert, D.L. and D.L. Lindberg, *Managing Climate Change Risk: Insurers Can Lead the Way.* Risk Hazards & Crisis in Public Policy, 2012. **3**(2): p. 1-16.

62.Soldatenko, S. and L.N. Karlin, *The Climate Change Impact on Russia's Wind Energy Resource: Current Areas of Research.* Energy and Power Engineering, 2014. **06**(11): p. 371-385.

63.Godschalk, D.R., et al., *Estimating the Value of Foresight: Aggregate Analysis of Natural Hazard Mitigation Benefits and Costs.* Journal of Environmental Planning and Management, 2009. **52**(6): p. 739-756.

64.Douglas, J. and A. Azarbakht, *Cost–benefit Analyses to Assess the Potential of Operational Earthquake Forecasting Prior to a Mainshock in Europe.* Natural Hazards, 2020. **105**(1): p. 293-311.

65.Grineski, S.E., et al., *Hurricane Harvey and Greater Houston Households: Comparing Pre-event Preparedness With Post-event Health Effects, Event Exposures, and Recovery.* Disasters, 2019. **44**(2): p. 408-432.

66.Poussin, J.K., et al., *Potential of Semi-Structural and Non-Structural Adaptation Strategies to Reduce Future Flood Risk: Case Study for the Meuse.* Natural Hazards and Earth System Science, 2012. **12**(11): p. 3455-3471.

67.Kastolani, W. and R. Mainaki, *Does Educational Disaster Mitigation Need to Be Introduced in School?* SHS Web of Conferences, 2018. **42**: p. 00063.

68.Lim, J.R., B.F. Liu, and A.A. Seate, *Are You Prepared for the Next Storm? Developing Social Norms Messages to Motivate Community Members to Perform Disaster Risk Mitigation Behaviors.* Risk Analysis, 2022. **42**(11): p. 2550-2568.

69.Whybark, D.C., *Co-Creation of Improved Quality in Disaster Response and Recovery.* International Journal of Quality Innovation, 2015. **1**(1).

70.Husna, C., et al., *Does Tabletop Exercise Enhance Knowledge and Attitude in Preparing Disaster Drills?* Nurse Media Journal of Nursing, 2020. **10**(2): p. 182-190.

71.Jonson, C.O., et al., *Short Simulation Exercises to Improve Emergency Department Nurses' Self-Efficacy for Initial Disaster Management: Controlled Before and After Study.* Nurse Education Today, 2017. **55**: p. 20-25.

72.Mejri, O. and P. Plebani, *SocialEMIS.* 2012.

73.Khorram-Manesh, A., et al., *Education in Disaster Management and Emergencies: Defining a New European Course.* Disaster Medicine and Public Health Preparedness, 2015. **9**(3): p. 245-255.

74.Zhang, R., et al., *Policy Implementation Challenges and the Ritualization of Public Health Emergency Plans: An Investigation of Urban Communities in Jiangsu Province, China.* Frontiers in Public Health, 2023. **10**.

75.Simpson, D., *Earthquake Drills and Simulations in Community-based Training and Preparedness Programmes.* Disasters, 2002. **26**(1): p. 55-69.

76.Perry, R.W. and M.K. Lindell, *Preparedness for Emergency Response: Guidelines for the Emergency Planning Process.* Disasters, 2003. **27**(4): p. 336-350.

77.Jiang, Y. and Y. Yuan, *Emergency Logistics in a Large-Scale Disaster Context: Achievements and Challenges.* International Journal of Environmental Research and Public Health, 2019. **16**(5): p. 779.

78.Rui, C., et al., *Coordination in Emergency Response Management.* Communications of the Acm, 2008. **51**(5): p. 66-73.

79.Feynman, J. and S. Martin, *The Initiation of Coronal Mass Ejections by Newly Emerging Magnetic Flux.* Journal of Geophysical Research Atmospheres, 1995. **100**(A3): p. 3355-3367.

80.Mandrini, C.H., et al., *Topological Analysis of Emerging Bipole Clusters Producing Violent Solar Events.* Solar Physics, 2013. **289**(6): p. 2041-2071.

81.McEntire, D.A. and A. Myers, *Preparing Communities for Disasters: Issues and Processes for Government Readiness.* Disaster Prevention and Management an International Journal, 2004. **13**(2): p. 140-152.

82.An, B. and S.-Y. Tang, *Lessons From COVID-19 Responses in East Asia: Institutional Infrastructure and Enduring Policy Instruments.* The American Review of Public Administration, 2020. **50**(6-7): p. 790-800.

83.Khair, F. and B.M. Sopha, *Evaluation of Location and Number of Aid Post for Sustainable Humanitarian Relief Using Agent Based Modeling (ABM) and Geographic Information System (GIS).* Iop Conference Series Earth and Environmental Science, 2017. **109**: p. 012001.

84.Lee, Y.-h., Y.-C. Kim, and H. Seo, *Selecting Disaster Waste Transportation Routes to Reduce Overlapping of Transportation Routes After Floods.* Sustainability, 2022. **14**(5): p. 2866.

85.Al-Kandari, H.A., *Epidemiological Disaster Management: Literature Survey and Analysis.* International Journal of Innovative Research and Scientific Studies, 2022. **6**(1): p. 49-63.

86.Lettieri, E., C. Masella, and G. Radaelli, *Disaster Management: Findings From a Systematic Review.* Disaster Prevention and Management an International Journal, 2009. **18**(2): p. 117-136.

87.Moatty, A., *Editorial.* Disaster Prevention and Management an International Journal, 2020. **29**(4): p. 515-521.

88.Coetzee, C. and D.v. Niekerk, *Tracking the Evolution of the Disaster Management Cycle: A General System Theory Approach.* Jàmbá Journal of Disaster Risk Studies, 2012. **4**(1).

89.Zurita, M.d.L.M., et al., *Towards New Disaster Governance: Subsidiarity as a Critical Tool.* Environmental Policy and Governance, 2015. **25**(6): p. 386-398.

90.Cicek, D. and B. Kantarcı, *Use of Mobile Crowdsensing in Disaster Management: A Systematic Review, Challenges, and Open Issues.* Sensors, 2023. **23**(3): p. 1699.

91.Lin, B.-C., *Conducting an Adaptive Evaluation Framework of Importance and Performance for Community-Based Earthquake Disaster Management.* Natural Hazards, 2022. **115**(2): p. 1255-1274.

92.Lopo, C., et al., *The Effect of Knowledge and Skills of Hospital Staff on the Hospitals' Alertness and Security in Encountering Earthquake in Palu City, Central Sulawesi, Indonesia.* Open Access Macedonian Journal of Medical Sciences, 2022. **10**(E): p. 1077-1081.

93.Seifi, B., G. Ghanizadeh, and H. Seyedin, *Disaster Health Literacy of Middle-Aged Women.* Journal of Menopausal Medicine, 2018. **24**(3): p. 150.

94.Rahmayanti, H., et al., *Environmental Learning About Flood Disaster in University: Students HOTS for Preliminary Analysis to Develop DIFMOL Model.* E3s Web of Conferences, 2020. **211**: p. 02016.

95.Heppner, P.P., *A Review of the Problem-Solving Literature and Its Relationship to the Counseling Process.* Journal of Counseling Psychology, 1978. **25**(5): p. 366-375.

96.Reedy, J.C., et al., *Nurse Leader Preparation for Disasters.* Jona the Journal of Nursing Administration, 2022. **52**(10): p. 536-541.

97.Tuladhar, G., et al., *Knowledge of Disaster Risk Reduction Among School Students in Nepal.* Geomatics Natural Hazards and Risk, 2013. **5**(3): p. 190-207.

98.Burby, R.J., *Hurricane Katrina and the Paradoxes of Government Disaster Policy: Bringing About Wise Governmental Decisions for Hazardous Areas.* The Annals of the American Academy of Political and Social Science, 2006. **604**(1): p. 171-191.

99.Witvorapong, N., R. Muttarak, and W. Pothisiri, *Social Participation and Disaster Risk Reduction Behaviors in Tsunami Prone Areas.* Plos One, 2015. **10**(7): p. e0130862.

100.Lusiana, N.A. and A. Widiyarta, *Disaster Mitigation as an Effort to Minimize the Impact of Floods in Lamongan District.* Dia Jurnal Ilmiah Administrasi Publik, 2021. **19**(1): p. 290-304.

101.Brown, L.M., J. Haun, and L. Peterson, *A Proposed Disaster Literacy Model.* Disaster Medicine and Public Health Preparedness, 2014. **8**(3): p. 267-275.

102.Fung, O.W.M., A.Y. Loke, and C.K.Y. Lai, *Disaster Preparedness Among Hong Kong Nurses.* Journal of Advanced Nursing, 2008. **62**(6): p. 698-703.

103.Sekartaji, D.A. and E.T.W. Mei, *The Effect of Disaster Knowledge on Community Preparedness in Dealing With Liquefaction Disaster in Palu City, Central Sulawesi.* Iop Conference Series Earth and Environmental Science, 2023. **1233**(1): p. 012069.

104.Kim, Y. and M.Y. Kim, *Factors Affecting Household Disaster Preparedness in South Korea.* Plos One, 2022. **17**(10): p. e0275540.

105.Lindell, M.K. and R.W. Perry, *The Protective Action Decision Model: Theoretical Modifications and Additional Evidence.* Risk Analysis, 2011. **32**(4): p. 616-632.

106.Lee, K.J., S. Malinen, and V. Nilakant, *The Dynamics of Cross-Sector Collaboration in Disasters.* Disaster Prevention and Management an International Journal, 2023. **32**(2): p. 337-351.

107.Park, C.L., *Meaning Making in the Context of Disasters.* Journal of Clinical Psychology, 2016. **72**(12): p. 1234-1246.

108.Walsh, L., et al., *Core Competencies for Disaster Medicine and Public Health.* Disaster Medicine and Public Health Preparedness, 2012. **6**(1): p. 44-52.

109.Uchida, Y., Y. Takahashi, and K. Kawahara, *Changes in Hedonic and Eudaimonic Well-Being After a Severe Nationwide Disaster: The Case of the Great East Japan Earthquake.* Journal of Happiness Studies, 2013. **15**(1): p. 207-221.

110.Kapucu, N. and S. Khosa, *Disaster Resiliency and Culture of Preparedness for University and College Campuses.* Administration & Society, 2013. **45**(1): p. 3-37.

111.Li, H., et al., *Mining Emergency Event Logs to Support Resource Allocation.* Ieice Transactions on Information and Systems, 2021. **E104.D**(10): p. 1651-1660.

112.Ludík, T. and J. Ráček, *Process Methodology for Emergency Management.* 2011: p. 302-309.

113.Rivera, J.D. and C.C. Knox, *Defining Social Equity in Emergency Management: A Critical First Step in the Nexus.* Public Administration Review, 2022. **83**(5): p. 1170-1185.

114.Walker, S. and A. Sheikh, *Managing Anaphylaxis: Effective Emergency and Long-term Care Are Necessary.* Clinical & Experimental Allergy, 2003. **33**(8): p. 1015-1018.

115.Goode, N., et al., *Defining Disaster Resilience: Comparisons From Key Stakeholders Involved in Emergency Management in Victoria, Australia.* Disasters, 2016. **41**(1): p. 171-193.

116.Doberstein, B., *Post-Disaster Assessment of Hazard Mitigation for Small and Medium-Magnitude Debris Flow Disasters in Bali, Indonesia and Jimani, Dominican Republic.* Natural Hazards, 2009. **50**(2): p. 361-377.

117.Kim, P.S. and J.E. Lee, *Emergency Management in Korea and Its Future Directions.* Journal of Contingencies and Crisis Management, 1998. **6**(4): p. 189-201.

118.Wu, W., K. Chang, and Y.-E. Tso, *If Only We Knew What We Know: Factors for Mobilizing Citizen Participation in Community-Based Emergency Preparedness.* Chinese Public Administration Review, 2016. **7**(1): p. 77-109.

119.Gani, A., R. Singh, and A.H. Najar, *Rebuilding Tourist Destinations From Crisis: A Comparative Study of Jammu and Kashmir and Assam, India.* Worldwide Hospitality and Tourism Themes, 2021. **13**(3): p. 437-454.

120.Wang, H., et al., *Evaluation and Obstacle Analysis of Emergency Response Capability in China.* International Journal of Environmental Research and Public Health, 2022. **19**(16): p. 10200.

121.Herstein, J.J., et al., *Emergency Preparedness: What Is the Future?* Antimicrobial Stewardship & Healthcare Epidemiology, 2021. **1**(1).

122.Albayrak, Ö., *Small Satellite Utilization for Disaster Management Information Systems.* 2005: p. 452-460.

123.Cheng, R., L. Hou, and S. Xu, *A Review of Digital Twin Applications in Civil and Infrastructure Emergency Management.* Buildings, 2023. **13**(5): p. 1143.

124.Jensen, J., et al., *The County Emergency Manager's Role in Recovery.* International Journal of Mass Emergencies & Disasters, 2014. **32**(1): p. 157-193.

125.Majchrzak, A., S.L. Järvenpää, and A.B. Hollingshead, *Coordinating Expertise Among Emergent Groups Responding to Disasters.* Organization Science, 2007. **18**(1): p. 147-161.

126.Comfort, L.K., *Crisis Management in Hindsight: Cognition, Communication, Coordination, and Control.* Public Administration Review, 2007. **67**(s1): p. 189-197.

127.Simon, T., A. Goldberg, and B. Adini, *Socializing in Emergencies—A Review of the Use of Social Media in Emergency Situations.* International Journal of Information Management, 2015. **35**(5): p. 609-619.

128.Owen, C., et al., *Values and Complexities in Assessing Strategic-Level Emergency Management Effectiveness.* Journal of Contingencies and Crisis Management, 2016. **24**(3): p. 181-190.

129.Morakabati, Y., S.J. Page, and J. Fletcher, *Emergency Management and Tourism Stakeholder Responses to Crises.* Journal of Travel Research, 2016. **56**(3): p. 299-316.

130.Norris, F.H., et al., *Community Resilience as a Metaphor, Theory, Set of Capacities, and Strategy for Disaster Readiness.* American Journal of Community Psychology, 2007. **41**(1-2): p. 127-150.

131.Wang, K., et al., *Study on the Evaluation of Emergency Management Capacity of Resilient Communities by the AHP-TOPSIS Method.* International Journal of Environmental Research and Public Health, 2022. **19**(23): p. 16201.

132.Cohen, O., et al., *Confidence in Health-Services Availability During Disasters and Emergency Situations—Does It Matter?—Lessons Learned From an Israeli Population Survey.* International Journal of Environmental Research and Public Health, 2019. **16**(19): p. 3519.

133.Zhao, Z.-x., et al., *Research on Emergency Management of Community Public Health Emergencies Based on Cr Theory.* 2021.

134.Pfefferbaum, B., R.L. Pfefferbaum, and R.L.V. Horn, *Community Resilience Interventions.* American Behavioral Scientist, 2014. **59**(2): p. 238-253.

135.Sobelson, R.K., C.J. Wigington, and B.A.V. Harp, *A Whole Community Approach to Emergency Management: Strategies and Best Practices of Seven Community Programs.* Journal of Emergency Management, 2015. **13**(4): p. 349-357.

136.Muir, L., *Whose Plan Is It? The Importance of Place.* Australian Journal of Emergency Management, 2021. **10.47389/36**(No 2): p. 54-58.

137.Alexander, D., *Resilience and Disaster Risk Reduction: An Etymological Journey.* Natural Hazards and Earth System Science, 2013. **13**(11): p. 2707-2716.

138.Winarni, E.W. and E.P. Purwandari, *Disaster Risk Reduction for Earthquake Using Mobile Learning Application to Improve the Students Understanding in Elementary School.* Mediterranean Journal of Social Sciences, 2018. **9**(2): p. 205-214.

139.Bradley, D., M. McFarland, and M. Clarke, *The Effectiveness of Disaster Risk Communication: A Systematic Review of Intervention Studies.* Plos Currents, 2014.

140.Wamsler, C., *Mainstreaming Risk Reduction in Urban Planning and Housing: A Challenge for International Aid Organisations.* Disasters, 2006. **30**(2): p. 151-177.

141.Damayani, N.A., et al., *The Local Wisdom-Based Disaster Mitigation Literacy of the Indigenous Pangandaran Community.* Jurnal Studi Komunikasi (Indonesian Journal of Communications Studies), 2022. **6**(2): p. 424-439.

142.Partini, D. and A.N. Hidayaht, *Disaster Risk Reduction Efforts Through Education in Indonesia: A Literature Review.* Iop Conference Series Earth and Environmental Science, 2024. **1314**(1): p. 012049.

143.Kunguma, O., M.O. Mokhele, and M. Coetzee, *Investigating the Prevention and Mitigatory Role of Risk Communication in the COVID-19 Pandemic: A Case Study of Bloemfontein, South Africa.* Jàmbá Journal of Disaster Risk Studies, 2021. **13**(1).

144.Lamidi, L., *Analysis of Policy Implementation in Tanjungpinang Flood Disaster Risk Reduction.* Journal of Social Science (Joss), 2022. **1**(3): p. 105-115.

145.Rijal, S., S. Adhikari, and A. Shrestha, *Guiding Documents for Disaster Risk Reduction and Management in Health Care System of Nepal.* Journal of Nepal Medical Association, 2020. **58**(230).

146.Rofiah, N.H., N. Kawai, and E.N. Hayati, *Key Elements of Disaster Mitigation Education in Inclusive School Setting in the Indonesian Context.* Jàmbá Journal of Disaster Risk Studies, 2021. **13**(1).

147.Stough, L.M. and D. Kang, *The Sendai Framework for Disaster Risk Reduction and Persons With Disabilities.* International Journal of Disaster Risk Science, 2015. **6**(2): p. 140-149.

148.Alabi, A.S., et al., *Stakeholders' Role in Disaster-Risk-Reduction of Fire Occurrences in Lagos Metropolis.* International Journal of Disaster Resilience in the Built Environment, 2017. **8**(4): p. 425-440.

149.Masten, A.S. and F. Motti-Stefanidi, *Multisystem Resilience for Children and Youth in Disaster: Reflections in the Context of COVID-19.* Adversity and Resilience Science, 2020. **1**(2): p. 95-106.

150.Kennedy, M.G., et al., *Building Back Better: Local Health Department Engagement and Integration of Health Promotion Into Hurricane Harvey Recovery Planning and Implementation.* International Journal of Environmental Research and Public Health, 2019. **16**(3): p. 299.

151.Morris, S., *Resilient Health System and Hospital Disaster Planning.* 2022.

152.Georgieva, M., R. Kostadinov, and M. Semerdjieva, *Disaster Medical Support Plan as an Element of the Hospital Disaster Resilience.* Folia Medica, 2022. **64**(3): p. 507-512.

153.Jones, K., et al., *Facilities Management and Earthquake Risk Reduction: The TURNkey Project.* Iop Conference Series Earth and Environmental Science, 2022. **1101**(6): p. 062008.

154.Chen, J., et al., *Public–Private Partnerships for the Development of Disaster Resilient Communities.* Journal of Contingencies and Crisis Management, 2013. **21**(3): p. 130-143.

155.Filimonau, V. and D.D. Coteau, *Tourism Resilience in the Context of Integrated Destination and Disaster Management (DM²).* International Journal of Tourism Research, 2019. **22**(2): p. 202-222.

156.Bhati, A., A. Upadhayaya, and A. Sharma, *National Disaster Management in the ASEAN-5: An Analysis of Tourism Resilience.* Tourism Review, 2016. **71**(2): p. 148-164.

157.Hawkins, C.V. and S.A. Andrew, *Linking Community Development and Disaster Resiliency: An Exploratory Study of County Government Agencies in Central Florida.* Public Administration Quarterly, 2021. **45**(2): p. 123-142.

158.Drennan, L., *Community Narratives of Disaster Risk and Resilience: Implications for Government Policy.* Australian Journal of Public Administration, 2017. **77**(3): p. 456-467.

159.Gloria, C., et al., *Partnerships for Community Resilience: Perspectives From the Los Angeles County Community Disaster Resilience Project.* Public Health, 2015. **129**(9): p. 1297-1300.

160.Scholten, K. and S. Schilder, *The Role of Collaboration in Supply Chain Resilience.* Supply Chain Management an International Journal, 2015. **20**(4): p. 471-484.

161.Drakaki, M. and P. Tzionas, *Community-Based Social Partnerships in Crisis Resilience: A Case Example in Greece.* Disaster Prevention and Management an International Journal, 2017. **26**(2): p. 203-216.

162.Bryan, J., J.M. Williams, and D. Griffin, *Fostering Educational Resilience and Opportunities in Urban Schools Through Equity-Focused School–Family–Community Partnerships.* Professional School Counseling, 2020. **23**(1_part_2): p. 2156759X1989917.

163.Ampratwum, G., R. Osei-Kyei, and V.W.Y. Tam, *A Scientometric Review of Public-Private Partnership in Critical Infrastructure Resilience.* Iop Conference Series Earth and Environmental Science, 2022. **1101**(5): p. 052007.

164.Stewart, G.T., R. Kolluru, and M. Smith, *Leveraging Public-private Partnerships to Improve Community Resilience in Times of Disaster.* International Journal of Physical Distribution & Logistics Management, 2009. **39**(5): p. 343-364.

165.Dharmasena, M., M. Toledano, and C.K. Weaver, *The Role of Public Relations in Building Community Resilience to Natural Disasters: Perspectives From Sri Lanka and New Zealand.* Journal of Communication Management, 2020. **24**(4): p. 301-317.

166.Upadhyay, A. and A. Sa-ngiamwibool, *A Systematic Literature Review of Community Disaster Resilience: Main and Related Research Areas and Agendas.* Continuity & Resilience Review, 2021. **3**(2): p. 192-205.

167.Snyder, A., et al., *Island Communities and Disaster Resilience: Applying the EnRiCH Community Resilience Framework.* Public Health Nursing, 2021. **39**(1): p. 62-70.

168.Giuliani, L., et al., *Social and Technological Aspects of Disaster Resilience.* International Journal of Strategic Property Management, 2016. **20**(3): p. 277-290.

169.Aksha, S.K. and C.T. Emrich, *Benchmarking Community Disaster Resilience in Nepal.* International Journal of Environmental Research and Public Health, 2020. **17**(6): p. 1985.

170.Simonović, S.P., *From Risk Management to Quantitative Disaster Resilience – A Paradigm Shift.* International Journal of Safety and Security Engineering, 2016. **6**(2): p. 85-95.

171.Khalili, S., M. Harré, and P. Morley, *A Temporal Social Resilience Framework of Communities to Disasters in Australia.* Geoenvironmental Disasters, 2018. **5**(1).

172.Xu, H., et al., *A Scientometric Review of Urban Disaster Resilience Research.* International Journal of Environmental Research and Public Health, 2021. **18**(7): p. 3677.

173.Dwiningrum, S.I.A., et al., *School Resilience Policy Development and Strategic Steps to Disaster-Resilient Communities.* Iop Conference Series Earth and Environmental Science, 2022. **989**(1): p. 012017.

174.Cole, S., *Information and Empowerment: The Keys to Achieving Sustainable Tourism.* Journal of Sustainable Tourism, 2006. **14**(6): p. 629-644.

175.Zhong, S., et al., *Validation of a Framework for Measuring Hospital Disaster Resilience Using Factor Analysis.* International Journal of Environmental Research and Public Health, 2014. **11**(6): p. 6335-6353.

176.Hakkyong, K., *Learning From UK Disaster Exercises: Policy Implications for Effective Emergency Preparedness.* Disasters, 2014. **38**(4): p. 846-857.

177.Zhou, H., W. Xi, and J.a. Wang, *A Way to Sustainability: Perspective of Resilience and Adaptation to Disaster.* Sustainability, 2016. **8**(8): p. 737.

178.Djalante, R., C. Holley, and F. Thomalla, *Adaptive Governance and Managing Resilience to Natural Hazards.* International Journal of Disaster Risk Science, 2011. **2**(4): p. 1-14.

179.Zhang, Q., *Land Use and Adaptive Governance Under Climate Change: Analysis of Four Cases in Pastoral Areas of China.* Frontiers in Environmental Science, 2023. **11**.

180.Munaretto, S., G. Siciliano, and M. Turvani, *Integrating Adaptive Governance and Participatory Multicriteria Methods: A Framework for Climate Adaptation Governance.* Ecology and Society, 2014. **19**(2).

181.Sun, Y., et al., *Farmers' Response to Agricultural Drought in Paddy Field of Southern China: A Case Study of Temporal Dimensions of Resilience.* Natural Hazards, 2011. **60**(3): p. 865-877.

182.Almeida, M.M.d., et al., *Hospital Resilience After the 2015 Earthquake in Nepal: Results From Semi-Structured Interviews With Hospital Staff.* Frontiers in Public Health, 2021. **9**.

183.Labarda, C., M. Labarda, and E.E. Lamberte, *Hospital Resilience in the Aftermath of Typhoon Haiyan in the Philippines.* Disaster Prevention and Management an International Journal, 2017. **26**(4): p. 424-436.

184.Lotto, R.D., V.G.C.M.D. Popolo, and E.M. Venco, *From Resilience to Flexibility: Urban Scenario to Reduce Hazard.* 2016: p. 429-439.

185.Çorbacıoğlu, S., S. Çelik, and U. Saran, *Self-Adaptation in Dynamic Disaster Environments: Response to the 2006 Avian Influenza Crisis in Turkey.* Journal of Asian and African Studies, 2016. **51**(6): p. 742-759.

186.Henley, L., et al., *Social Work in the Time of COVID-19: A Case Study From the Global South.* The British Journal of Social Work, 2021. **51**(5): p. 1605-1622.

187.Zhong, S., et al., *Development of Hospital Disaster Resilience: Conceptual Framework and Potential Measurement.* Emergency Medicine Journal, 2013. **31**(11): p. 930-938.

188.Radianti, J., T. Gjøsæter, and W. Chen, *Universal Design of Information Sharing Tools for Disaster Risk Reduction.* 2019: p. 81-95.

189.Almeida, M.M.d., et al., *Hospital Resilience After the 2015 Earthquake in Nepal: Results From Semi-Structured Interviews With Hospital Staff.* 2020.

190.Acharibasam, J.B. and R. Datta, *Enhancing Community Resilience to Climate Change Disasters: Learning Experience Within and From Sub-Saharan Black Immigrant Communities in Western Canada.* Sustainable Development, 2023. **32**(2): p. 1401-1411.

191.Firdaus, A., K.S. Pribadi, and M. Abduh, *The State of Sustainable and Disaster-Resilient Infrastructure in Indonesia.* Iop Conference Series Earth and Environmental Science, 2024. **1314**(1): p. 012007.

192.Boon, H., et al., *Bronfenbrenner's Bioecological Theory for Modelling Community Resilience to Natural Disasters.* Natural Hazards, 2011. **60**(2): p. 381-408.

193.Ma, Z., et al., *Community Disaster Resilience and Risk Perception in Earthquake-Stricken Areas of China.* Disaster Medicine and Public Health Preparedness, 2022. **17**.

194.Pfefferbaum, B., R.L.V. Horn, and R.L. Pfefferbaum, *A Conceptual Framework to Enhance Community Resilience Using Social Capital.* Clinical Social Work Journal, 2015. **45**(2): p. 102-110.

195.Wenger, C., *The Oak or the Reed: How Resilience Theories Are Translated Into Disaster Management Policies.* Ecology and Society, 2017. **22**(3).

196.Habiba, U., R. Shaw, and Y. Takeuchi, *Drought Risk Reduction Through a Socio-Economic, Institutional and Physical Approach in the Northwestern Region of Bangladesh.* Environmental Hazards, 2011. **10**(2): p. 121-138.

197.Alan, H., et al., *Nurses' Disaster Core Competencies and Resilience During the COVID-19 Pandemic: A Cross-sectional Study From Turkey.* Journal of Nursing Management, 2022. **30**(3): p. 622-632.

198.Lee, J., et al., *Community Resilience, Psychological Resilience, and Depressive Symptoms: An Examination of the Mississippi Gulf Coast 10 Years After Hurricane Katrina and 5 Years After the Deepwater Horizon Oil Spill.* Disaster Medicine and Public Health Preparedness, 2017. **12**(2): p. 241-248.

199.Cox, R.S. and K.-M.E. Perry, *Like a Fish Out of Water: Reconsidering Disaster Recovery and the Role of Place and Social Capital in Community Disaster Resilience.* American Journal of Community Psychology, 2011. **48**(3-4): p. 395-411.

200.Song, J., B. Huang, and R. Li, *Measuring Recovery to Build Up Metrics of Flood Resilience Based on Pollutant Discharge Data: A Case Study in East China.* Water, 2017. **9**(8): p. 619.

201.Olshansky, R. and L.A. Johnson, *The Evolution of the Federal Role in Supporting Community Recovery After U.S. Disasters.* Journal of the American Planning Association, 2014. **80**(4): p. 293-304.

202.Xu, J. and Y. Qiang, *Spatial Assessment of Community Resilience From 2012 Hurricane Sandy Using Nighttime Light.* Remote Sensing, 2021. **13**(20): p. 4128.

203.Little, C., et al., *Using Rapid Improvement Events for Disaster After-Action Reviews: Experience in a Hospital Information Technology Outage and Response.* Prehospital and Disaster Medicine, 2018. **33**(1): p. 98-100.

204.Rogers, P., et al., *Collaboration and Communication.* Disaster Prevention and Management an International Journal, 2016. **25**(1): p. 75-90.

205.Lestari, P., E.T. Paripurno, and A.R.B. Nugroho, *Disaster Risk Reduction Based on Community Through a Contingency Plan for Mount Sinabung.* Jurnal Ilmu Sosial Dan Ilmu Politik, 2018. **21**(3): p. 231.

206.Azad, M.A.K., et al., *Community-Based Disaster Management and Its Salient Features: A Policy Approach to People-Centred Risk Reduction in Bangladesh.* Asia-Pacific Journal of Rural Development, 2019. **29**(2): p. 135-160.

207.Andreastuti, S., A. Budianto, and E.T. Paripurno, *Integrating Social and Physical Perspectives of Mitigation Policy and Practice in Indonesia.* 2017: p. 307-320.

208.Wambede, M.N. and R. Tweheyo, *Community Based Flood Risk Management Approach in Northeastern Uganda.* Ghana Journal of Geography, 2022. **14**(2): p. 107-134.

209.Masten, A.S., *Resilience in Children Threatened by Extreme Adversity: Frameworks for Research, Practice, and Translational Synergy.* Development and Psychopathology, 2011. **23**(2): p. 493-506.

210.Παπαδόπουλος, Θ., et al., *The Role of Big Data in Explaining Disaster Resilience in Supply Chains for Sustainability.* Journal of Cleaner Production, 2017. **142**: p. 1108-1118.

211.Dentoni, D., J. Pinkse, and R.J.B. Lubberink, *Linking Sustainable Business Models to Socio-Ecological Resilience Through Cross-Sector Partnerships: A Complex Adaptive Systems View.* Business & Society, 2020. **60**(5): p. 1216-1252.

212.Gazley, B. and J.L. Brudney, *The Purpose (And Perils) of Government-Nonprofit Partnership.* Nonprofit and Voluntary Sector Quarterly, 2007. **36**(3): p. 389-415.

213.Ge, Y.G., et al., *Building Community Resilience Through <scp>cross-sector</Scp> Partnerships and Interdisciplinary Research.* Public Administration Review, 2023. **83**(5): p. 1415-1422.

214.Busch, N.E. and A.D. Givens, *Achieving Resilience in Disaster Management: The Role of Public-Private Partnerships.* Journal of Strategic Security, 2013. **6**(2): p. 1-19.

215.Bromley, E., et al., *How Do Communities Use a Participatory Public Health Approach to Build Resilience? The Los Angeles County Community Disaster Resilience Project.* International Journal of Environmental Research and Public Health, 2017. **14**(10): p. 1267.

216.Li, J., et al., *Establishing a Risk Assessment Framework for Marine Assets and Assessing Typhoon Lekima Storm Surge for the Laizhou Bay Coastal Area of the Bohai Sea, China.* Journal of Marine Science and Engineering, 2022. **10**(2): p. 298.

217.Sherman–Morris, K., J.B. Houston, and J. Subedi, *Theoretical Matters: On the Need for Hazard and Disaster Theory Developed Through Interdisciplinary Research and Collaboration.* Risk Analysis, 2018. **41**(7): p. 1059-1065.

218.Shi, J., L. Cui, and Z. Shen, *Interannual Variation and Hazard Analysis of Meteorological Disasters in East China.* Journal of Risk Analysis and Crisis Response, 2020. **9**(4): p. 168.

219.Birnbaum, M.L., et al., *Research and Evaluations of the Health Aspects of Disasters, Part IX: Risk-Reduction Framework.* Prehospital and Disaster Medicine, 2016. **31**(3): p. 309-325.

220.Gill, J.C., et al., *Invited Perspectives: Building Sustainable and Resilient Communities – Recommended Actions for Natural Hazard Scientists.* Natural Hazards and Earth System Science, 2021. **21**(1): p. 187-202.

221.Shen, G., et al., *A Global Expected Risk Analysis of Fatalities, Injuries, and Damages by Natural Disasters.* Sustainability, 2018. **10**(7): p. 2573.

222.He, Z. and W. Weng, *A Risk Assessment Method for Multi-Hazard Coupling Disasters.* Risk Analysis, 2020. **41**(8): p. 1362-1375.

223.Chen, J., et al., *Risk Assessment of Urban Rainstorm Disaster Based on Multi-Layer Weighted Principal Component Analysis: A Case Study of Nanjing, China.* International Journal of Environmental Research and Public Health, 2020. **17**(15): p. 5523.

224.Hooghly Women's College, *Hazard Mapping: Definition and Techniques.* 2024.

225.Assam State Disaster Management Authority & Doctors For You, *Community Based Disaster Preparedness*. 2013.

226.Purnomo, M.S. and L. Esariti, *Mapping Urban Disaster Adaptation Typology of Cebolok Community of Semarang City.* Iop Conference Series Earth and Environmental Science, 2023. **1264**(1): p. 012015.

227.Asteria, D., et al., *Integration of Local Capacity Building in Countering False Information About Disaster Into Community-Based Disaster Risk Management.* Iop Conference Series Earth and Environmental Science, 2023. **1275**(1): p. 012028.

228.Cui, K., Z. Han, and D. Wang, *Resilience of an Earthquake-Stricken Rural Community in Southwest China: Correlation With Disaster Risk Reduction Efforts.* International Journal of Environmental Research and Public Health, 2018. **15**(3): p. 407.

229.Soriano, G.P., *Disaster Risk Reduction Knowledge Among Local People in a Selected Community in the Philippines.* Journal of Health and Caring Sciences, 2019. **1**(2): p. 92-99.

230.Shalih, O., et al., *Toward a Community Resilience Framework for Disaster Risk Management. A Case Study: Landslide Cisolok in Sukabumi 2018 and Sunda Strait Tsunami in Pandeglang 2018.* E3s Web of Conferences, 2020. **156**: p. 01011.

231.Ayuningtyas, D., et al., *Disaster Preparedness and Mitigation in Indonesia: A Narrative Review.* Iranian Journal of Public Health, 2021.

232.Rangarirai, W., C.S. Marnani, and A. Rahmat, *Analyzing the Impact of Community-Based Approaches on Disaster Preparedness to the Risk of Tropical Cyclone Induced Flooding in Chimanimani District, Zimbabwe.* Iop Conference Series Earth and Environmental Science, 2023. **1173**(1): p. 012070.

233.Aladhrai, S.A., et al., *Impact of the 2011 Revolution on Hospital Disaster Preparedness in Yemen.* Disaster Medicine and Public Health Preparedness, 2015. **9**(4): p. 396-402.

234.Roudini, J., H.R. Khankeh, and E. Witruk, *Disaster Mental Health Preparedness in the Community: A Systematic Review Study.* Health Psychology Open, 2017. **4**(1): p. 205510291771130.

235.Chan, E.Y.Y., et al., *Is Previous Disaster Experience a Good Predictor for Disaster Preparedness in Extreme Poverty Households in Remote Muslim Minority Based Community in China?* Journal of Immigrant and Minority Health, 2012. **16**(3): p. 466-472.

236.Tierney, K.J., *Disaster Governance: Social, Political, and Economic Dimensions.* Annual Review of Environment and Resources, 2012. **37**(1): p. 341-363.

237.Matsuo, Y. and M. Hirano, *Effectiveness of Disaster Preparedness Education in Helping Older People Prevent Isolation.* Public Health Nursing, 2021. **38**(5): p. 837-849.

238.Midtbust, L.G.H., A. Dyregrov, and H.W. Djup, *Communicating With Children and Adolescents About the Risk of Natural Disasters.* European Journal of Psychotraumatology, 2018. **9**(sup2).

239.Uhnoo, S. and S. Persson, *The Flip Side of the Coin: Perils of Public–private Disaster Cooperation.* Journal of Contingencies and Crisis Management, 2021. **30**(4): p. 440-450.

240.Pérez, E.C.d., et al., *Action-Based Flood Forecasting for Triggering Humanitarian Action.* Hydrology and Earth System Sciences, 2016. **20**(9): p. 3549-3560.

241.Aitsi-Selmi, A., et al., *Reducing Risks to Health and Wellbeing at Mass Gatherings: The Role of the Sendai Framework for Disaster Risk Reduction.* International Journal of Infectious Diseases, 2016. **47**: p. 101-104.

242.Seifi, B., H. Seyedin, and G. Ghanizadeh, *The Role of Academic Partnership in Disaster Risk Management: A Systematic Review.* Disaster Medicine and Public Health Preparedness, 2019. **13**(5-6): p. 1047-1058.

243.Shawe, R. and I. McAndrew, *How Leadership Impacts FEMA's Whole Community Approach During Emergency Management's Preparedness.* Open Journal of Social Sciences, 2023. **11**(04): p. 128-147.

244.Sheikhi, R.A., et al., *Role of Religious Institutions in Disaster Risk Management: A Systematic Review.* Disaster Medicine and Public Health Preparedness, 2020. **15**(2): p. 239-254.

245.Kilpatrick, S., S. Auckland, and J.J. Woodroffe, *Community Health Planning.* 2019: p. 287-295.

246.Jacobs, J.A., et al., *Tools for Implementing an Evidence-Based Approach in Public Health Practice.* Preventing Chronic Disease, 2012.

247.Vizer, L.M., et al., *"It's Not Just Technology, It's People": Constructing a Conceptual Model of Shared Health Informatics for Tracking in Chronic Illness Management.* Journal of Medical Internet Research, 2019. **21**(4): p. e10830.

248.Israel, B.A., et al., *REVIEW OF COMMUNITY-BASED RESEARCH: Assessing Partnership Approaches to Improve Public Health.* Annual Review of Public Health, 1998. **19**(1): p. 173-202.

249.Luke, D.A., et al., *The Program Sustainability Assessment Tool: A New Instrument for Public Health Programs.* Preventing Chronic Disease, 2014. **11**.

250.Nagy, S., *Participant-Oriented Evaluation Through Participatory Action Research: A Case Study of a Community Engagement Approach.* Arts and the Market, 2023. **14**(1): p. 58-77.

251.Cawaling, E.J.B., D.U. Cunanan, and R.P. Bernarte, *Sustainability Capacity of HIV Programs in National Capital Region, Philippines.* International Journal of Public Health Science (Ijphs), 2018. 7(2): p. 137.

252.Tarhan, Ç. and D. Deniz, *Sustainable Urban Planning and Risk Assessment of Earthquake Hazards in Turkey.* The International Archives of the Photogrammetry Remote Sensing and Spatial Information Sciences, 2013. **XL-4/W1**: p. 113-117.

253.Naser, W.N. and H.B. Saleem, *Emergency and Disaster Management Training; Knowledge and Attitude of Yemeni Health Professionals- A Cross-Sectional Study.* BMC Emergency Medicine, 2018. **18**(1).

254.Subbarao, I., et al., *A Consensus-Based Educational Framework and Competency Set for the Discipline of Disaster Medicine and Public Health Preparedness.* Disaster Medicine and Public Health Preparedness, 2008. **2**(1): p. 57-68.

255.Tam, G., Z. Huang, and E.Y.Y. Chan, *Household Preparedness and Preferred Communication Channels in Public Health Emergencies: A Cross-Sectional Survey of Residents in an Asian Developed Urban City.* International Journal of Environmental Research and Public Health, 2018. **15**(8): p. 1598.

256.Schilly, K., et al., *Evaluation of a Disaster Preparedness Curriculum and Medical Students' Views on Preparedness Education Requirements for Health Professionals.* Disaster Medicine and Public Health Preparedness, 2024. **18**.

257.Wang, Y., et al., *Disaster Preparedness Among Nurses in China: A Cross-Sectional Study.* Journal of Nursing Research, 2022. **31**(1): p. e255.

258.Guo, C., T. Sim, and G. Su, *Individual Disaster Preparedness in Drought-and-Flood-Prone Villages in Northwest China: Impact of Place, Out-Migration and Community.* International Journal of Environmental Research and Public Health, 2021. **18**(4): p. 1649.

259.Uhm, D.-C. and H.S. Oh, *Disaster Preparedness of Child Care Teachers: A Cross-Sectional Study in South Korea.* Disaster Medicine and Public Health Preparedness, 2017. **12**(3): p. 321-328.

260.Hidayat, Z. and M. Yatminiwati, *Role of Local Wisdom-Based Disaster Education and Training Through Education Levels in Disaster-Prone Areas.* International Journal of Accounting and Management Research, 2023. **4**(1): p. 1-8.

261.Uhm, D.-C., et al., *Factors Affecting the Disaster Response Competency of Emergency Medical Technicians in South Korea.* Asian Nursing Research, 2019. **13**(4): p. 264-269.

262.Azizpour, I., S. Mehri, and A.H. Soola, *Disaster Preparedness Knowledge and Its Relationship With Triage Decision-Making Among Hospital and Pre-Hospital Emergency Nurses - Ardabil, Iran.* BMC Health Services Research, 2022. **22**(1).

263.Pandey, C.L., *Making Communities Disaster Resilient.* Disaster Prevention and Management an International Journal, 2018. **28**(1): p. 106-118.

264.Ainuddin, S. and J.K. Routray, *Institutional Framework, Key Stakeholders and Community Preparedness for Earthquake Induced Disaster Management in Balochistan.* Disaster Prevention and Management an International Journal, 2012. **21**(1): p. 22-36.

265.Carpio, C.J., *Disaster Preparedness of the Selected Barangays in Rizal, Nueva Ecija.* International Journal of Advanced Engineering Management and Science, 2019. **6**(1): p. 15-17.

266.Shimazaki, T. and K. Takenaka, *Evaluation of Intervention Reach on a City-wide Health Behavior Change Campaign.* Health Education & Behavior, 2015. **42**(6): p. 793-804.

267.Milkovich, R., et al., *Public Health Detailing to Increase Expedited Partner Therapy for Chlamydia and Gonorrhea in Maryland: Changes in Awareness and Implementation Among Prescribing Community Providers.* Preventive Medicine Reports, 2021. **24**: p. 101530.

268.Noar, S.M., *A 10-Year Retrospective of Research in Health Mass Media Campaigns: Where Do We Go From Here?* Journal of Health Communication, 2006. **11**(1): p. 21-42.

269.Levey, A.S., et al., *Nomenclature for Kidney Function and Disease: Executive Summary and Glossary From a Kidney Disease: Improving Global Outcomes (KDIGO) Consensus Conference.* Kidney Medicine, 2020. **2**(4): p. 373-376.

270.Phinney, A., et al., *<i>Dementia Without Borders</I>: Building Community Connections to Reduce Stigma and Foster Inclusion.* Dementia, 2023. **22**(3): p. 550-560.

271.Jo, S. and T. Nabatchi, *Different Processes, Different Outcomes? Assessing the <scp>Individual-Level</Scp> Impacts of Public Participation.* Public Administration Review, 2020. **81**(1): p. 137-151.

272.Nganga-Good, C., M. Chayhitz, and P. McLaine, *Overcoming Barriers and Improving Public Health Nursing Practice.* Public Health Nursing, 2022. **40**(1): p. 114-123.

273.Lubis, N., et al., *Global Community Perception of 'Surgical Care' as a Public Health Issue: A Cross Sectional Survey.* BMC Public Health, 2021. **21**(1).

274.Allen, K.M., *Community-based Disaster Preparedness and Climate Adaptation: Local Capacity-building in the Philippines.* Disasters, 2006. **30**(1): p. 81-101.

275.Tariq, M.N.M., et al., *A Cluster-Randomized Trial Study on Effectiveness of Health Education Based Intervention (HEBI) in Improving Flood Disaster Preparedness Among Community in Selangor, Malaysia: A Study Protocol.* BMC Public Health, 2021. **21**(1).

276.Gowan, M.E., R. Kirk, and J.A. Sloan, *Building Resiliency: A Cross-Sectional Study Examining Relationships Among Health-Related Quality of Life, Well-Being, and Disaster Preparedness.* Health and Quality of Life Outcomes, 2014. **12**(1): p. 85.

277.Khan, A., et al., *Community Based Assessment of Behavior and Awareness of Risk Factors of Cystic Echinococcosis in Major Cities of Pakistan: A One Health Perspective.* Frontiers in Public Health, 2021. **9**.

278.DeYoung, S.E. and M. Peters, *My Community, My Preparedness: The Role of Sense of Place, Community, and Confidence in Government in Disaster Readiness.* International Journal of Mass Emergencies & Disasters, 2016. **34**(2): p. 250-282.

279.Paterson, B. and A. Charles, *A Global Comparison of Community-Based Responses to Natural Hazards.* Natural Hazards and Earth System Science, 2019. **19**(11): p. 2465-2475.

280.Al-Ali, N. and A.H.A. Ibaid, *Health-Care Providers' Perception of Knowledge, Skills and Preparedness for Disaster Management in Primary Health-Care Centres in Jordan.* Eastern Mediterranean Health Journal, 2015. **21**(10): p. 713-721.

281.Andrade, E., et al., *Resilience of Communities in Puerto Rico Following Hurricane Maria: Community-Based Preparedness and Communication Strategies.* Disaster Medicine and Public Health Preparedness, 2021. **17**.

282.Karunasena, G. and R. Amaratunga, *Capacity Gaps in Post Disaster Construction &Amp; Demolition Waste Management.* Engineering Construction & Architectural Management, 2015. **22**(4): p. 446-466.

283.Rajapaksha, N.U., et al., *Incidence Management System of the Healthcare Institutions for Disaster Management in Sri Lanka.* BMC Emergency Medicine, 2023. **23**(1).

284.Putri, F.A. and F. Lestari, *Student Perceptions of Faculty of Medicine, Dentistry, Nursing, and Pharmacy University of Indonesia in Facing Disaster as Efforts to Enhance Resilience in University 2017.* Kne Life Sciences, 2018. **4**(5): p. 462.

285.Karancı, A.N., B. Akşit, and G. Dirik, *Impact of a Community Disaster Awareness Training Program in Turkey: Does It Influence Hazard-Related Cognitions and Preparedness Behaviors.* Social Behavior and Personality an International Journal, 2005. **33**(3): p. 243-258.

286.Gouda, M. and Y. Yang, *Investigating the Impact of a Community Disaster Awareness Training on Subjective Disaster Preparedness: The Case of Myanmar's Ayeyarwaddy Region.* Disasters, 2023. **47**(4): p. 1047-1068.

287.Azhar, N., et al., *Application ofBehavioural Model toDisaster Preparedness inA Developing Country Malaysia: An Overview.* Journal of Social Transformation and Regional Development, 2022. **4**(2).

288.Susmini, S., et al., *The Effects of a Disaster Preparedness App on Community Knowledge and Intentional Behavior in Hurricane Risk Areas.* Disaster Medicine and Public Health Preparedness, 2022. **17**.

289.Palupi, L.S., *Towards Sustainable Cities and Communities: Is Psychological Preparedness Include in the Disaster Risk Reduction Policy Framework in Indonesia.* E3s Web of Conferences, 2022. **340**: p. 03009.

290.Tanner, T. and F. Seballos, *Action Research With Children: Lessons From Tackling Disasters and Climate Change*.* Ids Bulletin, 2012. **43**(3): p. 59-70.

291.Emaliyawati, E., et al., *The Effect of Disaster Education of Increasing Earthquake Disaster Preparedness : A Narrative Review.* Jurnal Keperawatan Komprehensif, 2022. **8**(4).

292.Basolo, V., et al., *The Effects of Confidence in Government and Information on Perceived and Actual Preparedness for Disasters.* Environment and Behavior, 2008. **41**(3): p. 338-364.

293.Lindell, M.K., S. Arlikatti, and C.S. Prater, *Why People Do What They Do to Protect Against Earthquake Risk: Perceptions of Hazard Adjustment Attributes.* Risk Analysis, 2009. **29**(8): p. 1072-1088.

294.Xu, D., P. Li, and X. Wang, *Influences of Risk Perception and Sense of Place on Landslide Disaster Preparedness in Southwestern China.* International Journal of Disaster Risk Science, 2018. **9**(2): p. 167-180.

295.Onuma, H., K.J. Shin, and S. Managi, *Household Preparedness for Natural Disasters: Impact of Disaster Experience and Implications for Future Disaster Risks in Japan.* International Journal of Disaster Risk Reduction, 2017. **21**: p. 148-158.

296.Putra, D.G.S., K.R. Putra, and N. As, *Emergency Nurse's Perceptions of Hospital Facility Support and Disaster Preparedness.* International Journal of Public Health Science (Ijphs), 2020. **9**(4): p. 347.

297.Malmin, N.P., *Historical Disaster Exposure and Household Preparedness Across the United States.* Disaster Medicine and Public Health Preparedness, 2020. **15**(1): p. 58-64.

298.Pratama, P.Y. and A. Nurmandi, *Collaborating Network in Managing Post the Mount Merapi's Disruption, Indonesia.* Jàmbá Journal of Disaster Risk Studies, 2020. **12**(1).

299.Al-Shareef, A.S., et al., *Evaluation of Hospitals' Disaster Preparedness Plans in the Holy City of Makkah (Mecca): A Cross-Sectional Observation Study.* Prehospital and Disaster Medicine, 2016. **32**(1): p. 33-45.

300.Gausche-Hill, M., *Pediatric Disaster Preparedness: Are We Really Prepared?* Journal of Trauma and Acute Care Surgery, 2009. **67**(2): p. S73-S76.

301.Atreya, A., et al., *Adoption of Flood Preparedness Actions: A Household Level Study in Rural Communities in Tabasco, Mexico.* International Journal of Disaster Risk Reduction, 2017. **24**: p. 428-438.

302.Guo, W., et al., *Text Quality Analysis of Emergency Response Plans.* Ieee Access, 2020. **8**: p. 9441-9456.

303.Sutrisno, A., C.E.V. Wuisang, and A. Yusupa, *Disaster Readiness Assessment Model Using Integrated Statistical Variance and Proximity Value Index.* International Journal of Emergency Services, 2023. **12**(2): p. 197-212.

304.Aitsi-Selmi, A., et al., *The Sendai Framework for Disaster Risk Reduction: Renewing the Global Commitment to People's Resilience, Health, and Well-Being.* International Journal of Disaster Risk Science, 2015. **6**(2): p. 164-176.

305.Heidari, M., et al., *Analysis of the Man-Made Causes of Shiraz Flash Flood: Iran, 2019.* Prehospital and Disaster Medicine, 2020. **35**(5): p. 588-591.

306.Reinhardt, G.Y. and L. Drennan, *Local Emergency Management Special Issue: Guest Editors' Introduction.* Local Government Studies, 2019. **45**(3): p. 293-301.

307.Raju, E. and K.d. Costa, *Governance in the Sendai: A Way Ahead?* Disaster Prevention and Management an International Journal, 2018. **27**(3): p. 278-291.

308.Radel, K., A. Sukumaran, and C. Daniels, *Incorporating First Nations Knowledges Into Disaster Management Plans: An Analysis.* Australian Journal of Emergency Management, 2023. **10.47389/38**(No 2): p. 36-41.

309.Kelman, I., *Climate Change and the Sendai Framework for Disaster Risk Reduction.* International Journal of Disaster Risk Science, 2015. **6**(2): p. 117-127.

310.Australian Institute for Disaster Resilience, *Emergency Planning*. 2020.

311.O'Neill, E., et al., *The Impact of Perceived Flood Exposure on Flood-Risk Perception: The Role of Distance.* Risk Analysis, 2016. **36**(11): p. 2158-2186.

312.Werritty, A., *Sustainable Flood Management: Oxymoron or New Paradigm?* Area, 2006. **38**(1): p. 16-23.

313.Yannopoulos, S., et al., *Implementing the Requirements of the European Flood Directive: The Case of Ungauged and Poorly Gauged Watersheds.* Environmental Processes, 2015. **2**(S1): p. 191-207.

314.Shah, M.A.R., A. Rahman, and S.H. Chowdhury, *Challenges for Achieving Sustainable Flood Risk Management.* Journal of Flood Risk Management, 2015. **11**(S1).

315.Lin, Z., et al., *Weather and Seasonal Climate Prediction for Flood Planning in the Yangtze River Basin.* Stochastic Environmental Research and Risk Assessment, 2005. **19**(6): p. 428-437.

316.Paruthi, S., *Collaboration and Coordination: The Building Blocks of Effective Emergency Response & Disaster Management* 2023.

317.United States Agency for International Development. *Identify Current and Potential Stakeholders*. 2024 [cited 2024 13/5/2024]; Available from: .

318.AngloAmerican. *Task 3 – Develop a co-ordinated approach with key external stakeholders*. 2024 [cited 2024 13/5/2024]; Available from: .

319.Shi, W., L. Jiang, and X. He, *Precision Augmentation of Medical Surge Capacity for Disaster Response.* Emergency Medicine International, 2020. **2020**: p. 1-6.

320.Cox, R.S. and M. Hamlen, *Community Disaster Resilience and the Rural Resilience Index.* American Behavioral Scientist, 2014. **59**(2): p. 220-237.

321.Lee, E.-M. and H. Lee, *Disaster Awareness and Coping: Impact on Stress, Anxiety, and Depression.* Perspectives in Psychiatric Care, 2019. **55**(2): p. 311-318.

322.UN Office for Disaster Risk Reduction. *Essential Nine: Ensure Effective Disaster Response*. 2024 [cited 2024 14/5/2024]; Available from: .

323.Safiudin, S.I.b. and N.F.b.M. Kutty, *The Rationale for Collaborative Approach With Military Involvement to Strengthen Urban Disaster Management Strategy: A Case Study of Malaysia.* International Journal of Academic Research in Business and Social Sciences, 2023. **13**(3).

324.Ashraf, A., *Lessons Learned From COVID-19 Response for Disaster Risk Management.* Natural Hazards, 2021. **107**(2): p. 2027-2032.

325.Everhart, A., R. Patel, and N.A. Errett, *Engaging Local Health Departments in Disaster Research: A Washington State Survey.* Disaster Medicine and Public Health Preparedness, 2019. **14**(2): p. 163-167.

326.Manuel, M.P., M. Faied, and M. Krishnan, *A Novel LoRa LPWAN-Based Communication Architecture for Search &Amp; Rescue Missions.* Ieee Access, 2022. **10**: p. 57596-57607.

327.Mishra, B., et al., *Drone-Surveillance for Search and Rescue in Natural Disaster.* Computer Communications, 2020. **156**: p. 1-10.

328.Berawi, M.A., et al., *Optimizing Search and Rescue Personnel Allocation in Disaster Emergency Response Using Fuzzy Logic
.* International Journal of Technology, 2019. **10**(7): p. 1416.

329.Pham, N.H. and M.D. Nguyen, *An Evolutionary Algorithm for Optimal Multi-Direction Search Route in Search and Rescue Operation.* International Journal on Advanced Science Engineering and Information Technology, 2019. **9**(4): p. 1199-1204.

330.Albanese, A.A., V. Sciancalepore, and X. Costa-Pérez, *SARDO: An Automated Search-and-Rescue Drone-Based Solution for Victims Localization.* Ieee Transactions on Mobile Computing, 2022. **21**(9): p. 3312-3325.

331.Lozano, J.J.F., et al., *Integration of a Canine Agent in a Wireless Sensor Network for Information Gathering in Search and Rescue Missions.* 2018.

332.Kriheli, B., et al., *A Fast Algorithm for Scheduling Detection-and-Rescue Operations Based on Data From Wireless Sensor Networks.* Research in Computing Science, 2015. **104**(1): p. 9-21.

333.Tang, J., et al., *Simulation Optimization of Search and Rescue in Disaster Relief Based on Distributed Auction Mechanism.* Algorithms, 2017. **10**(4): p. 125.

334.Agrawal, J., M. Kapoor, and R. Tomar, *A Ferry Mobility Based Direction and Time-aware Greedy Delay-tolerant Routing (FM-DT-GDR) Protocol for Sparse Flying Ad-hoc Network.* Transactions on Emerging Telecommunications Technologies, 2022. **33**(9).

335.Bartolucci, A., D. Walter, and T. Redmond, *Comparative Review on the Cost-Effectiveness Analysis of Relief Teams' Deployment to Sudden-Onset Disasters.* Prehospital and Disaster Medicine, 2019. **34**(04): p. 415-421.

336.Casper, J. and R.R. Murphy, *Human-Robot Interactions During the Robot-Assisted Urban Search and Rescue Response at the World Trade Center.* Ieee Transactions on Systems Man and Cybernetics Part B (Cybernetics), 2003. **33**(3): p. 367-385.

337.Nasar, W., et al., *The Use of Decision Support in Search and Rescue: A Systematic Literature Review.* Isprs International Journal of Geo-Information, 2023. **12**(5): p. 182.

338.Li, T., Q. Wang, and Z. Xie, *Disaster Response Knowledge and Its Social Determinants: A Cross-Sectional Study in Beijing, China.* Plos One, 2019. **14**(3): p. e0214367.

339.Staupe-Delgado, R., et al., *Preparedness for Slow-onset Environmental Disasters: Drawing Lessons From Three Decades of El Niño Impacts.* Sustainable Development, 2018. **26**(6): p. 553-563.

340.Miller, A., et al., *Integrating Health Research Into Disaster Response: The New NIH Disaster Research Response Program.* International Journal of Environmental Research and Public Health, 2016. **13**(7): p. 676.

341.Lee, J.-W., J.L. Irish, and R. Weiss, *Real-Time Prediction of Alongshore Near-Field Tsunami Runup Distribution From Heterogeneous Earthquake Slip Distribution.* Journal of Geophysical Research Oceans, 2023. **128**(1).

342.Sugiura, M., et al., *Psychological Processes and Personality Factors for an Appropriate Tsunami Evacuation.* Geosciences, 2019. **9**(8): p. 326.

343.Yabusakki, S. and K. Asai, *Estimation of Groundwater and Spring Water Residence Times Near the Coast of Fukushima, Japan.* Ground Water, 2023. **61**(3): p. 431-445.

344.Sato, M., et al., *Displacement Above the Hypocenter of the 2011 Tohoku-Oki Earthquake.* Science, 2011. **332**(6036): p. 1395-1395.

345.Rabinowitz, H.S., et al., *Earthquake Slip Surfaces Identified by Biomarker Thermal Maturity Within the 2011 Tohoku-Oki Earthquake Fault Zone.* Nature Communications, 2020. **11**(1).

346.Sawai, Y., et al., *Shorter Intervals Between Great Earthquakes Near Sendai: Scour Ponds and a Sand Layer Attributable to <scp>A.D.</scp> 1454 Overwash.* Geophysical Research Letters, 2015. **42**(12): p. 4795-4800.

347.Ando, M., et al., *Interviewing Insights Regarding the Fatalities Inflicted by the 2011 Great East Japan Earthquake.* Natural Hazards and Earth System Science, 2013. **13**(9): p. 2173-2187.

348.Sharp, E.N. and H. Carter, *Examination of How Social Media Can Inform the Management of Volunteers During a Flood Disaster.* Journal of Flood Risk Management, 2020. **13**(4).

349.Vishnu, C.L., et al., *Satellite-Based Assessment of the August 2018 Flood in Parts of Kerala, India.* Geomatics Natural Hazards and Risk, 2019. **10**(1): p. 758-767.

350.Sherpa, S.F., et al., *Probabilistic Mapping of August 2018 Flood of Kerala, India, Using Space-Borne Synthetic Aperture Radar.* Ieee Journal of Selected Topics in Applied Earth Observations and Remote Sensing, 2020. **13**: p. 896-913.

351.Unnithan, S.L.K., B. Biswal, and C. Rüdiger, *Flood Inundation Mapping by Combining GNSS-R Signals With Topographical Information.* Remote Sensing, 2020. **12**(18): p. 3026.

352.Mishra, V., et al., *The Kerala Flood of 2018: Combined Impact of Extreme Rainfall and Reservoir Storage.* 2018.

353.Raman, K., *<i>Ecospatiality</I>: Transforming Kerala's Post-Flood 'Riskscapes'.* Cambridge Journal of Regions Economy and Society, 2020. **13**(2): p. 319-341.

354.Jament, J., et al., *Covid on the Coast: Pandemic Governance and Protests in Fishing Villages in South Kerala, India.* Journal of South Asian Development, 2023. **18**(2): p. 295-320.

355.Ulahannan, J.P., et al., *A Citizen Science Initiative for Open Data and Visualization of COVID-19 Outbreak in Kerala, India.* 2020.

356.Sarani, B., et al., *The Academic Medical Centre and Nongovernmental Organisation Partnership Following a Natural Disaster.* Disasters, 2012. **36**(4): p. 609-616.

357.Lusk, J.L. and R. Andre, *Aid Relief in Haiti After the Earthquake: Haitians' Preferences for Food and Other Basic Commodities.* Development Policy Review, 2017. **35**(S2).

358.Sapat, A., A.M. Esnard, and A. Kolpakov, *Understanding Collaboration in Disaster Assistance Networks: Organizational Homophily or Resource Dependency?* The American Review of Public Administration, 2019. **49**(8): p. 957-972.

359.Kabra, G. and A. Ramesh, *Analyzing Drivers and Barriers of Coordination in Humanitarian Supply Chain Management Under Fuzzy Environment.* Benchmarking an International Journal, 2015. **22**(4): p. 559-587.

360.Shultz, J.M., et al., *Psychological Consequences of Indirect Exposure to Disaster Due to the Haiti Earthquake.* Prehospital and Disaster Medicine, 2012. **27**(4): p. 359-368.

361.Nolte, I.M. and S. Boenigk, *Public–nonprofit Partnership Performance in a Disaster Context: The Case of Haiti.* Public Administration, 2011. **89**(4): p. 1385-1402.

362.Robinson, S.a., et al., *'We Are a People': Sovereignty and Disposability in the Context of Puerto Rico's Post-Hurricane Maria Experience.* Geographical Journal, 2022. **189**(4): p. 575-583.

363.Kapucu, N., T. Arslan, and M. Collins, *Examining Intergovernmental and Interorganizational Response to Catastrophic Disasters.* Administration & Society, 2010. **42**(2): p. 222-247.

364.Schneider, S.K., *Who's to Blame? (Mis) Perceptions of the Intergovernmental Response to Disasters.* Publius the Journal of Federalism, 2008. **38**(4): p. 715-738.

365.Shughart, I.I.W.F., *Katrinanomics: The Politics and Economics of Disaster Relief.* Public Choice, 2006. **127**(1-2): p. 31-53.

366.Sobel, R.S. and P.T. Leeson, *Government's Response to Hurricane Katrina: A Public Choice Analysis.* Public Choice, 2006. **127**(1-2): p. 55-73.

367.Mitchell, J.K., *The Primacy of Partnership: Scoping a New National Disaster Recovery Policy.* The Annals of the American Academy of Political and Social Science, 2006. **604**(1): p. 228-255.

368.Johar, A., W.R.S. Osman, and A.A. Aziz, *Amateur Radio Communication Technology Contingency Communication in Emergency Situation.* SHS Web of Conferences, 2017. **33**: p. 00023.

369.Kutner, N.G., et al., *Effect of Hurricane Katrina on the Mortality of Dialysis Patients.* Kidney International, 2009. **76**(7): p. 760-766.

370.Campbell, V.A., et al., *Preparing for and Responding to Pandemic Influenza: Implications for People With Disabilities.* American Journal of Public Health, 2009. **99**(S2): p. S294-S300.

371.Anderson, A.H., et al., *Missed Dialysis Sessions and Hospitalization in Hemodialysis Patients After Hurricane Katrina.* Kidney International, 2009. **75**(11): p. 1202-1208.

372.Reid, M., *Social Policy, "Deservingness," and Sociotemporal Marginalization: Katrina Survivors and FEMA.* Sociological Forum, 2013. **28**(4): p. 742-763.

373.Weisler, R.H., J.G. Barbee, and M.H. Townsend, *Mental Health and Recovery in the Gulf Coast After Hurricanes Katrina and Rita.* Jama, 2006. **296**(5): p. 585.

374.Bala, H., et al., *If the Worst Happens: Five Strategies for Developing and Leveraging Information Technology-Enabled Disaster Response in Healthcare.* Ieee Journal of Biomedical and Health Informatics, 2016. **20**(6): p. 1545-1551.

375.Kopp, J.B., et al., *Kidney Patient Care in Disasters.* Clinical Journal of the American Society of Nephrology, 2007. **2**(4): p. 814-824.

376.Condon, S.K., et al., *"Operation Helping Hands": Massachusetts' Health and Medical Response to Hurricane Katrina.* Prehospital and Disaster Medicine, 2010. **25**(1): p. 80-86.

377.Stivers, C., *"So Poor and So Black": Hurricane Katrina, Public Administration, and the Issue of Race.* Public Administration Review, 2007. **67**(s1): p. 48-56.

378.Kapucu, N., et al., *Coordinating Non-established Disaster Relief Groups: A Case Study of Hurricane Irma in Florida, United States.* Disasters, 2021. **45**(3): p. 717-737.

379.Mori, N., et al., *Local Amplification of Storm Surge by Super Typhoon Haiyan in Leyte Gulf.* Geophysical Research Letters, 2014. **41**(14): p. 5106-5113.

380.Field, J., *What Is Appropriate and Relevant Assistance After a Disaster? Accounting for Culture(s) in the Response to Typhoon Haiyan/Yolanda.* International Journal of Disaster Risk Reduction, 2017. **22**: p. 335-344.

381.Cuesta, J.G., et al., *The Impact of Typhoon Haiyan on Health Staff: A Qualitative Study in Two Hospitals in Eastern Visayas, the Philippines.* Frontiers in Public Health, 2018. **6**.

382.Cabello, K.E., et al., *Post-Disaster Assessment of Mangrove Forest Recovery in Lawaan-Balangiga, Eastern Samar Using Ndvi Time Series Analysis.* Isprs Annals of the Photogrammetry Remote Sensing and Spatial Information Sciences, 2021. **V-3-2021**: p. 243-250.

383.Buitre, M.J.C., H. Zhang, and H. Lin, *The Mangrove Forests Change and Impacts From Tropical Cyclones in the Philippines Using Time Series Satellite Imagery.* Remote Sensing, 2019. **11**(6): p. 688.

384.McKay, D. and P.L. Perez, *Citizen Aid, Social Media and Brokerage After Disaster.* Third World Quarterly, 2019. **40**(10): p. 1903-1920.

385.Al-Hajj, S., et al., *Beirut Ammonium Nitrate Blast: Analysis, Review, and Recommendations.* Frontiers in Public Health, 2021. **9**.

386.Rigby, S.E., et al., *Preliminary Yield Estimation of the 2020 Beirut Explosion Using Video Footage From Social Media.* Shock Waves, 2020. **30**(6): p. 671-675.

387.Kattan, C. and J. Kattan, *Accommodation With Anticancer Drug Shortage: A Lebanese Harmful Solution.* Frontiers in Oncology, 2023. **12**.

388.Kawa, N., *The Beirut Explosion: Medical Response and Resilience.* 2021(53).

389.Helou, M., N.E. Osta, and E.S. Weinstein, *Beirut Explosion: Challenge of Hospital Emergency Preparedness.* Disaster Medicine and Public Health Preparedness, 2022. **16**(6): p. 2419-2421.

390.Kheir, W.J., et al., *Ophthalmic Injuries After the Port of Beirut Blast—One of Largest Nonnuclear Explosions in History.* Jama Ophthalmology, 2021. **139**(9): p. 937.

391.Hashim, H.T., et al., *Beirut Explosion Effects on COVID-19 Situation in Lebanon.* Disaster Medicine and Public Health Preparedness, 2021. **16**(5): p. 1703-1704.

392.Ali, H.M., et al., *Investigating Organizational Learning and Adaptations for Improved Disaster Response Towards "Resilient Hospitals:" an Integrative Literature Review.* Prehospital and Disaster Medicine, 2022. **37**(5): p. 665-673.

393.Aruru, M., H.-A. Truong, and S.P. Clark, *Pharmacy Emergency Preparedness and Response (PEPR): A Proposed Framework for Expanding Pharmacy Professionals' Roles and Contributions to Emergency Preparedness and Response During the COVID-19 Pandemic and Beyond.* Research in Social and Administrative Pharmacy, 2021. **17**(1): p. 1967-1977.

394.Chaiban, C.G., et al., *The Experience of ER Nurses in Lebanese Hospitals, During the COVID-19 Outbreak: A Qualitative Study.* Disaster Medicine and Public Health Preparedness, 2023. **17**.

395.Zeenny, R.M., et al., *Assessing Knowledge, Attitude, Practice, and Preparedness of Hospital Pharmacists in Lebanon Towards COVID-19 Pandemic: A Cross-Sectional Study.* Journal of Pharmaceutical Policy and Practice, 2020. **13**(1).

396.Australian Institute for Disaster Resilience. *National Principles for Disaster Recovery.* 2024 [cited 2024 15/5/2024]; Available from: .

397.Meyer, M.A., et al., *Resilience in Recovery? Understanding the Extent, Structure, and Operations of Nonprofits Meant to Address Disaster Survivors' Unmet Needs.* Nonprofit and Voluntary Sector Quarterly, 2022. **52**(4): p. 979-1005.

398.Bogati, R. and M.S. Gautam, *Disaster Recovery Toward Attaining Sustainable Development Goals.* 2020: p. 1-10.

399.Curnin, S. and D. O'Hara, *Nonprofit and Public Sector Interorganizational Collaboration in Disaster Recovery: Lessons From the Field.* Nonprofit Management and Leadership, 2019. **30**(2): p. 277-297.

400.Bisri, M.B.F., *≪b>Observing Partnership Innovation Through Inter-Organizational Network Analysis on Emergency Response of the Great East Japan Earthquake and Tsunami 2011</B>.* Japan Social Innovation Journal, 2016. **6**(1): p. 27-41.

401.Hayashi, H., *Long-Term Recovery From Recent Disasters in Japan and the United States.* Journal of Disaster Research, 2007. **2**(6): p. 413-418.

402.Johnson, L.A. and H. Hayashi, *Synthesis Efforts in Disaster Recovery Research.* International Journal of Mass Emergencies & Disasters, 2012. **30**(2): p. 212-238.

403.Kennedy, M.G., S.A. Gonick, and N.A. Errett, *Are We Ready to Build Back "Healthier?" an Exploratory Analysis of U.S. State-Level Disaster Recovery Plans.* International Journal of Environmental Research and Public Health, 2021. **18**(15): p. 8003.

404.Khatri, J., G. FitzGerald, and M.B.P. Chhetri, *Health Risks in Disaster Responders: A Conceptual Framework.* Prehospital and Disaster Medicine, 2019. **34**(02): p. 209-216.

405.Tope, P., et al., *Social Economic Analysis of Disaster Recovery Index Sigi District CT.* 2022.

406.Li, Z. and X. Tan, *Disaster-Recovery Social Capital and Community Participation in Earthquake-Stricken Ya'an Areas.* Sustainability, 2019. **11**(4): p. 993.

407.Zhao, L., H.E. Fanneng, and C. Zhao, *A Framework of Resilience Development for Poor Villages After the Wenchuan Earthquake Based on the Principle of "Build Back Better".* Sustainability, 2020. **12**(12): p. 4979.

408.Shi, M., et al., *A Conceptual Framework Integrating "Building Back Better" and Post-Earthquake Needs for Recovery and Reconstruction.* Sustainability, 2021. **13**(10): p. 5608.

409.Vahanvati, M. and I. Rafliana, *Reliability of Build Back Better at Enhancing Resilience of Communities.* International Journal of Disaster Resilience in the Built Environment, 2019. **10**(4): p. 208-221.

410.Webb, G.R., K.J. Tierney, and J.M. Dahlhamer, *Predicting Long-Term Business Recovery From Disaster: A Comparison of the Loma Prieta Earthquake and Hurricane Andrew.* Environmental Hazards, 2002. **4**(2): p. 45-58.

411.Haynes, G.W., S.M. Danes, and K. Stafford, *Influence of Federal Disaster Assistance on Family Business Survival and Success.* Journal of Contingencies and Crisis Management, 2011. **19**(2): p. 86-98.

412.Wiatt, R.D., et al., *The Effect of Cash Flow Problems and Resource Intermingling on Small Business Recovery and Resilience After a Natural Disaster.* Journal of Family and Economic Issues, 2020. **42**(1): p. 203-214.

413.Marshall, M.I. and H.L. Schrank, *Sink or Swim? Impacts of Management Strategies on Small Business Survival and Recovery.* Sustainability, 2020. **12**(15): p. 6229.

414.Egbelakin, T., et al., *Preparation of Small to Medium-Sized Enterprises to Earthquake Disaster.* Bulletin of the New Zealand Society for Earthquake Engineering, 2018. **51**(4): p. 171-182.

415.Danes, S.M., et al., *Determinants of Family Business Resilience After a Natural Disaster by Gender of Business Owner.* Journal of Developmental Entrepreneurship, 2009. **14**(04): p. 333-354.

416.Rijkers, B., et al., *Which Firms Create the Most Jobs in Developing Countries? Evidence From Tunisia.* Labour Economics, 2014. **31**: p. 84-102.

417.Arnedo, E.G., J.A.V. Matas, and A.S. Bayón, *Spanish Tourist Sector Sustainability: Recovery Plan, Green Jobs and Wellbeing Opportunity.* Sustainability, 2021. **13**(20): p. 11447.

418.E, G.A., A.S. Bayón, and S. Fj, *European Recovery and Green Jobs Beyond the Energy Sector: Wellbeing Opportunity in Spanish Tourism Sector.* 2021.

419.Alves, G., G. Burdín, and A. Dean, *Workplace Democracy and Job Flows.* SSRN Electronic Journal, 2014.

420.Davis, S.J. and J. Haltiwanger, *Gross Job Creation and Destruction: Microeconomic Evidence and Macroeconomic Implications.* Nber Macroeconomics Annual, 1990. **5**: p. 123.

421.Трусова, Н.В., et al., *Attracting Foreign Investment in Cyclic Imbalances of the Economy.* Scientific Horizons, 2022. **25**(5).

422.Bruneckienė, J., et al., *Assessment of Investment Attractiveness in European Countries by Artificial Neural Networks: What Competences Are Needed to Make a Decision on Collective Well-Being?* Sustainability, 2019. **11**(24): p. 6892.

423.Krishna, R. and J. Mukherjee, *Revitalizing Infrastructure Sector to Accelerate Economic Recovery in India.* Vision the Journal of Business Perspective, 2021. **27**(3): p. 295-299.

424.Bello, M.F. and N.A.A. Neba, *An Examination of the Effectiveness of Economic Recovery and Growth Plan in Nigeria.* International Journal of Governance and Public Policy Analysis, 2023. **4**(01).

425.Martin, R., et al., *How Regions React to Recessions: Resilience and the Role of Economic Structure.* Regional Studies, 2016. **50**(4): p. 561-585.

426.He, D., P. Miao, and N.A. Qureshi, *Can Industrial Diversification Help Strengthen Regional Economic Resilience?* Frontiers in Environmental Science, 2022. **10**.

427.Brooks, S.K., et al., *Social and Occupational Factors Associated With Psychological Distress and Disorder Among Disaster Responders: A Systematic Review.* BMC Psychology, 2016. **4**(1).

428.Domínguez, D. and C.J. Yeh, *Social Justice Disaster Relief, Counseling, and Advocacy: The Case of the Northern California Wildfires.* Counselling Psychology Quarterly, 2018. **33**(3): p. 287-311.

429.Aten, J.D., et al., *Spiritually Oriented Disaster Psychology.* Spirituality in Clinical Practice, 2014. **1**(1): p. 20-28.

430.O'Connell, E., R.P. Abbott, and R.S. White, *Religious Struggles After Typhoon Haiyan: A Case Study From Bantayan Island.* Disaster Prevention and Management an International Journal, 2017. **26**(3): p. 330-347.

431.Felix, E.D., et al., *The Influence of Flood Exposure and Subsequent Stressors on Youth Social-Emotional Health.* American Journal of Orthopsychiatry, 2020. **90**(2): p. 161-170.

432.Lee, S. and M. Jang, *The Effect of Group Sandplay Therapy on Psychological Health and Resilience of Adolescent Survivors of Nepal Earthquake.* Journal of Symbols & Sandplay Therapy, 2020. **11**(2): p. 45-78.

433.Mash, H.B.H., et al., *Responding to Repeated Disasters: Time to Recovery in Public Health Workers.* Disaster Medicine and Public Health Preparedness, 2022. **17**.

434.Rosenberg, H., N.A. Errett, and D. Eisenman, *Working With Disaster-Affected Communities to Envision Healthier Futures: A Trauma-Informed Approach to Post-Disaster Recovery Planning.* International Journal of Environmental Research and Public Health, 2022. **19**(3): p. 1723.

435.Deshmukh, A. and M. Hastak, *Enhancing Post Disaster Recovery by Optimal Infrastructure Capacity Building.* International Journal of Research in Engineering and Technology, 2014. **03**(28): p. 5-12.

436.Κεπαπτσόγλου, K., et al., *Planning Postdisaster Operations in a Highway Network.* Transportation Research Record Journal of the Transportation Research Board, 2014. **2459**(1): p. 1-10.

437.Peters, K. and L.E.R. Peters, *Terra Incognita: The Contribution of Disaster Risk Reduction in Unpacking the Sustainability–peace Nexus.* Sustainability Science, 2021. **16**(4): p. 1173-1184.

438.Sawaneh, I.A. and F. Luo, *The Mediating Role of Disaster Policy Implementation in Disaster Risk Reduction and Sustainable Development in Sierra Leone.* Sustainability, 2021. **13**(4): p. 2112.

439.Kelman, I., J.C. Gaillard, and J. Mercer, *Climate Change's Role in Disaster Risk Reduction's Future: Beyond Vulnerability and Resilience.* International Journal of Disaster Risk Science, 2015. **6**(1): p. 21-27.

440.Kong, F., *<scp>Post-Disaster</Scp> Governance in Southeast Asia: Response, Recovery, and Resilient Societies. Andri N.R.Mardiah, Robert B.Olshansky<i>and</i> Mizan B.F.Bisri<i>(eds)</i>. Springer Nature Singapore Pte Ltd, Singapore, 2022, Pp. Xiv + 307. <scp>ISBN</Scp> 978-9-811-67400-6 (Hbk).* Singapore Journal of Tropical Geography, 2023. **45**(1): p. 155-159.

441.Holcinger, N. and Z. Šimac, *Importance of National Platforms in Disaster Risk Governance.* 2021.

442.Tissier, M.L. and H. Whyte, *Why Does Making Connections Through Resilience Indicators Matter?* 2021: p. 23-44.

443.Alifagusta, Y.N., D.G. Suharto, and R.D. Wahyuningsih, *Village Funds and Disaster Risk Reduction: Challenges to Deal With the Poverty Cause by Cultural Belief Systems.* 2019.

444.Thomalla, F., et al., *Reducing Hazard Vulnerability: Towards a Common Approach Between Disaster Risk Reduction and Climate Adaptation.* Disasters, 2006. **30**(1): p. 39-48.

445.Lopez-Cantu, T.P., A.F. Prein, and C. Samaras, *Uncertainties in Future U.S. Extreme Precipitation From Downscaled Climate Projections.* Geophysical Research Letters, 2020. **47**(9).

446.Hutter, G., et al., *Building Resilience to Natural Hazards at a Local Level in Germany—Research Note on Dealing With Tensions at the Interface of Science and Practice.* Sustainability, 2021. **13**(22): p. 12459.

447.Hunt, A. and P. Watkiss, *Climate Change Impacts and Adaptation in Cities: A Review of the Literature.* Climatic Change, 2010. **104**(1): p. 13-49.

448.Vargas-Hernández, J.G. and J. Zdunek-Wielgołaska, *Urban Green Infrastructure as a Tool for Controlling the Resilience of Urban Sprawl.* Environment Development and Sustainability, 2020. **23**(2): p. 1335-1354.

449.Hallegatte, S. and J. Li, *Investing in Resilience and Making Investments Resilient.* Plos Climate, 2022. **1**(10): p. e0000077.

450.Nkombi, Z. and G. Wentink, *The Role of Public Participation in Disaster Risk Reduction Initiatives: The Case of Katlehong Township.* Jàmbá Journal of Disaster Risk Studies, 2022. **14**(1).

451.Aitsi-Selmi, A., et al., *Reflections on a Science and Technology Agenda for 21st Century Disaster Risk Reduction.* International Journal of Disaster Risk Science, 2016. **7**(1): p. 1-29.

452.Lassa, J., et al., *Measuring Political Will: An Index of Commitment to Disaster Risk Reduction.* International Journal of Disaster Risk Reduction, 2019. **34**: p. 64-74.

453.Winoto, P.M.P., L. Wijayanti, and M.G.R. Pandin, *Literatur Review : Development of Disaster Education in Multi Agent Based Early Emergency Handling in the Pre-Hospitals Area.* 2022.

454.Ke, K.-Y., et al., *Enhancing Local Disaster Management Network Through Developing Resilient Community in New Taipei City, Taiwan.* International Journal of Environmental Research and Public Health, 2020. **17**(15): p. 5357.

455.Adams, R.M., D. Eisenman, and D.C. Glik, *Community Advantage and Individual Self-Efficacy Promote Disaster Preparedness: A Multilevel Model Among Persons With Disabilities.* International Journal of Environmental Research and Public Health, 2019. **16**(15): p. 2779.

456.Cvetković, V.M., et al., *Capacity Development of Local Self-Governments for Disaster Risk Management.* International Journal of Environmental Research and Public Health, 2021. **18**(19): p. 10406.

457.Amri, A., et al., *Disaster Risk Reduction Education in Indonesia: Challenges and Recommendations for Scaling Up.* Natural Hazards and Earth System Science, 2017. **17**(4): p. 595-612.

458.Lü, Y., et al., *Participatory Child-Centered Disaster Risk Reduction Education: An Innovative Chinese NGO Program.* Disaster Prevention and Management an International Journal, 2021. **30**(3): p. 293-307.

459.Pickering, C.J., et al., *"I Believe This Team Will Change How Society Views Youth in Disasters": The EnRiCH Youth Research Team: A Youth-Led Community-Based Disaster Risk Reduction Program in Ottawa, Canada.* Can J Public Health, 2021. **112**(5): p. 957-964.

460.Ali, T., et al., *Facilitating Sustainable Disaster Risk Reduction in Indigenous Communities: Reviving Indigenous Worldviews, Knowledge and Practices Through Two-Way Partnering.* International Journal of Environmental Research and Public Health, 2021. **18**(3): p. 855.

461.Apronti, P.T., et al., *Education for Disaster Risk Reduction (DRR): Linking Theory With Practice in Ghana's Basic Schools.* Sustainability, 2015. 7(7): p. 9160-9186.

462.Cabilao-Valencia, M.I., et al., *Integration of Disaster Risk Reduction in the Curriculum of Philippine Educational Institution.* 2019.

463.Myšiak, J., et al., *Brief Communication: Strengthening Coherence Between Climate Change Adaptation and Disaster Risk Reduction.* Natural Hazards and Earth System Science, 2018. **18**(11): p. 3137-3143.

464.Helgeson, J. and C.M. O'Fallon, *Resilience Dividends and Resilience Windfalls: Narratives That Tie Disaster Resilience Co-Benefits to Long-Term Sustainability.* Sustainability, 2021. **13**(8): p. 4554.

465.Ágústsdóttir, A.M., *Ecosystem Approach for Natural Hazard Mitigation of Volcanic Tephra in Iceland: Building Resilience and Sustainability.* Natural Hazards, 2015. **78**(3): p. 1669-1691.

466.Feagin, R.A., et al., *Shelter From the Storm? Use and Misuse of Coastal Vegetation Bioshields for Managing Natural Disasters.* Conservation Letters, 2010. **3**(1): p. 1-11.

467.Yousefpour, R., N. Nakamura, and N. Matsumura, *Forest Management Approaches for Climate Change Mitigation and Adaptation: A Comparison Between Germany and Japan.* Journal of Sustainable Forestry, 2020. **39**(6): p. 635-653.

468.Bernello, G., E. Mondino, and L. Bortolini, *People's Perception of Nature-Based Solutions for Flood Mitigation: The Case of Veneto Region (Italy).* Sustainability, 2022. **14**(8): p. 4621.

469.Metri, B.A., *Disaster Mitigation Framework for India Using Quality Circle Approach.* Disaster Prevention and Management an International Journal, 2006. **15**(4): p. 621-635.

470.Donkor, F.K., et al., *SDG Final Decade of Action: Resilient Pathways to Build Back Better From High-Impact Low-Probability (HILP) Events.* Sustainability, 2022. **14**(22): p. 15401.

471.Putri, R.F., et al., *A Review Disaster Mitigation of Jakarta Land Subsidence Areas.* E3s Web of Conferences, 2021. **325**: p. 01002.

472.Woodroffe, C.D., et al., *Mangrove Sedimentation and Response to Relative Sea-Level Rise.* Annual Review of Marine Science, 2016. **8**(1): p. 243-266.

473.Kauffman, J.B., et al., *Total Ecosystem Carbon Stocks of Mangroves Across Broad Global Environmental and Physical Gradients.* Ecological Monographs, 2020. **90**(2).

474.Ezcurra, P., et al., *Coastal Landforms and Accumulation of Mangrove Peat Increase Carbon Sequestration and Storage.* Proceedings of the National Academy of Sciences, 2016. **113**(16): p. 4404-4409.

475.Marchio, D.A., et al., *Carbon Sequestration and Sedimentation in Mangrove Swamps Influenced by Hydrogeomorphic Conditions and Urbanization in Southwest Florida.* Forests, 2016. 7(12): p. 116.

476.Igwe, V., B. Salehi, and M. Mahdianpari, *State-Wide Wetland Inventory Map of Minnesota Using Multi-Source and Multi-Temporalremote Sensing Data.* Isprs Annals of the Photogrammetry Remote Sensing and Spatial Information Sciences, 2022. **V-3-2022**: p. 411-416.

477.Aziz, T. and P.V. Cappellen, *Economic Valuation of Suspended Sediment and Phosphorus Filtration Services by Four Different Wetland Types: A Preliminary Assessment for Southern Ontario, Canada.* Hydrological Processes, 2021. **35**(12).

478.Mahdianpari, M., et al., *Meta-Analysis of Wetland Classification Using Remote Sensing: A Systematic Review of a 40-Year Trend in North America.* Remote Sensing, 2020. **12**(11): p. 1882.

479.Nyanga, C., *The Role of Mangroves Forests in Decarbonizing the Atmosphere.* 2020.

480.Adame, M.F., et al., *Future Carbon Emissions From Global Mangrove Forest Loss.* Global Change Biology, 2021. **27**(12): p. 2856-2866.

481.Vignola, R., et al., *Ecosystem-Based Adaptation for Smallholder Farmers: Definitions, Opportunities and Constraints.* Agriculture Ecosystems & Environment, 2015. **211**: p. 126-132.

482.Bergstrom, D.M., et al., *Combating Ecosystem Collapse From the Tropics to the Antarctic.* Global Change Biology, 2021. **27**(9): p. 1692-1703.

483.Agol, D., et al., *Ecosystem-Based Adaptation in Lake Victoria Basin; Synergies and Trade-Offs.* Royal Society Open Science, 2021. **8**(6): p. 201847.

484.Hernández-Blanco, M., et al., *Ecosystem Health, Ecosystem Services, and the Well-being of Humans and the Rest of Nature.* Global Change Biology, 2022. **28**(17): p. 5027-5040.

485.Marín, S.M.C., I. Restrepo-Tarquino, and D.F.C. Marín, *Methodological Strategy for the Conservation of Ecosystem Services.* Journal of Scientific Research and Reports, 2022: p. 14-27.

486.Slootweg, R., *Environmental Impact Assessment for Wetlands: Overview.* 2016: p. 1-12.

487.Mercer, J., et al., *Framework for Integrating Indigenous and Scientific Knowledge for Disaster Risk Reduction.* Disasters, 2009. **34**(1): p. 214-239.

488.Hiwasaki, L., et al., *Process for Integrating Local and Indigenous Knowledge With Science for Hydro-Meteorological Disaster Risk Reduction and Climate Change Adaptation in Coastal and Small Island Communities.* International Journal of Disaster Risk Reduction, 2014. **10**: p. 15-27.

489.Dube, E. and E. Munsaka, *The Contribution of Indigenous Knowledge to Disaster Risk Reduction Activities in Zimbabwe: A Big Call to Practitioners.* Jàmbá Journal of Disaster Risk Studies, 2018. **10**(1).

490.Kelman, I., *Lost for Words Amongst Disaster Risk Science Vocabulary?* International Journal of Disaster Risk Science, 2018. **9**(3): p. 281-291.

491.Taylor, L., et al., *Enablers and Challenges When Engaging Local Communities for Urban Biodiversity Conservation in Australian Cities.* Sustainability Science, 2021. **17**(3): p. 779-792.

492.Howitt, R., *Decolonizing People, Place and Country: Nurturing Resilience Across Time and Space.* Sustainability, 2020. **12**(15): p. 5882.

493.Rumbach, A. and D. Foley, *Indigenous Institutions and Their Role in Disaster Risk Reduction and Resilience: Evidence From the 2009 Tsunami in American Samoa.* Ecology and Society, 2014. **19**(1).

494.Nakamura, N. and Y. Kanemasu, *A Minority Group's Response to a Severe Climatic Event: A Case Study of Rural Indo-Fijians After Tropical Cyclone Winston in 2016.* Disasters, 2021. **46**(1): p. 206-225.

495.Reyes, J.A.L., et al., *Indigenous Knowledge in Disaster Risk Reduction.* The Copenhagen Journal of Asian Studies, 2020. **37**(1): p. 103-132.

496.Lee, S.H. and Y.J. Chen, *Indigenous Knowledge and Endogenous Actions for Building Tribal Resilience After Typhoon Soudelor in Northern Taiwan.* Sustainability, 2021. **13**(2): p. 506.

497.Ali, S. and A. George, *Fostering Disaster Mitigation Through Community Participation- Case of Kochi Residents Following the Kerala Floods of 2018 and 2019.* Natural Hazards, 2021. **111**(1): p. 389-410.

498.Abdulrashid, L., *The Use of Indigenous Knowledge in Flood Disaster Forecasting for Flood Disaster Risk Reduction in Northern Katsina State.* Fudma Journal of Sciences, 2021. **4**(4): p. 469-476.

499.Muyambo, F., Y.T. Bahta, and A. Jordaan, *The Role of Indigenous Knowledge in Drought Risk Reduction: A Case of Communal Farmers in South Africa.* Jàmbá Journal of Disaster Risk Studies, 2017. **9**(1).

500.Maina, N.J., F.O. Okaka, and P. Omondi, *Landslide Disasters' Causal/Trigger Factors as Understood by the Indigenous People in Murang'a County, Kenya.* Journal of Geography Environment and Earth Science International, 2022: p. 5-16.

501.Nepstad, D.C., et al., *Slowing Amazon Deforestation Through Public Policy and Interventions in Beef and Soy Supply Chains.* Science, 2014. **344**(6188): p. 1118-1123.

502.Sakurai, M. and Y. Murayama, *Information technologies and disaster management – Benefits and issues.* Progress in Disaster Science, 2019. **2**: p. 100012.

503.Haas, J., et al., *Introducing "Best Single Template" Models as Reference Baseline for the Continuous Automated Model Evaluation (CAMEO).* Proteins Structure Function and Bioinformatics, 2019. **87**(12): p. 1378-1387.

504.Plough, A.L., et al., *Building Community Disaster Resilience: Perspectives From a Large Urban County Department of Public Health.* American Journal of Public Health, 2013. **103**(7): p. 1190-1197.

505.Burns, A., *Doubting the Global War on Terror.* M/C Journal, 2011. **14**(1).

506.Sampath, S.K., et al., *Review on Human-like Robot Manipulation Using Dexterous Hands.* Cognitive Computation and Systems, 2023. **5**(1): p. 14-29.

507.Moro, A.I., et al., *Key Factors in the Implementation of E-Proctoring in the Spanish University System.* Sustainability, 2022. **14**(13): p. 8112.

508.Adewole, D.O., et al., *The Evolution of Neuroprosthetic Interfaces.* Critical Reviews in Biomedical Engineering, 2016. **44**(1-02): p. 123-152.

509.Akter, S. and S.F. Wamba, *Big Data and Disaster Management: A Systematic Review and Agenda for Future Research.* Annals of Operations Research, 2017. **283**(1-2): p. 939-959.

510.Madanian, S., A.C. Norris, and D. Parry, *Disaster eHealth: Scoping Review.* Journal of Medical Internet Research, 2020. **22**(10): p. e18310.

511.Mansourian, A., et al., *Using SDI and Web-Based System to Facilitate Disaster Management.* Computers & Geosciences, 2006. **32**(3): p. 303-315.

512.Wiratmaja, I.G., et al., *Participatory Mapping Framework for Smart Web-Gis Disaster Monitoring in Slawi Urban Area, Tegal Regency.* Iop Conference Series Earth and Environmental Science, 2023. **1264**(1): p. 012004.

513.Zhou, L., et al., *Design of Internet of Things and Big Data Analytics-Based Disaster Risk Management.* Soft Computing, 2021. **25**(18): p. 12415-12427.

514.Molina, M. and S. Bayarri, *A Multinational SDI-based System to Facilitate Disaster Risk Management in the Andean Community.* Computers & Geosciences, 2011. **37**(9): p. 1501-1510.

515.Aydınoğlu, A.Ç. and M.S. Bilgin, *Developing an Open Geographic Data Model and Analysis Tools for Disaster Management: Landslide Case.* Natural Hazards and Earth System Science, 2015. **15**(2): p. 335-347.

516.Bhandari, V., *Use of Technology in Disaster Management.* Unity Journal, 2022. **3**(01): p. 292-304.

517.Aldrich, D.P. and M.A. Meyer, *Social Capital and Community Resilience.* American Behavioral Scientist, 2014. **59**(2): p. 254-269.

518.Haque, C.E., M.A.K. Azad, and M.-U.-I. Choudhury, *Social Learning, Innovative Adaptation and Community Resilience to Disasters: The Case of Flash Floods in Bangladesh.* Disaster Prevention and Management an International Journal, 2022. **31**(5): p. 601-618.

519.Bednář, P., L. Danko, and L. Smékalová, *Coworking Spaces and Creative Communities: Making Resilient Coworking Spaces Through Knowledge Sharing and Collective Learning.* European Planning Studies, 2021. **31**(3): p. 490-507.

520.Lauriola, P., et al., *On the Importance of Primary and Community Healthcare in Relation to Global Health and Environmental Threats: Lessons From the COVID-19 Crisis.* BMJ Global Health, 2021. **6**(3): p. e004111.

521.Horgan, D. and B. Dimitrijević, *Social Innovation in the Built Environment: The Challenges Presented by the Politics of Space.* Urban Science, 2020. **5**(1): p. 1.

522.Folke, C., et al., *Resilience Thinking: Integrating Resilience, Adaptability and Transformability.* Ecology and Society, 2010. **15**(4).

523.Hills, J.M., E. Michalena, and K. Chalvatzis, *Innovative Technology in the Pacific: Building Resilience for Vulnerable Communities.* Technological Forecasting and Social Change, 2018. **129**: p. 16-26.

524.Quaranta, G., J. Brandt, and R. Salvia, *The Local Food Processing House: A Social Innovation for Rural Development in Campania.* Rivista Di Studi Sulla Sostenibilita, 2017(2): p. 227-236.

525.Bergami, M., et al., *Being Resilient for Society: Evidence From Companies That Leveraged Their Resources and Capabilities to Fight the COVID-19 Crisis.* R and D Management, 2021. **52**(2): p. 235-254.

526.Spaans, M. and B. Waterhout, *Building Up Resilience in Cities Worldwide – Rotterdam as Participant in the 100 Resilient Cities Programme.* Cities, 2017. **61**: p. 109-116.

527.Béné, C., et al., *Resilience: New Utopia or New Tyranny? Reflection About the Potentials and Limits of the Concept of Resilience in Relation to Vulnerability Reduction Programmes.* Ids Working Papers, 2012. **2012**(405): p. 1-61.

528.Gil-Rivas, V. and R.P. Kilmer, *Building Community Capacity and Fostering Disaster Resilience.* Journal of Clinical Psychology, 2016. **72**(12): p. 1318-1332.

529.Meerow, S., P. Pajouhesh, and T.R. Miller, *Social Equity in Urban Resilience Planning.* Local Environment, 2019. **24**(9): p. 793-808.

530.Leitner, H., et al., *Globalizing Urban Resilience.* Urban Geography, 2018. **39**(8): p. 1276-1284.

531.Cheek, W. and K. Chmutina, *Measuring Resilience in the Assumed City.* International Journal of Disaster Risk Science, 2022. **13**(3): p. 317-329.

532.Sutherland, C., D. Roberts, and J. Douwes, *Constructing Resilience at Three Scales: The 100 Resilient Cities Programme, Durban's Resilience Journey and Water Resilience in the Palmiet Catchment.* Human Geography, 2019. **12**(1): p. 33-49.

533.Galderisi, A., G. Limongi, and K.-D. Salata, *Strengths and Weaknesses of the 100 Resilient Cities Initiative in Southern Europe: Rome and Athens' Experiences.* City Territory and Architecture, 2020. **7**(1).

534.Bradford, R.A., et al., *Risk Perception – Issues for Flood Management in Europe.* Natural Hazards and Earth System Science, 2012. **12**(7): p. 2299-2309.

535.O'Sullivan, J., et al., *Enhancing Flood Resilience Through Improved Risk Communications.* Natural Hazards and Earth System Science, 2012. **12**(7): p. 2271-2282.

536.Khuwaja, A.H., et al., *Vulnerability, Preparedness, and Previous Experience of Disasters Among the Population of a High Hazard Region—Rural Southern Sindh, Pakistan.* Disaster Medicine and Public Health Preparedness, 2024. **18**.

537.Hamann, C., et al., *Disaster Preparedness in Rural Families of Children With Special Health Care Needs.* Disaster Medicine and Public Health Preparedness, 2016. **10**(2): p. 225-232.

538.McCormick, L.C., J. Pevear, and R. Xie, *Measuring Levels of Citizen Public Health Emergency Preparedness, Jefferson County, Alabama.* Journal of Public Health Management and Practice, 2013. **19**(3): p. 266-273.

539.Wakui, T., et al., *Disaster Preparedness Among Older Japanese Adults With Long-Term Care Needs and Their Family Caregivers.* Disaster Medicine and Public Health Preparedness, 2016. **11**(1): p. 31-38.

540.Kivi, H.K., M. Peyravi, and M.A. Marzaleh, *Investigating the Preparedness of Iranian Families in the Face of Disasters.* Disaster Medicine and Public Health Preparedness, 2022. **17**.

541.Wallis, A., R. Fischer, and W. Abrahamse, *Place Attachment and Disaster Preparedness: Examining the Role of Place Scale and Preparedness Type.* Environment and Behavior, 2021. **54**(3): p. 670-711.

542.Rushton, S., et al., *Re-examining Critiques of Resilience Policy: Evidence From Barpak After the 2015 Earthquake in Nepal.* Disasters, 2022. **46**(3): p. 768-790.

543.Aryal, K., P.S. Thapa, and D. Lamichhane, *Revisiting Agroforestry for Building Climate Resilient Communities: A Case of Package-Based Integrated Agroforestry Practices in Nepal.* Emerging Science Journal, 2019. **3**(5): p. 303-311.

544.Reynolds, C., et al., *Does "Greening" of Neotropical Cities Considerably Mitigate Carbon Dioxide Emissions? The Case of Medellin, Colombia.* Sustainability, 2017. **9**(5): p. 785.

545.Naef, P.J., *Resilience as a City Brand: The Cases of the Comuna 13 and Moravia in Medellin, Colombia.* Sustainability, 2020. **12**(20): p. 8469.

546.Sharifi, A. and A.R. Khavarian-Garmsir, *The COVID-19 Pandemic: Impacts on Cities and Major Lessons for Urban Planning, Design, and Management.* The Science of the Total Environment, 2020. **749**: p. 142391.

547.Castillo-Palacio, M., R. Harrill, and A. Zúñiga-Collazos, *Back From the Brink.* Worldwide Hospitality and Tourism Themes, 2017. **9**(3): p. 300-315.

548.Baró, F., et al., *Contribution of Ecosystem Services to Air Quality and Climate Change Mitigation Policies: The Case of Urban Forests in Barcelona, Spain.* Ambio, 2014. **43**(4): p. 466-479.

549.Chew, M.Y.L., et al., *Evaluating the Roadmap of 5G Technology Implementation for Smart Building and Facilities Management in Singapore.* Sustainability, 2020. **12**(24): p. 10259.

550.Kong, L. and O. Woods, *The Ideological Alignment of Smart Urbanism in Singapore: Critical Reflections on a Political Paradox.* Urban Studies, 2018. **55**(4): p. 679-701.

551.Li, Y., A. Taeihagh, and M.d. Jong, *The Governance of Risks in Ridesharing: A Revelatory Case From Singapore.* Energies, 2018. **11**(5): p. 1277.

552.Yeo, S.J.I., *Prospecting Digital Urban Futures in Practice.* Area, 2022. **55**(4): p. 473-480.

553.Demirel, D., *The Impact of Managing Diversity on Building the Smart City a Comparison of Smart City Strategies: Cases From Europe, America, and Asia.* Sage Open, 2023. **13**(3).

554.Laurent, B., et al., *The Test Bed Island: Tech Business Experimentalism and Exception in Singapore.* Science as Culture, 2021. **30**(3): p. 367-390.

555.Low, S.T.H., et al., *Attitudes and Perceptions Toward Healthcare Technology Adoption Among Older Adults in Singapore: A Qualitative Study.* Frontiers in Public Health, 2021. **9**.

556.Tan, I.B., et al., *Prevalence and Outcomes of SARS-CoV-2 Infection Among Migrant Workers in Singapore.* Jama, 2021. **325**(6): p. 584.

557.Yoon, S., et al., *Spillover Effects of COVID-19 on Essential Chronic Care and Ways to Foster Health System Resilience to Support Vulnerable Non-Covid Patients: A Multistakeholder Study.* Journal of the American Medical Directors Association, 2022. **23**(1): p. 7-14.

558.Tan, G., *Citizens Go Digital: A Discursive Examination of Digital Payments in Singapore's Smart Nation Project.* Urban Studies, 2021. **59**(12): p. 2582-2598.

559.Tintswalo, S., et al., *Management of Records at Statistics South Africa: Challenges and Prospects.* Information Development, 2021. **38**(2): p. 286-298.

560.He, R., et al., *Preparedness and Responses Faced During the COVID-19 Pandemic in Belgium: An Observational Study and Using the National Open Data.* International Journal of Environmental Research and Public Health, 2020. **17**(21): p. 7985.

561.Mortimer, A., T. Egbelakin, and W. Sher, *Policy Interventions for Disaster-Related Internal Displacement in Australia.* Iop Conference Series Earth and Environmental Science, 2022. **1101**(2): p. 022030.

562.Song, Y.S., et al., *Improvement Measure of Integrated Disaster Management System Considering Disaster Damage Characteristics: Focusing on the Republic of Korea.* Sustainability, 2020. **12**(1): p. 340.

563.Huang, L., Q. Yu, and Q. Wang, *Construction of Public Health Core Competence and the Improvement of Its Legal Guarantee in China.* Frontiers in Public Health, 2023. **11**.

564.Nepal, P., N.R. Khanal, and B. Sharma, *Policies and Institutions for Disaster Risk Management in Nepal: A Review.* Geographical Journal of Nepal, 2018. **11**: p. 1-24.

565.Adini, B., et al., *Learning Lessons in Emergency Management: The 4th International Conference on Healthcare System Preparedness and Response to Emergencies and Disasters.* Disaster and Military Medicine, 2016. **2**(1).

566.Hashmi, A., M. Ahmad, and M.A. Nawaz, *The Role of Coordination, Decision Making and Special Data Infrastructure on the Disaster Management in Pakistan: Moderating Role of Information System.* Review of Applied Management and Social Sciences, 2021. **4**(1): p. 79-91.

567.Malik, M.H.A., E.N. Omar, and S.N. Maon, *Humanitarian Logistics: A Disaster Relief Operations Framework During Pandemic Covid-19 in Achieving Healthy Communities.* Advances in Business Research International Journal, 2020. **6**(2): p. 101.

568.Arifin, S., et al., *Disaster Resilient Village-Based Approach to Disaster Risk Reduction Policy in Indonesia: A Regulatory Analysis.* Jàmbá Journal of Disaster Risk Studies, 2021. **13**(1).

569.Altay, N. and W.G. Green, *Or/MS Research in Disaster Operations Management.* European Journal of Operational Research, 2006. **175**(1): p. 475-493.

570.Wang, Y. and B. Sun, *Multiperiod Equitable and Efficient Allocation Strategy of Emergency Resources Under Uncertainty.* International Journal of Disaster Risk Science, 2022. **13**(5): p. 778-792.

571.Wang, Y., *Multiperiod Optimal Allocation of Emergency Resources in Support of Cross-Regional Disaster Sustainable Rescue.* International Journal of Disaster Risk Science, 2021. **12**(3): p. 394-409.

572.Li, H., et al., *A Dynamic Disastrous CGE Model to Optimize Resource Allocation in Post-Disaster Economic Recovery: Post-Typhoon in an Urban Agglomeration Area, China.* Environmental Research Letters, 2022. **17**(7): p. 074027.

573.Pradhananga, R., et al., *An Integrated Resource Allocation and Distribution Model for Pre-Disaster Planning.* Computers & Industrial Engineering, 2016. **91**: p. 229-238.

574.Persad, G. and E.A. Largent, *COVID-19 Vaccine Refusal and Fair Allocation of Scarce Medical Resources.* Jama Health Forum, 2022. **3**(4): p. e220356.

575.Ibrahim, J.E., *A Proactive Nursing Home Risk Stratification Model for Disaster Response: Lessons Learned From COVID-19 to Optimize Resource Allocation.* Journal of the American Medical Directors Association, 2021. **22**(9): p. 1831-1839.e1.

576.Hu, X.-B., et al., *A New Method for Resource Allocation Optimization in Disaster Reduction and Risk Governance.* International Journal of Disaster Risk Science, 2016. **7**(2): p. 138-150.

577.Wang, Y. and B. Sun, *A Multiobjective Allocation Model for Emergency Resources That Balance Efficiency and Fairness.* Mathematical Problems in Engineering, 2018. **2018**: p. 1-8.

578.Ahmadi, G., et al., *A Decision Support Model for Robust Allocation and Routing of Search and Rescue Resources After Earthquake: A Case Study.* Operational Research, 2020. **22**(2): p. 1039-1081.

579.Waugh, W.L. and G. Streib, *Collaboration and Leadership for Effective Emergency Management.* Public Administration Review, 2006. **66**(s1): p. 131-140.

580.Feiock, R.C., *Rational Choice and Regional Governance.* Journal of Urban Affairs, 2007. **29**(1): p. 47-63.

581.Barbarossa, G., et al., *Hexa-Helix Approach for Smart Disaster Governance Framework in Developing Cities, Case Study: Slawi Urban Area, Tegal Regency.* Iop Conference Series Earth and Environmental Science, 2023. **1264**(1): p. 012029.

582.O'Sullivan, T., et al., *Unraveling the Complexities of Disaster Management: A Framework for Critical Social Infrastructure to Promote Population Health and Resilience.* Social Science & Medicine, 2013. **93**: p. 238-246.

583.Terblanche, T., L.O.d. Sousa, and D.v. Niekerk, *Disaster Resilience Framework Indicators for a City's Disaster Resilience Planning Strategy.* Jàmbá Journal of Disaster Risk Studies, 2022. **14**(1).

584.Courtney, B., et al., *Legal Preparedness.* Chest Journal, 2014. **146**(4): p. e134S-e144S.

585.Whittaker, J., B. McLennan, and J. Handmer, *A Review of Informal Volunteerism in Emergencies and Disasters: Definition, Opportunities and Challenges.* International Journal of Disaster Risk Reduction, 2015. **13**: p. 358-368.

586.Hodge, J.G., D. Hanfling, and T. Powell, *Practical, Ethical, and Legal Challenges Underlying Crisis Standards of Care.* The Journal of Law Medicine & Ethics, 2013. **41**(S1): p. 50-55.

587.Wang, J., et al., *Evaluation of Public Health Emergency Management in China: A Systematic Review.* International Journal of Environmental Research and Public Health, 2019. **16**(18): p. 3478.

588.Hodge, J.J.G., *The Evolution of Law in Biopreparedness.* Biosecurity and Bioterrorism Biodefense Strategy Practice and Science, 2012. **10**(1): p. 38-48.

589.Friesen, L., *Targeting Enforcement to Improve Compliance With Environmental Regulations.* Journal of Environmental Economics and Management, 2003. **46**(1): p. 72-85.

590.Moulton, A.D., et al., *What Is Public Health Legal Preparedness?* The Journal of Law Medicine & Ethics, 2003. **31**(4): p. 672-683.

591.Botoseneanu, A., et al., *Achieving Public Health Legal Preparedness: How Dissonant Views on Public Health Law Threaten Emergency Preparedness and Response.* Journal of Public Health, 2010. **33**(3): p. 361-368.

592.Kapucu, N., *Collaborative Emergency Management: Better Community Organising, Better Public Preparedness and Response.* Disasters, 2008. **32**(2): p. 239-262.

593.Surianto, S., et al., *Regional Policy for Disaster Risk Management in Developing Countries Within the Sendai Framework: A Systematic Review.* Open Access Macedonian Journal of Medical Sciences, 2019. **7**(13): p. 2213-2219.

594.Cubie, D. and T. Natoli, *Coherence, Alignment and Integration: Understanding the Legal Relationship Between Sustainable Development, Climate Change Adaptation and Disaster Risk Reduction.* 2021: p. 45-64.

595.Liu, J., et al., *A Study on the Mechanism and Strategy of Cross-Regional Emergency Cooperation for Natural Disasters in China—Based on the Perspective of Evolutionary Game Theory.* International Journal of Environmental Research and Public Health, 2021. **18**(21): p. 11624.

596.Lü, Y., et al., *An NGO Disaster Relief Network for Small and Medium-Scale Natural Hazards in China.* Natural Hazards, 2021. **106**(3): p. 2689-2709.

597.Albris, K., K.C. Lauta, and E. Raju, *Disaster Knowledge Gaps: Exploring the Interface Between Science and Policy for Disaster Risk Reduction in Europe.* International Journal of Disaster Risk Science, 2020. **11**(1): p. 1-12.

598.Tang, P., et al., *Understanding the Collaborative Process and Its Effects on Perceived Outcomes During Emergency Response in China: From Perspectives of Local Government Sectors.* Sustainability, 2021. **13**(14): p. 7605.

599.Hercegová, K. and V.Y. Chernova, *Open Borders and Cross-Border Cooperation in Regional Development.* E3s Web of Conferences, 2021. **301**: p. 01003.

600.Kurowska-Pysz, J. and K. Szczepańska-Woszczyna, *The Analysis of the Determinants of Sustainable Cross-Border Cooperation and Recommendations on Its Harmonization.* Sustainability, 2017. **9**(12): p. 2226.

601.Kurowska-Pysz, J., *Opportunities for Cross-Border Entrepreneurship Development in a Cluster Model Exemplified by the Polish–Czech Border Region.* Sustainability, 2016. **8**(3): p. 230.

602.Lane, L. and M. Hesselman, *Governing Disasters: Embracing Human Rights in a Multi-Level, Multi-Duty Bearer, Disaster Governance Landscape.* Politics and Governance, 2017. **5**(2): p. 93-104.

603.Grad-Rusu, E., *Exploring Cross-Border Cooperation in Eastern Europe: What Kind of Initiatives Have Developed in the Romanian-Hungarian Border Area?* Észak-Magyarországi Stratégiai Füzetek, 2021. **18**(2): p. 35-43.

604.Tang, P., H. Chen, and S. Shao, *Examining the Intergovernmental and Interorganizational Network of Responding to Major Accidents for Improving the Emergency Management System in China.* Complexity, 2018. **2018**: p. 1-16.

605.Khmeleva, G.A., et al., *Determinants of Sustainable Cross-Border Cooperation: A Structural Model for the Hungarian Context Using the PLS-SEM Methodology.* Sustainability, 2022. **14**(2): p. 893.

606.Silapunt, P., et al., *Impact of the ARCH Project on National Capacity Development on Disaster Health Management Among the ASEAN Member States and Japan.* Prehospital and Disaster Medicine, 2022. **37**(S1): p. s44-s50.

607.Belligoni, S., *Held in the Grip: Political Status, Governing Institutions, and Emergency Management Procedural Arrangements in the Cases of Florida and Puerto Rico.* Politics &Amp Policy, 2024. **52**(2): p. 349-364.

608.Hu, Q., C.C. Knox, and N. Kapucu, *What Have We Learned Since September 11, 2001? A Network Study of the Boston Marathon Bombings Response.* Public Administration Review, 2014. **74**(6): p. 698-712.

609.Du, E., et al., *Impacts of Human Behavioral Heterogeneity on the Benefits of Probabilistic Flood Warnings: An Agent-Based Modeling Framework.* Jawra Journal of the American Water Resources Association, 2016. **53**(2): p. 316-332.

610.Vujanovic, A.A. and M.W. Gallagher, *Psychological Impact of Natural Disasters in Adults*. 2017, University of Houston.

611.Ehlers, A., A. Hackmann, and T. Michael, *Intrusive Re-experiencing in Post-traumatic Stress Disorder: Phenomenology, Theory, and Therapy.* Memory, 2004. **12**(4): p. 403-415.

612.Sareen, J., *Posttraumatic Stress Disorder in Adults: Impact, Comorbidity, Risk Factors, and Treatment.* The Canadian Journal of Psychiatry, 2014. **59**(9): p. 460-467.

613.Bourla, A., et al., *E-Ptsd: An Overview on How New Technologies Can Improve Prediction and Assessment of Posttraumatic Stress Disorder (PTSD).* European Journal of Psychotraumatology, 2018. **9**(sup1).

614.Ra, M., et al., *Fear Learning Circuitry Is Biased Toward Generalization of Fear Associations in Posttraumatic Stress Disorder.* Translational Psychiatry, 2015. **5**(12): p. e700-e700.

615.Webb, J. and S. Keane, *MDMA for the Treatment of Misophonia, a Proposal.* Frontiers in Psychiatry, 2022. **13**.

616.Musicaro, R., B.W. Bellet, and R.J. McNally, *Is Avoidance the Only Issue? A Case Study of "Self-Triggering" in Combat-Related Posttraumatic Stress Disorder.* Psychological Trauma Theory Research Practice and Policy, 2023. **15**(6): p. 961-968.

617.Busso, D.S., K.A. McLaughlin, and M.A. Sheridan, *Media Exposure and Sympathetic Nervous System Reactivity Predict PTSD Symptoms After the Boston Marathon Bombings.* Depression and Anxiety, 2014. **31**(7): p. 551-558.

618.Peirce, J.M., et al., *Assessing Traumatic Event Exposure: Comparing the Traumatic Life Events Questionnaire to the Structured Clinical Interview for DSM-IV.* Psychological Assessment, 2009. **21**(2): p. 210-218.

619.Lu, B., et al., *≪p>Prevalence and Influencing Factors of Post-Traumatic Stress Disorder Among Survivors in the Hard-Hit Areas Ten Years After the Wenchuan Earthquake: A Cross-Sectional Study</P>.* Neuropsychiatric Disease and Treatment, 2020. **Volume 16**: p. 933-941.

620.Acharibasam, J.W., B. Chireh, and H.G. Menegesha, *Assessing Anxiety, Depression and Insomnia Symptoms Among Ebola Survivors in Africa: A Meta-Analysis.* Plos One, 2021. **16**(2): p. e0246515.

621.Barkin, J.L., et al., *Effects of Extreme Weather Events on Child Mood and Behavior.* Developmental Medicine & Child Neurology, 2021. **63**(7): p. 785-790.

622.Lotzin, A., et al., *The SOLAR Group Program to Promote Recovery After Disaster and Trauma—A Randomized Controlled Feasibility Trial Among German Trauma Survivors.* Psychological Trauma Theory Research Practice and Policy, 2022. **14**(1): p. 161-171.

623.Raker, E.J., et al., *Twelve Years Later: The Long-Term Mental Health Consequences of Hurricane Katrina.* Social Science & Medicine, 2019. **242**: p. 112610.

624.Kino, S., et al., *Long-Term Trends in Mental Health Disorders After the 2011 Great East Japan Earthquake and Tsunami.* Jama Network Open, 2020. **3**(8): p. e2013437.

625.Shiba, K., et al., *Long-Term Associations Between Disaster-Related Home Loss and Health and Well-Being of Older Survivors: Nine Years After the 2011 Great East Japan Earthquake and Tsunami.* Environmental Health Perspectives, 2022. **130**(7).

626.Hikichi, H., et al., *Persistent Impact of Housing Loss on Cognitive Decline After the 2011 Great East Japan Earthquake and Tsunami: Evidence From a 6-year Longitudinal Study.* Alzheimer S & Dementia, 2019. **15**(8): p. 1009-1018.

627.Beaglehole, B., et al., *Psychological Distress and Psychiatric Disorder After Natural Disasters: Systematic Review and Meta-Analysis.* The British Journal of Psychiatry, 2018. **213**(6): p. 716-722.

628.Reifels, L., *Reducing the Future Risk of Trauma: On the Integration of Global Disaster Policy Within Specific Health Domains and Established Fields of Practice.* International Journal of Environmental Research and Public Health, 2018. **15**(9): p. 1932.

629.Woodhall-Melnik, J. and C. Grogan, *Perceptions of Mental Health and Wellbeing Following Residential Displacement and Damage From the 2018 St. John River Flood.* International Journal of Environmental Research and Public Health, 2019. **16**(21): p. 4174.

630.Ritter, J.D., et al., *Mental Health Correlates of Post Disaster Increases in Alcohol and Cigarette Smoking: A Vietnamese Study.* International Journal of Mental Health and Addiction, 2009. **9**(1): p. 118-125.

631.Stroever, S., et al., *Emergency Department Utilization for Mental Health Conditions Before and After the COVID-19 Outbreak.* The American Journal of Emergency Medicine, 2021. **47**: p. 164-168.

632.Choi, Y.J., M.-R. Won, and D.-H. Cho, *Efficacy of a Community-Based Trauma Recovery Program After a Fire Disaster.* International Journal of Mental Health Promotion, 2022. **24**(1): p. 85-94.

633.Chou, J.L., et al., *Couple/Marriage and Family Therapist Extent of Training for Working With Families Impacted by Substance Use.* Family Relations, 2022. **71**(4): p. 1658-1678.

634.Epel, E.S., et al., *Accelerated Telomere Shortening in Response to Life Stress.* Proceedings of the National Academy of Sciences, 2004. **101**(49): p. 17312-17315.

635.Juster, R.P., B.S. McEwen, and S.J. Lupien, *Allostatic Load Biomarkers of Chronic Stress and Impact on Health and Cognition.* Neuroscience & Biobehavioral Reviews, 2010. **35**(1): p. 2-16.

636.Schneiderman, N., G. Ironson, and S.D. Siegel, *Stress and Health: Psychological, Behavioral, and Biological Determinants.* Annual Review of Clinical Psychology, 2005. **1**(1): p. 607-628.

637.Warren, K.R., et al., *Role of Chronic Stress and Depression in Periodontal Diseases.* Periodontology 2000, 2013. **64**(1): p. 127-138.

638.Baum, A., J.P. Garofalo, and A.M. Yali, *Socioeconomic Status and Chronic Stress: Does Stress Account for SES Effects on Health?* Annals of the New York Academy of Sciences, 1999. **896**(1): p. 131-144.

639.Kopp, M., et al., *Chronic Stress and Social Changes.* Annals of the New York Academy of Sciences, 2007. **1113**(1): p. 325-338.

640.Umucu, E. and B. Lee, *Examining the Impact of COVID-19 on Stress and Coping Strategies in Individuals With Disabilities and Chronic Conditions.* Rehabilitation Psychology, 2020. **65**(3): p. 193-198.

641.Rakshasa, A.M. and M. Tong, *Making "Good" Choices: Social Isolation in Mice Exacerbates the Effects of Chronic Stress on Decision Making.* Frontiers in Behavioral Neuroscience, 2020. **14**.

642.Hernández, D., D. Phillips, and E.L. Siegel, *Exploring the Housing and Household Energy Pathways to Stress: A Mixed Methods Study.* International Journal of Environmental Research and Public Health, 2016. **13**(9): p. 916.

643.Girma, A., E. Ayalew, and G. Mesafint, *Covid-19 Pandemic-Related Stress and Coping Strategies Among Adults With Chronic Disease in Southwest Ethiopia.* Neuropsychiatric Disease and Treatment, 2021. **Volume 17**: p. 1551-1561.

644.Wickrama, K.A.S., E.T. Klopack, and C.W. O'Neal, *How Midlife Chronic Stress Combines With Stressful Life Events to Influence Later Life Mental and Physical Health for Husbands and Wives in Enduring Marriages.* Journal of Aging and Health, 2020. **33**(1-2): p. 14-26.

645.Arthur, C.M., *Little Rain Each Day.* Californian Journal of Health Promotion, 2007. **5**(SI): p. 58-67.

646.Seib, C., et al., *A Longitudinal Study of the Impact of Chronic Psychological Stress on Health-Related Quality of Life and Clinical Biomarkers: Protocol for the Australian Healthy Aging of Women Study.* BMC Public Health, 2014. **14**(1).

647.Condon, E.M., *Chronic Stress in Children and Adolescents: A Review of Biomarkers for Use in Pediatric Research.* Biological Research for Nursing, 2018. **20**(5): p. 473-496.

648.Tidal Basin, *The Psychological Effects of Disasters: Recognizing and Addressing Mental Health in Emergency Management*. 2024.

649.Australian Red Cross, *Psychological First Aid: Supporting people affected by disaster in Australia*. 2020.

650.Cain, D.S., et al., *Weathering the Storm: Persistent Effects and Psychological First Aid With Children Displaced by Hurricane Katrina.* Journal of Child & Adolescent Trauma, 2010. **3**(4): p. 330-343.

651.Schoultz, M., et al., *Psychological First Aid for Workers in Care and Nursing Homes: Systematic Review.* BMC Nursing, 2022. **21**(1).

652.Movahed, M., et al., *The Impact of Psychological First Aid Training on the Providers: A Systematic Review.* Disaster Medicine and Public Health Preparedness, 2022. **17**.

653.Jacobs, G.A., et al., *Disaster Mental Health and Community-Based Psychological First Aid: Concepts and Education/Training.* Journal of Clinical Psychology, 2016. **72**(12): p. 1307-1317.

654.Kim, H.-W. and Y.J. Choi, *A Simulation-Based Nursing Education of Psychological First Aid for Adolescents Exposed to Hazardous Chemical Disasters.* BMC Medical Education, 2022. **22**(1).

655.Allen, B., et al., *Perceptions of Psychological First Aid Among Providers Responding to Hurricanes Gustav and Ike.* Journal of Traumatic Stress, 2010. **23**(4): p. 509-513.

656.Solikhah, F.K. and R.S. Aditya, *Healing in Nurses After Assignment in Natural Disasters.* Folia Medica Indonesiana, 2022. **58**(4): p. 377-382.

657.Dieltjens, T., et al., *A Systematic Literature Search on Psychological First Aid: Lack of Evidence to Develop Guidelines.* Plos One, 2014. **9**(12): p. e114714.

658.Forbes, D., et al., *Psychological First Aid Following Trauma: Implementation and Evaluation Framework for High-Risk Organizations.* Psychiatry, 2011. **74**(3): p. 224-239.

659.Kim, E.Y. and S.-W. Han, *Development of Psychological First Aid Guidelines for People Who Have Experienced Disasters.* International Journal of Environmental Research and Public Health, 2021. **18**(20): p. 10752.

660.Jung, H.-O. and S.-W. Han, *Implementing Psychological First Aid Ontology.* Plos One, 2021. **16**(6): p. e0252891.

661.Greca, A.M.L. and W.K. Silverman, *Treatment and Prevention of Posttraumatic Stress Reactions in Children and Adolescents Exposed to Disasters and Terrorism: What Is the Evidence?* Child Development Perspectives, 2009. **3**(1): p. 4-10.

662.Wang, L., et al., *Psychological First Aid Training: A Scoping Review of Its Application, Outcomes and Implementation.* International Journal of Environmental Research and Public Health, 2021. **18**(9): p. 4594.

663.World Health Organization, *Psychological first aid: Guide for field workers.* 2011: Geneva.

664.Cuthbertson, J., F. Archer, and A. Robertson, *Special Report: WADEM Climate Change Position Statement.* Prehospital and Disaster Medicine, 2018. **33**(4): p. 428-431.

665.The World Association for Disaster and Emergency Medicine, *WADEM Climate Change Position Statement.* Prehospital and Disaster Medicine, 2017. **32**(4): p. 351-351.

666.Jenkins, S.G., *Resilience: The New Paradigm in Disaster Management—An Australian Perspective.* World Journal of Engineering and Technology, 2015. **03**(03): p. 129-139.

667.Oxfam International. *5 natural disasters that beg for climate action.* 2024 [cited 2024 19/5/2024]; Available from: .

668.Rowley, M., *Future Challenges for Emergency Management.* 2024, Columbia Southern University.

15

Index